82. (.45)
     .45
    410
   328
  ─────────
   36.90   37
           32
           15
          ───
          84

The
Management of
Business Logistics

The Management of Business Logistics

2nd Edition

JOHN J. COYLE
Pennsylvania State University

EDWARD J. BARDI
University of Toledo

WEST PUBLISHING COMPANY
St. Paul   New York   Los Angeles   San Francisco

COPYRIGHT © 1976 By WEST PUBLISHING CO.

COPYRIGHT © 1980 By WEST PUBLISHING CO.
50 West Kellogg Boulevard
P.O. Box 3526
St. Paul, Minnesota 55165

Printed in the United States of America

2nd Reprint—1981

Library of Congress Cataloging in Publication Data

Coyle, John Joseph, 1935-
    The management of business logistics.

    Bibliography: p.
    Includes index.
    1. Business logistics. I. Bardi, Edward J.,
1943- joint author. II. Title.
HD38.5.C69 1980   658.7'8   79-27030
ISBN 0-8299-0325-9

Dedicated to Dr. Robert D. Pashek
Teacher, administrator, and friend

Contents

Preface

Business logistics is a relatively new field of study in business administration. The concept of logistics/distribution first took hold in the early 1960s and has developed rapidly since then. The newness of the field lies in the approach used to manage the various subfunctions of traffic, transportation, inventory management, warehousing, packaging, order processing, and materials handling. The new aspect is the systems approach, which recognizes the interrelationships among the traditional functions of logistics and the other areas of a business. During the past few years, more and more companies, from well-established basic businesses to new high-technology firms, have recognized the potential increase in profitability possible through managed logistics activities.

The authors have been constantly encouraged with the positive comments and acceptance of the first edition of this text. This edition retains the basic thrust of the first edition to provide an introductory level text that emphasizes the nature of logistics functional relationships. Attention has been given to a thorough explanation of the basics of logistics: the how's, the why's, and wherefore's. Since logistics does not operate in a vacuum, a serious attempt is made to acquaint the reader with the interrelationship of logistics to other functional areas of the firm. Thus, the text blends a working knowledge of the logistics functional areas with the integrative nature of logistics to other departments in a company. This edition strengthens this blending by utilizing real-world examples and cases.

The authors of this text have purposely oriented the material toward the introductory level, blending both the marketing and production impacts of logistics. Examples are used wherever possible to explain various concepts and techniques, and short cases are available to permit written and/or classroom discussion of major points. Appendices are added to certain chapters so that the reader can gain exposure, if desired, to the application of quantitative techniques. Substantial pretesting of the text in the introductory logistics course has enabled the authors to include sufficient background material to provide the reader with a sound basis for understanding the fundamental nature and character of logistics in our dynamic business world.

The link-node concept is utilized as the framework upon which the text is built. The node is the fixed point in the logistics system where commodities are at rest and the link is the transportation system that connects the nodes. The link-node structure permits a discussion of the overall nature of logistics in a business, the various logistics management areas and responsibilities within each, and the coordination necessary between the two and between their respective functions to achieve logistics efficiency through the systems approach. Part One introduces the overall character of the link and node in logistics and the firm; Part Two discusses the nodal functions of inventory management, warehousing, materials handling, and packaging; Part Three presents the link functions of transportation and traffic management; and Part Four provides the link-node integration decision making areas of customer service, nodal location, nodal linking, and management and control.

Many individuals have been most helpful and encouraging throughout the preparation of this manuscript. To all the unnamed colleagues, students, and practitioners who have offered suggestions and criticisms, we wish to express our sincere appreciation.

Special appreciation should be expressed to a number of individuals: Dr. Joseph Carroll for his contributions to the material on inventory; Mr. Michael Dobson for his contributions to the material on warehousing and his assistance with the study questions; Major Walter Bawell for his contributions to the material on inventory and on management information systems; Dr. Joseph Cavinato for his contributions to the material on organization; Paul Anderson, Thomas Craig, Bud Colin, Howard Fishbein, and Robert Raines for their assistance; John Rasmussen for his assistance with the material on customer service; J. Duane Weeks for his contributions to the inventory chapters; Tom Kryger, Bob Novack, and George Roman for their help with the cases; Gary Kogon for his help in Chapter 12; Crystal Stover, Helen Spicher, and LuAnn Jaworski for their typing assistance; the thousands of Penn State Students from B.Log. 102 who offered comments; and finally to Barbara and Carol and our children, John and Susan and Susan and Pamela for their support throughout the preparation of this edition.

Part I

The introductory section treats two major topics, *viz.,* the framework of logistics and the logistics environments. The former essentially exposes the reader to the basic nature of logistics in an organization. Logistics is defined and the interest in the area is explained. In addition, the systems aspect of logistics analysis is discussed and some basic techniques of systems analysis are explored.

The second topic looks at the various environments of logistics. Initially, logistics is examined from the perspective of the economy and its role in the economy is explored. Second, logistics is viewed as it operates in the firm or company with an exploration of its relationship to areas such as marketing and production. Finally, logistics is examined introspectively to look at basic internal trade-offs of the logistics component.

The introductory section of two chapters should provide the reader with the background for an in-depth study of logistics functional areas and for the integrative decision-making areas.

| **Chapter 1** | Logistics Management: An Overview |

After studying this chapter you should be able to:

- Present a definition of business logistics.
- Demonstrate the different approaches that can be used to analyze logistics systems.
- Discuss the development of the logistics concept, including a rationale for the growing interest in it and its development.
- Discuss the systems approach in logistics and demonstrate the systems concept.

Business organizations have long recognized production, finance, and marketing as areas of functional importance with a need for a separate slot or box in the organizational structure. But business logistics was accorded little attention in a coordinated or systems sense until the early 1950s—it is a post-World War II phenomenon.

World War II Origins

In fact, it could be argued that the origin of the business logistics concept can be traced quite logically to the military supply or logistics effort of World War II. There is little doubt that the logistics effort, particularly of the United States, was a key factor in the outcome of the war, particularly in the European Theatre. Given the environment of the post-World War II era, which shall be discussed subsequently, it is not surprising that the military logistics expertise that continued to develop after World War II would be modified and applied in the private sector to resolve some of the problems.

Early Developments

During the 1950s, one began to see reference to such terms as *physical distribution, materials management, supply management,* and *distribution management* in business periodicals. In the 1960s the relevant titles began to show up in the organization charts of companies, e.g., Director of Physical Distribution, Materials Manager, etc. Also, during the 1960s other descriptive terms were coined, such as *marketing logistics, industrial logistics, logistical management,* and, of course, *business logistics.* As indicated, a number of different titles or terms have been applied to the set of activities in business organizations that will be treated in this text.

While much space could be devoted to arguing the appropriateness of each of these terms or labels, and perhaps the coining of yet another descriptive title, it would not appear to contribute significantly to the objectives of this text. The relative "newness" of the area accounts for the proclivity to develop different labels in the search for the most descriptive term. Also, there seems to be a fairly widespread acceptance for two terms, viz., physical distribution management and business logistics; and the latter is used for this text since it seems most appropriate for the broader perspective used herein. Our efforts would be better spent developing a definition of business logistics.

DEFINITION OF BUSINESS LOGISTICS

There are a number of different ways one could portray or define the area of business logistics, such as:

> Business Logistics is the planning, organizing, and controlling of all move-store activities that facilitate product flow from the point of raw material acquisition to the point of final consumption, and of the attendant information flows, for the purpose of providing a sufficient level of customer service (and associated revenues) consistent with the costs incurred for overcoming the resistance of time and space in providing the service.[1]

Another author used the following description:

> . . . this field deals with the development of distribution systems necessary to support the raw material and finished product flows of the business firm. Thus, all of the activities required to sustain a physical flow of materials and products from points of origin through the various stages of production, and on to points of final consumption, are essential elements of this subject. Characteristically, major areas of activity include transportation, inventory control, warehousing, material handling and industrial packaging, location of plants and warehouses, and information systems. The goal . . . is to combine these essential elements into a system of activities which permits attainment of a firm's . . . goals in the most efficient manner possible.[2]

The prestigious National Council of Physical Distribution Management (NCPDM) offers the following definition, which is similar to the Ballou definition:

> The term describing the integration of two or more activities for the purpose of planning, implementing and controlling the efficient flow of raw materials, in-process inventory and finished goods from point-of-origin to point-of-consumption. These activities *may* include, but are not limited to, customer service, demand forecasting, distribution communications, inventory control, material handling, order processing, parts and service support, plant and warehouse site selection, procurement, packaging, return goods handling, salvage and scrap disposal, traffic and transportation and warehousing and storage [Italics added].[3]

The definition offered above by the NCPDM is worth discussing briefly at this point for several reasons. First, their definition has changed over the fifteen-year history of the organization and is much more comprehensive now. The emphasis was initially on the finished goods side of the activities, i.e., what happened after manufacturing in terms of movement and storage. Now, the raw material side, i.e., what happens in terms of movement and storage prior to production or manufacturing, is accorded equal treatment. The latter we shall define subsequently as physical supply.

The other aspect that should be noted is the comprehensive list of activities in a business organization that are mentioned as being associated with physical distribution or what is defined as business logistics in this text. The use of the qualifier, *may,* in the NCPDM definition should be kept in mind. As shall be discussed, not all organizations will include all of these activities in their logistics or distribution area. However, the list does provide an excellent coverage of the activities that impact directly on the logistical function in an organization and does indicate how a comprehensive department or area could be set up in some organizations.

While there are many other definitions that could be presented, we can see the essential ingredients of business logistics management from the definitions offered above. In its most concise form, logistics can be defined as *the physical movement of goods from supply points to final sale to customers and the associated transfer and holding of such goods at various intermediate storage points, accomplished in such manner as to contribute to the explicit goals of the organization.*

The above definition indicates that "goods: (raw materials, semifinished, and finished goods) must be transported varying distances between supply points, plants, storage areas (warehouses) and markets (customers) and arrangements made to hold these goods safely and in sufficient quantities to meet anticipated needs of the organization.

If we dissect the description even further, we can discern that our interest is in two basic activities that are very interrelated—movement and storage. The movement aspect requires the selection and use of a mode or modes of transportation based upon criteria which will be discussed. The modern transportation system offers a variety of different for-hire carriers with each having a variety of services as well as the option of private transportation. The selection of the best transportation alternative(s) is often a formidable task.

The second activity, storage, is concerned with the number, size, design, type, and location of storage areas or warehouses as well as the appropriate order sizes, reorder points, stocking locations, and other related matters of inventory. Decisions made in transportation will affect inventory. For example, a slower and less reliable form of transportation usually requires the carrying of more inventory. Also, the number and location of warehouses will affect our transportation decisions in terms of shipment size and perhaps what modes are available for our use.

The successful management of logistics in an organization requires the careful coordination and manipulation of both movement and storage. The management also requires knowledge and interest in related areas such as materials handling and industrial packaging. These latter two areas are deserving of special attention at the interfaces between storage and movement. For example, the size and type of packaging affects our use of transportation equipment (stacking and use of cubic space) and our use of warehouse space as well as the transfer between transport equipment and the warehouse.

Perhaps our definition could be simplified even further. We could define logistical management as having the right product or material in the right quantity at the right time in the right place with the right customer and in the right physical condition.

The NCPDM definition indicated other areas that could also be included and would need careful coordination and control to achieve overall efficiency in the logistics area. We will discuss those activities in more detail subsequently. At this point, it would be useful to discuss the development of business logistics. The presentation will offer additional insights into the nature and scope of logistics.

DEVELOPMENT OF INTEREST IN LOGISTICS

The developing interest in business logistics has been documented by a number of different sources,[4] but one of the more interesting perspectives was that presented by Peter Drucker wherein he argued that logistics is essentially a last frontier along the road to overall efficiency of the business organization.[5]

Production Orientation

Interest in logistics developed as a part of a rather complicated evolution of industrial development in the United States. In the first stages emphasis was quite naturally upon production. Organizational principles and technological developments were applied to the area of production. The U.S. was behind England in terms of development and much effort was devoted by indigenous operations to overcoming the gap.[6]

Financial Developments

Mass production, however, required a capital investment. As it became evident in some industries that larger scale production offered increased efficiencies, we entered into a second stage in the industrial development in the U.S. The large corporations which were formed turned attention to financial practices for raising capital. Business became more sensitive to changing economic conditions and sought growth and less competitive market situations. One-man management was outgrown to a large extent and management teams and administrative ability became the focus of interest.[7]

Marketing Requirements

The appearance of large corporations almost coincided with the next stage in the evolutionary development of U.S. industry. We reached a point where the market could no longer regularly absorb the increased output and it became necessary for the business organization to cultivate and expand sales often within geographically imposed limits. So the marketing area received increased attention in this third stage. Marketing experts were necessary to maintain or expand competitive positions.[8]

Distribution Problems

The focus of attention upon production, engineering, finance, and sales brought into play many new developments including sales promotion, product research and development, stepped up unit production, etc. However, it was becoming increasingly difficult to keep the flow of products moving efficiently from the end of the manufacturing line to the consumer. There was often a bottleneck at the end of the production line. The problems and need for action ushered in a fourth stage, i.e., logistics or distribution.[9]

In the early part of the distribution stage, the warehousing of stocks at different points to meet sales needs became more popular. But even warehousing did not always place goods where they were most needed. "Rush" shipments at premium rates became necessary and some shippers even turned to private trucking to solve their problems.

Concurrent with the aforementioned developments were other increased burdens placed upon logistics and distribution activities in the firm because of a variety of marketing, manufacturing, legal, and other post-World War II economic developments.

*Production
Proliferation*

For example, a number of developments in recent years are due to changes in product-line characteristics. During earlier stages of the U.S. development, products were largely functional. Then, style and individuality became strong competitive weapons resulting in variations in color, packaging, and other features in a great number of lines of consumer goods. Variations in grade, color, and size have similarly taken place in industrial goods.[10]

The growth and change in product-line characteristics meant that manufacturers had more items to make, and distribution systems had more items to handle and stock. This meant lower volume per item and higher unit handling and inventory costs. The general rule is that the larger the sales volume of an item, the lower the inventory need be relative to sales. In the typical firm in the consumer and industrial goods fields, ten to twenty percent of the total items in the product line characteristically yield eighty percent of the sales. Half of the items stocked often account for less than four percent of the sales. This bottom half of the product line imposes a great deal of expense and investment in the distribution system.[11] In Chapter 4 we will discuss these relationships in some detail.

*Increased Freight
Rates*

Also, the freight rates of common carriers have steadily increased since the end of World War II. As a result, the geographical markets supplied from given market locations have been narrowed, and rate relationships that existed between sellers in common markets prior to World War II have been changed. The intensive competition which has developed between the forms of transportation makes it difficult to maintain any arbitrary system of rates. The net effect of these changes has been to reduce the market area of sellers with respect to given plant locations.[12]

Legal Rulings

Another factor limiting the market area which can be served profitably from a given plant location is the legal rulings which have cast doubt on the legality of uniform delivered pricing systems. Delivered pricing systems are sometimes aimed at promoting identical delivered prices among sellers at any destination by adjusting the total distribution costs of the sellers. The effect of this type of system was that buyers located close to the origin point paid a premium charge for transportation, and those located far from the origin point were subsidized through these excessive collections and thus sellers were able to enter previously unprofitable market areas. Legal rulings have cast doubt upon the legality of uniform delivered pricing systems, at least on an industry basis, and thus producers face the alternatives of dropping these peripheral market areas, selling at reduced profits, or relocating plants.[13]

Production planning became increasingly difficult because of the proliferation of products which necessitated shorter production runs of each type and made economies of scale difficult to achieve. It also made liaison more important between production and marketing because total demand as input information was no longer acceptable since effective control necessitated knowing something about the colors, models, etc. This made a strong case for someone or group to control the physical supply of such items and act as a go-between for production and marketing.

Higher Valued
Products

Related to the above, U.S. business firms in the post-war period manufactured increasingly higher valued goods. This was attributable to the increased affluence of the consumer and also to our higher labor costs precluding production of many low-valued, labor intensive products. These higher-valued products resulted in higher transportation cost,* and also increased inventory cost because of the larger amounts of money invested in inventory.

All of the above factors of a cost nature brought the related areas of logistics to the attention of many firms and pointed up the need of reducing such cost and introducing more effective controls. Investigation showed that we really did not know much in many instances about the physical flow of product from raw material through finished goods. But, it became increasingly apparent that there was a relationship between these elements of transportation. inventory, warehousing, and other areas which could be exploited in terms of reducing cost. However, it was necessary to be organized in such a fashion as to be able to meaningfully explore these relations and so more and more firms adopted formal organization structures which brought these activities under "one roof."

As a number of authors have suggested, the need to offer good service to customers was also a precipitating factor.[14] The increased competition of firms in oligopolistic markets often took the form of service competition.

Facilitating
Developments

In addition to the factors mentioned above which helped to focus attention upon the logistics area, there were two other developments which contributed to the emergence of logistics. First, the logistics area lends itself well to quantitative analysis because of the emphasis upon cost. The improvement and development of quantitative techniques in the post-World War II era has been noteworthy and such developments have helped to accomplish the analyses necessary to the logistics area, e.g., linear programming, simulation, etc. The second item was the computer which enabled people in the logistics area to analyze problems which were complex in terms of the number of variables that had to be handled.[15] The computer was particularly helpful in inventory control.

The discussion of the development of business logistics may have led to some unintended conclusions so some qualifications are probably necessary. First, the areas of marketing, finance, and production are still quite important today. Firms still experience problems in these areas and are continually analyzing and making improvements. What was said above merely implies that more progress has been made in improving production,

---

* As will be discussed in a later chapter, our rate structure has rates for higher valued products because of traditional value of service ratemaking and increased cost of moving higher valued commodites.

finance, and marketing practices. Second, some firms will not find it in their best interest to focus much attention upon logistics. For example, where transportation, warehousing, etc., are a small percentage of total cost, then it probably would not be worthwhile to emphasize this area or do much with it. Finally, logistics problems are generally symptomatic of maturity. Therefore, new firms will generally worry about production and marketing long before they turn their attention to logistics.

Much of what has been discussed thus far has indicated logistics as an area of management interest that requires the analysis of the elements of the logistics area from a systems perspective. In other words, there is a need to analyze the elements of logistics for possible changes which would result in lower cost. In the next section approaches to logistics systems analysis are reviewed.

APPROACHES TO ANALYZING LOGISTICS SYSTEMS

Physical Supply vs.
Physical
Distribution

The analysis and control of logistics activities requires grouping or classifying such activities in several different ways. We noted in the introductory section the number of different terms or labels that have been used in the logistics and distribution area. One such term is physical distribution, which is most appropriately associated with the movement and storage of finished goods and quite obviously of interest to the marketing area. In fact, another term often used synonymously with physical distribution is marketing logistics. Physical distribution is, therefore, concerned with the movement and storage of finished goods from the end of the production line to the customer.[16] (See Figure 1-1.)

Our previous definition of logistics indicated, however, an interest in the movement and storage of raw materials and/or semi-finished goods which suggests a broader view. In other words, the latter also includes an interest in the activities surrounding movement and storage up to the manufacturing point. Some authors have referred to this area as *physical supply*.[17] Another term frequently used synonymously is materials management. This facet of logistics is of interest to the production or manufacturing area in the firm.

The division or classification of logistics into physical supply and physical distribution is a very useful managerial or control perspective of the logistics activities in an organization. Frequently, there are important differences in the movement and storage aspects of raw materials and finished products in a firm. For example, if we think of a steel company, the movement of the required raw materials of iron ore and coal may be accomplished by barge and large rail carload movements. The storage aspects may require nothing more elaborate than an area of land where these items can be dumped and piled for future use. On the other hand, the finished steel will very often be moved by motor carrier and, obviously, the

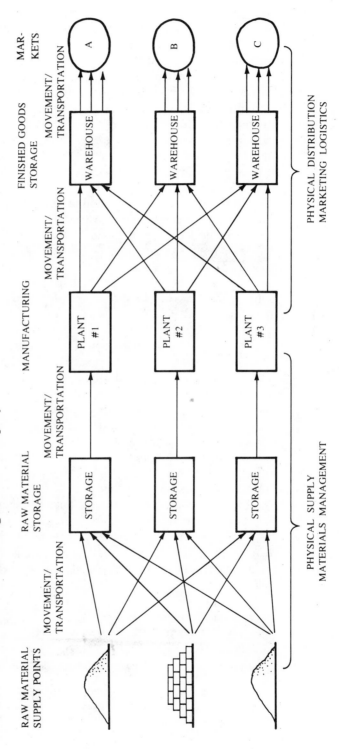

FIGURE 1-1 A view of business logistics in a company.

storage will require an enclosed facility for protection against the elements and, perhaps, elaborate materials handling equipment.

The differences which may exist between physical supply and physical distribution in terms of logistics requirements may have important implications for the design of the logistics system for the organization. Consequently, the differences may be so great as to result in a somewhat different design of logistics systems for physical supply and physical distribution. Companies may find it convenient to view their logistics system from these two perspectives and it may result in somewhat different management approaches for each. We should note, however, that coordination between physical supply and physical distribution is still necessary in spite of such differences.

Cost Centers

In the definitions from Ballou, Bartlett, and the National Council of Physical Distribution used previously, mention was made of the functional management activities included in the logistics area by many firms, viz., transportation, warehousing, inventory, materials handling, industrial packaging, etc. Emphasis was also placed upon the necessity for looking at these activities as being highly interrelated. As shall be discussed in some detail subsequently, we look at these activities as cost centers and analyze possible trade-offs between and among them that could result in lower overall cost and/or better service.

So the breaking down of the logistics area into the various cost centers or activity centers represents a second perspective on logistics or a second approach to viewing the logistics system. It should be easy to understand why logistics is frequently analyzed on the basis of activity centers since most frequently the possibility for reducing total logistics costs and/or improving service will occur by trading off one of these activity centers against another. For example, a shift from rail to motor carrier may result in lower inventory costs because of faster and more reliable service which will offset the higher motor carrier rate. (See Table 1-1.) Another possibility might be increasing the number of warehouses which would increase warehousing and inventory costs but may reduce transportation costs and increase sales enough to lower total costs. (See Table 1-2.)

The activity or cost center perspective is a very useful one in a variety of analytical and decision making situations where various trade-offs are being reviewed for lower cost and/or improved service to customer or the plant(s).

Nodes vs. Links

A third approach to viewing or analyzing the logistics system in an organization is in terms of nodes and links.* (See Figure 1-2.) The nodes are the established spatial points where the movement of goods is stopped for storage and/or processing. In other words, the nodes are the plants and warehouses of the organization where there are planned activities for storage

---

* Some authors refer to this breakdown as fixed points and transportation network. See, for example, J.L. Heskett, Robert M. Ivie, and Nicholas A. Glasowsky, Jr., *Business Logistics: Management of Physical Supply and Distribution* (New York: The Ronald Press Company, 1973), p. 43.

TABLE 1-1

Analysis of Total Logistics Cost
with Change to Higher Cost Mode of Transport

Cost Centers	System 1 (Rail)	System 2 (Motor)
Transportation	$ 500.00	$ 600.00 (↑)
Inventory Cost	1,000.00	900.00 (↓)
Packaging	300.00	250.00 (↓)
Total Cost	$1,800.00	$1,750.00

TABLE 1-2

Analysis of Total Logistics Cost
with Change to More Warehouses

Cost Center or Service Area	System 1 (1 Whse.)	System 2 (3 Whse.)
Transportation	$1,000,000.00	$ 700,000.00 (↓)
Inventory	3,000,000.00	3,300,000.00 (↑)
Cost of Lost Sales*	250,000.00	100,000.00 (↓)
Total Cost	$4,250,000.00	$4,100,000.00

*Based upon improved service to customers from the closer proximity of additional warehouses.

of materials for conversion into finished products or goods being held in finished form for sale to customers (equalization of supply and demand).

The other part of the system is the links, which represent the transportation network connecting the nodes in the logistics system. The transportation network can be made up of all the various modes of transportation (rail, motor, air, water, pipelines) as well as combinations and variations which will be discussed later.

We can appreciate that from a node/link perspective the complexity of logistics systems can vary enormously from systems with one node where the plant and warehouse are located with a simple network between suppliers and the plant to perhaps customers in one relatively small market area. At the other end of the spectrum are the large multiple product firms with multiple plant and warehouse locations. The transportation networks of the latter are also quite complex including three or four different modes and perhaps private as well as for-hire transportation.

In a sense the node and link perspective allows analyzing the two basic elements of a logistics system and therefore represents a convenient basis for

FIGURE 1-2   Nodes and links in a logistics system.

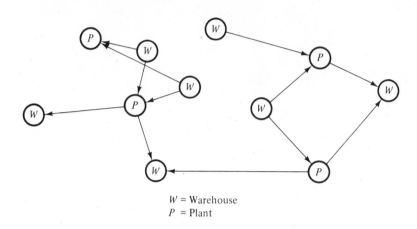

W = Warehouse
P = Plant

looking for possible improvements in the system. As has been noted elsewhere, the complexity of a logistics system is often a direct relationship to the variety of time and distance relationships between the nodes and the links and the degree of regularity and predictability as well as the volume of the flow of goods entering, leaving, and within the system.

A node and link perspective has been chosen in the major divisions of this text for the aforementioned reasons as well as others. However it should be noted that all three approaches or views of a logistics system are interrelated and are incorporated into the text. So for example the node analysis section of the book includes an activity or cost center breakdown of activities. It is useful for a number of reasons to look at the activities which take place at the nodes since they have important interrelationships when changes are being contemplated in the transportation network.

Logistics Channel   A fourth view or approach to logistics is an analysis of the logistics channel, i.e., the network of intermediaries engaged in various functions such as transfer, storage, handling, and communication that contribute to the efficient flow of goods.[18] The logistics channel can be viewed as part of the total distribution channel which includes, in addition to the logistical flows, a flow of transactions of specific interest to the marketing specialist.[19]

The logistics channel can be simple or complex. In Figure 1-3, we see a simple channel where an individual producer deals directly with a final customer. The control in the channel would be relatively simple in this case. The individual manufacturer should be able to exercise control of the logistical flows since they would be dealing directly with the customer.

Figure 1-4 presents a more complex multi-echelon channel with a market warehouse and retailers. The market warehouse could be a public warehouse. In this instance, the control would be more difficult because of the additional storage and transportation.

FIGURE 1-3 Simple logistics channel.

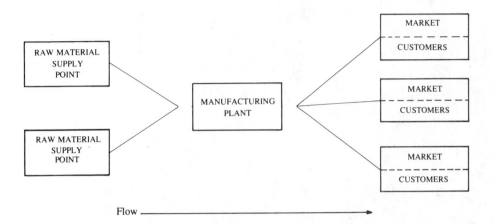

In Figure 1-5, a complex, comprehensive channel is illustrated. In this instance, it is easy to understand the more formidable task involved in achieving an effective logistical flow in the channel. However, this figure is a very realistic picture of the situation confronting many large organizations operating in the United States.

FIGURE 1-4 Multi-echelon logistics channel.

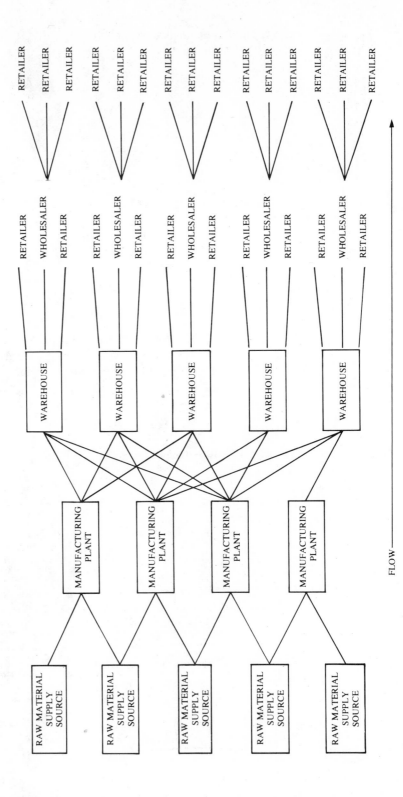

FIGURE 1-5 Complex logistics channel.

In some instances where a basic good like steel, aluminum, chemicals, or some other item is produced, the situation is further complicated by the fact that companies may be a part of more than one channel. For example, the steel may be sold to auto manufacturers, container manufacturerers, file cabinet producers, etc. There can be duplication of storage facilities, small shipment transportation, conflict over mode choices, and other problems contributing to inefficiency in the channel. There can also be problems of communications.

In an effort to overcome some of the problems mentioned above, companies employ different strategies. For example, some organizations integrate vertically so that they control the product over several stages in the logistics channel. Some channels are dominated by a strong company which exercises leadership in the channel to achieve efficiency. In any case, the complicating factors of the complex channel can be appreciated.

The various approaches or views of logistics should provide some additional insights into the nature of the relevant activities. Our understanding of logistics will be further aided by a discussion of logistical activities which are important ingredients in effective management of logistics systems.

LOGISTICAL ACTIVITIES

A previous section discussed a definition of logistics or physical distribution presented by the National Council of Physical Distribution Management listing activities that could be included as part of the responsibilities of the logistics manager. These activities were as follows:

- traffic and transportation
- warehousing and storage
- industrial packaging
- materials handling
- inventory control
- order processing
- customer service levels
- demand forecasting
- procurement
- distribution communications
- plant and warehouse site location
- return goods handling
- parts and service support
- salvage and scrap disposal

As suggested before, the above list of activities is quite comprehensive and many companies with well-organized logistics areas would not have responsibility for all of these activities. For example, companies that have strictly a physical distribution focus would not include procurement in their logistics organization.

The section of this chapter which discussed the development of interest in logistics implies the growth in the activities associated with the logistics area. The growth in scope means that activities are being taken from other parts of the organization, including marketing and production. There is disagreement among corporate executives as to what activities to include, particularly between marketing and logistics officials. For example, a recent study indicated that marketing and logistics executives expressed substantial disagreement for responsibility over:[20]

- customer service levels
- inventory
- packaging
- order processing

Given the controversy over logistics activities, it would seem worthwhile to discuss the scope of such activities and their appropriateness to logistics.

Transportation

All authors indicate that transportation is a necessary part of the logistics system. As has been pointed out, one of the major focuses in logistics is upon the physical movement or flow of goods, or expressed another way, the network which moves the product. This network is composed of transportation agencies which provide the service for the firm. Therefore, the logistics area would generally be accorded responsibility for selecting a mode or modes of tranportation that would be used in moving the raw materials and finished goods of the firm.

Storage

A second area which is closely related to transportation is storage, and it involves two separate but very related activities namely, inventory management and warehousing. There is a direct relationship between the transportation agency being used and the level of inventory and number of warehouses required. For example if the firm uses a relatively slow means of transport, they usually have to keep higher levels of inventory and would usually have more warehousing space for this inventory. They may examine the possibility of using a faster means of transport to eliminate some of these warehouses and the inventory which is stored therein. As suggested previously, a number of firms have been able to reduce their total logistics cost by increasing the amount of money that they spend on transportation to reduce costs in inventory and warehousing.

More will be said about the inventory area and the basic concerns within the firm about this area in succeeding chapters. However, at this point we should note that there are possible organizational conflicts about the level of inventory which should be held and a strong interest in the level and location of inventory stocks. It should also be noted that there is a very close relationship between transportation and inventory levels and that if the systems approach is going to be taken, it usually requires close coordination between these two areas.

Packaging

A third general area which is frequently mentioned is industrial (exterior) packaging. It can be demonstrated that the type of transportation which is selected will have an impact on the packaging requirements for moving the product to the market and also will be important as far as raw materials are concerned. In regard to the former, it is generally conceded that rail or water transportation will require additional expenditures for packaging because of the greater possibility of damage. In the trade-offs analyzed for proposed changes in transportation agencies, we would generally look to see what impact the change will have upon packaging costs. In many instances, when we move to a premium means of transport, such as air, packaging costs will be reduced. Therefore, an argument can be made that packaging should be a part of the responsibility of the logistics area because of this relationship to the transportation agency and also to storage costs.

Materials Handling

A fourth area frequently mentioned as a logistics activity is materials handling which is also of interest to a number of areas in the typical business organization. It should be readily apparent that materials handling is important in the efficient operation of warehouses. Therefore, logistics managers would be concerned with the movement of goods into a warehouse, their placement in a warehouse, the movement from storage areas to order picking areas and eventually out of the warehouse to be loaded for transportation.

Materials handling is concerned with mechanical equipment for short distance movement, including such things as conveyors, fork-lift trucks, overhead cranes, containers, and items of this particular nature. It should be quite obvious that the production managers may want a particular pallet or type of container which may not be compatible with the logistics warehousing activities. Therefore, the materials handling designs must be coordinated in an effort to make sure that the types of equipment being used are congruent. In addition, the company may find it economical from a purchasing point of view if they could use the same type of fork-lift trucks.

The actual physical detail design of a conveyor system or specification with respect to the strengths of a pallet would generally not be a part of the working knowledge of many managers with logistics training. It would require someone with engineering expertise to do this type of analysis. Some firms may find it expedient to have a separate engineering function in the firm which considers these particular problems. It would be the responsibility of the logistics people to specify the design needs and allow the engineering people to come up with the particular system to meet the overall specifications.

Order Processing

Another area of activitiy which is sometimes specified for control in the logistics area is that of order processing, which generally consists of those activities involved with filling customer orders. Initially, one might express some doubt as to why the logistics area would be concerned directly with order processing. However, if one looks at logistics in a time perspective we can see that one of the things which is important on the physical distribution side is the lapsed time between the moment when a customer decides to place an order for a product and the time that those goods are actually delivered in a satisfactory condition.

Viewed in this perspective, we can see that the initial stage is concerned with some form of transmittal by the customer, the receipt by the firm of the order, some designation that the order be shipped out, and then the actual transportation of that item. The time lapse with the communications surrounding the processing can in some instances be quite significant. Previously we had talked about trade-offs between transportation agencies and inventory, and we have also recognized the growing pressures of oligopolistic market structures to give good service to customers. Consequently, a company may be forced to use premium means of transportation like motor carrier or air in order to meet service requirements. If order processing was a part of logistics then we might examine possible improvements in order processing which would require additional expenditures but allow us to decrease our transportation costs. For example, let us assume that the present system takes a total order cycle period of eight days for transmittal, processing, order preparation and shipping. The order processing part of this may take four days, and order preparation may take an additional two days, which means that the goods have to be transported in two days to the customer. The short delivery time may require premium means of transportation. If order processing was viewed as part of the logistics system, then the company might legitimately look at improvements in order processing such as telephone calls and the use of more computer equipment for processing to reduce order processing time to two days or one day. This would allow the firm to use less expensive means of transportation and still get the goods to the customer within eight days. Looking at logistics in a time perspective or in terms of total order cycle time, we can readily see that order processing can be quite important.

Forecasting

Another activity that is sometimes assigned to the logistics area is demand forecasting. One can also question why the logistics manager would be concerned with forecasting. Forecasting of sales is based upon knowledge of the markets as well as the manipulation of data with statistical techniques to make a forecast. Sales forecasting would frequently be an input to logistics received from marketing in order to be prepared to make deliveries to various market areas according to the projections. However, logistics managers may need to do their own forecasting for inventory purposes and may use sales forecasts as input.

It should be noted that the logistics manager should also be familiar with forecasting techniques, since it may be necessary for the logistics manager to recast the sales estimates, particularly in terms of geographic requirements. However, the basic responsibilities for sales forecasting should logically lie with marketing, and logistics would use such data as an input and attempt to meet these demand levels.

Production
Scheduling

Another area that is mentioned in discussing logistics systems is that of production scheduling, which requires decisions as to when goods should be produced and the number or quantities of goods that are produced. It is sometimes inferred that if production scheduling is the responsibility of logistics area then this would have the effect of logistics taking over production. Nothing could be further from the truth since it is the primary responsibility of the production area to determine how products will be made and what productive processes will be used as well as other decisions with respect to sampling technique, quality control, and production line balancing to achieve the lowest cost of operations. The type of scheduling we are talking about here is very similar to what the logistics people would receive from marketing. Logistics would inform production when certain types of goods would have to be produced and the numbers which are necessary. This type of information would be developed based upon sales forecast and the inventory levels in the company of the various products.

Purchasing

Purchasing is another activity which has been mentioned as being included in logistics and is in some business organizations. The basic rationale for including purchasing in logistics is that very often there is a direct relationship between transportation and the amounts and geographic location of raw materials and component parts which are purchased for the production needs of a company. Therefore, the logistics cost would be affected by the quantities purchased in terms of transportation cost and also inventory costs. Whether purchasing is actually included as a part of the logistics area is primarily a matter of which achieves the most effective coordination and lowest cost for the firm.

Site Location

Another area cited by the NCPDM organization is warehouse site location. The relevancy of this activity is discussed at some length in later chapters. At this point, the importance to logistics should be readily comprehendable. A change in location could alter time and place relationships between plants and markets or between supply points and the plants. Such changes will impact upon transportation rates and service, customer service, inventory requirements, and possibly other areas. Therefore, the logistics manager is quite interested in and concerned about location decisions. In fact, plant location is frequently as important as warehouse location and will be discussed.

Other Activities

Other areas such as parts and service support, return goods handling, and salvage and scrap disposal mentioned in the NCPDM definition are indicative of a very broad set of logistical activities being managed in one area in companies producing consumer durables and/or industrial products. Here it is argued that a very integrative approach is necessary. Therefore, logistical input is included into product design as well as maintenance and supply service activities since these areas are affected by transportation and storage decisions.

No attempt has been made in this section to specifically delineate what activities should be included in logistics. There are a number of possibilities depending upon the characteristics and environment of the indiividual firm. The intent at this point was to discuss all of the possibilities and cover the relationships to other areas. Later chapters will treat design of specific systems. The next section covers logistics and systems analysis.

LOGISTICS AND SYSTEMS ANALYSIS

The previous section on the development of logistics pointed out that improvements in techniques of analysis and methodologies facilitated the development of logistics. One such improvement was systems analysis or the systems concept. A convenient starting point for this section is a brief discussion of the basic nature of systems analysis.

Basic Nature Essentially a system is a set of interacting elements, variables, parts, or objects that are functionally related to each other and form a coherent group.[21] The concept of a system is actually something all of us have been exposed to at an early stage in our education. Early in our academic program we were given an introduction in science to the solar system and learned about the relations between the planets, the sun, and the moon and how these relathionships resulted in day and night, weather, etc. Later in biology we learned about the human body and once again took a systems perspective viewing the parts of the body and their relationships such as the heart, the blood vessels, etc.

Examples Perhaps in an auto mechanics class, we learned about engines in automobiles as a system. We were probably informed that parts of the engine like the pistons could have been designed for larger size and more efficiency but their very efficiency may have overloaded other parts of the engine so as to cause it to break down. So the pistons had to be designed in harmony with other parts of the engine. In other words, the overall performance of the engine was most important, not one part.

Cost Perspective The above analogy provides insights into the characteristics of business systems. If we are measuring efficiency by cost, then an individual part of the system may not be operating at its lowest cost but may contribute to the overall efficiency of the system. For example, in a logistics context, perhaps water transportation is the cheapest alternative available to some company. If the company optimizes transportation alone, then water movement would be the best approach. However, moving freight by water may require increased holdings of inventory with associated increases in warehousing space and other costs. These additional costs may then be greater than what is being saved by using water transportation. In other words, the transportation decision has to be made in harmony with the related areas of inventory and warehousing and perhaps packaging so that the overall system or subsystem is optimized instead of just transportation. The general tenet of the systems concept is that we do not focus upon individual variables but rather how they interact as a whole. Our objective is to operate the whole effectively, not the individual parts.

Levels of Optimality Another aspect of the systems concept that was implied above was that there are what might be called "levels of optimality" in the firm. It was just stated that transportation should not be optimized at the expense of related areas in the logistics system such as warehousing and packaging. At the same time, however, logistics is only one subsystem in the firm, and, therefore, it should not be optimized at the expense of another area in the firm. For example, the logistics manager may want to give five-day delivery service to some customers in order to eliminate some warehouses and inventory. However, this may conflict with marketing since the firm's competitors give three-day delivery service in the same sales area. Clearly, some compromise will have to be worked out after the situation is analyzed. In fact, logistics may have to accept the three-day service as a working constraint imposed because of competition and design the "best" system within this constraint. Some one or group at the senior executive level in the organization has to examine the trade-offs between the marketing and logistics area in terms of efficiency or profit of the total organization.

In addition to the marketing area, consideration has to be given to production, finance, etc. In other words, the overall firm is a system which should be optimized. The internal subsystems may have to be suboptimized in order to achieve the best position for the overall firm. Generally, this means that logistics has to work within certain constraints such as set delivery times, minimum production run orders, financial limits on warehouse improvements and construction. Such constraints are usually somewhat arbitrary and should be flexible within reasonable limits. Ideally such decisions as delivery times should be made on a more individual or short run basis, but the complexity of organizations is such that this cannot be done from an operational standpoint. A dynamic simulation model would help to solve some of these problems and allow more flexibility. However, there are many factors which deter companies from having such models. More will be said about this point in the chapters covering management of logistics systems.

One other point should be made about levels of optimality. As Heskett and others have pointed out or implied, firms operate very often in a channel or perhaps even in several channels if they produce intermediate goods such as steel or have a multiple line.[22] Therefore one might consider channel optimization or external effects of firm decisons as another higher level of optimality. For example, a container or pallet may be designed for shipping a firm's product which is consistent with the overall needs of the firm, but it may not be compatible with the ordering and receiving needs of customers. Therefore, in the final analysis such an improvement may be harmful to overall efficiency of the channel. (See Figure 1-6.)

In summary, a systems approach involves looking at related variables or elements and taking into consideration what impact a planned change in one or two variables will have on the others or, if you will, the effect on the total system. Logistics is, however, only one system or subsystem in the firm and, therefore, consideration must also be given to the overall firm and what effects changes in logistics have on other areas such as marketing and production. The firm itself operates in an economic, social and political environment which requires consideration being given to variables outside the company for an overall systems viability. Finally, it should be noted that a change in one of the elements in logistics may not necessarily have any impact upon the other parts of the logistics system but could affect some other system in the firm. For example, a change may be made from motor carrier A to motor carrier B, which has no effect on inventory, warehousing, etc., but the new motor carrier may have restrictions in their operating authority which affects deliveries to certain customers. While a good transportation manager would usually catch something of this nature, it points out the danger of too narrow a view of the effects of a change. Just because the subsystem of which the variable is a part does not change does not necessarily mean that there is no reaction to the change.

SYSTEM EVALUATION

The previous discussion indicated two important and related aspects of the systems approach which deserve emphasis and some amplification at this

FIGURE 1-6   Levels of optimality.

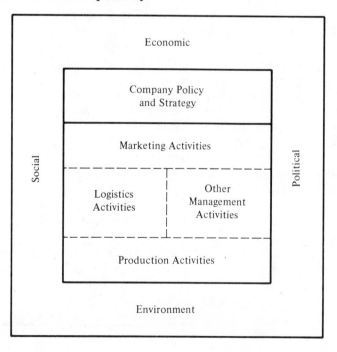

Total Cost Analysis

Trade-offs

juncture. It was pointed out that the effect of a change in the system is usually measured by some criterion such as cost and the emphasis is upon the total cost of the system. In other words, we maximize by reducing the total cost of the system. Implied in this total cost aspect is a second aspect, viz., trade-offs, which is frequently mentioned in the literature. When a change is made in one part of the system, it usually affects other variables. If the initial change represents an increased cost then we may be trading off against decreased costs in other variables or vice versa so that overall costs are reduced.* For example, a firm may change from a centralized warehousing system to one that is decentralized in various market areas. This change in warehousing would usually involve increased warehousing costs because of the increase in facilities and also increased inventory levels. These increases would usually be traded off against decreased transportation costs and perhaps increased sales through better service. If the overall effect was lower cost then the system would usually be adopted.

There is some tendency in logistics to emphasize cost, which is understandable because of the nature of the area. Cost then is very often the criterion used for evaluating system performance in logistics. As the reader will see, the example problems in logistics system analysis are approached in a cost context. Some individuals have warned that minimization of cost may be over emphasized.[23] While this may be true in some isolated instances, most authors writing in this area recognize that logistics has to contribute to the overall profitability of the firm. Therefore, profit maximization is a vital concern and is usually the most important objective for overall efficiency of the organization.

One should recognize that cost minimization is a natural focus for logistics since higher management will customarily measure performance in terms of cost within certain constraints which are imposed to maximize overall profit. For example, logistics cost might be lowest by having five-day delivery to customers in the southwestern states like Texas for an Ohio firm. But, competitors provide four-day delivery service which the company must meet to remain competitive and maximize profits. Perhaps logistics would like 4,000 units of a certain item in the product line for next month's deliveries, but production efficiency requires a minimum run of 5,000. These are constraints on logistics in terms of their cost, but they help the firm.

In analyzing possible changes in a logistics system and evaluating potential trade-offs, a method or technique for analysis is necessary. While we might choose to take this matter up in a later chapter and present a more sophisticated approach, it would help to illustrate some of the basic ideas that have been presented to consider techniques or methods of analysis at this point

---

* It should be noted that there is a need to look at overall impact on the firm, so that we do not lose sight of the overall objective of the firm which is to maximize profits.

TECHNIQUES OF LOGISTICS SYSTEM ANALYSIS

In this section, consideration is given to the techniques of total cost analysis for logistics systems. It should be pointed out that only some of the more basic methods are presented. In a later section, more sophisticated techniques of total cost analysis will be discussed. However, it is a good idea at this point to look at the basic approaches because it will tend to bring together some of the concepts we have been discussing thus far and will also provide a very meaningful background for some of the things which we are about to discuss in the next section of the book.

Two Aproaches

There are actually two general approaches that can be used in a total cost analysis of the type prescribed for business logistics. First, we can look at a very short-run situation and develop costs associated with the various cost centers of logistics previously described. Such cost information can be developed for each of the alternative systems we are considering. We would then select that system which had the lowest overall cost as long as it was consistent with other constraints imposed by the firm on the logistics area. Some authors refer to this short-run type of an analysis as static analysis.[24] Essentially they are saying that cost associated with the various components of a logistics system at one point in time or one level of output will be analyzed; for example, refer to Table 1-3.

Short Run/ Static Analysis

In this instance, a firm is presently using an all-rail route from the plant and the associated plant warehouse to the customers. At this plant warehouse the chemicals are bagged and then shipped by rail to the customer. A second system is being proposed using a market-oriented warehouse. The goods will be shipped from the plant to the market warehouse and then they would be packaged and sent to the customer. Instead of shipping it all by rail, now it will be shipped by barge to the warehouse taking advantage of low bulk rates to the warehouse. Then, movement would be by rail from the warehouse after it had been bagged for shipment to the customer.

The trade-off example is lower transportation costs against some increases in storage and warehousing. If the analysis is strictly static, i.e., at this level of output, we can see that the proposed system is more expensive than the present one. So, unless some additional information more favorable to the proposed system was provided, we would continue with our present system.

There are two reasons why the proposed system could be selected. First, there is no information about customer service requirements. The new market-oriented warehouse might provide better service to customers and therefore increase sales and profits which would offset some of the higher cost of System II. Second, if we use a longer run perspective (dynamic analysis) and look at the example (Figure 1-7) we can see that System I is giving us a lower cost at 50,000 units of output. But, at approximately 70,500 units of output, System II becomes cheaper than System I. Therefore, if the company is experiencing rapid growth in sales they may

TABLE 1-3

Static Analysis
(C & B Chemical Company
50,000 pounds of output)

	System 1	*System 2*
Plant Logistics Costs:*		
Packaging	$ 500	$ 0
Storage and handling	150	50
Inventory carrying	50	25
Administrative	75	25
Fixed cost	4,200	2,400
Transportation Costs:*		
To market warehouse	0	150
To customer	800	100
Warehouse Costs:*		
Packaging	0	500
Storage and handling	0	150
Inventory carrying	0	75
Administrative	0	75
Fixed cost	0	2,400
Total Cost:*	$5,775	$5,950

*In thousands of dollars.

want to plan the shift to System II now. The immediate planning may be necessary because of the start up time for the new warehouse.

Referring back to our previous commentary, a second reason why a firm might switch to System II, even though they are presently experiencing lower costs with another system, is that in the future they expect the second system to result in lower costs. Since it usually takes some period of time to set up a new system, they may initiate the change in the near future. If this firm is growing at a relatively rapid rate perhaps they will be able to achieve 70,500 units in a fairly short period of time.

Long Run/
Dynamic Analysis

The second way to determine the optimum system projecting into the future is to mathematically calculate the point of equality between the systems. So, in our example, System I and System II were equal at about 70,500 units of output. If the graph is used to determine the point of equality it is difficult to be completely accurate. For a mathematical solution all we need to do is start with the equation for a straight line $(y = a + bx)$. In this particular case, a would be the fixed costs and b would be the variable cost

FIGURE 1-7   Dynamic analysis.

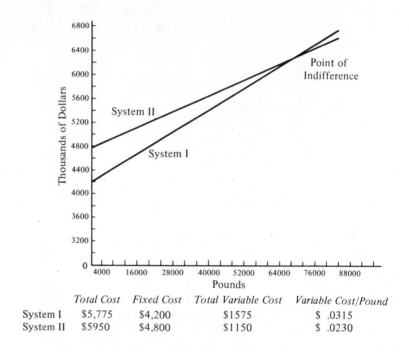

	Total Cost	Fixed Cost	Total Variable Cost	Variable Cost/Pound
System I	$5,775	$4,200	$1575	$ .0315
System II	$5950	$4,800	$1150	$ .0230

per unit. The x would be the level of output. If we want to solve for the point where the two systems are equal, we can set the two equations up as being equal to each other and plug in the appropriate cost information solving these equations, and we can quickly see as is demonstrated below that at approximately 70,500 pounds the two systems are equal and we experience a point of indifference between the two systems.

1. System I

Total Cost = Fixed Cost + Variable Cost/unit × Number of Units

$$y = 4200 + .0315\, x$$

2. System II

$$y = 4800 + .0230\, x$$

3. Trade-off Point

$$4800 + .0230\, x = 4200 + .0315\, x$$

$$600 = .0085\, x$$

$$x = 70,588 \text{ pounds}$$

It should be noted that there is no reason why a particular firm might not be considering more than two logistics systems at one time. In fact, many examples show three systems or sometimes four systems being considered by a particular firm. The same basic methodology for plotting and for mathematically solving for the points of indifference can be used regardless of how many systems we might be analyzing. It should also be noted that there is no reason why the cost functions have to intersect. It is possible in a particular situation where we are considering two systems that they in fact do not intersect so that one will be lower than the other over the entire range of output. Where we are considering three or more systems, two of them may intersect and the other occur at a higher level in the quadrant. In a situation where you have three systems with all three intersecting there are two relevant intersection points or two relevant points of indifference. A third intersection would occur at a point above some other cost function and would not be relevant.

SUMMARY

In this chapter, the basic aspects of logistics systems have been discussed and analyzed, and the important dimensions have been reviewed. One important aspect that has been referred to in a number of places is the relationship of logistics to other areas of the organization such as production and marketing. In addition, the importance of logistics in the economy and more detail on trade-offs, in the logistics system, must be developed. These topics are covered in the next chapter.

Study Questions

1. What factors contributed to the development of interest in business logistics? Which of those factors do you think were the most important and why?
2. What are three perspectives or approaches to viewing business logistics? Which one of the approaches would be used most frequently?
3. What is the basic nature of systems analysis? How is it used in business logistics?
4. What are the various levels of optimality for an organization?
5. How would you justify taking a logistics approach in a company?

Notes

1. Ronald H. Ballou, *Business Logistics Management* (Englewood Cliffs, New Jersey: Prentice-Hall., 1973), p.8.

2. Hale C. Bartlett, *Readings in Physical Distribution* (Danville, Illinois: The Interstate Printers and Publishers, 1972), p.1.

3. Lynn Edward Gill, "Organization for Effctive Physical Distribution," *Annual Meeting Proceedings—1977,* NCPDM, pp. 105-106.

4. See for example, "New Strategies to Move Goods," *Business Week,* September 24, 1966, pp. 112-36.

5. Peter F. Drucker, "The Economy's Dark Continent," *Fortune,* April 1962, pp. 103, 265-70.

6. E. Smykay, F. Mossman, D. Bowersox, *Physical Distribution Management* (New York: The Macmillan Company, 1961), pp. 7-10.

7. George Smerk, George Wilson, and John Spychalski, *Physical Distribution Management,* Vol. 1 (Bloomington, Indiana: Indiana University Press, 1964), pp. 4-60.

8. Smykay et al., *op. cit.,* pp. 7-11.

9. *Ibid.*

10. Smerk et. al., *op. cit.,* pp. 45-65.

11. Smykay et. al., *op. cit.,* pp. 11-14.

12. *Ibid.*

13. Smerk, *op. cit.,* pp. 20-30.

14. Donald J. Bowersox, Edward W. Smykay, and Bernard J. LaLonde, *Physical Distribution Management* (New York: The Macmillan Company, 1968), pp. 13-14; James Heskett, Robert Ivie and Nicholas A. Glaskowsky, Jr., *Business Logistics* (New York: Ronald Press, 1964), pp. 39-41; and John F. Magee, *Industrial Logistics* New York: McGraw-Hill Book Company, 1968), pp. 19-21.

15. *Ibid.,* p. 11.

16. Ballou, *op. cit.,* p. 7.

17. J. L. Heskett, Robert M. Ivie, and Nicholas A. Glaskowsky, Jr., *Business Logistics: Management of Physical Supply and Distribution* (New York: The Ronald Press Company, 1973), p. 26.

18. Donald J. Bowersox, *Logistical Management*, (New York: The Macmillan Company, 1974, pp. 36-37.)

19. *Ibid.*

20. Thomas W Speh. "Physical Distribution-Marketing Interfaces: Research and Managerial Implications," *NCPDM Proceedings,* Los Angeles, October 1977, p. 36.

21. E. J. Kelley and W. Lazor, *Managerial Marketing: Perspectives and Viewpoints* (Homewood, Illinois: Richard D.Irwin, Inc., 1967), p. 19.

22. Heskett et al., *op. cit.,* p. 42.

23. See for example: J. R. Grabner and James F. Robeson, "Budgeting for Profit in Physical Distribution," *Transportation and Distribution Management,* April 1969, pp. 41-47.

24. J.L.Heskett et al., *op. cit.,* pp. 454-69.

Case 1-1
Alpha Company

The Alpha Company, a major nationwide distributor of electrical components, is presently facing the problem of increased competition in its western
region, with most problems occurring in the Los Angeles metropolitan area.

The electrical components produced by Alpha have traditionally been
transported by motor carrier to the respective consignees on the West Coast.
The majority of the Alpha product line is used in the assembly of computers.
Alpha's production facilities are located in St. Louis.

Mr. Amadio, the vice-president of Alpha's logistics department, has
contracted the NO-IT-ALL Management Consulting Firm to look at the
possibility of adding a new distribution warehouse in the Los Angeles area.

In a meeting with Mr. Black, a NO-IT-ALL representative, Mr.
Amadio stated what he viewed as three possible alternatives open to Alpha
with respect to the Los Angeles problem. The alternatives were:

1. The firm could lease space in a public warehouse at a rate of $5.00 per
   unit of throughput. A unit of throughput is defined as a unit moved into
   the warehouse and then transported out to a consignee.
2. The firm could purchase a warehouse with a throughput capacity of
   60,000 units per year for an operating cost of $4,000 per month plus
   $3.00 per unit of throughput.
3. The firm could purchase a larger warehouse with an annual capacity of
   100,000 units at a cost of $8,000 per month plus $2.00 per unit of
   throughput.

Mr. Amadio has made it clear that Alpha wants to increase its
competitiveness in the Los Angeles area, but at this time, they are unsure as
to the level of throughput required.

You are employed by NO-IT-ALL in the logistics consulting department. Mr. Black has just explained the circumstances pertaining to the
Alpha Company and hands you a sheet of paper containing the following
orders. Assume the level of throughput to be constant each month.

1. Graph the alternatives and label each on the basis of monthly losses/
   throughput on a sheet of graph paper.
2. Solve for the relevant indifference points.
3. For what range of output would the firm choose to use each alternative?

   a) Public warehouse from _____ to _____ units/month
   b) Private warehouse capacity 60,000 from _____ to _____
      units/month.
   c) Private warehouse capacity 100,000 from _____ to _____
      units/month.

Case 1-2
L. Fox Manufacturing Company

The L. Fox Manufacturing Company is a large Chicago-based producer of children's wear. The market areas of L. Fox Manufacturing are concentrated on the East Coast, ranging from Maine to Florida.

In the past two years, Fox, a quite prosperous company, has suffered cuts in profit due to higher transportation costs and increased competition from a Los Angeles firm, Kiddie's Klothes, which has expanded into Fox's market and during this expansion has set up four distribution warehouses in the eastern region.

In a September meeting, scheduled by Mr. Lawrence Fox, president of the firm, all staff and ranking line members were called in to discuss the present problems which were plaguing the company in the eastern region.

THE SEPTEMBER MEETING

John J. Roberts, a staff person employed in the logistics department, argues that the present system (I) being used by L. Fox is quite efficient and that transport costs would be reduced if marketing would give some advanced notice as to when they were going to run specials or have changes made in the package design of the product.

The director of marketing, Tom Schultz, responds by quoting sales and market demand figures and states that the present system (I) is inefficient and must be upgraded with the combination of common carrier trucks (II) to the logistics system.

The production manager, Harry Kalahan, believes that the firm could realize increased savings by extending production runs and thus achieving economies of scale. Additionally, he argues that the incorporation of a rail common carrier (III) into the distribution channel would be more efficient and effective and help cut costs throughout the firm.

Mr. Fox, a clothes designer, possesses very little knowledge of logistics, marketing, and production, and thus contacts a local consulting firm to carry out a cost study, reviewing all three of the proposed systems.

Analysis

Use the information presented in the following table to conduct the cost study.

	Total Fixed Costs	Variable Costs
1. Private Truck (present system) (I)	$2,000	$4/cwt
2. Common Carrier Truck (II)	$0	$6/cwt
3. Rail (III)	$6,500	$1/cwt

1. Graph the three systems on a sheet of graph paper.
2. Compute the relevant indifference points.
3. At the following levels of output, which system should be used and what is the cost? 350 cwt; 1100 cwt; 1500 cwt; 2000 cwt.

Chapter 2	# Logistics Environments

After studying this chapter, you should be able to:

- Provide a macro perspective on business logistics in our society.
- Discuss the relationships between logistics and other functional areas in a business organization.
- Analyze the various factors which affect logistics costs.

The preceeding chapter provided a basic exposure to logistics and its various activities along with a look at how logistics systems can be analyzed. Some perspective was provided about the relationship of logistics to other areas. It is important that such relationships be delineated more specifically and that the several dimensions of these relationships be explored. In effect, there are several environments that interact with logistics. See Figure 2-1 for a representation of the several environments and relationships of logistics.

FIGURE 2-1   The environments and relationships of logistics.

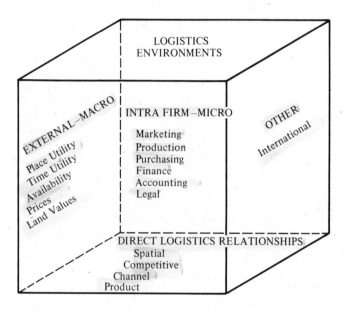

If we limit the scope of our investigation of logistics relationships, direct cost variables such as competitive relations, spatial relations, etc., would be a part of the analysis. If broadened somewhat, then the investigation would focus on logistics as one important subsystem in an organization which has to function in harmony with other subsystems such as marketing and production.

An even broader perspective is possible which explores the role of logistics in the economy and the associated contributions and relationships of logistics on a macro basis. The major objective of this chapter is to review and analyze all three environments and discuss the important aspects of such relationships. Initially, the broad external view of logistics will be investigated. Then, the intra-firm relations will be discussed followed by the more direct relations. The international dimension will be discussed in Chapter 9.

LOGISTICS IN THE ECONOMY: THE MACRO-EXTERNAL ENVIRONMENT

Micro vs. Macro

Generally in analyzing business logistics, we explore the micro dimension. The micro dimension of business logistics implies a study of the logistics area from the perspective of the individual firm. In this section, we will take another viewpoint by looking at logistics as it relates to the economy. This is sometimes referred to as the macro dimension of business logistics.

In a previous section discussing the development of the logistics concept, it was pointed out that during the economic development which occurred in the United States during the 19th and early 20th centuries there was a tremendous focus upon production efficiency. This encompassed a movement within the economy to specialize in the production of certain types of output in regions where particular economic advantages existed.

Specialization

This tendency to specialize and to produce at lower costs was a normal development of economic growth in the sense described by Adam Smith and other economists. This leads one to question why specialization of labor, if it does result in lower cost and lower prices, did not advance more rapidly or why the United States does not specialize more than it does at the present time. Perhaps one might also raise the question of underdeveloped countries and why they do not practice specialization of production in order to aid in their economic development.

Limits on Specialization

Adam Smith answered this question when he indicated that specialization or division of labor is limited by the extent of the market or the volume of demand for the product. In other words, it does not pay nor is it beneficial to an organization to practice specialization to a greater degree if the fruits of this specialization, the additional output, cannot be sold to consumers. The additional output would have no economic value unless it could be moved from the point of production surplus to the point or points where demand is unfulfilled. Logistics provides the means to capitalize on comparative cost advantages in the production of goods and services.

Place Utility

Logistics performs one of its roles by moving goods from points of surplus to points *where* demand exists. Logistics extends the physical boundaries of the market thus adding economic value to the goods. This addition to the economic value of the goods or services by movement from points of excess to points of demand is known as the value of place utility. Place utility is primarily created through transportation.

Time Utility

Not only must goods and services be available where they are needed, but they must also be at that point *when* they are demanded. This is called time utility or the economic value added to a good or service by having it at a demand point at the time desired. Time utility is created through proper inventory maintenance and the strategic location of goods and services. To some extent transportation may also play a role in time utility creation by quicker movement of something to a point of demand. An example of this concept is the addition of time utility by using air transportation as a substitute for warehousing.

As we have seen logistics is concerned with the creation of time and place utility yet nothing has been mentioned about promotion, the other aspect of distribution. Promotion may be defined as the effort, through direct and indirect contact with the customer, to increase the desire to possess a good or benefit from a service. In other words, promotion is concerned with the creation of possession utility. The role of logistics in the economy is based upon the existence of possession utility for if no demand exists at a given point, it makes little sense to move the unwanted commodity to that point. (See Figure 2-2.)

FIGURE 2-2   Fundamental utility creation in the economy.

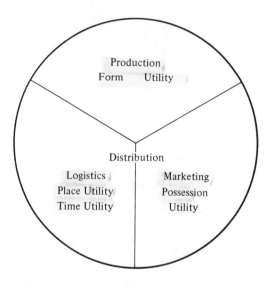

So we see that logistics is basically concerned with adding time and place utility to goods in the economy. The emphasis during the production stage of economic development was upon the place utility function, being able to move goods as efficiently as possible to the various points. Consequently, during the 19th and early 20th centuries the railroad dominated the transportation scene. It offered low rates and volume movement, factors quite important in a production oriented economy. As we have developed in the 20th century with higher-valued multiple-product line firms and affluent consumers with particular types of tastes, we have put increasing emphasis upon time utility. So now faster modes of transportation are important even though they may give rise to higher rates. Also warehousing and other related activities are very important in the successful role of products. Timing of deliveries in our modern economy has received an increasing amount of attention and in fact one might argue that this emphasis on time has been the most important factor giving rise to our

Increasing Importance of Time Utility

present concern in the logistics area. If we were only interested in optimizing movement or place utility, we would use slower forms of transport, which have lower rates, such as water or rail.

Specific Examples of the Impact of Logistics

The reader, at this point, may ask to what extent does logistics serve the economy. Its significance is far greater than one might imagine aside from its role of creating time and place utility; logistics and related activities provided jobs for over 14 million Americans in 1980, about 14% of the total labor force.[1] Investment in privately owned transportation and logistics facilities has been estimated at approximately 300 billion dollars.[2] This does not include public investment in such facilities since such is difficult to account for; public expenditure figures often fail to differentiate between capital investment and the operating and maintenance expenditures associated with present equipment. Furthermore, no allowance is made for the depreciation and obsolescence of older facilities. However, Heskett and others do provide us with an estimate of the total investment in freight and passenger logistics facilities at approximately 18.5% of the national wealth.[3] Another interesting item is the estimate that approximately 20%[4] of our expenditures for goods and services, directly and indirectly goes for logistics related expenditures. Clearly logistics is of major economic importance; the task of getting materials and services to the right place, at the proper time, and in the desired quantities not only affects the individual firm, but is an important aspect of the econony as well.

Some additional perspective can be gained on the importance of logistics to the economy by referring to Exhibit 2-1. For manufacturing companies, the cost of distribution activities averages almost 14% of the sales dollar. Also, it can be seen that for merchandising companies the average is almost 27% of the sales dollar. For manufacturing companies, there is a likelihood that the costs are underestimated because most of the activities listed emphasize the physical distribution component of logistics.

For purposes of comparison, it has been estimated that direct labor comprises from 12% to 14% of the cost of delivered goods. Therefore, logistics costs compare favorably in importance with other major cost components in business organizations and logistics is an area worthy of investigation for improving productivity.[5]

Variety of Goods

In addition to the time and place utility aspects of logistics, there are other dimensions of the relationships of logistics in the economy. One very important contribution is the volume and variety of goods available to consumers in areas far removed from where they are produced and at times often far removed from when they were manufactured or produced.

We often take this availability of a wide assortment of goods for granted but it is very much dependent upon the effective performance of the movement and storage functions (logistics) in all the firms in the economy. The total of all these logistics operations provides the economy with the link and storage network that is so crucial to a modern economy.

Lower Prices

As was implied in the discussion of time and place utility, the logistics systems contribute to lower prices for goods. It enables firms to extend their

EXHIBIT 2-1 Logistics costs as a percentage of sales dollar.

	Outbound trans- portation	Inventory carrying	Ware- housing	Adminis- tration	Receiving and Shipping	Packaging	Order Processing	Total
All manufacturing companies	6.2%	3.6%	3.6%	0.5%	0.8%	0.7%	0.5%	13.6%
Chemicals and plastics	6.3	1.6	3.3	0.3	0.7	1.4	0.6	14.1
Food manufacturing	8.1	0.3	3.5	0.4	0.9	-	0.2	13.4
Pharmaceutical	1.4	-	1.2	0.7	0.5	0.1	0.5	4.4
Electronics	3.2	2.5	3.2	1.2	0.9	1.1	1.2	13.3
Paper	5.8	0.1	4.6	0.2	0.3	-	0.2	11.2
Machinery and tools	4.5	1.0	2.0	0.5	0.5	1.0	0.5	10.0
All other	6.8	1.0	2.9	1.2	1.4	0.4	0.4	14.1
All merchandising companies	7.4%	10.3%	4.2%	1.2%	0.6%	1.2%	0.7%	25.6%
Consumer goods	8.1	8.5	4.0	1.3	0.9	0.9	0.5	24.2
Industrial good	5.9	13.7	2.9	0.7	0.2	2.0	1.0	26.4

Source: B. J. LaLonde and P. H. Zinszer, Customer Service: Meaning and Measurement (Chicago, National Council of Physical Distribution Management, 1976).

markets in time and space which aid production costs and also the total set of logistics systems is a very efficient deliverer of goods. As we improve our logistics systems from both a technical and managerial perspective, we see further fruits of the effect on prices and availability of goods.

Land Values   Logistics also affects other aspects of our economic system, for example, the transportation segment often has an effect upon land values when technical improvements occur. When a new interstate highway is built in an area, land values near the highway usually go up because it becomes more accessible to other areas. Manufacturing and storage facilities are often attracted to the interchange areas of such highway facilities. There are also social and political aspects besides the economic effects with improved logistics systems.

The next section will treat the role and relations of logistics in the company organization. Some of the points raised above about time and place utility will be further emphasized in the micro framework. It is hoped that the reader will gain some understanding of when logistics will be important to the firm.

LOGISTICS IN THE ORGANIZATIONAL ENVIRONMENT: INTRA-FIRM RELATIONS

Previous discussion has indicated the importance of the systems perspective in logistics. For example, comment has been made about relationships between transportation and warehousing; transportation and packaging; materials handling and warehousing; etc. In addition, there has been some mention of the role of logistics in the organization or company and the importance of the relationships between logistics activities and other areas such as production or finance, but such relationships have received very brief treatment.

In line with the objectives of this chapter, it is important to delineate in more detail the intra-organizational environment for logistics. Logistics is only one "subsystem" in a company and other managerial areas will be examined in this section as far as interactions between and among logistics activities are concerned. The emphasis is upon how decisions in these other areas affect logistics and also how logistics decisions affect these areas. The interactions are quite important in designing a logistics system and developing managerial policies and strategies for the organization.

Figure 2-3 attempts to show the dynamic nature of the interrelationships which exist in many business organizations. The emphasis in the illustration is quite obviously on the physical distribution side of the logistics system. The *Ct* figure is used to indicate cost trade-offs between relevent activity or cost centers. Also, the rectangular figures used to enclose certain areas, such as advertising and manufacturing, have overlaps with the so-called distribution environment. The overlap is shown as a dashed line to indicate the important interface which exists.

Figure 2-3 indicates, for example, the impact of advertising upon the consumer, which in turn impacts upon customer service criteria (requirements). Then, we have to consider the trade-offs between customer service and inventory, i.e., is it worthwhile to increase inventory to improve

FIGURE 2-3 Managing the distribution function as one subset of the firm's system of activities.

Source: Unpublished Master's Paper of J. Duane Weeks, *The Effect of Inventory Control and Stockout Costs on the Management at a Multi-Echelon Distribution System* (University Park: Pennsylvania State University, 1974).

customer service? Our subsequent discussion would add to your understanding of the interrelationships between these functional areas and contribute to a knowledge of the appropriate cost trade-offs.

Mention should be made at the outset that other authors have suggested that the relationships between logistics and areas such as production and marketing may be specified as restrictions or constraints on logistics systems.[6] In other words, the logistics manager may be informed that there are certain boundaries within which a logistics system has to be designed because of the importance or necessity to meet requirements in other areas. For example, between logistics and marketing, if customer service is quite competitive, delivery times may have to be relatively short. After an analysis of the costs and benefits of varying lead times or replenishment times to customers, a decision may be made in the organization to establish maximum delivery times of five days. In a sense then, this is a boundary or constraint within which the logistics system will have to operate. As has already been suggested in the previous chapter, it would be much better if we had a dynamic "model" which would be able to analyze such constraints or restrictions quickly and change them if conditions were substantially changed but this is often not possible or feasible. Constraints or definitive relationships tend to be developed in general areas and allow some latitude for system design. There are then many aspects of the relationships between managerial areas in a firm that should be discussed and analyzed which is our immediate objective.

Marketing

Logistics has sometimes been referred to as the other half of marketing. The rationale for this definition is that the physical distribution part of a logistics system is responsible for the physical movement and storage of goods for customers and quite obviously has an important role with respect to selling a product. In some instances physical distribution may be the key variable in selling a product, i.e., your ability to provide the product at the right time in the right quantities may be the critical element in making the sale. When one defines marketing, there are certain key decision areas that are always mentioned, i.e., product, price, promotion, packaging, and channels of distribution. Our discussion will focus on each of these areas and how they relate to logistics.

Pricing   Decisions about price are very important where demand is relatively elastic or even where price is relatively inelastic since it is important to set that price which maximizes the organizational objective(s) whether that be profit or a combination of profit and some social objectives. A decision about price is one that requires the processing of a number of variables that affect demand for a product and supply costs. A detailed analysis of such variables is not appropriate for this discussion but we can mention such things as competitive products, style, income, economic conditions, etc.

These are all variables that may affect the price that customers are willing to pay and the organization can charge.

From a logistics perspective, it may be quite important to adjust quantity prices to conform with appropriate shipment sizes by transportation companies. Mention has been made before of truckload vs. less-than-truckload shipments and carloads vs. less-than-carload shipments, Railroads, for example, publish minimum weight requirements for carload lots, e.g., 30,000 lbs. Motor carriers typically publish four or five rates that will apply on the same commodity between two points depending upon the size (weight) of the shipment. The larger the size, the lower will be the rate charged. In other words, there is a price discount schedule for shipping larger volumes at one time because of the economies experienced by the transportation company if larger shipments are sent.

Companies selling products typically provide a discount schedule also for larger purchase quantities. If such discount schedules in terms of weight are related to transportation rate discount schedules then the company may be able to save itself some money or save money for customers depending on the terms of the sale. For example, if a company sells on a delivered price basis (price includes transportation charges) and if their price schedule matches the transportation shipping requirements on a weight basis, they should be able to get lower rates with larger purchases and thus save themselves some money. So when they calculate the number of units that they want to sell to a customer for a particular price they should see how the weight of that number of units compares with the weight requirement for a transportation rate. For example, if they were thinking about giving a discount for the purchase of 150 units, the weight of the 150 units could be 3,900 pounds. By adjusting the price discount up to 160 units, they would be entitled to the 4,000-pound rate which would usually be lower if shipped by motor carrier. Even if the goods were being sold on an F.O.B. point of origin basis (transportation charges paid by buyer), by setting the prices in this fashion, their customers could qualify for the 4,000-pound rate and save money.

While it is not always possible or feasible to adjust to meet rate breaks and have a convenient quantity to deal with, such possibilities should be investigated. Some organizations have their entire pricing schedule set up to conform to various quantities that can be shipped by motor and railroad or other modes of transportation. It should be noted that under the Robinson-Patman Act and related legislation, transportation cost savings are a valid reason for offering a price discount.

In addition, the logistics manager may be interested in the volume sold under different price schedules because this will have some impact on inventory requirements, replacement times, and other aspects of customer service. While this is more difficult to analyze, some consideration may be given to the logistics manager's ability to make available sufficient volumes generated by an attractive price schedule. Such a situation may be particularly true when there are price specials run at particular times of the year to generate extra sales. It is quite important that the logistics manager be apprised of such specials so that he/she can consequently adjust inventory requirements to meet projected demand.

Product Design   Another decision made in the marketing area concerns products, particularly the physical attributes. Much has been written about the number of new products that come on the market each year in the United States. Decisions about new products have an effect upon the logistics system. The size, shape, weight, packaging, and other physical dimensions of the products will have an impact upon logistics and its ability to move and store the item. Therefore, there should be some input from the logistics manager when decisions are being made about new products in terms of their physical dimensions. The logistics manager can supply appropriate information about the movement and storage aspects of the new products. In addition to new products, old products are frequently refurbished in one way or another to improve and maintain sales. Very often such change may take the form of a new package design and perhaps package size changes. The physical dimensions of products affect the use of storage and movement systems. They affect carriers that can be used, equipment needed, damage rates, ability to store, use of materials handling equipment such as conveyors and pallets, exterior packaging, and many other aspects of logistics.

It is very difficult to convey the frustration that some logistics managers experience when they discover a change in the form of a product package that makes the use of standard size pallets uneconomical, or makes inefficient use of trailer or boxcar space that could lead to damage. These things often seem mundane and somewhat trivial to people concerned about making sales to customers, but in the long run they become important factors affecting the overall success and profitability of an organization. There are no magic formulas which can be developed to spell out what should be done in these cases but merely keep in mind that interaction should take place so the logistics manager can provide input about these possible negative aspects of decisions being made. It may well be that nothing can be done and the importance of the sale would be the overriding factor. But often small changes can be made that will make the product much more amenable to the movement and storage aspect of a logistics system with no real effect upon the sales of the product itself.

Promotion   Promotion is an area of marketing which receives much attention in an organization. Thousands and thousands of dollars are often spent on advertising campaigns and other promotional practices of an organization to improve the sales position. If there is going to be a promotional effort to stimulate sales then certainly the logistics manager should be informed so that there will be sufficient quantities in inventory available for distribution to the customer.

We should look beyond the obvious relation and analyze basic strategies in the promotion to see how they affect the logistics department. Marketing people often classify their promotion strategies into two basic categories, "push" or "pull." What they are implying is that they can try to "push" the product through the channel of distribution to the customer or "pull" it through the channel of distribution.

Channels of distribution will be discussed subsequently in more detail, but for our purposes here let us say that channels of distribution are the institutions that handle the product after it is manufactured but before it is sold to the ultimate consumer. It would include such organizations as wholesalers and retailers.

There is frequently competition among producers to get the channels of distribution to give their products the sales effort they feel they deserve. For example, a producer of a cereal product may want to be sure that it is given enough space on the retailer's shelf or that wholesalers hold the proper quantities of the product to satisfy demand of retailers and ultimately the final consumer. The retailer and the wholesaler will be influenced, of course, by the demand for the product. They want to sell popular products so that they can improve their profitability. The higher the turnover of the product, the more likely they will make a profit and the happier they are going to be with the particular product and willing to give it the space and the better position in the store.

Therefore, companies can attempt to improve their sales by pulling their product through the channel of distribution with national advertising. The promotional advertising attempts to create or stimulate sales to customers and get them going into the retail store asking for a particular product that they have seen advertised in a magazine, heard advertised on a radio or, more likely, have seen advertised on television. The purchases will likely influence the retailer and the retailer will influence the wholesaler if purchased through a wholesaler. So many companies feel that the best approach for them in promoting a product is to try to pull it through the channels of distribution by stimulating demand directly at the consumer level.

The other basic approach is the "push" method. Implied in the push approach is cooperation with the channels of distribution to stimulate customer sales, in other words, cooperating with retailers or wholesalers with local advertising, perhaps paying part of the advertising costs or having a special display in the store to stimulate sales. Cooperating with the wholesaler, it is also possible that they can give a special price to retailers at a particular period of time to stimulate demand for the product. The emphasis is upon having the channel of distribution work with the company in stimulating demand for the product. This is in contrast to the pull approach where the company stimulates sales somewhat independently of the retailer by national advertising or broad scale regional advertising of their product.

There are many arguments that can be offered pro and con for these two approaches. In fact, some companies use a combination of the two in their promotion efforts. From the logistics managers point of view, however, there often is a difference between "push" and "pull" as far as requirements for the logistics system are concerned. The pull approach is more likely to generate erratic demand which is difficult to predict and may cause emergency demands being placed upon the logistics system. Broad scale national advertising has the potential of being extremely successful, but for new products, it is often difficult to predict what consumer response will be. And it may put a lot of stress and strain on the logistics system and require emergency type shipments and higher transportation rates. Frequent stock-outs may also result which may require adding to inventories in hopes of alleviating such conditions. On the other hand, a push approach very often has a more orderly type demand pattern with it. The cooperation with the retailer allows the "pipeline" to be filled somewhat in advance of the stimulated sales instead of filling the "pipeline" quickly on an almost emergency basis as retailers and consumers clamor for some successfully promoted new product.

Therefore, from the logistics manager's point of view, the push approach is often more desirable with its more orderly filling of the pipeline in preparation for the sales. The pull approach can lead to tremendous demand that may cause some problems but if the logistics manager is involved in the coordination and some of the planning, he can be better prepared to meet any emergency situation.

Channels of Distribution

Mention was made above about channels of distribution, and the fact that marketing managers in their responsibilities have to make decisions about the type and number of channels of distribution they should use. For example, are wholesalers necessary or should they distribute their products directly to retailers? Should they use sales agents or special channels? Should they distribute in some areas to wholesalers and in another area to retailers? These are very, very important decisions that have to be made by the marketing manager and the design of a multi-echelon channel system for distributing the product is quite important, particularly to multi-product companies.

From the logistics manager's point of view such decisions affect logistics systems requirements. Companies, for example, that deal only with wholesalers will probably have less problems from a logistics point of view than companies that deal only with retailers. Wholesalers on the average tend to purchase in larger quantities than the retailers and manage their inventories and place their orders in a much more predictable fashion which makes the logistics manager's job easier. Retailing establishments, particularly those of a smaller variety, often order in small quantities and do not always allow sufficient lead time for replenishment before stockouts. They may require rush shipments to get products to them. While it may be necessary to sell to smaller retail stores as opposed to dealing with wholesalers some attention should be paid to the effects of this upon the logistics system.

Consumer Packaging

Another area of marketing that impacts upon logistics is the consumer packaging area. Consumer packaging is often regarded by the marketing manager as a "silent" salesman. For sales of products at the retail level, the package may be a determining factor in influencing the sales. The marketing manager will be concerned about the appearance of the package, the provision of information, and other related aspects so if a customer is comparing several products on the retailer's shelf, the consumer package may make the sale. The consumer package is important to the logistics manager for several reasons. The consumer package usually has to be fitted into what we call the industrial package or the external package. The size, shape and other dimensions of the consumer package will affect the use of industrial packages. The logistics manager will also have to be concerned about the amount of protection that is given by the consumer package. The physical dimensions and the protection aspect of consumer packages affect the logistics system in the transportation area, materials handling and warehousing.

From the above, it is easy to see why there are such strong relationships between the logistics and the marketing area. In addition to what has already been cited, we could mention such things as sales forecasting which is generally a responsibility of the marketing area. The sales forecast is information that has to be analyzed by the logistics manager in making provisions for inventory during future time periods. While the sales forecasting area is not a decision center in the same sense as some of the other marketing areas discussed in this section, it is nevertheless an important piece of information for making certain logistics decisions. Therefore, there should be some interaction as far as making realistic forecasts so that the logistics manager can be prepared to meet the future demands for products of the organization.

Decisions in the logistics area also impact with marketing. For example, decisions about transportation agencies with varying service characteristics will affect the ability to make deliveries at certain times and in certain places. The location and number of warehouses, the amount of inventory which is stored are decisions which will affect customer service. So many of the topics discussed and analyzed in forthcoming sections of the book are areas quite important to the marketing manager and he should provide input to the logistics manager in making decisions in such areas.

Production

Production Runs and Inventory

Another area of concern is production or manufacturing. We have already indicated that the production manager and the logistics manager have to cooperate and interact. For example, the manufacturing or production manager is usually quite interested in having relatively long production runs so as to improve the cost per unit of production and also the quality of production. If the production manager has to make manufacturing line changes in products frequently, this means the assembly line or manufacturing line will be closed down while the changes and switch overs are made. Also many companies find that efficiency is lowest at the initial stages of a new production run and that efficiency improves as the run lengthens out. The same is often true about product quality. Therefore, the production manager would like to have as long a production run as possible and not make frequent changes. The obvious problem with long "runs" is it means inventories are going to have to be accumulated when we produce far ahead of projected demands. So decisions about the length of production runs and the scheduling of products in a production run are going to have an effect upon the logistics system costs. So it is important that these decisions be worked out and some attempt made to minimize cost or maximize profits. Thus, a trade-off exists between inventory carrying costs and the average production costs.

Seasonal Demand   The production manager is also interested in avoiding seasonal rushes as much as possible. This will usually result in overtime and other scheduling problems. Seasonal demand for products places manufacturing or production under serious strain at times. This is particularly true when the seasonal demand is concentrated in a 30-60 day or 90-day period and the sales can be very erratic depending upon such things as weather. For example, sale of equipment used in the snow such as skis or snowmobiles is influenced by the amount of cold weather and snow in various parts of the country. Production managers in order to keep their costs low and avoid overtime and rush types of situations would usually like to produce well ahead of the season and produce a maximum amount to be prepared for the demand schedule. Such advanced production may not be very practical or feasible because of the high cost associated with storing inventory. However, some consideration has to be given to this particular problem in an attempt to keep the cost down. Therefore, the logistics department in conjunction with production or manufacturing must be prepared to accept seasonal types of inventory; and sometimes because of the necessity of filling up the pipeline far in advance, seasonal inventories can start to accumulate 3 to 6 months before sales occur. It is necessary, however, to be cautious about inventories and not over stock in case there might be problems with sales or sales might be affected by factors such as weather at a later date.

We should also make note of the important relationship which exists between production and logistics on the supply side since the logistics manager will generally be responsible for the inbound movement and storage of raw materials which in effect will feed the production line. Any stockout situations or serious delays will cause shut downs and, of course, higher production costs. Therefore, just like the case with marketing, an attempt must be made to have a supply of materials available to meet the demand of the production schedule. It is typically easier to project production requirements because schedules are made up in advance. The close relationship between the production schedule and forecast demand must be noted. Once we accept a given projection about demand, the production schedule is typically made up to meet that projection. The logistics manager then is responsible for having the raw materials available at the right time in the right quantities to meet that production schedule. Sometimes a firm may attempt to minimize their inventories and work with a pretty close schedule on raw materials in an attempt to keep cost down. However, the cost of a stockout is very high for production, so adequate safety stock must be kept on hand or rush shipments must be used to bring in raw materials if delays occur.

*Logistics as a
Mediator*

Special note might be made of the important interrelationship between marketing, production and logistics. Some authors have referred to this relationship as logistics providing a bridge between production and marketing. There are a number of implications about such a statement. First, the logistics department can provide a reasonable feedback mechanism for transmitting information from marketing to production so that they are advised of market needs and have adequate time so as to avoid overtime or special production sequences. In addition, having logistics effect interface between production and marketing will usually contribute to lower inventory costs because in both areas there may be some tendency to build up inventories for the reasons indicated previously. Also, effective coordination can be provided with purchasing and sales forecasting which are often related to production and marketing as previously indicated.

Other Areas

*Financial Function
Relationships*

While production and marketing are usually the most important other functional areas in a manufacturing organization in terms of relationships for logistics, mention should be made of several others. First, the financial management aspect of the organization is obviously quite important. The logistics manager will often be competing for capital of the organization just like other areas such as marketing and production. For example, a private warehouse might be part of a suggestion which comes out of a logistics study or a fleet of private trucks to provide better service. These are assets which require capital which is a scarce and expensive resource. Justification usually has to be provided as to why it would be more worthwhile for the company to invest in such facilities as opposed to a new machine or a new advertising program or some other investment.

In addition, another area of great importance is the inventory. All inventories are expected to be sold but in the short run inventory represents capital of the company being "tied up" and as indicated previously, some charge has to be assessed because capital in the inventory represents an opportunity cost for the firm. So the accumulation of inventory often has to be coordinated with the financial manager.

Purchasing

The purchasing area in an organization as has been indicated is often an area of importance to logistics. Purchasing makes decisions about where the company will purchase supplies and in what quantities they are going to purchase such supplies. Both aspects of the decision have an effect upon logistics costs. The "where" aspect is important particularly if such goods are purchased F.O.B. point of origin since arrangements will have to be made to transport the goods to the plant(s). The distance from the vendors to the plant(s) will affect transportation cost. Also the goods purchased in large quantities will have to be stored or warehoused.

Decisions made by purchasing affect the cost of logistics but if the logistics manager doesn't do his job properly then this can cause problems for the purchasing area. For example, if adequate arrangements are not made for transportation or there is inadequate space for storing materials then this will cause problems for the purchasing area. In some instances, it might be noted that the relationship between purchasing and logistics is so important that the purchasing responsibilities are placed under the jurisdiction of logistics. This very frequently tends to be the case for industries selling in industrial markets which use large quantities of raw materials such as chemicals and where the logistics responsibilities are labeled materials management.

Accounting

Another area of importance is accounting. As has been indicated in the previous chapter in discussing analysis of cost in logistics and trade-offs, it is quite evident that good cost information is quite important to logistics. Without adequate cost information, it is difficult to accomplish basic types of analysis suggested in the previous chapter, let alone more sophisticated types of simulation models. Very often logistics departments have some problems because the accounting systems are designed to give good financial data for financial analyses and/or data for tax information purposes.

Information about such things as warehousing costs may be very difficult to come by and very often are considered as part of the overhead cost of operation which makes their analyses for logistics purposes very difficult. This has become an item of special concern in some areas. The National Council of Physical Distribution funded a major study on cost analysis in logistics to point out some of the problems in this particular area.[7] As you would expect, cost information is often a very critical problem when a company first sets up a logistics department. Many of the costs of concern to a logistics department will be spread around other areas and very often will be lumped into overhead charges.

While some other areas might be discussed as having important relationships with logistics, the major ones have been discussed in this section. Other areas that have interactions with logistics will be discussed in subsequent sections of the text. The discussion in this section should provide insights into the important intra-firm relationships of logistics and the need for effective coordination. The next section treats more specifically some of the factors which affect logistics costs more specifically.

THE INTERNAL LOGISTICS ENVIRONMENT: DIRECT FACTORS AFFECTING LOGISTICS COSTS

It would be useful at this point to discuss factors which tend to affect logistics directly and influence the cost of logistics. This analysis will also provide a perspective on why logistics is important to certain business organizations. Looking at this in another manner, the focus is upon those characteristics which make logistics an area of management concern.

Spatial Relationships

One area of importance to logistics costs is spatial relationships, that is, the location of nodes or fixed points in the logistics system with respect to market and supply points. Spatial relationships are very important in terms of transportation costs since these costs tend to increase with distance. Consider the following example, which is illustrated by Figure 2-4.

FIGURE 2-4   Logistics spatial relations.

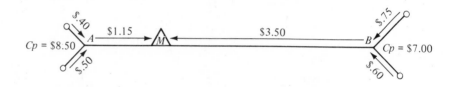

Example

The firm located at B has a $1.50 production cost advantage over firm A since the former produces at $7.00/unit as opposed to $8.50/unit for firm A. However, firm B pays $1.35 for inbound raw materials (.60 + .75) and $3.50 for outbound movement to the market or a total of $4.85 in per unit transportation charges. Firm A pays $.90 for inbound raw materials and $1.15 for outbound movement for a total of $2.05 in transportation charges. The $1.50 production cost disadvantage of firm A is offset by its $2.80 transportation cost advantage. Firm B may wish to look at alternative strategies for its logistics system in order to compute more effectively at M. For example, firm B's $3.50/unit transportation cost for shipping to the market may be based on less than truckload rates (low volume movements). The firm may wish to examine the possibility of using a warehouse at M and shipping in higher volume rail carload lots at lower transportation costs.

The distance factor or spatial relationships may affect logistics costs in other ways besides transportation costs. For example, if a firm is located a great distance from one or more of its markets, it may be necessary to use a market oriented warehouse to make deliveries to customers in a satisfactory time period. Therefore, distance can add to warehousing and inventory carrying costs. It may also be a factor in increased order processing costs.

Distance or spatial relationships are of such importance to logistics cost that site location is, as was indicated, an activity included in logistics area responsibilities. Location or site analysis will be considered in some detail in Part Four of the text.

Competitive Relationships

As was indicated in the previous chapter, competition is sometimes too narrowly defined. When people think of competition they often consider only price competition. There is no doubt that in many markets price competition is very important. However, in other markets or sometimes in the same markets where price competition is important, service to the customers is also a very important form of competition. For example, if a company is able to provide its customers with its product(s) in a relatively short period of time on a reliable basis, then their customers are often in a position to minimize inventory cost. The minimization of inventory costs cuts expenses which is just as important as lower product prices since it will help to make more profit or in turn enable them to be more competitive with their customers. Therefore, customer service is something that should be given consideration for the logistics area.

It is a well-accepted principle of logistics management that order cycle length directly affects inventory requirements, or stated in another way, the shorter the order cycle, the less inventory required.[8] We will discuss order cycles in some detail in the chapters dealing with inventory. For our purposes at this point, we can define order cycle as the length of time it takes for a customer to receive an order once they have decided to place the order. It would include such activities as order transmittal time, order preparation time, transportation time, etc. The relationship can best be described by referring to Figure 2-5.

The impact depicted in Figure 2-5 shows rather clearly that longer order cycles require higher inventories. Therefore, if a firm can improve customer service by shortening customer order cycles, then its customers should be able to operate with less inventory. It follows then that such a cost reduction would be as important as a price reduction.

Substitutability   The importance of customer service is very often affected by what is referred to as substitutability. In other words, if a product is one that is similar to other products, then consumers may be willing to substitute a competitive product if a stockout occurs. Therefore, customer service is more important for highly substitutable products than situations where customers may be willing to wait or back order a particular product. This is one of the reasons why some firms spend so much money in advertising to make customers conscious of their brands. They want consumers to ask for their brand, and if their brand is not available, temporarily they would like consumers to wait for their brand to come in or be available.

There is much variation among products in terms of substitutability of one product for another. Usually, the more substitutable a product, the higher the level of customer service that is required. As far as a logistics

FIGURE 2-5   Relationship between required inventory and length of order cycle.

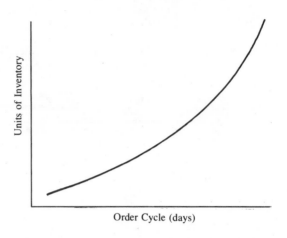

manager is concerned, if a firm would like to reduce its cost of lost sales which is a measure of customer service and substitutability, then they can either spend more money on inventory or money on transportation.

Inventory versus Lost Sales

Referring to Figure 2-6(a), one can see that as inventory costs increase (either by increasing the level of inventory or by increasing reorder points) firms can usually reduce cost of lost sales. There is, in other words, an inverse relationship between the cost of lost sales and the inventory cost. We should also note by referring to the total cost curve that we are only willing to do this to the point where total costs start to go up. We would typically be willing to spend increasing amounts for inventory to decrease the cost of lost sales by larger amounts. In other words, up to the point when the marginal savings from reducing the cost of lost sales equals the marginal cost of the added amount of inventory.

Transportation versus Lost Sales

A similar kind of relationship exists with transportation as can be seen from Figure 2-6(b). Companies can usually trade off increased transportation cost against decreased cost of lost sales. For transportation, this additional expenditure takes the form of either buying a better transportation service, for example, switching from water to rail or rail to motor or motor to air. Also the higher transportation cost could result from shipping more frequently in smaller quantities at higher rates. So, as indicated in Figure 2-6(b), we can reduce the cost of lost sales by spending more on transportation service to improve customer service. Once again as can be seen from the total cost curve, we are only willing to do this up to the point where the marginal savings in cost of lost sales equals the marginal increment associated with the increased transportation cost. While it is convenient to show inventory cost and transportation costs separately, we should note that companies will very often spend more for inventory and

FIGURE 2-6(a)   **General relationship of the cost of lost sales to inventory cost.**

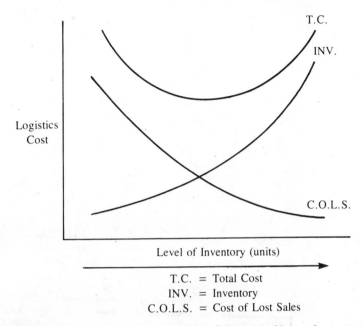

T.C. = Total Cost
INV. = Inventory
C.O.L.S. = Cost of Lost Sales

FIGURE 2-6(b)   **General relationship of the cost of lost sales to transportation cost.**

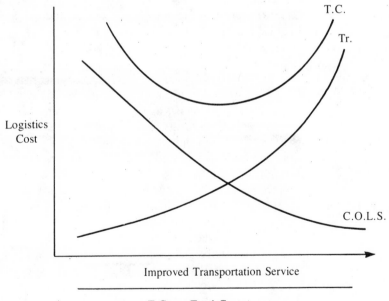

T.C. = Total Cost
Tr. = Transportation Cost
C.O.L.S. = Cost of Lost Sales

more for transportation almost simultaneously to reduce the cost of lost sales. In fact, improved transportation will usually result in lower inventory cost.* In other words, the situation is much more interactive and coordinated than indicated.

Product Relationships

There are a number of aspects of the product which will have a direct bearing on logistics cost. First, the dollar value of the product will typically affect warehousing costs, inventory costs, transportation costs, packaging costs, and even materials handling costs. As indicated in Figure 2-7, as the dollar value of the product increases, typically the costs in each of the indicated areas will also go up. The actual slope and level of the cost functions will vary with particular products.

Dollar Value

Transportation rates reflect risk associated with the movement of the goods. There is often more chance for damage with higher valued goods; and if there is damage, there will be a larger amount for the transportation company to reimburse. Also transportation companies tend to charge higher rates for higher value products because typically they can afford to pay a higher rate. There is a relationship between the value of the product and amount of the rate in our transportation rate structures.

Warehousing and inventory cost will also go up as the dollar value of products increase. Higher value means more capital in inventory with higher total capital costs. In addition, the risk factor for storing products of higher value will increase the possible cost of obsolescence and depreciation. Also, the physical facilities required to store higher value products are more sophisticated and therefore warehousing cost will increase with increased dollar value.

Packaging cost will also usually increase because protective packaging is used in an attempt to minimize damage. More effort is spent in packaging the product to protect it against damage and/or loss of it has higher value. Finally, materials handling equipment is very often more sophisticated to meet the needs of higher valued products. Firms are usually willing to use more capital intensive and expensive equipment to speed higher value goods through the warehouse and to minimize the chance of damage.

Density

Density is another factor which affects logistics cost. Density refers to a weight/space ratio. An item which is light in weight compared to the space which it occupies, for example, household furniture has low density. Transportation and warehousing cost are affected by density; this can be seen from Figure 2-8. As we move from low density to high density, warehousing cost and transportation cost will tend to go down.

Transportation companies in establishing their rates take into consideration how much weight they can get into their vehicles since their rates are

---

* The lower inventory costs stem from smaller carrying capacity and faster transit times.

FIGURE 2-7 **General relationship of dollar value of product to various logistics costs.**

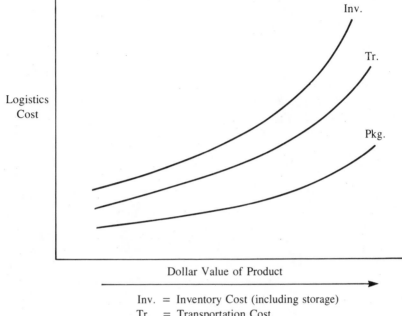

Inv. = Inventory Cost (including storage)
Tr. = Transportation Cost
Pkg. = Packaging Cost

quoted in terms of cents per hundred pounds. Therefore, on high density items they can afford to give a lower rate per hundred pounds because they can get more weight into a car. Warehousing costs are also affected, the higher the density the more weight can be stored in area of space in the warehouse, i.e., The more efficiently you can use the warehousing space. So warehousing cost also tends to follow the same kind of relationship as transportation cost.

Susceptibility to Damage

The third product factor affecting logistics cost is susceptibility to damage. (See Figure 2-9.) The greater the risk of damage, the higher the transportation and warehousing cost. Transportation companies will charge higher rates with the expectation of greater damage of a product and warehousing cost will go up either because of damage or protection measures which are taken for reducing the risk of damage.

Special Handling

A fourth factor related to damage susceptibility but nevertheless somewhat distinct, is special handling requirements for products. Some products may require oversize transportation units for movement or they may require refrigeration or they may require heating or they may require stopping in-transit. Special handling requirements whether for transportation purposes or for warehousing purposes will generally increase logistics cost.

FIGURE 2-8 General relationship of the weight density of a product to logistical costs.

Tr. = Transportation Cost
Inv. = Inventory Cost (including storage)

FIGURE 2-9 General relationship of product susceptibility to loss and damage to logistical cost.

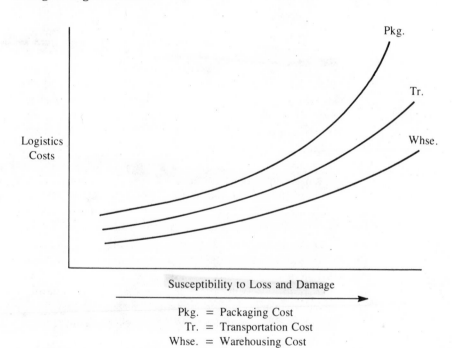

Pkg. = Packaging Cost
Tr. = Transportation Cost
Whse. = Warehousing Cost

Channel Relationships

Most organizations are not completely integrated from initial raw materials to the final ultimate customer. In other words, they operate in a channel of distribution. The manufacturer usually has firms which supply raw materials. After the producer has finished manufacturing a product other organizations will wholesale and/or retail the product before it reaches the final customer.

The relationship of firms in a channel is one that is sometimes overlooked but nevertheless it is one that is very important. Therefore, some consideration has to be given to the channel relationships and location in a channel. (See Figure 2-10.) If firms are at mid-points in a distribution channel then they find themselves typically with responsibility for inbound raw materials and storage as well as outbound finished products. This will tend to make their logistics cost higher than a firm that is located at the starting point or ending point in the logistics channel which would only have responsibility for one part of the total logistics cost.

Let us begin by looking at the suppliers: their function is to obtain raw materials from various supply sources and store this for sale to the manufacturing firm. Suppliers tend to locate closer to their sources and hence will have lower inbound movement costs than those associated with the outbound haul, the spatial relationships being very important in this instance relative to product value. Also associated with the suppliers is the storage function: since the product is usually low in value, it may be stored in abundance.

Next we come to the manufacturer, who may or may not be concerned with physical supply costs depending upon the purchase terms from the suppliers (specifically, whether or not raw materials are shipped on a delivered price basis which includes the price of transportation). The firm will be very interested in its outbound costs since, in this instance it has the responsibility of paying freight charges to the distribution warehouse. The cost of these outbound movements will be higher (per hundred pounds) than that of the inbound movements due to the fact that value has been added at the point of manufacture. The manufacturer is also faced with storage costs at the plant and at its distribution warehouse. He is also concerned with material handling expense: everytime a good is unloaded, moved within a nodal facility, or reloaded, materials handling expenses occur. Often these costs are observed as part of the movement or storage costs.

Who bears responsibility for transportation depends upon the terms of sale from the distribution warehouse to the wholesaler: if the goods are sold F.O.B., warehouse, then the wholesaler will pay for the movement. If the goods are sold F.O.B., wholesaler, then the manufacturer agrees to pay for the movement. Similar is the case with the wholesaler-retailer transaction.

The total logistics cost at any point in the channel will be equal to or greater than the costs incurred in the product's path there. In the case of the retailer, logistics costs will be equal to or greater than the total of the following:

FIGURE 2-10   Logistics cost and channel relations.

Supplier movement and storage cost
Manufacturer movement and storage cost
Warehouse movement and storage cost
Wholesaler movement and storage cost

As such, one can easily see that the location within a channel of distribution has a great impact on the amount and type of costs that firms must bear.

SUMMARY

An attempt has been made here to provide a complete picture of the environment for logistics. We took a look at the economic or macro perspective of a logistics system, looking at some of the important variables affecting logistics and some of the contributions of logistics and other areas of the firm. Finally we looked at a more specific kind of environment, the almost day-to-day environment in which logistics has to operate in making decisions for the firm, and it is convenient for us to end the chapter at this point to take up a consideration of the next chapter of what we have labeled *Nodal Activities*.

Study Questions

1. How does logistics contribute to our society?
2. What is the most important role of logistics in our society and why?
3. How does business logistics interact with marketing and production?
4. Discuss the various elements of the logistics system and their relation to each other.

Notes

1. J. Heskett, R. Ivie and N. Glaskowsky, *Business Logistics* (New York: Ronald Press, 1973), p. 9. Figures updated by authors.
2. D. P. Locklin, *Economics of Transportation* (Homewood, Illinois: Richard D. Irwin, Inc., 1972), p.12.
3. Heskett et. al., *op, cit.,* p. 15.
4. Locklin *op. cit.,* p. 13.
5. David P. Herron, "Managing Physical Distribution for Profit," *Harvard Business Review,* May-June 1979, pp. 121-23.
6. Heskett et. al., *op. cit.,* pp. 153-54.
7. Michael Schiff, *Accounting and Control in Physical Distribution Management* (Chicago: National Council of Physical Distribution, 1972).
8. Roy Dale Voorhees and Merrill Kim Sharp, "Principles of Logistics Revisited," *Transportation Journal*, Fall 1978, pp. 69-84.

Case 2-1
Contemporary Foods, Inc.

Contemporary Foods, Inc., a major United States food products company located in New York, has developed a new type of coffee and plans to test market the coffee nationwide. In addition to the test marketing, Contemporary wants to saturate the ''coffee market'' with its new product by selling the coffee at a $2.50 per pound introductory price for one week. The second week of the introduction campaign, Contemporary is planning to increase the price per pound to $2.75, but all one-pound cans will be three inches larger due to a free stainless steel measuring scoop enclosed.

Two weeks prior to the product introduction, the marketing department using all forms of media, advertised quite heavily throughout the United States. Posters, billboards, newspapers, radio, and television all carried advertisements for the new coffee.

Raffle drawings were established in all the major grocery store chains nationwide with Contemporary Foods, Inc. providing the prizes

In conjunction with the marketing department, production runs for the new coffee started one month prior to the introduction. Estimated demand for the new product was 1,000,000 units for the first week and 1,250,000 units for the second week. Production runs had to be started early in order to meet the estimated product demand and also because of a break in the production for the second week, in order to set up for the new size cans.

Questions:

1. Describe what interactions must take place between the marketing, production, and logistics departments. Explain the logistics department's role in the introduction of the new produce.

2. Why is it necessary that the logistics department be cognizant of all the planned changes in the promotion and production schedules for the new product introduction. (Discuss various problems which may arise, i.e., the second week change in can size and weight, and what the logistics department's responsibilities will be with respect to changes.)

Case 2-2
Comp-Data Company

The Comp-Data Company is located in Boston, Massachusetts. The company was founded in 1952 and began operations by offering a product line which consisted primarily of computer hardware. From 1952 through late 1977, Comp-Data's major customers were larger business firms which used the computers in their daily operations. Beginning in early 1978, a new market segment had developed in the data-processing industry—smaller, portable systems for use in smaller business as well as for home use.

Joe DiMaio is the distribution manager for Comp-Data and is facing the problem of exactly how to coordinate the distribution of these new, more consumer-oriented computers. Joe has recently met with Comp-Data's national sales manager, Ed McHugh, and the two are undecided as to the channel of distribution which will be most effective for their product. McHugh seems to feel that the new mini-computers should be sold in small electronics stores (such as Radio Shack) in which the typical consumer would be more confident in making such a purchase. Joe agrees with McHugh; however, he feels that some serious complications may arise.

Specifically, Joe feels that since this market segment is anticipated to become quite competitive, Comp-Data may not receive the in-store sales promotion it needs. (Two other leading competitors in the industry are already planning a "small retailer" approach.) In addition, Joe seems to feel that the smaller outlets may not be as willing to encounter the relatively high costs associated with carrying a significant number of Comp-Data's mini-computers in inventory. Joe would like to see the computer distributed in some of the larger retail outlets in the country (such as Sears, and J. C. Penney). DiMiao feels as if the computer would get more exposure and be more readily available to "cash-and-carry" consumers.

Joe and Ed must report to the Chief Executive Officer of Comp-Data with a specific recommendation for the distribution of the mini-computers. You have been hired as a consultant to aid in making this decision. How do you address the problem at hand? Who's position do you support? Why? What are your own recommendations? Why do you feel they would be more successful?

SELECTED BIBLIOGRAPHY FOR PART I

BALLOU, RONALD H., *Basic Business Logistics*. Englewood Cliffs, New Jersey: Prentice-Hall, Inc., 1978, Chapters 1 and 2.

BALLOU, RONALD H., *Business Logistics Management*, 2nd Edition. Englewood Cliffs, New Jersey: Prentice-Hall, Inc., 1979, Chapters 1 and 4.

BARTLETT, HALE C., Editor, *Readings in Physical Distribution*, 3rd Edition. Danville, Illinois: The Interstate Printers and Publishers, Inc., 1972.

BOWERSOX, DONALD J., *Logistical Management*, 2nd Edition. New York: Macmillan Publishing Company, Inc., 1974, Chapters 1 and 2.

BOWERSOX, DONALD J., BERNARD J. LaLONDE, and EDWARD W. SMYKAY, Editors, *Readings in Physical Distribution Management*. New York: The Macmillan Company, 1969, Part I.

DANIEL, N. and J. R. JONES, *Business Logistics*. Boston: Allyn and Bacon, 1969.

DRUCKER, PETER F., "The Economy's Dark Continent," *Fortune*, April 1962, p. 103.

HESKETT, JAMES L., NICHOLAS A. GLASKOWSKY, JR., and ROBERT M. IVIE, *Business Logistics*, 2nd Edition. New York: The Ronald Press Company, 1973, Chapters 1 and 2.

JOHNSON, JAMES C. and DONALD F. WOOD, *Contemporary Physical Distribution*. Tulsa, Oklahoma: Petroleum Publishing Company, 1977, Chapters 1 and 2.

KOTLER, PHILIP, *Marketing Management*, 3rd Edition. Englewood Cliffs, New Jersey: Prentice-Hall, Inc., 1976.

MAGEE, JOHN F., *Industrial Logistics*. New York: McGraw-Hill Book Company, 1968, Chapters 1 and 2.

ROSE, WARREN, *Logistics Management*. Dubuque, Iowa: Wm. C. Brown Company, 1979, Chapter 1.

SMYKAY, EDWARD W., DONALD J. BOWERSOX and FRANK H. MOSSMAN, *Physical Distribution Management*. New York: The Macmillan Company, 1961, Chapter 1.

Part II

The second major segment of the text examines those activities that take place at the nodes, i.e., the points in a logistics system where goods have been temporarily held. Attention is first devoted to the general nature of inventory management and, second, to how the important inventory decisions are made. In this era of spiraling costs, effective management of inventory in conjunction with other parts of the logistics systems is the subject of much attention.

The third chapter of this part of the text examines warehousing activities. The inventory decisions have to be made in conjunction with warehousing. In particular, such questions as private versus public warehousing, how many warehouses are needed to fill the firm's needs, are all decisions which have to be made and affect warehousing decisions.

The fourth chapter in Part II examines materials handling and packaging. The two topics are quite important to logistics and provide an important integration with linking decisions discussed in Part III. The efficiency of warehouse operations depends upon materials handling systems and the effective interchange between the warehouse and the transportation agency. Packaging interacts with materials handling and transportation in terms of size and shape of the package and the protection provided by the package.

Chapter 3	# Inventory in the Logistics System

After studying this chapter, you should be able to:

- Present a general overview of inventory in the logistics system, including the basic nature and importance of inventory.

- Develop a rationale for physical supply and physical distribution inventories.

- Provide an explanation of the importance of inventory to other functional areas in a company.

- Explain the nature of relevant cost categories used in inventory analysis and other related concepts necessary for an understanding of inventory decision models.

The discussion in Chapter 1 of the rationale for the increasing interest in business logistics pointed out several developments that have important inventory control implications. For example, it was indicated that competition has led many consumer product companies to increase the variety of sizes, colors, weights, packages, etc., in an attempt to reach various market segments.

Factors Leading to Increased Inventory Cost

The increased variety in product lines has caused the level of inventory to expand. For example, a company may have estimated (forecasted) sales of paper hand towels at 100,000 rolls for the next sales period. However, this is a gross estimate and will have to be broken down by color, package size (one roll, two rolls, etc.), ply, etc. So instead of a basic inventory of 100,000 rolls plus an additional 5,000 to 10,000 rolls for safety stock, the company will most likely need a total inventory (basic plus safety) of 120,000 to 125,000 units because of the need to carry safety stock for each of the varieties of sales units.

In addition, the increasing cost of labor, taxes, and supplies associated with the general inflationary trend of the 1970s and 1980s has caught many companies in a profit squeeze, as was also pointed out in Chapter 1. The cost of carrying inventory for most companies has also increased. At the same time, many manufacturing companies have been faced with pressure to increase their inventories to help maintain their competitive position with their channels of distribution. That is, retailers and wholesalers want lower inventories for themselves but need fast customer service to offset the risk of stockouts, which necessitates higher inventories at the manufacturing level.

Cost Effect of Increased Inventory

To illustrate the effect on costs of increased inventory, let us assume that the Happy Valley Manufacturing Company has had an average inventory of $2,000,000. As shall be explained in this chapter, annual inventory carrying costs are generally calculated as a percentage of the dollar value of average inventory. Assuming that this percentage has been calculated at 25 percent (a very realistic figure for many U.S. companies), then the annual cost of holding a $2,000,000 inventory is $500,000 ($2,000,000 × 25%)—a significant figure. If they have to increase their inventory to $3,000,000, their annual cost of carrying the inventory is now $750,000 ($3,000,000 × 25%).

Sales versus Reduced Inventory

Looking at inventory from another perspective, the investment in inventory often represents a significant percentage of a company's total assets. While this may vary from company to company, there are many instances when investment in inventory is 50 percent or more of the total investment in current assets. If the investment in inventory is reduced by $500,000, for example, this could represent a cost savings of $125,000 ($500,000 × 25%). There are many companies whose profit ratio is only 5% of sales. Therefore, a reduction in inventory cost of $125,000 is equivalent to an additional $2,500,000 in sales ($2,500,000 × 5%). Therefore, good inventory management and control is important to most companies.

The above comments are not meant to imply that we always seek to reduce inventory. We can establish a conscious policy to increase inventory as long as the additional expenditure for inventory leads to compensating cost reductions in other areas, such as transportation and/or perhaps additional sales with extra profits to cover the increased cost. In other words, a trade-off perspective, as was discussed in Chapters 1 and 2, is necessary. In fact, it is very important to view inventory in a positive manner, that is, as a possible strategy to achieve cost savings and/or sales increments. A convenient introduction to this positive perspective on inventory can be provided by a discussion of the problems of a municipal water authority.

THE MUNICIPAL WATER AUTHORITY ILLUSTRATION

As is the case with most businesses, a municipality experiences fluctuations in demand for water. There is a daily fluctuation that occurs because less water is used at night. During the day, most people are awake and use water to bathe, to cook, and for other purposes. A sharp increase in demand for water is consequently experienced in the morning—and continues throughout most of the day. There is even variation during the day, such as meal times, and in the evening when many people bathe.

The Problem of Peak Demand
There is also a significant difference in the demand for water between the summer and the winter months in many sections of the country. In summer, consumers spend more time watering their grass, filling their swimming pools, washing their cars, and bathing. Consequently, there is more demand for water in the summer than in the winter months when some of these activities are performed infrequently or not at all.

One of the problems that the municipality faces is the amount of pumping capacity it should have. Should it be sufficient to meet peak demand on that hot day in July when the temperature is 100 degrees and the relative humidity is 95 percent? If the municipality builds pumping capacity to meet peak demand, many times during the year its pumping facility will be working at 10 percent of capacity or less, which is very costly. In some instances, the facility may even have to shut down during the night, which is also very expensive.

Consequently, most municipalities have some type of storage facility for water so that they are able to use their pumps on a more uniform basis, that is, they do not have to have productive capacity to meet peak demand. Water is taken from the storage facilities during the times of peak demand. During the periods when the demand for water is low, the excess water is pumped into the storage facility so that it is ready when needed for consumption. The water storage facility allows the municipality to "smooth out" production by producing ahead of or in anticipation of demand with consequent efficiencies; it also allows the municipality to reduce the size of production facilities; and finally, it provides better service for customers during peak periods.

Several points about our discussion of the municipal water authority need to be emphasized. As suggested previously, the storage cost of municipal water is a very positive contribution to the reduction of overall cost. It allows lower capital investment in pumping or productive capacity; the pumping facilities can function more efficiently because they can operate at near capacity most of the time; customers will get better service with less risk of stockouts. In other words, the accumulation of inventory leads to significant savings in total costs.

Business firms have problems similar to that of the municipal water authority. If they build production capacity to meet peak demand, then they can usually expect periods when their productive capacity is going to be underutilized. While a certain amount of underutilization is to be expected, it can be quite expensive if they build a plant sufficient to meet peak seasonal demand. For example, some companies experience 60-70 percent of their yearly sales during the two- to three-month Christmas season. Consequently, businesses also may find it attractive to have warehousing or storage facilities that will enable them to reduce production costs by not working overtime at peak demand periods, to reduce capital equipment needs, and so on.

Another point is that business organizations have a more comprehensive inventory environment than water authorities, with additional trade-offs, e.g., transportation, and more intricate or complex interrelationships, e.g., different classes of customers with differing service requirements. Also, the value of the items to be stored, unlike water, may be very high, which is an additional consideration. However, the municipal water authority case provides us with a good overview and introduction to the importance and nature of inventory management and control. This background is desirable for our discussion in the next section, which gives a general explanation of why inventory is accumulated and lists some of the trade-offs.

GENERAL RATIONALE FOR INVENTORY

In our discussion of nodal activities, we have noted that interruptions or stops in the flow of goods for the accumulation of inventory increase the operating expense of the business. However, these additional expenditures can contribute to positive reductions in cost in other areas and/or increased sales.

Our objective in this section is to explore in some detail why business organizations hold or accumulate inventory. To fit in with the discussions in Chapters 1 and 2, it would be useful to approach our discussion in terms of physical supply inventory and physical distribution inventory.

*Purchase
Economics*

One reason for accumulating an inventory of raw materials is that the company may be able to realize purchase economies. In other words, firms may buy raw materials in large quantities because of the price discounts that are available. Although they will have to store what they are not going to use immediately, their inventory costs are frequently less than what they can save by buying in large quantities. One can quickly see that they are trading off between a purchase price discount and storage costs, and as long as the storage costs are less than the amount saved on the purchase price, they are willing to do it.

Transportation Discounts

A second reason for accumulating physical supply inventory may be transportation economies. Frequently, the opportunity to realize transport savings is associated with the purchase economies discussed above. When large quantities are purchased, large quantities can be shipped. As will be recalled from previous comments, many firms ship raw materials in carload, truckload, or bargeload lots because they can decrease transportation costs. In some instances, shipments can be made in multiple carloads or even trainloads at an even lower rate per hundredweight.

The transportation cost usually represents a significant part of the final selling price of raw materials. Even a small reduction in the per hundredweight rate can often be quite important because of the volume moved and the importance of transportation. At the same time, the value and nature of raw materials are such that inventory and warehousing costs are often relatively low. For example, a raw material like coal can often be dumped on the ground without any storage shelter. Consequently, total costs can often be reduced if transportation costs are reduced through increased volume movement, since inventory and warehousing costs may not increase as much as the transport cost is decreased.

Stockouts

A third reason for physical supply inventory would be to prevent a production shutdown because of an emergency. In other words, a firm will usually hold a certain amount of inventory as buffer or safety stock in case there is a delay in shipping or some problem in filling orders. Most firms would not want to shut down an assembly line because raw materials were out of stock, since the cost may run into thousands of dollars per hour. The amount of raw materials held will vary, depending upon the probability of the events that could delay delivery and the volume of raw materials utilized. At this point, we should note that like our previous examples, this one also involves a cost trade-off analysis, *viz.*, the cost of holding the inventory (safety stock) measured against the cost of a stockout. However, it also involves using probability theory to develop the expected costs for safety stock and stockouts, as does the next example.

Speculative Purchase

A fourth possible reason for physical supply inventory is for speculative purchases. Some firms may face uncertainty with respect to the future supply of raw materials. For example, there may be some fear of a price increase in the near future, so a company may buy a large quantity in advance of the price increase. There may be a threat of a labor strike, which would mean a discontinuance of supply. For example, when there is a threat of a strike in the steel industry, the automobile industry starts to accumulate steel in case the strike takes place. Another example is a firm that imports raw materials from a foreign country. If there is a possibility of a political coup, the supply might be interrupted. As was the case with the previous example of possible stockouts from delays in transportation or order processing, the firm in this case has to measure the cost of holding the inventory as safety stock against the expected cost of one of the events described above.

Seasonal availability of supply is a fifth reason for accumulating physical supply inventory. Agricultural products such as wheat or other grains are good examples of items that are available only at certain times of the year, necessitating accumulation of supply to meet demand throughout the year. In some cases, the means of transportation may cause the seasonal availability. For example, iron ore moves across the Great Lakes or down the St. Lawrence River. The supply of iron ore is interrupted each winter because the waterways are closed because of ice. In these cases, the firm trades off the inventory and warehousing cost of the accumulated inventory against the lower costs from balanced production, i.e., being able to produce all year without interruption.

A sixth reason for holding physical supply inventory is to maintain supply sources. Large manufacturing firms very often find it expedient to make use of small vendors or suppliers who manufacture subassemblies or semifinished goods for them even though they may have the same production facilities. They use the vendor or supplier much the same way a company may use a public warehouse; that is, when you do not have enough productive capacity to meet your peak demands, you buy from the vendor or supplier.

One of the problems, however, is that small vendors or suppliers are often "captive." In other words, their only clients may be one or two large manufacturers. If during certain times of the year the large manufacturer does not buy from the small vendor, the small vendor could be cut off completely. It would then have to close down and lay off its employees. When the large manufacturer again needs materials from the small vendor, the small vendor would have to try to hire its employees back again, which could cause costs to go up or quality to go down. So quite often the large manufacturer will find it expedient to give the small vendor a certain amount of business during the off-season to keep it in operation—at least at partial capacity. This course of action would mean the accumulation of a certain amount of inventory, but it may be chaper to do this than to change vendors or to try to get a small vendor started up again. The trade-off in this instance is usually lower vendor prices against the holding cost of the inventory.

The above factors represent six major reasons for holding physical supply inventory. In all cases, there are certain economies or cost reductions that the firm should be trading off against the increased warehousing and inventory cost. As mentioned above, the cost of storing physical supply inventory is often relatively low because elaborate storage facilities are not required. This is in direct contrast to finished goods, which often require very elaborate and sophisticated storage facilities because of their value or perishability. At this point, an analysis should be provided for the accumulation of finished goods inventory.

One reason why companies may accumulate physical distribution inventory (finished goods) is similar to one of the reasons mentioned above

Transportation Savings

for raw materials, i.e., transportation economies. By shipping in carload or truckload lots as opposed to less-than-carload or less-than-truckload shipments, the company will experience lower transportation rates. As long as the transportation economies are less than the warehousing costs, the firm will be better off to ship in larger quantities. Also, the company may experience better service (faster transit times), which should reduce other costs such as in-transit inventory cost and cost of lost sales.

The transportation economies associated with physical distribution inventory are frequently associated with the use of market-oriented warehouses. Companies ship from their plants to strategically located market-oriented warehouses in carload or truckload quantities. The items can then be shipped shorter distances to customers in less-than-carload or less-than-truckload quantities to minimize costs.

Production Savings

The second reason why firms may accumulate physical distribution inventory is because of production economies. As indicated by the water tank analogy, a firm may find it expedient to minimize its unit cost of production of an item by having relatively long production runs without stopping or changing to another product item. This generally means that the company will be producing somewhat in advance of demand, i.e., it will not immediately be able to sell all it produces. The firm would be trading off the lower production costs and perhaps better quality against the increased inventory cost.

Seasonal Demand

A third reason, related to the above reason for accumulating finished goods, is that a company may have seasonal demand for its product. It may not be efficient to have productive capacity to meet the peak seasonal demand, and the company would be better off producing on a more regular basis throughout the year with a smaller plant. Such a strategy would mean having warehousing facilities to store finished goods during the period of the year when they are not in great demand so as to stabilize their production for lower cost. Once again the inventory cost would be traded off against lower production costs and perhaps decreased plant investment.

Customer Service

A fourth reason, and one that is very important from a marketing point of view, is that physical distribution inventory may be held to improve customer service, or using previous terminology, to reduce the cost of lost sales. We talked about the concept of substitutability previously and the effect of this on sales and cost. Where the substitutability is high, firms may choose to have finished-goods inventories available in reasonable proximity to their customers to allow expedient deliveries. The trade-off is between cost of lost sales and inventory cost.

The above are four of the major reasons for accumulating finished goods inventory. Before turning to the next section, some of the important interrelationships of the above reasons should be noted and some mention made of the special concerns of logistics.

It is probably apparent that some of the reasons for accumulating inventory may occur simultaneously. For example, in the discussion on finished-goods inventory, it was noted that reduced transportation costs through carload shipments to market-oriented warehouses may provide the rationale for accumulating inventory. At the same time, the market-oriented warehouses would probably enable the firm to provide better delivery times to customers and thus perhaps to increase sales. Other costs, such as in-transit inventory cost, might also be decreased.

In addition to the above relationships, we should also mention that some of the reasons provided for raw materials inventory may actually result in finished-goods inventory instead. For example, perishable seasonal items such as fresh vegetables may have to be processed immediately. In other instances, it may be more convenient to hold items in finished form, particularly if there is great loss of weight.

Functional Types of Inventory

Our discussion has essentially discussed two types of inventory— physical supply and physical distribution. Another way of classifying inventory would be to view it in terms of the four functions of inventory. First, we would have process inventory of two types—*goods in process* because of time taken to manufacture goods and *goods in transit*. Both types of process stocks are important. In a logistics context, the inventory in-transit is particularly important to analyze, and we shall consider it in detail subsequently.

The second type of functional inventory is lot size, or what is sometimes called cycle stock. In other words, when items are purchased or manufactured they last for some time, i.e., all of them are not used immediately. There is a certain economic lot size or order quantity that is decided upon after analyzing appropriate costs, and this lot size or order quantity will be used up or sold over time.

A third type of functional inventory is safety or buffer stocks to guard against changes in customer buying patterns and other variations or unexpected events in the logistics system. A fourth type of inventory is seasonal stocks, which are the accumulation of inventory before a season begins. For example, Christmas toys may start being produced in August and September, which will necessitate accumulating inventory until October when shipments begin.

Whether we talk about physical supply inventory and physical distribution inventory or look at cycle, process, safety, and seasonal inventory, we still approach it the same way, i.e., we analyze the trade-offs.

The last item of direct concern in this section is that logistics will be involved to differing degrees in the reasons offered for holding or increasing inventory depending upon the situation and the firm. Some of the trade-offs are external to the logistics area to a certain extent, and the logistics manager may be involved only to provide information about availability and cost. For example, if a company purchases raw materials in a large quantity because of possible increases in price or possible severe shortages, the primary impetus may come from another area of the firm. The logistics manager may be called upon to provide information on how the logistics costs of operation are going to be affected, but otherwise logistics would be privy to the decision. The optimizing strategy would be occurring at a higher level or, stated differently, across functional areas. Another example might be when a company keeps employees working during slack time and is willing to accumulate the inventory to maintain good employee relations. However, because of the importance of inventory to other functional areas, some attention should be devoted to a discussion of inventory to other functional areas.

The Importance of Inventory in Other Functional Areas

In an earlier chapter, some of the important interfaces with other functional areas in an organization such as marketing, management, etc., were explored. Nowhere is the interface usually more prominent than in the area of inventory. As background to our analysis of the importance of inventory in the logistics system, we should examine inventory from the perspective of those other function areas. They could be summarized as follows:

- Marketing—desiring high customer service levels and well replenished inventory stocks in order to meet customer needs as quickly and completely as possible.
- Manufacturing—desiring long production runs and lowest procurement costs as well as early production of seasonal items in order to minimize manufacturing costs.
- Finance—desiring low inventories in order to increase turnover, reduce current assets, and achieve high capital utilization.

From the statements above, one can quickly discern the interest in inventory of the three functional areas. Also, it appears fairly obvious that the objectives of the finance area will lead to some conflict with marketing and manufacturing.

A more subtle conflict will sometimes arise with marketing and manufacturing, although both areas appear interested in high inventory levels. The long production runs that manufacturing may demand could cause shortages of some products needed by marketing for customer sales. For example, manufacturing may want to continue a particular production run up to 5000 units at a time when some other product is in short supply.

A case can be made in many companies for having a formal logistics organization as a means of resolving the conflicts in the inventory objectives indicated above. Inventory obviously has an important impact on logistics, and in many logistics organizations, it is the pivotal activity for logistics. The logistics manager can play an important role in analyzing inventory trade-offs not only with other areas in logistics but also among the functional areas discussed above. In a sense, this can almost be an arbitrator's role in some instances.

Proper inventory management and control has an impact on customers, on suppliers, and on major functional departments in an organization.

Therefore, the role of logistics in the inventory area is of great importance to the success of most companies, since all movement and information flows are directly related to inventory. Also, the company's internal and external relationships regarding product flows center on inventory.[1]

The rationale for inventory and its importance to an organization has been presented. It is indeed an area that is at the very nerve center of most manufacturing and distribution companies. Our discussion has touched upon but has not really explored the nature of the inventory decisions and what we hope to achieve. So let us turn our attention to this topic.

Basic Decisions for Inventory Control

The magnitude of the potential cost in the inventory area and its importance to the success of most organizations leads us to set forth a statement of what a company desires to achieve through inventory control. A succinct statement of the desired objective of most manufacturing and distribution companies would be to *achieve the designated customer service level within a reasonable level of cost*. Another way to state this would be *to have the right product at the right place at the right time at the right cost to the organization*.

The above statements imply balancing costs associated with holding inventory against the customer service needs. This familiar trade-off perspective necessitates trying to achieve what is best overall and not achieving 100 percent customer service nor the lowest possible inventory holding or carrying costs.

The general nature of this relationship between inventory and customer service can be seen in Figure 3-1. While this does not depict the balancing of the costs, it does show the impact of customer service upon inventory.

How Much Inventory

The inventory models to be discussed in the next chapter enable us to achieve the best balance or trade-offs in given situations. These are designed to aid us with certain critical inventory decisions. First, the question of "how much" should be ordered or "how much" should be produced or "how much" should be shipped must be answered. Based upon balancing certain costs to be discussed, the decision to be made is: What is the most economic quantity to order, to produce, or to ship? As we shall see, the model used to resolve this question of "how much" is most often referred to as the economic order quantity model (EOQ).

Whether it is an order situation or production situation will depend upon the circumstances. When we are concerned with physical supply, then we are usually talking about ordering some economic quantity of raw materials or other supplies to meet our production line requirements. Physical distribution, on the other hand, is often concerned with how much of a product should be produced and held in inventory to meet customer requirements. On the physical distribution or physical supply side, we may be concerned with how much to ship to a warehouse or a plant.

FIGURE 3-1   Customer service level as a percentage.

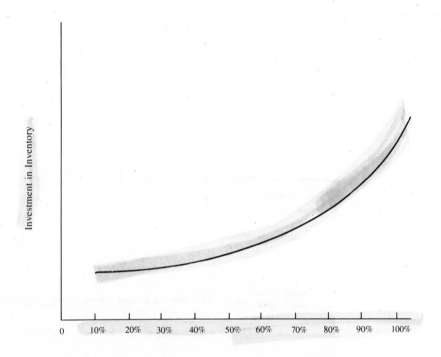

The "When" of Inventory

The second question is "when" to order or produce. This decision is related to how much lead time or replenishment time will be required for the goods to arrive and to be available for the customer or for production. The amount of time required will depend upon a variety of variables: production rates, transportation times, order processing times, order preparation time, etc. Essentially, one has to estimate the length of time required for getting the goods and how much inventory will be needed for production or sales during this interval. In some situations, however, the timing for orders is fixed or occurs at certain intervals, as we shall see in a later section.

In summary, inventory decisions are primarily concerned with the questions of "how much" and "when." The difficulty of answering these two questions will depend upon the circumstances under which the company operates and the willingness to accept simplifying assumptions. Generally speaking, the more complex the circumstances, the more sophisticated the model required to answer the questions. This will be treated at length in another section.

A third question relevant to inventory is "where" the inventory should be stocked or located. However, we will consider this in another section since the basic inventory models do not handle this particular decision.

The two decisions discussed above may seem relatively simple. However, as we shall see, these decisions are relatively complex in terms of the cost and demand information required for analysis in certain types of models. For companies with thousands of items of inventory, it is neither practical nor feasible to devote the same attention to all items of inventory, since they are not of equal importance. Maintaining close surveillance and control with sophisticated inventory models over a product line that may include over twenty thousand or more stockkeeping units is too expensive for the benefits received. Therefore, for effective management and control, inventory should be classified in terms of importance.

Classification of Inventory

The problem of multiple product lines and inventory control mentioned above requires companies to focus their attention on the most important items of inventory, i.e., apply the more sophisticated controls. Inventory classification, then, is usually a first step in effectuating good control. Consequently, we could logically have saved this section for the next chapter which deals with the tools of inventory control. However, we decided to cover the topic at this point since it demonstrates an important aspect of the nature of most inventory situations.

"ABC" Analysis

Ford Dicky of General Electric was one of the first people to recognize the need to rank inventory items in terms of their importance. He suggested that items be classified according to relative cash flows, lead time, or stockout costs. He used what is commonly referred to as "ABC analysis" for his classification scheme. In other words, items were assigned to three groups according to an appropriate criterion. The most important items were placed in the A group, then the B, and then the C.[2]

The significance and viability of such a classification can best be demonstrated by referring to Figures 3-2 and 3-3. Here we can clearly see that over 50 percent of the sales volume is associated with about 10 percent of the items in the product line of Company A (Figure 3-2) while Company B (Figure 3-3) has 20 percent of its product line accounting for 80 percent of its sales. Table 3-1 shows a specific breakdown of the importance of the various items, and we can see how a relatively small number of items can account for a major portion of the sales volume or value of inventory. These relationships are quite typical for most companies.

"80-20" Rule

This phenomenon is prevalent in many situations. For example, marketing people frequently find that 20 percent of the customers account for 80 percent of the total sales. Universities find that 20 percent of their courses generate 80 percent of their student credit hours. This is the basis of the so-called "80-20" rule. While it is most frequently associated with inventory, it nevertheless is also common in other situations.

A number of explanations help account for the "80-20" rule in inventory situations. In some instances, firms may have very successful new products but must retain old, slower moving products to maintain sales. In other cases, because their customers expect it, companies feel obligated to

FIGURE 3-2   ABC analysis of company *A*.

FIGURE 3-3   ABC analysis of company *B*.

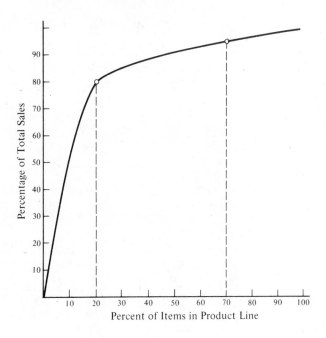

maintain a complete array of items even though some are not large contributors to sales. Sometimes the C items are necessary for the sales of A products, or the C items may be new products that are expected to be successful. In some cases, the C items can be very profitable, and while sales are small, the items are still important contributors to profit.

Actually the classification in terms of ABC is relatively simple. The first decision is the selection of some criterion such as sales volume or value for developing the ranking. The next step is to rank the items according to this characteristic or criterion in descending order of importance and then sum up the total number of items as the total value of the ranking criterion. Working from the top, or most important item, the next step is to calculate the number and percentage of total items as well as the cumulative amount and percentage of the total ranking criterion represented by the instant item being dealt with and all those above it. This last step is clearly illustrated in Table 3-1.

The last step requires assigning the items into the ABC groups.* This step is the most difficult, and there is no simple technique to use. To a large extent the decision is somewhat arbitrary, requiring a subjective judgment on the part of the decision maker. As one examines the rankings of items, significant natural breaks will often be discovered. But in other instances this is not the case and a decision will have to be made based on the cost of the control system and the importance of the item.

Before leaving the specifics of ABC analysis, we should mention that products or items are very often described by an item code. Also, the

TABLE 3-1

ABC Distribution for Happy Valley Associates

Item Code	Units Sold	Price	$1000/yr Sales	Cumulative Sales	Cumulative %
647BQ	40100	$ 20.00	802	802	54.2
8944C	282	1000.00	282	1084	73.2
6869R	1730	100.00	173	1257	84.9
1287B	5100	200.00	102	1359	91.8
2246R	595	100.00	59.5	1418.5	95.0
4973Z	8	4000.00	32	1450.5	98.0
8924A	83	2000.00	16.6	1467.1	99.1
9937D	796	100.00	7.96	1475.06	99.6
5321J	3270	1.00	3.27	1478.33	99.89
6777K	118	10.00	1.18	1479.51	99.97
4222F	31	10.00	.31	1479.82	99.99
5664G	3	10.00	.03	1479.85	100.00
8437F	10	.10	.001	1479.851	100.00

* More groups can be used if deemed necessary.

calculations described above are obviously ones that can be performed most readily by a computer. This is particularly appropriate where there are a large number of items to be analyzed.

While the classification technique for inventory is usually referred to as "ABC" analysis as indicated, it is acceptable to use more than three groups. In fact, when classification is initially done or when an existing classification is redone at an appropriate interval, companies frequently add a fourth category: "D" items. Sometimes this is an abbreviation for the "dead" items, i.e., those that should be eliminated from the product line and/or inventory. While occasionally a five item classification is used, it is usually not a cost-effective approach for control purposes.

This brings us to an important point: Remember that ABC analysis is a tool for control. The objective is to identify the items that contribute the most to sales, overall usage, etc. In other words, we want to focus the most attention on the most important items. Other things being equal, we will focus the most attention upon the so-called A items regarding inventory management techniques and review; the B items will generally be accorded less sophisticated treatment and review; and the C items will receive even less attention.

Some companies find that ABC analysis is not entirely satisfactory from an inventory control perspective because some C items may be accorded insufficient attention. For example, shoelaces may be a C item of inventory to a distributor or wholesaler of shoes, but a stockout of shoelaces could cause some loss of shoe sales. In the manufacture of sophisticated consumer products like refrigerators or automobiles, some small bolt or other part may be a C item based upon a cost/usage measure and yet a stockout could shut down the production line, Therefore, some companies utilize an approach developed by the military called Critical Value Analysis.[3]

Critical Value Analysis

The essence of a Critical Value Analysis is a classification of inventory items with point values assigned for three to five categories. An example would be as follows:

#1 (top priority): no stockouts—critical item
#2 (high priority): essential but limited stockouts permitted
#3 (medium priority): necessary but occasional stockouts permitted
#4 (low priority): desirable but stockouts allowed.

Critical Value Analysis is obviously a more subjective approach than the straightforward quantitative approach of ABC analysis. Consequent care must be used in the assignment process because there is always a tendency to assign too high a priority. Additionally, this classification by critical value would have to be combined with ABC analysis if all items were classified by the Critical Value Analysis approach.

One can easily discern that having to classify an inventory of 10,000 or more items by the critical value approach would be a formidable undertaking. Therefore, it is not unusual for a survey to be made of various inventory items in order to decide which ones are vital according to the established criterion—these items would be given an A classification. In this way, there is a more consistent, less awkward, and more objective approach used.

In the final analysis, it must be remembered that the ABC classification of inventory is a control technique subject to limitations. However, it is an easily implementable system that allows an organization to focus attention on the more important items of inventory for a more effective utilization of resources. Companies will want to use the more sophisticated, and consequently the more expensive, inventory management techniques where they can get the best returns, i.e., the A items. An understanding of the basic forms of inventory models will help in this regard.

FORMS OF THE INVENTORY MODEL

As discussed in a previous section, there are several important questions that have to be answered in the area of inventory control. The two most important are "how much" and "when." Inventory control models take two general approaches or forms in helping to answer these questions: a fixed quantity model or a fixed interval model.

Fixed Quantity Model

In regard to the first form of the model, companies will, as the name implies, place an order for a fixed amount each time based upon the cost and demand characteristics which they experience. When firms use this form or approach, it generally necessitates developing a minimum stock level when the fixed quantity is to be reordered. This is usually called the reorder point. When the number of items in inventory reaches the predetermined level, the fixed economic order quantity is "automatically" ordered. In a sense, the predetermined level for ordering acts as a trigger for setting the wheels in motion for the next order, and hence the reference made to the trigger principle by some authors.

Certain authors also refer to the fixed quantity model as the two bin system. When the first bin is empty, an order is placed. The amount of stock in the second bin represents how much inventory is needed until the new order arrives. Both notions (trigger and bin) imply that stock will be reordered or produced when it reaches some predetermined level. As stated above, the amount ordered will depend upon the cost and/or demand characteristics of the firms which will be discussed in a later section. Also, the level (number of units) at which the stock will be ordered depends upon the length of time it takes to get the new order and the demand for the product or sales rate during that time, i.e., how many units are sold per day, per week, etc. For example, if it takes two weeks for a new order to come in and 10 units per day are sold, then the reorder point will be 140 units (14 days × 10 units/day).

The fixed quantity model is shown in Figure 3-4. As can be seen, there are three inventory cycles or periods depicted. In each instance, the cycle period starts off with 4000 units, which is the fixed quantity ordered or produced. However, the length of time in the cycle periods varies, i.e., 5 weeks, 7 weeks, and 4 weeks. Likewise, the point in time when the level of inventory reaches the reorder level or point of 1500 units also varies in the three cycles depicted.

As suggested above, the purpose of establishing the reorder point is to provide a signal or trigger as to when to reorder the fixed quantity. For example, most people implicitly have reorder points for personal purchases such as gasoline. On a trip one may customarily stop to fill the tank when the needle indicates that one-eighth of a tank is left. One who buys cartons of cigarettes may decide to buy a new carton when the last pack is taken out of the previous carton.

In business inventory decisions, the reorder point is based upon the concept of lead time or replenishment time, i.e., the length of time that it takes for an order to be replenished or the fixed quantity to be manufactured.

The constant or perpetual monitoring necessary to determine when the reorder point is reached makes the fixed quantity model more expensive to administer. However, it has good control features built into it which allows it to be sensitive to demand without carrying too much excess inventory.

Fixed Interval Model

The second form of the model is fixed interval (period) ordering, which is sometimes referred to as fixed period review. In other words, inventory is ordered at fixed or regular intervals, and generally the amount ordered will vary depending upon how much is in stock at the time of the review. It is

FIGURE 3-4 Fixed quantity model.

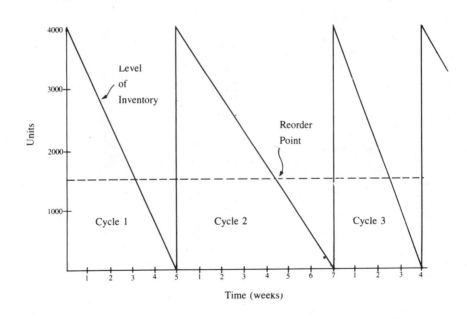

customary to make a count of inventory near the end of the interval and reorder based on what is on hand at that time.

Figure 3-5 depicts the basic nature of a fixed interval mode. As can be easily discerned, the length of time in each inventory period or cycle is the same, namely, 5 weeks, but the amount reordered varies each time.

The advantage of the fixed interval model is that it is less expensive to monitor. Close surveillance is not necessary. Low-valued items can be ordered infrequently in large quantities with infrequent checks to determine levels. Therefore, this approach is customarily used with C items. In some instances, the fixed period model or approach is necessitated by delivery schedules and/or salespersons' visits. This is frequently the case in retail food stores, where deliveries may be daily on some items, weekly or bi-weekly on others, and monthly on others. Therefore, some desired level of inventory can be decided upon and enough is ordered each time to bring the number of units up to that desired level. As indicated in Figure 3-5, the amount ordered each time will usually vary and will be a function of demand in the prior period. For example, if a company decides to start each period with 4000 units and it has experienced 2500 units of sales since the last order then it will have to reorder 2500 units plus the anticipated sales during lead time to bring inventory up to the desired level of 4000 units at the beginning of the period.

In summary, we should note that under the first form of the inventory model, the quantity ordered is fixed and the intervals between orders will usually vary. The second form requires fixed intervals and will usually have

FIGURE 3-5   Fixed interval model.

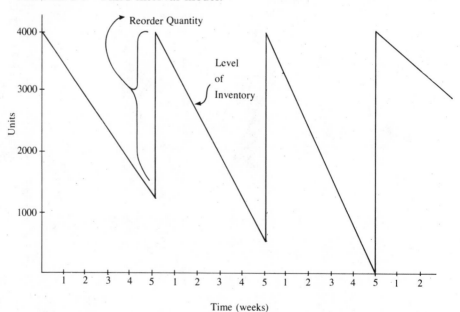

Time (weeks)

varying order quantities. Some authors have argued that there are four basic forms of the inventory model, namely, fixed quantity-fixed interval, fixed quantity-irregular interval, irregular quantity-fixed interval, and irregular quantity-irregular interval. In actuality, the first of these forms represents a situation where we are dealing with the fixed quantity model under special circumstances—known demand or certainty. When we examine the simple EOQ model we will see that fixed orders and intervals occur because of a constant rate of demand. The fourth form implies no control in the usual sense. So, in essence, we are left with the two forms discussed in this section.

We will examine the mathematical aspects of these two forms in a later section. However, mention of the use of the two basic forms of the model should again be made. Customarily, fixed quantity models are used when dealing with the more important inventory items, that is, A items, since close scrutiny must be kept over the number of items on hand for reordering purposes. The close surveillance is usually expensive and would be done only for the more important items. The other version of the model does not require the close monitoring of inventory levels but rather a check at stated intervals. Therefore, this approach is very often used for less expensive items. This version may also be mandatory where it is only possible to order at certain intervals.

Whether a fixed order quantity model or a fixed interval model is used, the costs associated with inventory levels play a critical role in answering the questions *how much* and *when* posed previously. The mathematical aspects of inventory costs appear overwhelming to some individuals. However, if one understands the basic nature and logic of inventory costs, the mathematics is relatively easy. The next section examines the various costs associated with inventory.

INVENTORY COSTS

The usual discussion and analysis of inventory costs includes three basic categories of cost: inventory carrying (holding) cost, ordering (acquisition) or setup cost, and stockout cost. These costs are, as suggested, categories or classifications of various expenses associated with inventory. Each of the three types of cost has a unique nature and a number of different expenses or costs included in its particular calculation. We will examine each of these costs in some detail.

Carrying Cost   First, carrying cost generally includes the handling cost associated with moving a product into and out of inventory and the storage cost, such as rent, heat, light, and so on; that is, the physical storage and handling cost. The level of such costs varies considerably. For example, raw materials can often be dumped out of rail cars and stored outside, whereas finished goods require safer handling and more sophisticated storage facilities. In some instances warehousing costs is delineated separately from carrying cost.

Another component of carrying cost is insurance and taxes. Depending upon the value and the type of product, the risk of loss or damage may be such as to require high insurance costs. Also, some states impose a tax on the value of inventory, sometimes on a monthly basis. The higher the level of inventory, the higher the tax costs. Both tax and insurance costs may vary considerably from product to product, but they must be taken into consideration in calculating carrying cost.

A third component of carrying cost is depreciation and obsolescence. When goods are held in storage there is a chance that they might depreciate in value or become obsolete. This is easiest to comprehend with fresh fruits and vegetables, where the quality deteriorates over time and/or the price goes down. However, even manufactured products may face the same risk, although not usually to the same degree. Styles may change, technology may change, etc., which may make goods in inventory less desirable and, therefore, less valuable.

The final major component of carrying cost is interest or opportunity cost. In other words, what does it cost us to have capital tied up in inventory? Since the interest or opportunity cost on inventory investment and inventory losses usually account for the largest portion of holding cost and are usually expressed as a percentage rate of the dollar value of inventory, a cost estimate representing all elements of holding cost is usually expressed the same way. For example, suppose a company has $300,000 worth of items in inventory. This is a capital asset of the company, figured just like a machine or any other investment. Therefore, if the company figures its opportunity cost on capital at 15 percent, and its average inventory value throughout the year is $300,000 then the opportunity cost is $45,000 (15% × $300,000) per year.

The additional cost categories associated with carrying cost, i.e., the storage and handling cost, insurance and taxes, and depreciation and obsolescence, can be expressed as a percentage as indicated and can add to the opportunity cost figure, giving a figure such as 25 percent or 30 percent as the percentage rate to be multiplied against the dollar value of average inventory.

Items with substantially the same holding costs should use the same estimate of holding cost per dollar of inventory. Separate cost estimates may be needed, however, for items subject to rapid obsolescence or for items which require servicing to prevent deterioration. The estimate of holding cost per dollar of inventory expressed as a percentage of the inventory value carried during the year will reflect how holding costs change with inventory value. The nature of this relationship is indicated in Table 3-2.

As can be seen from Table 3-2, as average inventory increases, i.e., as the level of inventory increases, annual carrying cost will increase and vice versa. In other words, carrying cost is a variable cost and the basic EOQ model to be discussed handles carrying cost as being directly proportional to the number of units of average inventory or the average value of inventory.

It should also be noted that annual cost associated with carrying inventory will increase with increases in the percentage carrying cost and

TABLE 3-2

Inventory and Carrying Cost

Average Inventory*	Order Period	Average Value of Inventory†	Annual Carrying Cost of Inventory‡
150	1 month	$ 15,000	$ 3,750
300	2 months	30,000	7,500
450	3 months	45,000	11,250
600	4 months	60,000	15,000
900	6 months	90,000	22,500
1800	12 months	180,000	45,000
3600	24 months	360,000	90,000

*Expressed in units where 1 month's supply is 300 units
†Value per unit is $100
‡Percentage carrying cost 25%

also with increases in the value per unit of inventory. In the short run, it is usually assumed that value per unit and the percentage carrying cost will remain constant and the size of the order or *production run* will be the only factor affecting carrying cost and the other costs that are to be discussed.

Order or Set-up Cost

A second cost, indicated previously, that affects total inventory cost is ordering cost (acquisition cost), which is incurred because an order has been placed for inventory. In some instances, we refer to set-up costs when we are filling an inventory order from our own manufacturing facility. Ordering cost usually refers to the cost of placing an order for inventory with a vendor or supplier.

As indicated, ordering or acquisition cost encompasses direct costs such as clerical personnel, paper and supplies, mailing, etc., as well as indirect costs such as managerial cost and other costs of securing and maintaining sources of supply. In more detail, the cost of placing an order may include the cost associated with the following operations: (1) review of the level of stock in inventory; (2) preparing and processing an order requisition or purchase request; (3) selection of a supplier (which may involve comparison of several alternatives); (4) preparation and processing the purchase order; (5) preparing and processing receiving reports; (6) checking and inspecting stock; and (7) preparing and processing payment. It is easy to overlook these costs, but they are important when one considers the total spectrum of activities associated with placing and receiving an order.

Production set-up costs may be more obvious than ordering or acquisition cost. Set-up costs are those expenses which are incurred each time a company stages a production line to produce a different item for inventory. Such expenses include the opportunity cost associated with the delay in setting up the line and the associated personnel costs for setting up. In some instances, such expenses are referred to as change-over costs.

TABLE 3-3

Order Frequency and Order Cost

Number of Orders per Year	Total Annual* Order Costs
48	$9600
36	7200
24	4800
20	4000
15	3000
12	2400
10	2000
8	1600
5	1000
3	600
1	200

*Assuming the cost per order is $200

Irrespective of the source of the order, both situations typically incur a fixed or constant cost or charge *per order* or *per set-up*. Therefore, total order cost per year are affected by the number of orders or set-ups per year, which in turn is affected by the size of the order placed or the number of units produced per set-up (length of production run). The general relationship can perhaps be best viewed in Table 3-3.

As can be seen from Table 3-3, when the number of orders decreases, i.e., the size of the order or length of production run increases, then total order costs decrease. We would expect this to happen in light of our explanation of order or set-up costs, i.e., they are fixed per order.

Therefore, as long as yearly sales or demand stays the same, we would expect total annual order or set-up costs to decrease or increase with the size of the order or production run. That is, if the size of the order increases (fewer orders), total cost will decrease. On the other hand, if the size of the order decreases (more orders), then total order costs will increase.

As should be evident, order or set-up costs respond in an opposite fashion to carrying or holding costs. The former will decrease on an annual basis as the size of the order or production run increases due to the smaller number of orders. The latter cost will increase as the size of the order or length of production run increases, since this will mean a larger number of units of average inventory on hand. By combining Tables 3-2 and 3-3 into Table 3-4 we can visualize this relationship.

As can be seen in examining Table 3-4, order costs and carrying cost respond in an opposite manner to a change in the number of orders or size of the order. Also, it can be seen that total cost is also responding to the changing order size. Close examination indicates an interesting relationship. Order costs are decreased more rapidly than carrying cost increases initially,

TABLE 3-4

Inventory Carrying Cost and Order Cost

Number of Orders	Average Inventory	Total Order Costs	Total Carrying Cost	Total Cost
36	50	$7200	$1250	$ 8450
		⟩ -2400	⟩ + 625	
24	75	4800	1875	6675
		⟩ - 800	⟩ + 375	
20	90	$4000	2250	6250
		⟩ - 400	⟩ + 250	
18	100	$3600	2500	6100
		⟩ - 600	⟩ + 500	
15	120	$3000	$3000	6000
		⟩ - 600	⟩ + 750	
12	150	2400	3750	6150
		⟩ - 400	⟩ + 750	
10	180	2000	4500	6500
		⟩ - 400	⟩ +1128	
8	225	1600	5625	7225
		⟩ - 600	⟩ +3375	
5	360	1000	9000	10000

which brings total costs down. In other words, there is a "positive trade-off" since the marginal earnings from order cost are more than the marginal increment in inventory costs. However, we reach a point where this relationship changes. That is, total costs start to increase since there is a negative trade-off due to the fact that the marginal savings from order cost are less than the marginal increase in carrying cost. This set of relationships can be viewed in terms of cost curves as shown in Figure 3-6.

As can be seen more readily in Figure 3-6, carrying cost is increasing with increasing order sizes (or length of production run) and order (or set-up cost) is decreasing. Total cost takes a "U" shape, indicating positive trade-offs up to a point and then negative trade-offs. In other words, total cost is decreasing initially because the savings from order costs is more than the increase in carrying cost. However, we reach a point where this is no longer true, i.e., the savings from decreasing order cost are not enough to offset the increasing carrying cost. Then, total costs begin to go up. As will be explained in more detail in a later section, the objective of inventory decisions is to minimize total cost. So the best decision is the one that puts us at the low cost point on the total cost curve.

Stockout Cost   A third type of cost that may occur in inventory related situations is stockout cost, i.e., the opportunity cost of not having something available when it is demanded or needed. When an item cannot be supplied to

FIGURE 3-6   Inventory costs.

customers, they may substitute a competitor's product, thus causing a direct loss of profit. It is also possible to experience an indirect or longer-run cost in the same situation, i.e., a customer could be lost. On the physical supply side, a stockout may result in no new materials or semifinished goods or parts, meaning idle machine time or even the shutdown of an entire manufacturing facility.

Safety Stock
Most companies facing the possibility of a stockout (which can occur for a variety of reasons, as we shall see in a later section) will build a certain amount of safety stock or buffer stock into their inventory. The difficulty for the inventory decision maker is to decide how much buffer or safety stock to have on hand. To have too much will mean excess inventory, whereas not having enough will mean stockouts and lost sales.

Developing the appropriate information for deciding what level of safety stock is necessary is a difficult task. The measurement of the carrying cost associated with different levels of safety stock can be approached in the same fashion as suggested earlier in our general discussion of carrying cost, i.e., determining a percentage carrying cost which would include the same categories previously discussed, e.g., interest or opportunity cost, physical storage and handling, etc. This percentage figure would then be multiplied by the value per unit and the number of units. Two points should be made here. First, it is likely that the same carrying cost would be used as previously determined for the carrying cost decision. Second, most decision models involve probability analysis in relation to safety stock levels. An example is offered in Appendix A of Chapter 4.

Cost of Lost Sales   While the determination of the cost of carrying safety stock inventory may be relatively easy, determining the loss (cost) of not having an item available for sale may be much more formidable. If a company is dealing with raw materials or supplies for a production line, a stockout would mean shutting down operations in whole or in part. The opportunity loss from such a shutdown would have to be calculated. Most companies would be able to determine the hourly or daily production rates, which could be multiplied by the loss of profit on the number of units not produced. For example, if the plant is shut down for four hours with an hourly production rate of 1,000 units and a per unit profit of $100, the loss would be $400,000. However, this figure is possibly a conservative estimate of the loss (cost). For example, consideration may have to be given to labor if wages have to be paid irrespective of idle time. Also, overhead costs may need to be considered, since they are often assigned or allocated to each production unit. Finally, the shutdown may inconvenience customers, causing further potential losses as explained below.

It should be apparent by this time that there are some important decisions that have to be made in estimating the stockout cost when making decisions about how much inventory to hold and store for production purposes. In fact, because the cost of carrying raw materials is often low (since they can be stockpiled outside), companies may calculate what amounts to an infinite cost for being stocked out of raw materials, i.e., they carry large inventories. On the other hand, some companies buy expensive and sophisticated parts on which the carrying cost is too great to justify excess inventory. Consequently, they would want to be very careful in calculating the stockout cost and arriving at an appropriate level of safety stock, i.e., they do not want too much excess inventory (safety stock).

In addition to the stockout cost associated with raw materials and/or supplies for production lines, it may also be necessary to calculate a different stockout cost for finished-goods inventory. In fact, the only concern of some organizations, such as wholesalers or retailers, is the stockout cost for finished goods.

The calculation of stockout costs for finished goods where a customer will be affected is usually a more formidable task than for raw material stockout cost. There are three possible events which can occur: a backorder, a lost sale, or a lost customer. From the viewpoint of most companies, these three possible outcomes of a stockout are stated from best to worst in terms of desirability.

Backorder Costs   Technically, a backorder can occur in one of two ways. The item(s) stockout cost can be replenished at the time of the next regular order or an expedited backorder can be used. If the customer is willing to wait until the next regular order, then the company has really not had any loss. There is always the risk, of course, that if this occurs repeatedly, the customer will take the business elsewhere. Assuming that this does not happen, then there really is no loss.

If a stocked out item has to be backordered, the expenses will be incurred for special order processing and transportation. The extra order processing time is usually attributable to the additional paperwork that accounts for and traces the movement of the backorder, in addition to the normal processing for regular replenishments. The extra transportation charges are usually attributable to the fact that a backorder is typically a smaller size shipment and often incurs higher rates. Also, the backordered item may be shipped a longer distance, e.g., from a plant or warehouse in another region of the country. In addition, it may be necessary to ship the backorder by a faster and more expensive means of transportation. Therefore, the backorder cost could be estimated based on an analysis of additional order processing and additional transportation expense. In the event that customers always backordered stocked out items, then this would be our estimate of the cost of stockouts and could be compared with costs of excess inventory.

Most firms find that while some customers may backorder, others will turn to alternative sources of supply. In other words, most companies have competitors producing substitute products, and when one source does not have an item available, it will be ordered from another source. In such cases, the stockout has caused a lost sale. The direct loss to the seller is the loss of profit on the item(s) which was not available when the customer wanted it. In other words, we could calculate the profit on an item basis and multiply it by the number ordered by the customer. For example, if the order was for 100 units and the profit is $10 per unit, the loss is $1000.

Two additional points should be made about lost sales. First, in addition to the loss of profit, we might include an amount for the cost of a salesperson that may have made the initial sale. In other words, the sales effort with the associated order was wasted effort and in that sense an opportunity loss. Whether such a cost inclusion is valid would depend upon whether salespersons are used in the marketing effort of the company. Second, it may be difficult to determine the amount of a lost sale in some circumstances. For example, there are numerous companies where telephone orders are customary. In such cases, the customer may initially just inquire as to the availability of items without specifying how much is desired. If an item is out of stock, the customer may never indicate a quantity desired and we would therefore not know the amount of the loss. Also, it is often difficult to develop a systematic way of recording lost sales in telephone order situations. While this poses a problem in those situations, it is not insurmountable and can be overcome through sampling techniques.

In the event that lost sales will probably be sustained with stockouts of inventory, a cost will have to be assigned along the lines suggested above. Then an analysis should be made of the expected number of stockouts associated with different possible levels of inventory. (An example of this technique is offered in a later section.) The expected number of lost sales then will be multiplied by the profit loss plus additional assigned cost, if any, and analyzed against the cost of carrying the safety stock.

Customer Loss

The third possible event that can take place with a stockout, in addition to the backorder or lost sale, is the loss of a customer, i.e., the customer permanently switches to another brand. If a customer is lost, a future stream of income is lost. The estimation of customer loss associated with stockouts is rather difficult. Marketing researchers have been concerned with brand switching for some time. Such an analysis will often use management science techniques along with more qualitative marketing research methods. Given this information, we attempt to develop the probability of a lost customer and multiply this by an estimated loss of profit in future time periods.

In addition to the loss of profit, we may also be concerned with the loss of goodwill from stockouts. Goodwill is difficult to measure and often ignored in inventory decisions, but it can be very important to the overall profits of the corporation.

As can be seen from the above discussion, estimating the cost of a stockout is a difficult but necessary task. Otherwise, an organization may find itself with almost continuous conditions of excess inventory or, on the other hand, almost continuous out-of-stock situations. Neither extreme is desirable. While it is almost impossible to achieve perfect balance between safety stock and stockouts, a reasonable balance can be achieved with proper management.

In effect, the critical question in safety stock analysis is determining the level of customer service that is desired. The answer to this question will lie in an analysis of the trade-offs between safety stock cost and the costs of stockout. If the latter is low, then the service level can be low. On the other hand, if the latter is high, a higher safety level is necessary.

Perhaps a convenient way to summarize our discussion of stockout cost is to examine Figure 3-7. You will note that ''Total Stock Out Costs'' is a function of the three variables we have mentioned, *viz*., cost of backorders, cost of lost sales, and cost of lost customers. Each of those in turn are described as a function of the factors we have discussed.

Cost of Carrying Inventory In Transit

Another possible cost associated with inventory is the cost of carrying inventory in transit. This particular cost may not be as apparent as the three previously discussed. However, under certain circumstances, companies may have to consider the cost of carrying inventory in transit. For example, if a company sells its product F.O.B., destination, this means that the company is responsible for transporting the product to its customer, since title does not pass until it reaches the customer's facility. So in other words, although it is still the company's inventory, it is going to be contained in the vehicle of a transportation company or perhaps even in the company's private carrier.

Since this ''moving'' inventory is still company-owned until it is delivered to the customer, the time it takes to be delivered may be a concern. The faster the order is delivered, the sooner the bill can be collected. Typically, however, faster delivery means higher-cost transportation, so the company may want to analyze the trade-off between transportation cost and the cost of carrying inventory in transit.

The question for us at this point is how to calculate the cost of carrying inventory in transit, i.e., what variables should be considered. It will be recalled that in calculating the cost of carrying inventory in a warehouse four basic categories were considered. First, storage and handling cost was included for warehouse carrying cost, which would usually not be relevant for in-transit inventory since the carrier usually provides the equipment as a part of the price or rate of the service and the handling for loading is

FIGURE 3-7   A method for estimating hard and soft stockout costs.

Source: Unpublished Master's Paper of J. Duane Weeks, *The Effect of Inventory Control and Stockout Costs on the Management of a Multi-Echelon Distribution System* (University Park: Pennsylvania State University, 1974).

included in the warehouse carrying cost. Second, depreciation and obsolescence may be relevant but typically are not considered because the time period involved is relatively short with not much likelihood of depreciation or obsolescence occurring. Also, the carrier has insurance. Third, taxes and insurance were included. Taxes would generally not be relevant for inventory in transit, and whether insurance should be considered would depend upon the type of transportation utilized. For example, common carriers are held to a high degree of liability under the law and, therefore, you may choose not to carry insurance. On the other hand, if private carriage is being utilized, then insurance would probably be appropriate. The fourth type of cost that was discussed was the interest or opportunity cost on the capital invested in the inventory. This particular cost is a major component of inventory in transit and in many instances is the only type of cost that needs to be considered.

The discussion has focused upon the four major types of cost that have a major effect upon inventory cost. The analysis has been somewhat lengthy but a thorough understanding of the nature of these costs will make the coverage of the mathematical models for inventory control decisions much easier to understand.

SUMMARY

As indicated at the outset of this chapter, the basic objective was to introduce the complex topic of inventory control and management. Starting with an explanation of why organizations accumulate inventory and ending with a discussion of the important types of inventory costs. At this point, you should have a good enough background to proceed with the more conceptual and theoretical presentation of inventory models.

Study Questions

1. How would the inventory situation of a steel company be similar to that of a water authority?
2. Select some company and discuss their reasons for holding inventory in terms of physical supply inventory and physical distribution inventory.
3. You have been called in as a consultant to a large drugstore chain which has 24,000 line items of inventory. Explain how inventory classification could help this company to better control their inventory.
4. Explain why and under what circumstances you would use a fixed quantity inventory model.
5. Explain the difference between inventory carrying costs and order costs.
6. Why are stockout costs so difficult to calculate?

Notes

1. Warren Rose, *Logistics Management* (Dubuque, Iowa: Wm. C. Brown, 1979), pp. 142-143.

2. David P. Herron, "ABC Data Correlation," in Business Logistics in American Industry, edited by Karl Ruppenthal and Henry A. McKinnel, Jr. (Stanford, California: Stanford University, 1968), pp. 87-90.

3. Rose, *op. cit.*, p. 153.

Case 3-1
Byte Size Computer Company

Joe Homan, Vice President of Logistics in the Byte Size Computer Company, found the following memo on his desk early one morning:

> Joe:
>
> What is your department trying to do? Do you realize that our production line had to be shut down for the second time this month? We are constantly running out of physical supply for the manufacture of our computers. This is costing the company millions of dollars. Please reevaluate your parts inventory policy and get back to me as quickly as possible.
>
> Mike Parrish
> Vice-President, Production

Mr. Homan immediately called a meeting of his managers to review the situation. The apparent cause of the inventory depletions, according to Mr. Homan's staff, is the nature of the computer industry. Being a very specialized piece of equipment, a computer is usually made to order using customer specifications. Although many parts are basic to all computers, some models require special components. This, compounded by the dynamic nature of consumer demand, prompts the logistics managers to hold inventory levels to a minimum. Because of the low inventory levels, more orders must be placed in order to satisfy the inventory requirements. Mr. Homan's managers considered this to be an appropriate and cost-effective trade-off for the logistics department because computer parts have high carrying costs.

Mr. Parrish, on the other hand, considers this cost to be unimportant when compared to the cost of his department of shutting down the production line. He has suggested to the president of the company that the logistics department carry a full array, in adequate quantity, of every part needed in the manufacture of their full line of computers. He further substantiates his suggestion by stating that order costs per year would decrease (a big savings to the logistics department) and production runs would be smooth and continuous.

The president of the company has asked Mr. Homan to formulate his position on the present situation and be ready to present it at next week's board meeting.

If you were Mr. Homan, how would you suggest the situation be resolved? What variables must be considered? Is it acceptable to the firm for one department to attempt to maximize at the expense of another department? Explain.

Case 3-2
Pin-Pal Company

The Pin-Pal Company of Cincinnati, Ohio, is a manufacturer of bowling balls. They began operations only four months ago and are doing quite well in light of their age. This is attributable to the fact that they are the originators of a new type of molded plastic ball with gyroscopically balanced weights within the ball. Many professional bowlers around the country have used the ball and regard it highly. The new Pin-Pal ball has not yet been approved by the American Bowling Council (ABC) and therefore is not permitted to be used in any professional competition or in local bowling leagues which are sanctioned by the ABC (this constitutes about 90 percent of all leagues in the country). It has been estimated that 70 percent of all the bowling in the United States is conducted in conjunction with a bowling league. Bowling ball experts have told the Pin-Pal executives that the new ball stands about an 80 percent chance of being approved by the ABC.

Ed Norton is the materials manager at Pin-Pal. He has been with the company for all of its four months but has 35 years experience as a top-notch materials manager. Tom Arnold, a recent graduate of a major university's business logistics curriculum, is Ed's able assistant. Ed has set up the current system for the control of incoming raw materials. Since there are only two raw materials involved in the production of the ball—plastic (very expensive) and the lead weights (these are molded prior to Pin-Pal's purchasing)—Ed feels that ordering a fixed amount (1000 units) of each raw material when triggered by a reorder point of 500 units is adequate during this time of steady and moderate demand (approximately 500 balls are sold each week).

If the ball is approved by the ABC, demand is expected to reach from three to five times the current level. Anticipating the approval, Tom has developed a plan for Pin-Pal to switch to an ordering system in which a fixed amount of raw materials is ordered each week. Tom feels this type of arrangement is superior to the current plan because it eliminates the need to keep an on-going count on the amount of raw materials in stock.

Ed has reviewed Tom's plan for the change in raw materials inventory policy and does not agree wholeheartedly with the recommendations because there is an uncertainty as to the level of demand which will be experienced should the ball be approved. Ed thinks this may result in costly inadequacies or excesses in raw materials inventory.

Which manager's position do you support? Why? Do you have any suggestions of your own as to a more efficient inventory policy? Specifically, how will your ideas benefit Pin-Pal? Do you perceive any conflict between the two managers which may be independent of the problem at hand?

Chapter 4	Inventory Control Decisions

After studying this chapter, you should be able to:

- Explain how the important inventory decisions of *how much* and *when* are made using an inventory model.

- Demonstrate through the use of an inventory model how the trade-offs occur between inventory carrying costs and order costs in reaching a decision about how much should be ordered or produced.

- Present and explain various adaptations in the basic inventory model to aid the logistics manager in making logistics-related decisions.

The preceding chapter developed at some length the rationale for inventory in a logistics system and some of the other fundamental aspects of inventory management. A very important component of the preceding chapter was the discussion and analysis of the major categories of cost for inventory decisions, i.e., carrying cost at the warehouse, carrying cost in transit, order or set-up cost, and stockout cost.

In this chapter, the background previously developed, particularly the basic cost categories, is put to use in the discussion of the inventory models for decision making. The Basic or Simple EOQ model is presented initially and is followed by logistics-related adjustments being made in the basic model to accommodate such decisions as inventory in-transit, larger shipment sizes, and private trucking. In addition, there are two important appendices covering topics which may be taken up in some classes, *viz.*, inventory decisions under conditions of uncertainty, and inventory decisions with inexcess rates.

INVENTORY CONTROL MODELS

In many situations when business decisions must be made, the number of variables affecting the decision is almost overwhelming. Therefore, when models are developed to aid in the decision process, they abstract from reality or represent reality in a simpler manner. In other words, models generally make some simplifying assumptions about the nature of the real world they are attempting to represent. This is particularly true for the basic or simple EOQ model for inventory decisions.

The complexity and accuracy of the models are related to the assumptions which are made. Generally, the more that is assumed away in the model, the easier it is to work with and understand; however, the output of the simple model is often less accurate. There are trade-offs usually between the two (simplicity and degree of accuracy) that require analyzing. The developer or user of models attempts to achieve the proper balance. One usually attempts to use or develop models which are as simple as possible but yet do not assume away too much of reality.

As indicated previously, there are two general types of inventory control models. First, there is the fixed order quantity model. In this case, the number of units ordered or produced (the lot size) is fixed until there is a change in the cost and or demand factors. In addition, there is a critical level of stock which is also fixed that triggers or signals a replenishment order or production run. This reorder level or point is also based upon certain variables such as transit time, cost, etc.

As previously noted, the length of time which elapses between orders or production runs under the fixed quantity model will vary depending upon demand. This is in direct contrast to the other type of model, the fixed interval or periodic review model. In the latter situation, the intervals between orders or production runs are fixed but the amount ordered or produced will vary depending upon what is needed to bring inventory up to the predetermined level.

The type of model selected will depend upon the particular product or firm involved as discussed at some length in the preceding chapter. Our attention will focus primarily upon fixed quantity models and we will move from the simple form to the more complex.

We should begin by delineating and explaining the more important assumptions of the simple EOQ model.

Assumptions of the   1. A continuous, constant and known rate of demand.
Simple EOQ Model   2. A constant and known replenishment or lead time.
     3. The satisfaction of all demand.
     4. Constant price or cost which is independent of the order quantity or time, e.g., purchase price, transport cost, etc.
     5. No inventory in-transit.
     6. One item of inventory or no interaction between items.
     7. Infinite planning horizon.
     8. No limit on capital availability.

The first three assumptions are very closely related and basically mean that we are dealing with conditions of certainty. We know exactly how much will be demanded each relevant time period (daily, weekly, or monthly) and exactly how long it takes to replenish our stock. That is, we assume no variations in demand or the length of time it takes us to receive or produce replenishment stock. Therefore, we do not have to be concerned about stockouts and, consequently, stockout costs.

The assumptions of certainty are ones that some individuals feel make the basic model too simplistic and consequently the output decisions not accurate enough. While this charge is true in many cases, there are several justifications for the simple form of the model. First, there are businesses where the variation in demand is so small that to make the model more complex is too costly for the extra accuracy achieved. Second, firms just beginning to develop inventory models find the simple EOQ model a convenient and necessary point of departure because of the data they have available. In fact, this is the form presented in this discussion. Some firms get "caught up" in sophisticated models with simple data and the end results are probably no more accurate than if they had used the simple form of the model.

Finally, from a pedagogical point of view, it is easier to work from the simple model to the complex. The simple EOQ model familiarizes the reader with the essential logic of the lot size model. If these essentials are grasped then the material which follows is easier to understand.

The assumption about no inventory in transit can be handled by assuming that goods are purchased on the delivered price basis (purchase price includes transportation for delivery) and are sold F.O.B. our plant (the buyer pays transportation charges). If we make these assumptions, then we will not have any responsibility for goods in transit, i.e., there are no in-transit inventory carrying costs.

The assumption about constant cost is necessary in the short run to reach a decision. While it is perhaps somewhat unrealistic, it is not particularly limiting because, as we shall see, the model can be adapted to handle cost changes. The cost information can be changed from time to time as the cost of carrying inventory, etc., changes. Also, if desirable, projected cost information can be fed into the model to see what changes might be forthcoming in lot size. It is the relative rates of change which are important as we shall see, e.g., if carrying cost increases faster than order cost then the size of the Economic Order Quantity will decrease.

As far as the availability of capital is concerned, while this may be important in some instances, it is a decision which is usually made outside of the logistics area. Therefore, if there is some restraint on capital for inventory this can be used as an upper limit on lot size.

While most firms have more than one item of inventory, the assumption made in this regard is not seriously limiting. Separate EOQ decisions can be made with regard to each important item of inventory. While some reality is lost because of the lack of effective interaction, the essential costs are considered.

Given the assumptions made, we only have to consider two basic types of cost in the simple EOQ model, *viz.*, inventory carrying cost and ordering or set-up cost. The decision reached in the simple model analyzes trade-offs between these two types of cost. If we only considered inventory carrying cost which is directly variable with increases in lot size, we would order as little as possible (see Figure 4-1). If we viewed only order cost or set-up cost which is fixed per order or set-up, we would place large orders to decrease the total order costs (see Figure 4-2). The decision reached about lot size compromises these two types of cost with the objective of minimizing total cost, i.e., carrying cost plus set-up or order cost (see Figure 4-3).

FIGURE 4-1   Inventory carrying cost.

FIGURE 4-2 Order or set up cost.

FIGURE 4-3 Inventory costs.

At this point it would be best to develop the model in standard mathematical form.

R = the annual rate of demand

Q = the quantity ordered or lot size

A = the cost of placing an order

V = the value or cost of one unit of inventory

W = carrying cost per dollar value of inventory per year expressed as a percentage

t = time in days

TAC = the total annual cost.

Given the assumptions that we made previously, the total annual cost can be expressed as follows:

$$TAC = \left(\frac{1}{2} \cdot Q \cdot V \cdot W\right) + \left(A \cdot \frac{R}{Q}\right)$$

Handwritten annotations: CARRING; LOST; ORDER COST; OR SET UP COST

Total Cost of
Simple EOQ Model

The first part of the equation refers to inventory carrying cost, and literally translated states that these costs are equal to the average number of units in the economic order quantity during the order cycle ($\frac{1}{2} Q$) multiplied by the value per unit (V) multiplied by the carrying cost (W). If you refer to Figure 4-4, which is the so-called saw tooth model, you can understand more readily the logic of the equation. The vertical line labeled Q represents the amount ordered or produced for our economic order size. We start each period with this amount. During the order cycle (t) we sell or use up this amount at the rate represented by the slanted line. Demand is known and constant and the inventory is used up at a constant or uniform rate over the period. The cost of carrying inventory during this period is affected by the average numbers of units we have on hand during the period. The average number we have on hand, given our constant rate of demand, is simply one-half the amount we start with (Q). The dashed horizontal line in Figure 4-4 represents average inventory. The logic can be proven very simply. Let us assume that Q is 100 and that daily demand is 10 units which means that the 100 units would last 10 days (t). At the half way point in the period, fifth day, we would still have 50 units left which is one-half of Q ($\frac{1}{2} \times 100$).

FIGURE 4-4   Sawtooth model.

Determining the average number of units is not enough as indicated in the equation. We still need the value per unit which will vary depending upon the nature of the product. We also need to know the percentage carrying cost which will also vary depending upon the product and the firm's warehousing operations. The larger the Q, the higher the inventory carrying cost will be. This general relationship was described before, i.e., increasing carrying cost with larger inventory lots or orders. As should be evident in our present context, larger order quantities of inventory will last longer and thereafter increase our carrying cost. In other words, on the average, we will have more inventory on hand as we increase the economic order size given a constant demand (see Figures 4-5(a) and 4-5(b)).

FIGURE 4-5 **Sawtooth models.**

(a)

(b)

The second part of the previous equation refers to order cost or set-up cost. As stated before, order cost is assumed to be constant per order or set-up. Therefore, if the size of Q is increased, there will be a smaller number of orders per year since annual demand is constant. It follows then that annual order costs will be lower with larger order quantities.

While the general nature of carrying cost and order cost have been explained, we are still not finished. It is still necessary to determine Q, our economic order quantity. As was indicated previously, this involves trading off between carrying cost and order cost. This can be handled mathematically by differentiating the TAC function with respect to Q as follows:

$$TAC = \frac{1}{2} Q \cdot V \cdot W + A \cdot \frac{R}{Q}$$

$$\frac{d\,(TAC)}{d\,Q} = \frac{VW}{2} - \frac{AR}{Q^2}$$

Setting this equal to zero and solving for Q gives

$$Q^2 = \frac{2RA}{VW}$$

or

$$Q = \sqrt{\frac{2RA}{VW}}$$

Let us assume the following to show how the formula would work:

Simple EOQ
Example

$V = \$100/\text{unit}$

$W = 25\%$

$A = \$200$

$R = 3600 \text{ units}$

If we solve for Q as indicated previously, it would be as follows:

$$Q = \sqrt{\frac{2RA}{VW}}$$

$$Q = \sqrt{\frac{(2)(3600)(\$200)}{(\$100)(25\%)}}$$

$$Q = 240 \text{ units}$$

The nature of the trade-offs and the logic of the above solution can probably be best demonstrated by referring to Table 4-1 and Figure 4-6. Here we see developed an array of different Q's from a low at 100 to a high of 500 with the associated inventory carrying cost and order cost of each as well as the total cost. These costs are plotted in Figure 4-6.

As can be seen in the table, at the lower Q's order costs are high, as we stated they would be, but carrying costs are low. As we increase Q up to 240, the ordering costs decrease because of the decrease in number of orders per year, but carrying costs increase because of the higher average inventories. Beyond 240 units, while total order cost decreases, the incremental decrease in order costs was less than the incremental increase in carrying cost so total costs increased.

TABLE 4-1

Total Costs for Various EOQ Amounts

Q	Order Cost (A) (R/Q)	Carrying Cost (1/2) (Q) (V) (W)	Total Cost
100	$7200	$1250	$8450
140	5140	1750	6890
180	4000	2250	6250
220	3270	2750	6020
240	3000	3000	6000
260	2770	3250	6020
300	2400	3750	6150
340	2120	4250	6370
400	1800	5000	6800
500	1440	6250	7690

FIGURE 4-6   Graphical representation of EOQ example.

We are defining our optimum Q in terms of total cost so we can quickly discern from the table that a Q of 240 is optimum in terms of the total cost as we have defined it. This is also demonstrated in Figure 4-6.

In previous discussion it was indicated that in addition to "how much" to order (which we have now solved) it was also necessary to know "when" to order. The "when" as we said, is generally referred to as a reorder point and defined in terms of some level of inventory, i.e., some number of units.

Under our assumptions of certainty, we just need enough inventory to last us during replenishment time or lead time. Therefore, if the length of lead time is known, we just have to multiply lead time by daily demand.

It should be noted in regard to replenishment time that it is generally defined as consisting of several components, e.g., order transmittal time, order processing, order preparation, and delivery. The length of time involved can vary considerably depending upon how the order is transmitted (mail, salesman, telephone), whether it has to be produced to order by the vendor or he has it in inventory, what mode of transportation is used, etc. So there are many variables that can affect lead time.

Reorder Point   In our previous example it will be assumed that it takes two days for an order to be prepared and transmitted, one day for the order to be prepared for shipping by the vendor, and seven days for transportation. This results in a total of ten days for replenishment time or lead time. Daily demand is ten units (3600/360); so our reorder point would be 100 units (10 days × 10 units).

Reviewing what we have said thus far, our analysis and example have allowed us to determine an economic order quantity which given certain costs associated with carrying or holding inventory and ordering gives us the lowest total cost. We have also determined the reorder point which is the signal to order another lot of our product. Given our assumptions, the reorder point is the minimum amount needed for sales during replenishment time. We have assumed that the new supply will be delivered exactly when the old supply is depleted which is shown in our sawtooth model.

At the outset, it was stated that the simple EOQ model, while somewhat unrealistic because of the number of assumptions, was still useful because it would aid in the understanding of the logic of inventory models. The simple EOQ model can be adjusted or developed to handle more complex situations. In fact, there are over two hundred variations of the simple model which have been developed to aid in making inventory related decisions in a number of areas. In the next several sections, we will discuss several variations of the simple EOQ model which can be used for helping the logistics manager to make inventory related decisions.

ADJUSTMENT OF THE SIMPLE EOQ MODEL FOR MODAL CHOICE DECISIONS—THE COST OF INVENTORY IN TRANSIT

In Chapter 1 we discussed the trade-off possibilities between transportation decisions regarding choice of modes and inventory costs. Implied in our discussion was the idea that longer transit times resulted in higher inventory costs. One of the reasons why inventory could be higher with longer transit times is that we may own the inventory in transit, and in effect, we are experiencing carrying costs on this inventory in transit similar to the carrying cost of inventory in the warehouse. There are differences, as we shall see, between inventory in transit and inventory in the warehouse, but basically they both represent situations where a company is responsible for inventory. There is always some cost attached to having inventory whether it be sitting in a warehouse or plant or moving to another point.

Therefore, if modes of transportation have different transit times and different rates with other variables being equal, then we should examine the trade-off between the transportation rates and the inventory cost associated with the transit times. The transportation rates are usually easy to obtain since, as we shall see in Chapter 8, regulated carriers are required to publish their rates. However, in order to calculate the costs of carrying inventory in transit, we will have to modify our basic or simple EOQ model.

You will recall that the simple EOQ model considered only the trade-off between order/set-up costs and the carrying cost associated with holding inventory in a warehouse. In order to consider transportation effects associated with different transit times, we will have to release one of the assumptions that we made in the basic EOQ model and adapt our model accordingly.

One of the assumptions that we made with the simple EOQ model was that we had no cost of inventory in transit because we purchased on a delivered price basis and we sold F.O.B., our plant. If we change the conditions so that we are either buying F.O.B., origin or selling on a delivered price basis then we would have to consider the cost of carrying inventory in transit. Figure 4-7 depicts a modified sawtooth model of inventory with the lower half showing the inventory in transit.

Comparing the lower half with the upper half, which depicts inventory in the warehouse, one can see two differences which are relevant for calculating the appropriate costs. First, inventory is in transit usually for only a part of the cycle period. In other words, we would typically expect that the number of days that it takes for inventory to be shipped would be less than the number of days that inventory would be on hand in the warehouse from the preceding EOQ replenishment that we received.

The second difference between the two types of inventory carrying cost is that while inventory is in transit it is not used up or sold as is the case of inventory in the warehouse. The two distinctions are represented in Figure 4-7.

Since the inventory in transit has these two distinctive characteristics, then our calculation of the cost of inventory in transit must be different than that for inventory in the warehouse. There are several ways that we can approach this cost. If we had a precise daily cost for inventory, we could multiply this by the number of days inventory is in transit. Such a cost might be developed by multiplying the value of the inventory in transit times a daily opportunity cost. This cost, after it had been multiplied by the number of transit days, could be multiplied by the number of orders per year or cycles per year for an annual cost of inventory in transit.

For our purposes, the same results can be achieved by following a slightly different but related approach. This different approach is suggested

FIGURE 4-7   Sawtooth model modified for inventory in transit.

since it follows closely what was done in calculating the cost of inventory in the warehouse.

Consider the following:

Y = cost of carrying inventory in transit (given)

V = value/unit of inventory (given)

t_m = inventory transit time (given)

M = "average" number of units of inventory in transit which is calculated as follows:

$$\frac{t_m}{t} = \text{percentage of time inventory is in transit per cycle period}$$

$$M = \frac{t_m}{t} \cdot Q$$

This could be rewritten as follows:

$$t \text{ (days in cycle)} = \frac{360 \text{ (days in year)}}{\frac{R}{Q} \text{ (cycles per year)}}$$

$$t = 360 \cdot \frac{Q}{R}$$

$$M = \frac{(t_m \cdot Q)}{360} \cdot \frac{R}{Q}$$

$$M = \frac{t_m}{360} \cdot R$$

Now that we have developed a way of calculating the "average" number of units in transit, all that remains to be done is to multiply this figure by the value per unit and the percentage annual carrying cost of inventory in transit. The result will be a dollar cost for inventory in transit comparable to the dollar cost of inventory in the warehouse:

$$\frac{t_m}{t} \cdot Q \cdot V \cdot Y$$

The new Total Cost Equation for inventory would appear as follows:*

$$TAC = \left[\frac{1}{2} Q \cdot V \cdot W\right] + \left[A \cdot \frac{R}{Q}\right] + \left[\frac{t_m}{t} \cdot Q \cdot V \cdot Y\right]$$

In order to demonstrate how we can measure the trade-off between transit times and transportation cost using the total cost formula that we developed above, let's review the information that was provided in the previous example we used to demonstrate the simple EOQ model:

Model Selection Example

$R = $ 3600 units (annual demand)

$A = $ \$200 (cost of one order or set-up)

$W = $ 25% (cost of carrying inventory in warehouse)

$V = $ \$100 (value per unit)

$Q = $ 240 units (this would remain the same)

Now let's assume that our hypothetical company is trying to choose between two modes of transportation (rail and motor) and that we have the following information:

Rail: 8 days transit time
$3 per hundred pounds

Motor: 6 days transit time
$4 per hundred pounds

We will be shipping the same amount by either mode, viz., 240 units. If we assume that each unit weighs 100 pounds, then this represents 24,000 pounds or 240 hundredweight. Also, we will assume that the cost of

---

*   It should be noted that if we differentiate and solve for Q with our expanded total cost formula that we still end up with the same form as previously, viz.,

$$Q = \sqrt{\frac{2 \cdot R \cdot A}{V \cdot W}}$$

carrying inventory in-transit (Y) is 10%. Given the above, let's examine our two alternatives using the formula we developed:

RAIL

(1) $\left(\dfrac{1}{2} \cdot 240 \cdot \$100 \cdot 25\%\right) + \left(\$200 \cdot \dfrac{3600}{240}\right) + \left(\dfrac{8}{24} \cdot 240 \cdot \$100 \cdot 10\%\right)$

(2) $\qquad$ \$3000 $\qquad + \qquad$ \$3000 $\qquad + \qquad$ \$800

(3) $\qquad\qquad\qquad\qquad$ \$6800

If we add the transportation cost to the inventory cost, our total cost would be:

(4) $\qquad\qquad\qquad$ \$6800 + (\$3 · 240 cwt)

(5) $\qquad\qquad\qquad$ \$6800 + 720

(6) $\qquad\qquad\qquad$ <u>\$7520 (total cost)</u>

MOTOR

(1) $\left(\dfrac{1}{2} \cdot 240 \cdot \$100 \cdot 25\%\right) + \left(\$200 \cdot \dfrac{3600}{240}\right) + \left(\dfrac{6}{24} \cdot 240 \cdot \$100 \cdot 10\%\right)$

(2) $\qquad$ \$3000 $\qquad + \qquad$ \$3000 $\qquad + \qquad$ \$600

$\qquad\qquad\qquad\qquad$ \$6600

Once again we should add the transportation cost of motor to the inventory costs:

(4) $\qquad\qquad\qquad$ \$6600 + (\$4 · 240 cwt)

(5) $\qquad\qquad\qquad$ \$6600 + \$960

(6) $\qquad\qquad\qquad$ <u>\$7560 (total cost)</u>

Given the above, we would choose the rail alternative. Before leaving this section, we should examine the trade-offs a little more closely. As can be seen, the rail alternative has a \$200 higher cost associated with the slower inventory, but this is offset by the \$240 savings in transportation cost, so the net effect is a \$40 savings by rail.

We should also note that we are still assuming conditions of certainty. Therefore, if there were variations in the transit times, we would have to establish probabilities and approach the solution in a more sophisticated manner.

ADJUSTMENT OF THE BASIC EOQ MODEL FOR VOLUME TRANSPORTATION RATES

The basic EOQ model previously discussed did not take into account possible reductions in transportation rates per hundredweight associated with larger volume shipments. For example, in our previous illustration it was decided that 240 units was the appropriate quantity to order or produce. If we assume again that each unit weighed 100 pounds, this would mean a shipment of 24,000 pounds. What if the rate per hundred pounds (cwt) was $3.00 on a shipment of 24,000 pounds (240 cwt) and the rate for a 40,000-pound shipment was $2.00 per cwt; would it be worthwhile to ship 400 units (40,000 lbs.) instead of 240 units?

The publication of volume rates on carload (rail) and truckload (motor carrier)* quantities are very commonplace as long as the shipper transports a specified minimum quantity (weight) or more. Therefore, the decision maker in inventory situations who is responsible for transporting goods should take into account the effect of the lower volume rate upon total cost. In other words, in addition to storage (holding) cost and order or set-up, the effect of lower transportation costs on total cost should be considered.

In those situations where the Economic Order Quantity decided upon by our previously presented basic model is less than the quantity necessary for a volume rate, it is possible to adjust it to consider the following cost relationships associated with shipping a larger volume than the basic EOQ determined:

1. *Increased inventory carrying cost for inventory in the warehouse* — The larger quantity required for the volume rate means a larger average inventory (½ Q) with consequent increased cost of inventory.
2. *Decreased order* or *set-up costs* — the larger quantity required for the reduced volume rate will reduce the number of orders (R/Q) with consequent decreased order or set-up cost since the cost of each order or set-up is fixed.
3. *Decreased transportation cost* — the larger quantity will reduce the cost per hundredweight of transporting the goods with consequent lower transportation costs.
4. *Decreased in-transit inventory carrying cost* — carload and truckload shipments usually have shorter transit times than shipments which are less-than-carload (LCL) or less-than-truckload (LTL) and the faster time means a lower cost for inventory in transit.

A graphical representation of the cost relationships taking into account possible transportation rate discounts (volume rates vs. less than volume rates) is shown in Figure 4-8. The total cost function "breaks" or is discontinuous at the quantity which permits use of the volume rate.

* The motor carriers, in fact, often publish different *LTL* rates on quantities of 500, 2,000, and 4,000 pounds and two truckload rates.

Therefore, the cost function for the transportation rate discount(s) cannot be "plugged into" the original EOQ formulation. Rather, the analysis is really what is referred to as sensitivity analysis or a sensitivity test to consider whether total annual costs are lower if a quantity larger than the basic EOQ amount is purchased. It should be noted that while Figure 4-8 indicates that use of the volume rate will lower total cost, this does not necessarily have to be the case. For example, if the dollar value of the goods was very high, then the increased storage (holding) costs could more than offset the reductions in order costs and transport costs.

FIGURE 4-8   EOQ costs considering volume transportation rate.

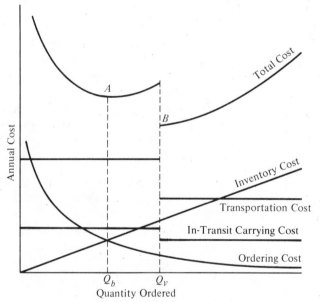

A = Total cost at basic EOQ (Q_b)
B = Total cost at quantity associated with transportation volume rate

Summarizing our above analysis, the relevant question is: "Should a quantity larger than the Economic Order Quantity be purchased so as to take advantage of a lower rate per hundredweight available for a larger volume shipment?" Using our trade-off framework we would respond: "Yes, a larger quantity should be purchased if the *total cost* associated with the larger quantity is less than the total cost of the Economic Order Quantity."

$$ANS \text{ (if any)} = TAC_b - TAC_v$$

Where:

ANS = Annual Net Savings (if any)

TAC_b = Total Annual Cost at basic EOQ

TAC_v = Total Annual Cost at volume rate quantity

Q_b = basic EOQ

Q_v = volume rate quantity

t_m = time in transit for less than volume shipment

t_n = time in transit for volume shipment

LVR = less than volume rate

VR = volume rate

S_r = $LVR - VR$ (i.e., savings per hundredweight between LVR and VR)

TAC = Inventory Carrying Cost + Order Cost + Transportation Cost + In-transit Inventory Carrying Cost

$$TAC_b = \left(\frac{1}{2}Q_b \cdot V \cdot W\right) + \left(A \cdot \frac{R}{Q_b}\right) + \left(LVR \cdot Q_b \cdot \frac{R}{Q_b}\right)$$
$$+ \left(\frac{t_m}{t} \cdot Q_b \cdot V \cdot Y\right)$$

$$TAC_v = \left(\frac{1}{2}Q_v \cdot V \cdot W\right) + \left(A \cdot \frac{R}{Q_v}\right) + \left(VR \cdot Q_v \cdot \frac{R}{Q_v}\right)$$
$$+ \left(\frac{t_n}{t} \cdot Q_v \cdot V \cdot Y\right)$$

$ANS = TAC_b - TAC_v$, then

$$ANS = \left[\left(\frac{1}{2}Q_b \cdot V \cdot W\right) + \left(A \cdot \frac{R}{Q_b}\right) + \left(LVR \cdot Q_b \cdot \frac{R}{Q_b}\right)\right.$$
$$\left. + \left(\frac{t_m}{t} \cdot Q_b \cdot V \cdot Y\right)\right] -$$
$$\left[\left(\frac{1}{2}Q_v \cdot V \cdot W\right) + \left(A \cdot \frac{R}{Q_v}\right) + \left(VR \cdot Q_v \cdot \frac{R}{Q_v}\right)\right.$$
$$\left. + \left(\frac{t_n}{t} \cdot Q_v \cdot V \cdot Y\right)\right]$$

Given the above methodology for analyzing possible savings in total annual cost associated with transportation rate discounts, we can illustrate how the model can be used with an addition to our previous problem.

LVR = \$3.00/cwt (assume each unit weighs one hundred pounds)

VR = \$2.00/cwt with a minimum of 40,000 pounds (with each unit weighing 100 pounds this would be 400 units or 400 cwt)

s_r = \$1.00/cwt or unit ($LVR - VR$)

t_n = 6 days—time in transit for volume movement

Y = 10%—carrying cost of inventory while in transit

Q_v = 400 units

From our previous problem we know:

R = 3600 units (3600 cwt)—annual sales

A = \$200—cost of placing an order or cost of set-up

V = \$100/cwt/unit—value per unit

W = 25%

Q_b = 240 units (240 cwt or 240,000 pounds)

t_m = 8 days—time in transit for LTL movement

In effect, we are asking the question: If we shipped in a volume quantity, would the savings offset the increased cost? In other words, would there be any annual net savings (ANS)? Filling in the appropriate information we could rewrite our equation as follows:

$$ANS = [(\frac{1}{2} \cdot 240 \cdot \$100 \cdot 25\%) + (\$200 \cdot \frac{3600}{240}) +$$

$$(\$3 \cdot 240 \cdot \frac{3600}{240}) + (\frac{8}{24} \cdot 240 \cdot \$100 \cdot 10\%)] -$$

$$[(\frac{1}{2} \cdot 400 \cdot \$100 \cdot 25\%) + (\$200 \cdot \frac{3600}{400}) +$$

$$(\$2 \cdot 400 \cdot \frac{3600}{400}) + (\frac{6}{40} \cdot 400 \cdot \$100 \cdot 10\%)]$$

$$ANS = [(\$3000) + (\$3000) + (\$10,800) + (\$800)] -$$
$$[(\$5000) + (\$1800) + (\$7200) + (\$600)]$$

$$ANS = [\$17,600] - [\$14,600]$$

$$ANS = \$3000$$

ADJUSTMENT OF THE BASIC EOQ MODEL FOR THE PRIVATE TRUCK CASE

Many companies that use their own fleet of trucks or lease trucks for private use assess a fixed charge per mile or per trip irrespective of how much is shipped at any one time. In other words, since operational charges do not change much with weight, e.g., you do not usually pay more to drivers or more for fuel, etc., and your fixed expenses do not change with weight, many companies find it convenient not to differentiate on a weight basis for a trip but rather to charge a flat amount per trip. Therefore, the decision maker can pose the question of what quantity should be shipped since there is no additional charge for extra weight.

The basic EOQ model can handle this analysis since the fixed trip charge is comparable to the order cost or set-up cost. Therefore, the larger shipment has to be traded off against the increased inventory carrying cost.

If we let T_c = trip charge, then the basic model can be rewritten as:

$$EOQ = \sqrt{\frac{(2)(R)(A + T_c)}{(V)(W)}}$$

From our previous example, we can add a charge of $100 per trip to illustrate the example as follows:

$$EOQ = \sqrt{\frac{(2)(\$3600)(\$200 + \$100)}{(\$100)(25\%)}}$$

$$= \sqrt{\frac{\$2,160,000}{25}}$$

$$= \sqrt{86400}$$

$$= 293.94$$

Therefore, the size of the EOQ has been increased from 240 units because of the additional fixed charges associated with private truck costs.

The three adjustments that we have discussed in the basic EOQ model have all been related to decisions important to the logistics manager—modal choice, volume rates, and private trucking. There are other adjustments that could be made, but the three discussed should be sufficient for our needs. It should be noted that all three still assume conditions of certainty. Some other adjustments require adjusting the model for conditions of uncertainty. In Appendix 4-B, an example of inventory decision making under conditions of uncertainty is demonstrated.

CONDITIONS OF UNCERTAINTY

Under the assumptions we have been using to this point, the reorder point was established on the basis of the amount of stock remaining in the warehouse. We assumed that the usage or sales rate was uniform and constant. As soon as the last unit of a particular EOQ amount was sold, another order or batch was received. No stockout costs (lost sales) were incurred. While it may be useful to assume conditions of certainty as was previously delineated, it would not be the usual operating circumstances for most organizations.

There are a variety of reasons why most companies would not find conditions of certainty to be normal. First, customers usually purchase products somewhat sporadically. Their usage rate of many items vary depending on weather, social needs, psychological needs, and a whole host of other factors. As a result, sales of most items vary day by day, week by week, season by season, etc.

In addition, there are factors that can cause variations in lead time or replenishment time. For example, transit times can and do change particularly for distances over 500 miles in spite of carrier efforts to the contrary. In fact, as is developed in a later section, reliability with respect to expected carrier transit times is an important factor in deciding what type of agency of transportation to use, or what particular transportation company to use once a particular mode has been decided upon.

Another factor that can cause variations in lead time or replenishment time is the processing of the order and the associated period for transmittal of the order. If the order is mailed in, there can be delays. Clerks can overlook a particular order or develop a backlog which delays their efforts. In fact, the problems in this area or the potential for problems in this area is one of the reasons why some firms have utilized computer systems for order processing and the associated activities.

If an item has to be produced or manufactured when we order it, then there obviously can be variations in production schedules for numerous reasons. There are other factors which could be mentioned as having an effect on lead time or replenishment time. But the reader should by this time realize or have a feel for why one can expect variations in lead time.

In addition to varying demand rates and replenishment times, the logistics manager can experience problems with merchandise being damaged or lost in transit. In this case, the goods would have to be reordered. While the carrier would usually be liable for the damage, it could cause a stockout situation in the short run resulting in lost sales.

The reader may at this point feel that the situation is hopeless and that there is no solution. Fortunately, this is not the case. The variables that have been mentioned above as causing variations are what the statistician calls stochastic variables or random variables. Consequently, experience with a particular company and associated study will enable the manager to develop for these variables probability distributions and to apply expected value analysis to determine the optimum reorder point.*

---

* Appendix 4-B to this chapter presents an approach for determining the optimum reorder point under conditions of uncertainty.

There are several ways that the problem can be approached for solution. However, an essential factor in any approach is the level of what is often called safety stock or buffer stock that will be required to cover the variations. It is, of course, necessary to analyze our requirements very carefully so as not to keep too much safety stock on hand because it results in excess inventory cost. On the other hand, if there is not enough safety stock, then a stockout will be experienced with consequent loss of sales.

SUMMARY

Our discussion and analysis in this chapter has focused upon the basic EOQ model, which is a very important tool for analysis. We have also seen how this methodology could be adjusted to consider other situations such as inventory in transit and volume rates. In fact there are other possible variations, some of which are illustrated in the Appendices attached to this chapter.

Study Questions

1. Explain the importance of the assumptions used in the simple EOQ model.
2. What is the relationship between carrying costs and ordering costs? Explain why it occurs.
3. How does the basic EOQ model change for inventory in transit?
4. What assumptions are changed for EOQ under uncertainty? What effect does this have?
5. What are the effects of stockout costs on the basic EOQ model?

Case 4-1
Perkalater Carriers

Perkalater Carriers is an intrastate common carrier located in Pennsylvania. Perkalater has eight terminals located throughout the state and for the majority of its movements uses eighteen-wheeled tractor-trailers.

Perkalater employs a large fleet of trucks, and in order to keep their fleet operations running smoothly, it must order 540 tires annually at a cost of $50 per tire. The tires are ordered by telegram from the Midland Tire Company in Cleveland, Ohio, with a cost per order of $12.

The tires purchased for Perkalater's fleet are stored in a central warehouse in Pittsburgh. The estimated carrying cost rate of holding an inventory of tires is set at 20 percent.

Mr. Mills, the Perkalater warehouse manager, is considering changing the present inventory procedures used for ordering and storing the tires. Before any changes are made, Mills needs to have four questions answered, so that any new decisions initiated, with regard to the tire inventory, will be based on correct information.

Questions

1. What is the firm's EOQ for tires? (Assume 360 days per year.)
2. What is the total annual cost associated with ordering and storage if the tires are purchased in EOQ size lots?
3. If the total lead time for the tires is 6 days, what is the reorder point (ROP)?
4. If the firm is required to buy tires F.O.B., origin, and the transit time is 4 days, what is the cost of inventory in transit? (Use and inventory in transit carrying cost rate of 10%.)

Case 4-2
Boxwell Soups

The Boxwell Soups Company is a large soups and food products manufacturer located in Boston, Massachusetts. For the production of their top of the line soup, "Chef's Surprise," Boxwell buys carrots from Supper-Veggies, a large produce distribution warehouse in Atlanta.

Boxwell's EOQ, the amount of carrots purchased for production, is in lots of 300 bags. Annually, they use 18,000 bags, each weighing 100 pounds, at a cost of $20 per bag. The ordering cost for Boxwell is $10; and the inventory carrying cost rate at the Boston warehouse is 20 percent.

Gritts Transfer, a carrier out of Atlanta, has offered Boxwell a volume rate on the transportation of carrots at a minimum weight of 400 cwt. per shipment.

Mr. Bean, Boxwell's traffic manager, estimates the proposed volume rate to save the firm 2 cents per cwt.

Questions for analysis

1. What are the annual net savings/or loss of using this volume rate?
2. Should Boxwell use the volume rate? Note: be sure to indicate whether it is a savings or loss.)

Appendix 4-A:
Application of EOQ Framework to Utilization and Establishment of Inexcess Rates*

The basic inventory analysis framework discussed in this chapter can be applied to the question of the utilization of an inexcess rate. An inexcess rate is an attempt by carriers to encourage heavier loadings by the shipper. The carrier offers a lower rate for weight shipped in excess of a specified minimum weight. The decision faced by a logistics manager is: Should the inexcess rate be used and, if so, how much should be shipped in each shipment?

Consider the following example: The C & B Railroad has just published a new inexcess rate on items that the XYZ company ship quite often. The present rate is $4.00/cwt with a 40,000 pounds minimum (400 cwt). The inexcess rate just published by C & B is $3.00/cwt on shipment weight in excess of 40,000 pounds up to 80,000 pounds. That is, a rate of $3.00/cwt applies only to the shipment weight in excess of 40,000 lbs. up to 80,000 lbs. The XYZ logistics manager presently ships in 400 cwt lots and wants to know if XYZ should use the inexcess rate and, if so, what quantity should be shipped per shipment?

The following data has been obtained from XYZ:

$R = 3,200,000$ lbs. (32.000 cwt), annual shipments

$V = \$200$, value of item per cwt

$W = 25\%$ of value, inventory carrying cost/unit value/year

Each item weighs 100 lbs.

The inexcess rate should be used as long as the annual transportation cost savings offsets the added cost of holding a larger inventory associated with the heavier shipment. That is, the realization of the inexcess rate transportation cost savings will cause XYZ to incur additional inventory carrying cost. The optimum shipment size occurs when the annual net savings is maximized, i.e., where the difference between the annual transportation savings minus the annual added inventory carrying cost is maximized.

---

* This is adapted from J. Heskett, R. Ivie, and N. Glaskowsky, *Business Logistics* (New York: Ronald Press, 1964), pp. 516-20.

In developing the savings and cost functions we will use the following symbols:

S_r = savings per cwt between present rate and new inexcess rate

Q = optimum shipment quantity in cwt

Q_m = old minimum shipment quantity in cwt

The annual net savings is equal to the annual transport savings minus the annual added inventory carrying cost, or: $ANS = S_y - C_y$

The annual transport savings equals the number of shipments per year times the savings per shipment, or:

$$S_y = \frac{R}{Q} \cdot S_r(Q - Q_m),$$

where R/Q is the number of shipments per year, $(Q - Q_m)$ is the amount of shipment weight to be shipped at the lower inexcess rate and $S_r(Q - Q_m)$ is the transportation savings per shipment. Rewriting the equation for S_y we get:

$$S_y = R \cdot S_r \left(1 - \frac{Q_m}{Q}\right)$$

The annual added inventory carrying cost, C_y is equal to the added inventory carrying cost of the consignor (shipper or seller) and of the consignee (buyer). The added inventory of the consignee (buyer) must be recognized since either the seller must pass this amount of savings on to the buyer as a form of price discount to encourage the buyer to purchase in larger quantities or the seller will incur this cost if the shipment goes to the seller's node (seller's warehouse, for example). The added average inventory, the difference between the average inventories with the larger shipment quantity and the smaller (present) shipment quantity, is:

Consignor's added inventory $= \frac{1}{2}Q - \frac{1}{2}Q_m$

Consignee's added inventory $= \frac{1}{2}Q - \frac{1}{2}Q_m$

The total added inventory $= 2\left(\frac{1}{2}Q - \frac{1}{2}Q_m\right) = Q - Q_m$

Then $C_y = (W)(V)(Q - Q_m)$, where $V(Q - Q_m) =$ the value of added inventory and $(W) =$ the inventory carrying cost per dollar value.

Table 4A-1 and Figure 4A-1 show the savings and cost relationships developed above.

The annual net savings function to be maximized is:

$$ANS = S_y - C_y = (R)(S_r)\left(1 - \frac{Q_m}{Q}\right) - (W)(V)(Q - Q_m).$$

TABLE 4A-1

Annual Savings, Annual Cost & Net Savings
By Various Quantities Using Incentive Rates

Q	S_y	C_y	ANS
400	0	0	0
410	781	500	281
420	1,524	1,000	524
430	2,233	1,500	733
440	2,909	2,000	909
450	3,556	2,500	1,056
460	4,174	3,000	1,174
470	4,766	3,500	1,266
480	5,333	4,000	1,333
490	5,878	4,500	1,378
500	6,400	5,000	1,400
505	6,654	5,250	1,404
510	6,902	5,500	1,402
520	7,385	6,000	1,385
530	7,849	6,500	1,349
540	8,296	7,000	1,296
550	8,727	7,500	1,227
560	9,143	8,000	1,143
570	9,544	8,500	1,044
580	9,931	9,000	931
590	10,305	9,500	805
600	10,667	10,000	667
610	11,017	10,500	517
620	11,355	11,000	355

Taking the first derivative and setting it equal to zero and solving for Q, we get:

$$\frac{d(ANS)}{dQ} = (R)(S_r) \frac{Q_m}{Q^2} - (W)(V) = 0$$

$$WV = \frac{RS_rQ_m}{Q^2}$$

$$Q^2 = \frac{RS_rQ_m}{WV}$$

$$Q = \sqrt{\frac{RS_rQ_m}{WV}}$$

FIGURE 4A-1   Net savings function for incentive rate.

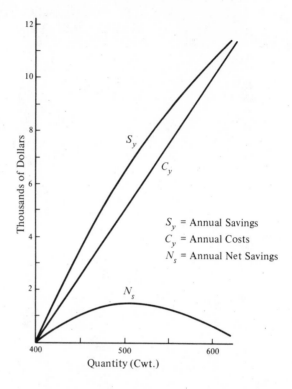

Now, taking the data from the problem posed in this section we find the solution is:

$$Q = \sqrt{\frac{(32,000)\,(\$1.00)\,(400)}{(.25)\,(\$200)}} = \sqrt{256,000} = 506 \text{ cwt}$$

The conclusion is that the XYZ company should use the inexcess rate and 50,600 lbs. should be shipped in each shipment.

Appendix 4-B:
Adjustment of EOQ Model for
Conditions of Uncertainty

It would probably be easiest for the reader if we dealt with only one of the factors which may cause uncertainty. The best and most common example would be the sales rate or usage rate. So that we can focus our attention on this variable, keep in mind that the following assumptions are still being made about the EOQ model:

1. Lead time is constant.
2. Inventory is purchased F.O.B., origin and sold F.O.B., our warehouse.
3. One line of inventory.
4. Constant cost.
5. Sufficient capital or funds for inventory.

In our approach to handling uncertainty in the sales area, we will be trying to "balance" the costs associated with carrying safety stock and stockouts (lost sales).

In a fixed quantity model with an established reorder level, the initial impact of introducing uncertainty into the analysis is the level of inventory needed to cover sales during lead time. The reader should recall in our chapter example under conditions of certainty that we established an EOQ amount of 240 units and a reorder point of 100 units. In other words we would start the inventory period with 240 units and when our inventory reached a level of 100 units we would reorder.

The fact that sales may vary, and the time elapsed between a level of 240 units and 100 units would also obviously vary, is not critical to our inventory problem with conditions of uncertainty. What is critical is whether the 100 units is the best amount to have on hand at the start of lead time or what we would call the replenishment cycle. In effect, that is where we build in our safety stock, i.e., by raising the reorder level. If we raise it too high then we will have too much stock on hand when the next order arrives. If we set it too low, we will sell out.

Using the framework of our previous problem, let us assume that our hypothetical firm experiences a range of demand during lead time from 100 units to 160 units with an average of 130 units. Furthermore, let us assume that we have a discrete distribution with demand varying in blocks of ten units and that we have established probabilities for these demand levels as they appear below in Table 4B-1.

In effect we have a possibility of seven different reorder points corresponding to the seven possible levels of demand listed in Table 4B-1.

TABLE 4B-1

**Probability Distribution of
Demand During Lead Time**

Demand	Probability
100 units	.01
110	.06
120	.24
130	.38
140	.24
150	.06
160	.01

Based on this information we can develop the matrix that appears as Table 4B-2.

While Table 4B-2 is quite useful to see all the *possible* situations confronting our hypothetical firm, it does not obviously make use of our probability distribution of demand. The use of the probability distribution of demand allows us to determine expected units "short" or "in excess" during lead time with each of the seven possible reorder points.

TABLE 4B-2

**Possible Units of Inventory "Short"
Or "In Excess" During Lead Time
With Various Reorder Points**

Actual Demand	Reorder Points 100	110	120	130	140	150	160
100	0	10	20	30	40	50	60
110	10	0	10	20	30	40	50
120	20	10	0	10	20	30	40
130	30	20	10	0	10	20	30
140	40	30	20	10	0	10	20
150	50	40	30	20	10	0	10
160	60	50	40	30	20	10	0

Let us assume that the firm experiences a stockout cost (k) of $10.00 per unit whenever a unit is demanded but not in stock. In other words, this is an opportunity cost for the profit lost on the immediate sale and future sales.

The inventory carrying cost associated with safety stock is calculated the same as our carrying cost for the simple EOQ model. The value per unit of inventory is still assumed to be $100.00 and the percentage annual inventory carrying cost is 25%. It should be remembered that the percentage figure is for annual cost of inventory in the warehouse. Therefore, the $25.00 that we derive by multiplying 25% by $100.00 is annual cost per unit of inventory in the warehouse. The $25.00 is in contrast to the $10.00 for stockout cost which is a unit cost per cycle or order period. Therefore, as will be done in Table 4B-3, we have to multiply by the number of cycles or orders per year to put this on an annual basis.

Table 4B-3 develops expected units "short" or "in excess" by multiplying across the matrix by the probabilities associated with each of the demand levels. Then, the number below (shorts) and above (excess) the diagonal line can be added as is done in the calculations below Table 4B-3 to develop the number of units we expect to be "short" or in "excess" with each of the seven possible reorder points.

Given the following:

$$e = \text{expected excess in units}$$

$$g = \text{expected shorts in units}$$

$$k = \text{stockout cost in dollars per unit stocked out}$$

$$G = (g) \cdot (k) = \text{expected stockout cost per cycle}$$

$$G \cdot \frac{R}{Q} = \text{expected stockout cost per year}$$

$$(e) \cdot (V) \cdot (W) = \text{expected carrying cost per year for excess inventory}$$

After calculations have been performed as delineated under Table 4B-3 we then have a Total Annual Cost for each of the seven reorder levels. The lowest total cost is that associated with the reorder point of 140 units. While this number does not always give us enough inventory in every cycle period and it may result in too much inventory in some period, overall it gives the lowest total cost, i.e., $390.00.

The reader no doubt noted that the Q used in step 5 of our calculations under Table 4B-3 came from our problem with conditions of certainty, i.e., 240 units. That was all the information that we had at this point. Our Total Cost Model should now be expanded to include the safety stock cost and stockout cost and it would appear as follows:

$$\text{T.C.} = \left(\frac{1}{2}Q \cdot V \cdot W\right) + \left(A \cdot \frac{R}{Q}\right) + \left(\frac{t_m}{360} \cdot R \cdot V \cdot Y\right)$$

$$+ (e \cdot V \cdot W) + \left(G \cdot \frac{R}{Q}\right)$$

TABLE 4B-3

Expected Number of Units Short or in Excess

Actual Demand Probabilities		Reorder Points						
		100	110	120	130	140	150	160
100	.01	0.0	0.1	0.2	0.3	0.4	0.5	0.6
110	.06	0.6	0.0	0.6	1.2	1.8	2.4	3.0
120	.24	4.8	2.4	0.0	2.4	4.8	7.2	9.6
130	.38	11.4	7.6	3.8	0.0	3.8	7.6	11.4
140	.24	9.6	7.2	4.8	2.4	0.0	2.4	4.8
150	.06	3.0	2.4	1.8	1.2	0.6	0.0	0.6
160	.01	0.6	0.5	0.4	0.3	0.2	0.1	0.0

C. Calculation of Lowest Cost Reorder Point

	100	110	120	130	140	150	160	
1. Expected excess per cycle (of values above line)	0.0	0.1	0.8	3.9	10.8	20.1	30.0	(e)
2. Expected carrying cost per year	0	2.50	20.00	97.50	270	502.50	750	(V.W.)
3. Expected shorts per cycle (of values below line)	30.0	20.1	10.8	3.9	0.8	0.1	0.0	(g)
4. Expected stockout cost per cycle	300	201	108	39	8	1	0	$(g \cdot k) = G$
5. Expected stockout costs per year	4500	3015	1620	585	120	15	0	$\left(G \cdot \dfrac{R}{Q}\right)$
6. Expected Total Cost per year (2 + 5)	$4500	$3017.50	$1640	$682.50	$390	$517.50	$750	

If we solve for our low cost we would have:

$$\frac{d(\text{T.C.})}{dQ} = \left[\frac{1}{2} V \cdot W\right] - \left[\frac{R(A + G)}{Q^2}\right]$$

If we set it equal to zero and solve for Q, we would have

$$Q = \sqrt{\frac{2 \cdot R \cdot (A + G)}{V \cdot W}}$$

Using our expanded model and the computed reorder point of 140 units, we can solve for a new Q as follows:

$$Q = \sqrt{\frac{2 \cdot 3600 \cdot (200 + 8)}{100 \cdot 25\%}}$$

$$Q = 242 \text{ (approximately)}$$

The reader should note that Q is now 242 units with conditions of uncertainty. Technically this would change our expected cost of stockouts for the various reorder points in Table 4B-3. However, the change is so small, it can be ignored in this instance. In other cases, we may have to go through another iteration of our calculations. This would be no problem with a computer. The optimum or best solution to our problem with conditions of uncertainty is a fixed order quantity (EOQ) of 242 units and this amount will be reordered when inventory reaches a level of 140 units (our calculated reorder point).

Our situation now requires a recalculation of our total annual cost:

$$\text{T.C.} = \left(\frac{1}{2} Q \cdot V \cdot W\right) + \left(A \cdot \frac{R}{Q}\right) + \left(\frac{t_m}{360} R \cdot V \cdot Y\right) + (e \cdot V \cdot W)$$

$$+ \left(G \cdot \frac{R}{Q}\right)$$

$$\text{T.C.} = \left(\frac{1}{2} \cdot 242 \cdot \$100 \cdot 25\%\right) + \left(\$200 \cdot \frac{3600}{242}\right) +$$

$$\left(\frac{8}{360} \cdot 3600 \cdot \$100 \cdot 10\%\right) + (10.8 \cdot \$100 \cdot 25\%) + \left(8 \cdot \frac{3600}{242}\right)$$

$$\text{T.C.} = \$3025 + \$2975 + \$800 + \$270 + \$119$$

$$\text{T.C.} = \$7189.00$$

The $7189.00 indicates what happens to total cost when conditions of uncertainty with respect to sales are introduced into our model. If we introduce other variations such as the lead time variable then we would expect costs to increase even more.

Chapter 5	# Warehousing

After studying this chapter, you should be able to:

- Provide a rationale for the warehousing function in a logistics system along with a discussion of its importance for effective logistics management.

- Present and discuss basic operations of a warehouse.

- Develop an understanding of the space requirements in a warehouse and how such space should be layed out to achieve effective utilization.

- Examine the basic, important decisions that face the logistics manager in the warehousing component of the logistics system.

- Discuss public warehousing its nature and services as an option to the manager.

As indicated in the preceding chapters on inventory, there is a strong relationship between the areas of inventory and warehousing. In fact, it could be argued that the two topics should be treated under a common label such as STORAGE. For example, the percentage figure (W) that was used for carrying cost in our discussion of inventory models included, you will recall, a component for storage and handling. In other words, it was implied that the goods had to be stored in some facility, a warehouse. As noted, the cost of such storage would vary depending upon the sophistication of the facility and the nature of the goods. Nevertheless, the strong relationship between warehousing and inventory is evident from the discussion of inventory models.

The approach used for including warehousing costs in inventory models and decisions, however, probably leaves individuals first being exposed to the area without a full appreciation of the dynamic interaction between inventory and warehousing. It appears in most inventory models that warehousing space is accepted as given or static. However, because of the variety of possible approaches to warehousing and the associated varying costs, inventory decisions should not view warehousing costs as static. Even in the short run, when a company has a given set of warehousing facilities, some alternatives are possible in stocking arrangements and, of course, public warehousing is an alternative. The inventory decision should not be made in a vacuum. The dynamic interaction with warehousing should be analyzed. This chapter will present, describe, and analyze the various alternatives and important questions as well as give the reader good exposure to the basic rudiments of warehousing.

The approach in this chapter will be to discuss, first of all, the basic nature and importance of warehousing. This will be followed by a discussion and description of the basic warehousing activities. Then, some of the basic questions or decisions which were introduced will be explored in detail.

NATURE AND IMPORTANCE OF WAREHOUSING

Warehousing is often defined as the storage of goods prior to their use.[1] Broadly interpreted, this definition includes a wide spectrum of facilities and locations which provide warehousing, such as open field storage of iron ore, storage of finished goods in the production facility, the storage of raw materials, industrial goods, finished goods while they are in transport, and highly specialized storage facilities such as farm product storage in bean and grain elevators, tobacco warehousing, potato cellars, products which require refrigeration, etc.

In a macro-economic sense, warehousing performs a very necessary function. Its major advantage lies in creation of time utility for raw materials, industrial, and finished products. The proximity of market oriented warehousing to the customer allows the customer to be served near points where desired. More importantly, warehousing increases the utility of goods by extending or broadening their availability on a time basis to prospective customer. In other words, by using warehouses, companies are able to make goods available *when* and *where* they are demanded. This function of warehousing continues to be increasingly important as companies and industries use customer service as a dynamic competitive tool.

The basic demand for warehousing is determined by the quantity and variety of commodities that require storage. Thus, warehousing exists because companies inventory commodities. Inventories, as indicated previously, can be divided into two general categories—physical supply (raw materials) and physical distribution (finished goods). Both types of inventories are stored for some of the same reasons. We discussed in a preceding chapter reasons for holding inventory which are essentially the same as the rationale for warehousing. However, a brief review will aid our discussion for a following section of this chapter where the role warehousing in a logistics system is discussed.

Transportation

In almost all companies, transportation and production economies are paramount reasons for creating inventories. By transporting commodities in bulk, rate savings can be realized since carload and truckload rates average approximately 80-110% lower than less-than-carload and less-than-truckload rates. The cost savings in transportation alone are sufficient to cause many companies to warehouse inventories in order to take advantage of this opportunity.

Purchase Economies

In addition to the financial benefits derived from bulk buying of raw materials, stopping the production line is usually prohibitively expensive. Never shutting down the line for lack of raw materials is a common rule in many companies. To avoid this situation, adequate stocks of raw materials are maintained. Efficient and balanced production runs for different products also dictate that sufficient warehouse space for finished goods be provided.

Raw materials are warehoused for a variety of other significant reasons. A prevalent pricing strategy of offering quantity discounts makes volume purchases advantageous, thus making it necessary to store the commodities until needed. For companies subcontracting or purchasing from suppliers, maintaining the viability of these supplies is necessary. The timing and quantity of purchases become more a function of maintaining the suppliers than one determined by strictly cost efficiencies for the firm. This is particularly true when the company is an important customer for the supplier or when the supplier's products are only needed seasonally.

Seasonality

Seasonal variability in obtaining required raw materials also necessitates storage. A multitude of situations can occur which alter the timing of replenishments. Some are expected, such as the seasonality of agricultural commodities and the inaccessibility of transportation during the winter months. These are all important reasons, depending upon the company, for maintaining warehouse facilities for raw materials.

Customer Service

A more elaborate rationale for customer service is an important reason for the extensive use of inventories and warehouses in finished goods. Since

World War II, there has been a growing reliance among companies to use customer service as a competitive tool. Logistics systems are sometimes designed based upon minimizing the time between the customer's order and receipt of the product. Examples of company customer standards include never being stocked-out, two-day delivery time, and a 95% customer service level. These stringent goals have multiplied inventory and warehousing requirements dramatically. The number of market oriented warehouses and production facility warehouses needed to serve a national market adequately is determined by each company's product philosophy. One firm felt that 350 different warehouse locations were necessary to meet its customer service requirements.[2] This continued emphasis on customer service can only increase the importance of finished goods inventories.

The industry, a firm's own philosophy, the particular product's characteristics, and the economy all can alter or highlight the foregoing reasons for storing inventory. Many industries are radically different in their orientation to inventory. For example, the distribution characteristics of the chemical and retail industries are individual and unique. Also, firms within an industry can have different philosophical approaches to marketing—for example, Avon and Max Factor in the cosmetics industry.

Numerous product characteristics affect the extent and type of distribution system required. The size, perishability, product lines, the substitutability, the intended market, obsolescence, dollar-density, and weight-density are a few of these product characteristics. The current shortage of plastic has quickly and acutely altered the inventory policies of plastics manufacturers.

Various types of production processes place different and unusual demands on the inventory and warehouse system. For companies marketing seasonal products, such as Christmas lights, lawn mowers, and packing cans, the storage of finished products assumes added importance and magnitude. It can readily be seen that the inventory methods, patterns, and warehousing philosophy change tremendously depending upon a multitude of variables.

Warehousing is of significant national economic importance. Every product manufactured, grown, or caught is warehoused at least once during the product's life cycle (creation to consumption). Unfortunately, neither the Federal Government nor any warehousing association has information on the total annual amount of warehousing done in the United States.

The cost of warehousing facilities has been estimated by various authorities at between 6-9% of sales.[3] This represents roughly 3% of the Gross National Product. The warehousing costs are quite significant considering that all transportation costs comprised 9% of the GNP.[4]

THE ROLE OF THE WAREHOUSE IN THE LOGISTICS SYSTEM—A BASIC CONCEPTUAL RATIONALE

The warehouse is a fixed point or node in the logistics system where raw materials, semi-finished goods or finished goods are stored or held for

FIGURE 5-1   Transportation consolidation.

PHYSICAL SUPPLY SYSTEM

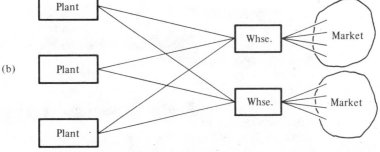

PHYSICAL DISTRIBUTION SYSTEM

varying periods of time. The holding of goods in a warehouse represents a stop or interruption in the flow of goods that adds cost to the product(s). The added cost associated with warehousing has at times been looked at in very negative fashion by some firms, i.e., it was to be avoided if at all possible. Other firms went to the opposite extreme, particularly distributors or wholesalers, and warehoused as many items as possible. Neither end of the spectrum is usually correct. As was implied in a preceding section of this chapter, items should only be held or stored if there are possible trade-offs in other areas.

Transportation Consolidation

The warehouse serves several very important roles in a logistics system, *viz.*, transportation consolidation, product mixing, service, contingency protection, and smoothing. As indicated previously and as is demonstrated in Figure 5-1, companies will at times be faced with less-than-truckload and less-than-carload shipments of raw materials and finished goods. By moving the LTL and LCL amounts relatively short distances to or from a warehouse, then the warehousing operation can perform the role of making possible consolidation of smaller shipments into a large shipment (carload or truckload) with significant transportation savings.

Mixing

A second function of warehousing may be product mixing for customer orders. Companies frequently produce a product line which contains thousands of "different" products if you consider color, size, shape, as well as other differences. Customers when placing orders will often want a mixture of the product line, e.g., 5 dozen 4-cup coffee pots, 6 dozen 10-cup coffee pots with blue trim and 10 dozen with the red trim; 3 dozen of the blue salad bowl sets, etc. The items are often produced at different plants; and, if the goods were not warehoused, then orders would have to be filled from several locations causing differing arrival times, more opportunity for mix-ups, etc. Therefore, a warehouse for a multiple product line leads to efficient order filling. (See Figure 5-2.)

In addition to product mixing for customer orders, it is not uncommon for companies using raw materials and/or semi-finished goods, e.g., auto manufacturers, to feel the need to move carloads mixed with items from several sources from a physical supply warehouse to a plant (see Figure 5-2). This strategy will become increasingly popular with higher transport costs related to fuel expenses and more sophisticated M.R.P. (materials requirements planning).

Service

A third function of a warehouse is to provide service. The obvious aspect of service is that provided to customers which we have mentioned in several instances. The availability of goods in a warehouse when an order is received from a customer, particularly if the warehouse is in reasonable proximity to the customer, will usually lead to customer satisfaction and enhance future sales. The service function may also be a factor for physical supply warehouses. However, in the latter instance, production schedules, which are made in advance, are easier to "service" than customers. This is attributable to the uncertainty of demand associated with serving customers considered in our discussion of inventory. Also, as suggested previously, stockout costs are usually regarded as infinite.

Contingencies

A fourth function of warehousing is protection against contingencies of various sorts, e.g., transportation delays, vender stockouts, strikes, etc. This particular function is usually very important for physical supply warehouses. However, contingencies occur with physical distribution warehouses, e.g., goods damaged in transit.

Smoothing

A fifth function for warehousing is to smooth operations or decouple successive stages in the manufacturing process. In our previous discussions, mention was made of seasonal demand and the needs for production runs of sufficient length to insure reasonable costs and quality. These are examples of smoothing, i.e., preventing operations under overtime conditions, or working at low levels of production. In effect, this strategy allows a company to reduce investment in manufacturing capacity.

FIGURE 5-2 Supply or product mixing.

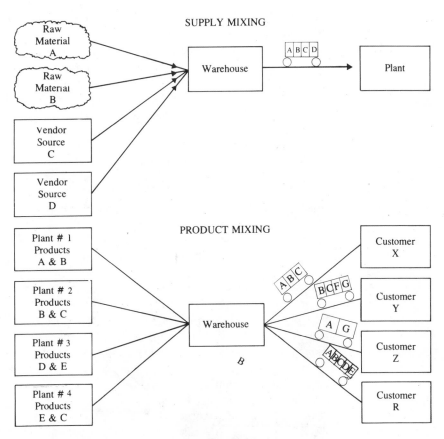

As can be discerned from the foregoing discussion of the functions of warehousing, the important contribution of warehousing to logistics systems and company operations can be readily understood. The potential contributions or benefits are apparent, but warehousing must be viewed in a cost or trade-off context, i.e., the contribution to profit must be better than the cost of the operation.

BASIC WAREHOUSING DECISIONS

Private versus Public Warehousing

In making arrangements for providing warehousing space, an organization has two basic alternatives, *viz.*, private ownership of facilities or making use of public warehouses.* The choice between the two or a combination of both is one of the major warehousing decisions that must be made. Many firms find a combination of public and private warehousing attractive because of

---

* A third alternative frequently cited is leased warehousing. Generally this means leasing a complete facility at a fixed fee per year. The basic nature of this arrangement closely resembles private warehousing so for our purposes they are treated synonymously.

varying regional market conditions and other things such as seasonality that will be discussed later.

As you would expect, the decision has to be approached in a cost trade-off framework. Certain types of operations lend themselves to private warehousing while others lend themselves best to public facilities where space is rented on a temporary basis according to need. The cost variations and conditions favoring one or the other of the alternatives as well as the advantages will be examined subsequently. At this point, the reader should be aware that the public-private ownership decision is important and has to be analyzed.

Related to the private warehousing decision are a series of interrelated decisions concerning design and layout of warehouses. Once it has been decided that a private warehouse is the most appropriate, then a number of decisions have to be made about how the facility is to be utilized in the most effective manner.

Centralized versus Decentralized Warehousing

Another important decision which has to be made in the warehousing area is whether the firm is going to use a centralized approach or a decentralized approach in providing warehousing facilities. This decision then is essentially concerned with how many warehouses should be provided by the firm. In some instances, the decision will be relatively simple to answer because of the size of the firm. That is, small and medium size firms with a single regional market area will often only need one warehouse. It is usually only the large firms with national or international coverage of market areas that need to examine the question in some detail.

As was the case with the private-versus-public warehousing decision, a cost trade-off framework has to be used in analyzing the need for warehouses in various areas. Certain demand and supply conditions will make one alternative more attractive than the others for particular firms. So, for example, if a firm manufactures or distributes a highly competitive and substitutable product on a national basis, it may be necessary to use highly decentralized warehousing to give rapid service in the market area.

The decision about number of warehouses has to be made in conjunction with or in close coordination with the decision about transportation (link) alternatives. For example, air freight makes possible rapid national market coverage from one or two strategically located warehouses. While the cost of air freight is relatively high, it nevertheless can be traded off against savings in warehousing and inventory costs. There are, as we shall see in the next section, a number of link or transportation alternatives which make the decision about numbers of warehouses a real challenge, particularly when it is considered in conjunction with the public-private warehouse alternative.

Warehouse Size and Location

Very closely related to the decision about number of warehouses or the centralized versus decentralized question are two other important warehousing decisions, *viz.*, warehouse size and warehouse location. If a firm is using public warehousing, the size question is important but usually space can be expanded or contracted according to needs at differing points in time.

Similarly, the location decision is reduced in magnitude in using public warehousing. While the firm has to decide the points to use public warehousing, the exact location is fixed and the decision is temporary and can be changed if necessary.

Therefore, the size and location questions are of paramount importance to firms using private warehousing; and, in particular, to firms who have to provide national or international market coverage. In addition to the four warehouse decisions cited above, firms also have to decide how the interior of the warehouse is going to be layed out. In other words, decisions have to be made about aisle space, shelving, equipment, and all the other physical dimensions of the interior warehouse. A second decision is how stock is going to be arranged in the warehouse for efficiency and cost purposes.

A final warehousing decision that has to be made is what items should be stocked and how much stock is to be assigned to various warehouses; but it is only relevant where firms have multiple warehouse locations. Where firms do have a number of locations, they have to decide whether all warehouses will carry the entire product line or will the warehouses each specialize to some extent or use some combination of specialization and general stocking of all items. Some aspects of this decision particularly where location of warehouses, size, and demand are known make a convenient linear programming type decision.

As one can see from this review, warehousing decisions are important and require close attention. Also, the warehouse decisions interact very closely with other areas of the logistics system. Some of these decisions will be explored in detail in this chapter. Before turning our attention to these questions, a conceptual discussion of the warehouse in the logistics system and its basic functions will be explored.

BASIC WAREHOUSE OPERATIONS

The basic warehouse operations are movement and storage. The latter is probably the most obvious warehouse operation whereas the former may seem incongruous to warehousing. However, the movement aspect of warehouses is short distance movement and a very vital aspect of warehousing.

Movement

The movement aspects of warehousing can be divided into four somewhat distinct operations: (1) receiving of goods into the warehouse from the link or transport network; (2) the transfer(s) of the goods into a particular location(s) in the warehouse; (3) selection of particular combinations of goods for orders from customers or raw materials for production; and (4) the loading of the goods for shipping to the customer or to the production line.

Distribution or market warehouses for finished goods are characterized by the movement function. Goods which are brought to so-called distribution or market warehouses "move" through the warehouse rapidly, i.e., there is rapid turnover of the inventory in such warehouses. While there are a number of reasons that can be offered for the rapid turnover of stock, the most fundamental is the high cost of holding finished goods inventory for long periods of time. You will recall our formulation of inventory cost from the previous chapter and the examples cited of inventory costs. Finished goods have high value, need more sophisticated storage facilities, have greater risks for damage, loss and obsolescence, etc., all contributing to higher inventory costs. So it is almost mandatory that goods be moved through the market or distribution warehouses quickly and efficiently. The visitor to a distribution warehouse can sense the activity level almost instantly. While modern technology for materials handling has made the movement activities more orderly in many warehouses, the movement functions are still nevertheless quite obvious in such warehouses.

One might still be a little confused about the movement function in a warehouse. In a sense, movement almost seems contradictory to a warehouse which by its very nature seems to suggest holding of goods. But even the novice logistician can appreciate, for example, the need for large firms to "collect" their various product lines from different plants at strategic points for the purpose of combining the appropriate mix of items to meet customer orders. This assembling, mixing and distribution of goods is the very essence of distribution or market warehousing. So while the term movement may seem inappropriate at "first brush," it is quite apropros to warehousing, and in particular to market or distribution warehousing.

Storage
The other very important function in warehousing is the more obvious one, *viz.*, storage or holding of goods. As indicated above, in some warehouses the storage or holding function is of a very temporary or short term nature. In fact, some items will "turn" in 24 to 48 hours. The holding of goods for longer periods of time (over 30 days) is often associated with raw materials or semi-finished goods. The reader can appreciate by this time why the holding of items for longer periods of time would usually occur with raw materials and semi-finished goods—lower value, less risk, less sophisticated storage facilities, possibility of quantity purchase discounts, etc.

We should note, however, that even finished goods may be held for longer periods of time than suggested by the comments above. In other words, one can find numerous examples of finished goods being held for periods longer than 30 days. In some instances, the longer time is for very obvious reasons. For example, alcoholic beverages which may be considered finished after processing will have to be stored for conditioning or aging purposes.

In addition, where firms are faced with conditions of very erratic demand for their goods, it is quite difficult to forecast inventory requirements accurately. If substitutability is an associated problem, then the firm may be forced to carry relatively large inventories to preclude stockout situations. While such an approach is costly, it is deemed necessary in some cases. Fashion goods are a good example of where such a problem occurs and the cost is passed off in the form of higher prices.

One of the most common reasons for holding finished goods for periods longer than 30 days is where seasonality of demand enters the picture and where the distribution channels or "pipeline" for distributing the goods to the ultimate consumer may be relatively long. For example, manufacturers of Christmas cards, paper, and accessories will start to accumulate inventory for the Christmas season in late June and July and the production of such items will often be completed by September. The products will start moving out to wholesalers and other middlemen in early September or even late August. But some will be retained by the manufacturers until mid-November or possibly later to satisfy stockouts by shipping quickly and directly to retailers. There are other companies in very similar situations and while they may not have to store items as long as card manufacturers, they nevertheless hold finished goods for periods longer than 30 days and very often for periods of 90 to 120 days. As indicated previously, seasonal goods may be stored for relatively longer periods as a trade-off against increased production costs. In other words by lengthening production runs and eliminating overtime, production costs can usually be reduced for a trade-off against increased storage costs.

All warehouses provide both the movement and the storage function. As discussed above, one function is usually more accentuated depending on the orientation of the warehouse in the system. So market oriented or distribution warehouses storing finished goods are characterized by the movement function. Goods move through the warehouse rapidly and may only be held for 24 to 48 hours. Very often such warehouses are decentralized to serve specific market areas. Raw materials, semi-finished goods, and seasonal finished goods are held very often for much longer periods of time. The warehouses in such instances are storage warehouses. Their design, location, and orientation reflect the fact that goods are held for longer periods of time. Even the casual observer can quickly discern the difference in tempo in such warehouses.

The basic operations of a warehouse are affected by the layout of the warehouse facility. While there is no magic formula for stating exactly what layout design should be used, the basic aspects can be considered.

WAREHOUSE LAYOUT AND DESIGN

In order to understand warehouse layout and design, it is necessary to have some background information on the basic space requirements in a typical warehouse. This discussion of space requirements will relate quite closely to our previous discussion of the basic warehouse operations. Before looking specifically at the types of space needed, a brief comment should be made about determining how much space is required.

Stating the situation as simply as possible, the first step in determining warehouse space requirements is developing a forecast of demand for our products. This means an estimate in units for the next relevant sales period (usually 30 day increments) by product category. Then, some decision will need to be made about economic order quantities of each of the items, usually including some allowance for safety stock. The next step is to convert the units into cubic footage requirements, which may have to be expanded to allow for pallets if they are utilized for our products. Usually some allowance such as 10-to-15 has to be made for growth over some relevant period. At this point we have an estimate of our basic space requirements. To this must be added additional space needs for aisles and other items to be discussed. It is not uncommon to have one-third of the total space devoted to nonstorage functions.

Link Interface

One of the space requirements in a warehouse is for providing adequate interface with the link part of the logistics system, i.e., receiving and shipping. While this could be one area, it is usually two separate areas for efficiency. In considering the space needs in this area, some consideration has to be given to whether we will be using the dock area outside the building or whether we will unload right out of the vehicle into the warehouse. Allowance will have to be made for turnaround space and possibly for storage of equipment and/or pallets. Also, there may be a need for space in this area for checking, counting, and inspecting. The volume and frequency of the throughput will be a critical factor in determining space needs for receiving and shipping.

Order Selection Space

Another type of space requirement in physical distribution warehouses is an area for order picking and assembly. The amount of space actually necessary for this function will depend upon the volume of orders and the nature of the product along with the material handling equipment. The layout in this area is critical to efficient operations and customer service. We will be discussing this aspect subsequently when we analyze layout requirements.

Storage Space

A third type of space is the actual storage space. It is essential in a warehouse that we use the full volume of the cubic storage space as efficiently as possible. The amount of storage space will be derived from the analysis described at the beginning of this section, and it will be the largest single area in the warehouse. Similar to the order picking area detailed consideration will have to be given to layout of the storage area which will be considered in a subsequent section.

Other Types of Space

The three additional types of space can be treated briefly for our purposes. First, many physical distribution warehouses have space for recoupering, i.e., an area to salvage undamaged parts of damaged cartons. Second, office space is generally required for administrative and clerical staff. Finally, there are miscellaneous space requirements for restrooms, employee cafeteria, utilities, and locker rooms. The amount of space required in those last three categories will depend on a number of variables. For example, recoupering space needs will be determined by the amount of damaged merchandise and the feasibility of repacking undamaged merchandise. The space requirement for cafeteria and locker rooms are a function of the number of employees.

FIGURE 5-3 **Basic warehouse configuration.**

Our discussion thus far has delineated the various space needs in a typical warehouse. We have also devoted some attention to layout, but we need to consider this area in more detail. First, we will consider some general principles of layout design and then examine layout in the context of the several categories of space previously discussed.

Layout Principles   The most commonly accepted principles of warehouse design and layout are first, use a one-story facility wherever possible since it usually provides more useable space per dollar of investment and very often is cheaper to construct. Second, straight line or direct flow of goods into and out of the warehouse should be used, as illustrated in Figure 5-3. Such an approach avoids backtracking and inefficiency in the warehouse operations. Implied in this principle is the need to avoid warehouse designs that are not laid out on a straight line, i.e., "L," "T" or any other odd shape.

A third principle is the use of efficient materials handling equipment and operations. We shall explore the fundamentals of materials handling in the next chapter. However, for our purposes here we should note that materials handling equipment helps to improve efficiency in operations as well as other benefits to be delineated.

A fourth principle is the use of an effective storage plan in the warehouse. In other words, the goods have to be placed in the warehouse in such a way as to maximize warehouse operations. If goods are not placed in the warehouse properly, this can also result in inefficiencies. Stated as simply as possible, we are seeking to achieve as complete and effective utilization of existing space as possible while at the same time providing adequate protection for the goods being stored.

A fifth principle of good layout is to keep aisle space to a minimum within constraints imposed by size, type, and turning radius of materials handling equipment. Also, consideration must be given to the products themselves and the contraints imposed by the products.

A sixth principle is to make maximum use of the height of the building, i.e., to utilize the cubic capacity of the building effectively. As shall be

FIGURE 5-4   General area configuration for order picking.

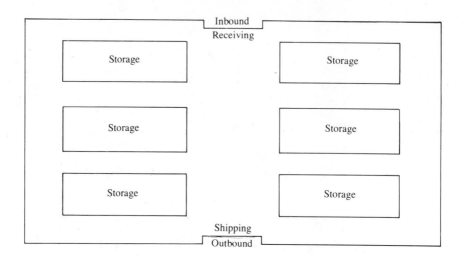

pointed out in the next chapter, this usually requires integration with materials handling.

With these general principles in mind, we will look at the design requirements of some of the basic space areas in the warehouse. With regard to the shipping and receiving areas, consideration will have to be given to whether stock will be placed temporarily in these areas and whether equipment has to be stored in these areas. Also, the turning requirements of materials handling equipment will influence our needs in this area. An analysis will also have to be made of the number of bays as well as their size and shape. The bay requirements will be influenced by the type of carrier utilized, product characteristics, and materials handling equipment.

In regard to the order picking and preparation area, it must be kept in mind that this section of the warehouse is characterized by almost constant movement if we are dealing with a physical distribution warehouse. It is difficult to utilize cubic space effectively because of the need to keep items within reaching distance for order pickers. However, this problem can be overcome to some extent by utilizing materials handling equipment. However, the problem will never be completely resolved, because constant movement requires more open space.

Layout for Order Picking and Preparation

There are two basic ways to lay out the order picking and preparation area. One is to use the general area approach where the order picking and preparation is basically mixed in with the storage area with appropriate racks and equipment for order preparation (see Figure 5-4).

The second basic layout for order picking and preparation is the modified area approach. This approach has a separate area for storage and for order preparation (see Figure 5-5). The order picking bays are usually

FIGURE 5-5   Modified area configuration.

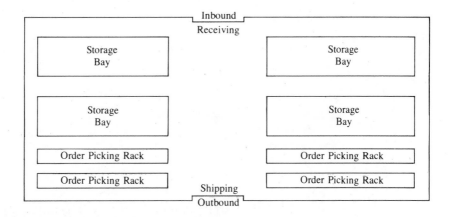

smaller than the storage bays to allow better access. The order picking bays will be stocked on a regular basis, and usually there will be provision made for partial and full boxes. The separation of order picking from storage offers the advantages of reducing picking time and distance, but reduces the flexibility of the facility.

As stated previously, an underlying principle of layout design in the storage area of the warehouse is to make full use of the cubic capacity. One of the design features of a storage area which lends itself to achieving this objective in the use of the larger storage bays with bays more limited access. However, the actual size of the storage bays will be affected by the level of turnover or throughput. For example, when turnover is very low, such as in physical supply warehouses, the bays can be wide and deep with limited access. Also, the aisles can be narrow. Increased turnover, however, necessitates better access, and consequently, smaller bays and wider aisles. The customer service requirements of the physical distribution warehouse necessitate quick access.

The protection and efficiency objectives of warehouse layout discussed above provide a good framework for deciding on the use of warehouse space. Looking first at the protection aspect for storing goods in a warehouse, some general guidelines can be developed. First, hazardous materials such as explosives, flammable items, and oxidizing items should be separated from other items so as to eliminate the possibility of damage. Second, products requiring special security should be safeguarded against pilferage by proper methods. Third, items requiring physical control such as refrigeration, heat, etc., should be properly accommodated. Fourth, items which are light or fragile will have to be treated carefully in terms of stacking and storage near other items that could cause them damage.

The efficiency aspect actually has two dimensions. One is the effective utilization of space in the warehouse which means using the height of the facility and minimizing aisle space.

The second aspect of efficiency is the placement of stock in the warehouse so as to minimize labor costs or handling costs. Efficiency is usually achieved by analyzing first the activity level of items, i.e., Are the items fast or slow moving? The faster-moving items should be stored in the most accessible areas. This could mean location near shipping areas or just simply positioning on shelves, i.e., not high or low. Second, size can have some effect on efficiency. Large and bulky items which are difficult to handle may be stored near the shipping area to minimize handling time. Third, if the load size is large compared to order size then the commodity should be stored close to shipping area to minimize handling costs.[5]

There are quite a number of ''common sense'' principles of warehouse layout which can be cited, i.e., do not exceed specified floorloads, aisles should be straight and clear of obstructions; stock should be rotated, etc. The reader should have sufficient background at this point to permit the turning of attention to the major warehousing decisions previously cited. The first of these is the ownership decision.

THE OWNERSHIP DECISION

In the introductory comments for this chapter, it was stated that one of the important decisions that had to be made in the warehousing area was whether to use private or public warehousing. In other words, should the company purchase or build its own warehouse(s) or should they rent space from a public warehouse on an as needed basis. There are advantages and disadvantages to both approaches. The decision is usually resolved in terms of cost, i.e., which of the two alternatives or combinations thereof will result in the lowest total cost. A simplistic view of the costs involved is presented in Figure 5-8.

Figure 5-8 attempts to show the important general relationships of a cost comparison between a public warehouse and a private warehouse. As can be quickly discerned the public warehouse is all variable cost. As the volume of throughput in the warehouse increases, more space has to be rented. This space is available at a specific charge per square foot or per cubic foot. Obviously, then the cost or expense will go up proportionately to the amount that has to be stored in the warehouse. The cost function is depicted as linear in this instance. As we shall see in the next section, it may be possible to obtain lower rates for larger volumes in a public warehouse; but the effect will be a tapering off of the curve at the upper end. The general relationship will remain the same, however.

The private warehouse as can be quickly seen has an element of fixed cost in its cost structure. The fixed cost is attributable to property taxes,

FIGURE 5-6 Layout of large warehouse.

TYPICAL MODERN WAREHOUSE LAYOUT

UTILIZING BIN SELECTION AND PACKING CONVEYOR SYSTEM COORDINATED WITH A BULK DRAGLINE CONVEYOR WITH AUTOMATIC SWITCHING

THE BIN LAYOUT EMPHASIZES A HOT LINE (FAST MOVING) PRINCIPAL OF STORAGE AND CONVEYOR ACCUMULATION OF ORDERS ASSEMBLED

CAPACITY OF WAREHOUSE ————————————————————— APPROXIMATELY 830,000 SQ. FT.

CAPACITY OF BIN AREA ————————————————————— APPROXIMATELY 90,000 SQ. FT.

Source: From *Warehouse Operations,* General Services Administration, U.S. Government Printing Office, Washington, D.C., 1964.

FIGURE 5-7 Typical small warehouse.

Source: From *Warehouse Operations*, General Services Administration, U.S. Government Printing Office, Washington, D.C., 1964.

FIGURE 5-8   Cost comparison of private and public warehousing.

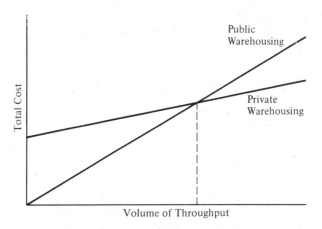

depreciation, etc. The variable cost from operating the warehouse would, of course, usually increase at a slower rate than the cost of the public warehouses. Consequently, at some point the two cost functions will meet or in other words be equal. The general relationship indicated is that at lower volumes of output, the public warehouse is the best alternative. As volume increases, we are able to use private facilities more efficiently, i.e., we can spread the fixed costs over the larger volumes of output.

In the form of Figure 5-8, the ownership decision can be made very much like our total cost problems presented in Chapter 1. The difference would be that the public warehouse, as depicted, would have zero fixed costs for the equation, $y = a + b(x)$. The decision maker could therefore find a solution to the problem in the same fashion, i.e., solve for the point of equality between the two cost functions.

Obviously, this is a somewhat simplistic view of the situation confronting many firms, particularly large multiproduct line companies who may be involved with anywhere from five to one hundred warehouses. However, even in those more complex situations of the large firms such a simplistic perspective may not be too far from reality for two reasons. First, warehouses are often added one at a time and the choice in each new instance could be between private and public because of different market and cost circumstances. Second, even where more than one warehouse is being added, the locational circumstances are often quite different and require each warehouse to be analyzed individually in terms of the ownership question.

At this point it would be appropriate to investigate some of the characteristics of firms and their products which result in their using private or public warehousing. Looking at Figure 5-8, it is possible to deduce some of the characteristics or factors which lead firms to one of the two choices.

If we take the private warehouse situation first, it is quite obvious that relatively high volume of throughput is necessary to make a private warehouse economical. This is attributable to the fixed cost associated with the private warehouse. The fixed costs are going to occur irrespective of use so it is necessary to have a sufficient volume to "spread out" the fixed cost so the average cost (fixed plus variable) for the private warehouse is lower than public. Implied in this analysis are two very important points. First, we are assuming as indicated by Figure 5-8 that the variable cost per unit (slope of the function) for the private warehouse is less than the cost per unit (only variable in Figure 5-8) for the public warehouse. Otherwise, the private warehouse would never be cheaper than public warehousing. The other important assumption is the usage rate or throughput is stable throughout most of the year. If this is not true, then we will have problems with the size decision and we will not be able to utilize our space efficiently.

The stability factor is often a critical one like it is in private trucking. Many products have seasonal sales. However, many large firms and some smaller firms have multiple product lines and this helps to stabilize the throughput in the warehouse. It also, of course, tends to help build the volume necessary for an economical private warehouse. A good example would be companies like General Foods or General Mills. In the summer when coffee sales drop off, they sell more tea for iced tea drinkers.

Another factor conducive to private warehousing is a dense market area relatively close to the warehouse or for physical supply warehouses having the vendor(s) relatively close. As was indicated in a previous section, small shipment rates (LTL or LCL) are relatively high per mile. Therefore, the savings that usually accrue by shipping in bulk (CL or TL) to a warehouse are quickly used up by having to pay the relatively high, small shipment rates. Consequently, in low population density areas, firms will often find it more economical to use several public warehouses in different locales as opposed to "putting together" enough volume for a private warehouse and having to serve a rather broad geographical area.

An additional reason why a private warehouse might be more beneficial to a firm is for control purposes. This can encompass physical control for such things as security or refrigeration and service control for customers or plants. Certain raw materials and finished goods are highly susceptible to theft or loss of value from damage or spoilage. While public warehouses are reputable firms and must exercise care in storing goods, the chances of loss may be higher than with private warehouses. Even if losses are paid for by the public warehousing company, the loss of customer goodwill or production efficiencies may be too great. Competition in the form of customer service is another "control" factor favoring private warehousing. While this rationale can lead to too much private warehousing as indicated previously, it nevertheless has become increasingly important as a reason for private warehousing. This is particularly true with more sophisticated computer based information systems which attempt to centralize and/or coordinate inventory control and order processing. There is no question that competition through customer service is an increasingly viable force that will justify varying kinds of strategies.

Companies currently using or contemplating using private warehousing find several of the above characteristics interacting to justify their use of private warehousing. In particular, firms with multiple product lines will often find private warehousing economical since on the physical distribution side they will have the volume, stability, and the denser markets and will need to exercise control for a variety of reasons. Also, because they usually have multiple plant operations, they find private warehousing most economical on the physical supply side also.

At this point, one might ask if public warehousing is ever economical and the answer is yes. In fact. if we reflect on the characteristics that made private warehousing economical, we can find many firms with different characteristics where public warehousing is most economical for their needs.

From the review of the contrasting cost structures of private and public warehousing, it was obvious that relatively large volume was important. Therefore, a company with no large accumulations of inventory or a very seasonable need for warehousing space would find a private warehouse could not be utilized in a consistent and efficient manner. If shipments from the warehouse were in small quantities for long distances (dispersed customers or plants), then companies would also usually find a public warehouse more economical.

Another possible reason for using public warehousing is when firms are entering into a new market area where there is uncertainty about the level and stability of sales. Such conditions will usually necessitate using a public warehouse until some effective market penetration is gained. If the market venture is successful and experience shows the volume and stability necessary then private warehousing can be instituted.

The above brief comments about public warehousing do not really do justice to this very important area. A more complete discussion is offered in a subsequent section. In using public warehousing, one should also have some knowledge of the various services offered as well as such things as regulation and pricing practices. Before covering each of these topics, the next two sections offer an overview of the importance of public warehousing and a historical development.

PUBLIC WAREHOUSING

In the previous section in offering a rationale for private warehousing some mention was made of the growth of private warehousing in conjunction with competition through customer service. This should not be interpreted to mean that public warehousing has declined or even maintained the status quo. The fact is that public warehousing has grown and prospered and has been a very dynamic and changing industry. In particular, general merchandise public warehousing which would be used most frequently by most companies has grown rapidly.

The Bureau of Census separates warehousing into six different areas

TABLE 5-1

Types of Public Warehouses

Category of Operation	Number	Total Revenue	Proportion of Total Revenue in 1972
Local trucking and storage (including household goods)	4687	823,959	38.79%
General Merchandise Warehousing	2170	610,566	28.74
Refrigerated Goods (including food lockers)	1534	351,668	16.55
Farm Products	744	154,536	7.30
Special Warehousing	468	136,861	6.42
Household Goods	423	46,698	2.20
Total	10026	2,124,288	100.00

(see Table 5-1). General merchandising warehouses rank second in the total proportion of revenue received.

General merchandise warehousing has continued to grow during the past several decades. The number of establishments has increased by over 80 percent and the amount of square feet available has increased by approximately 80 percent also. Table 5-2 provides an interesting historical perspective on the development of general merchandise warehouses.

Changes in marketing since World War II have enhanced the importance of all types of warehousing. Product proliferation and customer service, as previously noted, have been the two driving forces. The larger and more varied product lines of today are a different market strategy from their one-product ancestors. For each product manufactured, differentiation inventories need to be maintained. The increased emphasis on customer service has likewise increased the necessity of warehousing for companies.

A 1970 study of public warehousing provides an interesting insight into its composition.[6] The report stated that public warehousing was dominated by locally owned firms. Eighty percent of these firms did business in only one city and the firms who were multi-city had no significant national market share. However, some attempts have been made at integrating local warehouses under regional and national ownership. One highly touted national public warehousing firm, D. H. Overmyer Company, with 32 million square feet of warehouse space, filed for bankruptcy in New York in November 1973.[7] Its management's failure was not caused by its philosophy of warehousing, but this was a setback to progressive public warehousing regardless.

TABLE 5-2

General Merchandise Warehousing

Year	Number of Establishments	Occupiable Public Floor Space (000 sq. ft.)	Number of Paid Employees	Revenue ($000)
1954	1,197	108,315	22,283	$171,542
1958	1,512	119,325	22,496	200,934
1963	1,483	129,170	22,880	248,282
1967	1,677	163,168	28,295	379,910
1972	2,170	296,067	32,495	610,566

Source: 1972 Census of Selected Service Industries, Vol. 1, July 1976, p. 7-20.

A combination of factors has caused increased awareness and use of warehousing in recent years. Since 1972 a scarcity of raw materials and of industrial and finished products has motivated companies into buying to insure adequate supplies. Higher inventories create a demand for added warehouse space. The oil crisis and truckers' strikes have combined to cause more companies to maintain higher inventory levels. Such factors will contribute to more growth in public warehousing.

Rationale for Public Warehousing

As stated previously, when a company decides to increase the amount of warehousing, two distinct alternatives are available. The firm can either own its own warehouse or use public warehousing. When deciding between the alternatives, the desirability and economic feasibility of each needs to be considered. The five basic reasons for using public instead of private warehousing will be discussed in this section.

Limited Capital Investment

The first and most significant reason from a financial viewpoint is that by using public warehousing, no capital investment is required of the company. Clifford F. Lynch, Manager of Distribution Facilities for Quaker Oats Company, stated at a November 1971 warehousing conference that "you can spend $1-½ million to $2 million (on constructing a facility) without too much difficulty."[8] Today, this represents a conservative estimate considering inflation and the increased cost of construction. When a company builds, a long-term financial commitment for 20-40 years has been established. Therefore, the firm incurs the risks of capital payback through continued profitable use or sale of the facility. This assumes that the firm has adequately forecasted and located consumer demand and concentration, and that technological breakthroughs in construction, transportation, or warehouse systems will have a minimal effect. For automated warehouses, the consideration of facility obsolescence becomes even more acute. If the firm has not made accurate predictions, the warehouse might have to be sold or leased to continue the capital payback. By use of public warehousing, companies can avoid the capital investment and financial risks of owning their own warehouse.

Flexibility

A second advantage of public warehousing is the flexibilty it allows the company. Space can be rented for periods of 30 days. This enables the firm to react quickly to movements in demand or changes in the quality of transportation services. Location flexibility is required in exploring new markets. Public warehousing enables a firm to immediately launch, expand, or pull out in new untried markets without lingering distribution costs. The dynamic nature of market location and the quality of supporting transportation services makes the flexibility that public warehousing affords a serious advantage. Closely associated with flexibility is the ability of public warehousing to adequately fulfill the space requirements of companies. Added space can be quickly secured for promotional, spot demand, production balancing, or for large order storage purposes. For many firms, the seasonal concentration of raw materials or demand for finished goods makes public warehousing a much more feasible alternative than company owned or operated warehousing.

Reduced Managerial Responsibilities

The management difficulties that are avoided by using public warehousing are considered the third advantage of public warehousing. Problems that arise in private warehousing can be a tremendous drain on both the manpower and resources of the firm. Two examples will highlight this point. When a firm is experiencing a strike, the private warehousing can be picketed. Courts have ruled that a labor union does not have the right to picket a public warehouse when a union is in a labor dispute with a customer of the warehouse. This offers considerable advantages to firms which have contracts with many unions or have a history of strikes. Manpower training and management is a major problem for any type of warehouse. This problem is magnified for companies whose product movements or characteristics are irregular or seasonal in nature since it is difficult to maintain an experienced work force.

Increased Cash Flow

The fourth advantage is the ability of firms to increase their cash flow by using public warehousing. The legal contract between the shippers and the warehouseman enables him to issue negotiable warehouse receipts, thereby allowing the company the opportunity of discounting the receipts and initiating the cash flow earlier than a private warehouse without a field warehouse. The importance of this advantage depends on the company's need for cash and the inventory turnover rate.

Lower Taxes

Finally, taxes can be a twofold advantage. In a majority of states there are definite reasons not to own property within that state. The ownership of property denotes "doing business" in that state. Therefore, the company is subject to a variety of state taxes. The second advantage is that there often are tax shelters available through the use of public warehousing. Both these factors vary in importance depending upon the locality and the company.

TABLE 5-3

**Public Warehousing Services Offered by 120
Larger Public Warehousing Companies**

Service	Proportion of Firms Surveyed Offering Service
Inventory records	100%
Warehouse receipts	100
Storage	100
Break bulk handling	100
Marking and tagging	100
Over, short, damage reports	93
Prepaying freight	88
Local pickup and delivery	72
Accredited customer lists	72
Recoopering and repairing	68
Packaging	52
Field warehousing	32
Make bulk handling	28
Loans on goods in storage	23

Source: Public Warehouse Study, (Washington, D.C.: McKinsey and
Company, Inc., 1970).

Public Warehousing Services

The services offered by public warehousing are competitive in respect to the
majority of services provided by private warehousing.

Table 5-3 indicates that the normal services of inventory, records
storage, break bulk, and damage reports are offered by most of the larger
warehouses. Additional services, which were not identified, which some
public warehouses are currently performing are yearly physical inventory
counts, initiating orders to restock depleted inventories, and providing
customer ordering, processing and invoicing services, and the use of
electronic data-processing facilities. These specialized services are normally
offered only to major or special accounts. Competitive public warehousing
is trying to establish a service ability which would offer a feasible alternative
to private warehousing.

The services that public warehousing offers its many customers are
individualized. Attempts are made to tailor the services that public
warehouses offer to the individual needs aand requirements of the customer.
The great diversity of product characteristics, distribution systems utilized,
customer demand, and company operations and philosophy require that for
the most efficient service by the public warehouseman, the needs of each
customer must be considered individually.

The retiring president of the AWA, Don Haslett, recognized this
change in his opening address at the AWA annual meeting when he stated:

Now, we and our customers and potential customers think in terms of the total physical distribution concept in which there is no perfect pattern, no set of rules, that applies to every situation. The intelligent distribution executive plans carefully to make use of every possible tool in the distribution field to accomplish the effective distribution of his company's products. Public warehousing is one of these tools. The key to the importance of public warehousing as a tool is service.[9]

In the same address, Mr. Haslett went on to discuss the competitive importance of service.

More and more, business is placed with a public warehouse, or not placed with a public warehouse, on the basis of whether, first of all, any public warehouse in a particular area provides the proper location for a needed service, followed by the consideration of which public warehouse can best and most efficiently provide that service on a regular basis.[10]

These statements indicate the increasing importance of varying services being offered to users of public warehousing. General storage and associated handling has long been the major portion of the public warehouse business. But today public warehousing firms will, as cited above, manage your inventory, manage your order-processing, make transportation arrangements, design information systems for you—even design a complete warehouse with materials handling equipment and layed out to meet the needs of the user. So public warehousing services today can run the gamut from simple rental of warehouse floor space for a short period of time to perhaps a complete warehouse with trained personnel, order processing, inventory control and any thing in between.

In addition, mention should be made of two traditional public warehousing services that can be offered in a public warehouse or at a private facility by a public warehouseman. These services are a bonding service and field warehousing. In both instances, the public warehouseman is responsible for goods, issues a receipt for them and cannot release the goods unless certain conditions are met.

Bonded Warehousing

In the case of bonded warehousing, the user is usually interested in delaying the payment of taxes or tariffs or even in some cases avoiding their payment altogether. It is common knowledge that taxes are relatively high on certain items such as cigarettes and liquor. The seller is liable for the taxes and may want to postpone paying such taxes until the goods are immediately ready for sale. The same may be true of imported items that are to be held in inventory for awhile before sale. If a public warehouse holds the items in his custody, the tax or tariff does not have to be paid until they are released. The user of this service must usually pay what is appropriate at the time the public warehouseman releases the items or even before they are released.

In special cases, items may be imported and later exported without entering the "stream of commerce." In such instances, if the item(s) are held in bond, the tariff may be avoided altogether. The alternative would be to apply for a rebate after the goods are exported. Essentially the same thing is accomplished by using Free Trade Zones or Free Port Areas. Goods can be imported to these points and no tariff paid if they are later re-exported.

Field Warehouse

A field warehouse situation occurs when a receipt is issued for goods stored in a public warehouse or under the supervision of a public warehouseman in a private warehouse. In such cases, the warehouseman's receipt is usually going to be used for collateral for a loan. The receipt issued is a negotiable instrument whereby title to the goods is transferable. This type of service is attractive to individuals or companies who may have accumulated inventory for any of the reasons specified earlier and find themselves in need of working capital. While most attractive to small and medium size companies, it is potentially a valuable service that can be used by all companies.

All in all as has been suggested, public warehousing today offers many valuable services from the traditional storage function to complete management of inventories and associated services to customers. It is a dynamic dimension of the logistics industry that offers many possible alternatives to the logistics manager. There is an additional area about public warehousing that the logistics manager should know something about and that is the legal control aspects which will be considered in the next section.

Public Warehousing—Regulation

It is safe to say that in spite of the "for-hire" or public nature of public warehousing, there has been very little control exercised by government over the affairs of this industry. This is in sharp contrast to the transportation industry's "for-hire" segment particularly that of the common carrier discussed in the next major section of the book. There are probably a number of reasons for the difference in regulatory control but the underlying cause is the fact that the warehousing industry has never been in a position to discriminate against its users with consequent public clamor for regulation as was the case in the rail industry in the 19th century.

While there have been several regulatory acts affecting public warehousing, the most comprehensive and important was the *Uniform Warehouse Receipts Act of 1912*. In effect, this Act did several important things. First, it defined the legal responsibility of the warehouseman. However, it should be noted that the public warehouse operator is only liable for exercising *reasonable care*. So if the public warehouseman refused to pay for damages because he felt that the damage was basically beyond his control, the user would have the *burden of proof* to attempt to show that the warehouseman was liable.

Once again this is in sharp contrast to the common carrier situation where the burden of proof is upon the carrier when damage occurs and there are only several allowable excuses from the liability as we shall see. The comparison to the transportation industry should not be interpreted to mean that the public warehouse does assume any responsibility for damage or loss, i.e., liability. The situation is one of relative degrees of liability, and the comparison is offered to show the special case of the transportation industry.

In addition to setting up the legal responsibility of the public warehouseman, the Uniform Warehouse Receipts Act also defined the types of receipts that the public warehouseman can issue items stored, as is suggested in the title of the Act. Two basic types of receipts were recognized—negotiable and nonnegotiable. As indicated previously, if the receipt was negotiable then the title to the goods held by the public warehouseman could be transferred. So in effect the "holder" of the receipt owned the goods or in other words it could be signed over like a check.

In addition to recognizing the two basic types of receipts the Act also set forth certain requirements for information to be contained on receipts. The information required included the location of the warehouse, the date the receipt was issued, the rate that was to be charged for the warehousing service, a description of the goods, signatures of the parties and the type of instrument.

It is easy to discern that these requirements while they might appear somewhat mundane are very important and give protection primarily to the user of public warehousing and, of course, anyone taking advantage of the negotiable aspects of the receipts.

While the knowledge of regulation and service of public warehouseman are quite important, the logistics manager is very much interested in the rates or charges of the public warehouseman which is the topic of the next section.

Public Warehousing—Rates

The public warehouse sells service in terms of a facility which has fixed dimensions. The service is sold usually on a space basis per period of time, e.g., dollars per square foot per period of time. While the warehouse company in a sense has a more simplistic pricing structure than a transportation company, the logistics manager should have a basic understanding of the factors affecting rates, keeping in mind that rates are negotiable.

Value. As indicated previously, a public warehouse has a certain legally defined liability for goods they store. Consequently, the risk increases with higher valued goods, i.e., if there is liable damage they will have to pay out more. So consequently, rates generally reflect the higher risk of higher valued goods.

The logistics manager may be able to reduce his rate by exercising care in packaging. This can be done by protective packaging to decrease chance of damage and also marking packages to specify care in handling and perhaps in position if it is important. If the public warehouse can show that their risk is diminished by these efforts, the rates will reflect such items.

Fragility.   The general susceptibility to damage of commodities is something that has to be considered in setting warehouse rates because of the risk involved to the warehouse company. The logistics manager may be able to reduce the risk of damage by protective packaging and consequently, reduce the warehouse rates. Once again, the trade-off is between the reduction in the warehouse rates and the increased cost of packaging.

Damage to Other Goods.   In a public warehouse setting where there is often a variety of different commodities to be stored, there is always a risk of damage to goods not compatible with each other. In a sense, this is a two-way risk. Your product may cause damage to another or your product may be particularly susceptible to damage by some other product. Chemicals and food are obvious examples but there are other more subtle ones. For example, automobile tires may have an adverse effect on certain products even causing color change in some instances. It may be possible to reduce the risk by proper packaging but once again it should be viewed in a trade-off context.

Volume and Regularity.   As was indicated previously, the cost of *using* a public warehouse is generally a variable cost, but the warehouse company itself will experience fixed costs. Therefore, volume and regularity of use by customers will influence the rates since the company can ''spread'' their fixed costs, i.e., the volume and regularity will help them achieve efficiencies in terms of lower per unit costs. Many users of public warehouses may not be able to offer regularity in their use. They may use public warehouses to handle peak seasonal demands on their own facilities. However, in other cases a logistics manager may be able by proper planning to use the public warehouse in a systematic fashion and consequently reduce the warehouse rates.

Weight Density.   Warehouse rates are generally set on a space basis and usually on a square footage basis. However, there are instances when some warehouse charges will be based on weight density. In other words, like transportation charges they will be assessed on hundredweight basis. Therefore, light and bulky items will have to be assessed higher charges by the warehouseman. Even if its charges are not being assessed in this fashion, the users of public warehousing should be concerned about weight density because it will affect the ability to use the space they are renting efficiently. Assembled items which are light in weight will use up a lot of space per unit of weight. Perhaps the same number of items could be stored in a smaller space if the items were packaged unassembled.

Services.   As was stated previously, public warehousing is a comprehensive and sophisticated industry today, willing and able to offer a variety of services beyond the general storage function. Such services have charges associated with them and the more service, the higher the charge usually. However, it may be less costly to have the services provided by the public warehouse particularly in low sales density areas than providing them privately.

As can be seen from the above, the logistics manager has the opportunity to influence the level of his public warehouse rates. It will require analysis on the part of the logistics manager to determine whether it is economically justifiable but nevertheless the options should be explored.

THE NUMBER OF WAREHOUSES

As stated in the introduction to this chapter, one of the most important decisions made by logistics managers is in answer to the question of how many warehouses to have in the system. As was the case when we discussed the question of private versus public warehousing, it would probably be best to view the general trade-offs in such decisions.

Figure 5-9 depicts the important costs affected by increasing the number of warehouses in a logistics system on the physical distribution side. In effect, as the number of warehouses in the system are increased, transportation cost and the cost of lost sales decline while inventory cost and warehousing cost increase.

Transportation costs are decreased by the consolidation of shipments into carload and/or truckload lots with lower rates per hundredweight. On the outbound side, increasing the number of warehouses brings the warehouses closer to the customer and market area thus reducing the distance the goods have to be transported with consequent lower transport costs.

Warehousing costs increase because the total amount of space will always increase with a larger number of warehouses. For example, a firm with only one warehouse which may be a facility of 200,000 square feet, would not, if they operated two warehouses, be able to get away with two facilities with 100,000 square feet each at the same level of sales. First, as indicated in our diagrams of warehouses, there is a certain amount of space needed for maintenance, offices, lavatories, lunch rooms, etc., that is almost fixed in size. Also, aisles use up a higher proportion of space for smaller warehouses.

In addition, there is more total inventory carried when the number of warehouses increase which is why the cost function for inventory increases. The larger amounts of inventory associated with the increased number of warehouses means more total space being required. More inventory is necessary because the slower moving items in a product line will usually be carried at both facilities at almost the same level as with one facility because of the difficulty of predicting demand for the slower moving items. The

FIGURE 5-9 **Logistics costs related to the number of warehouses.**

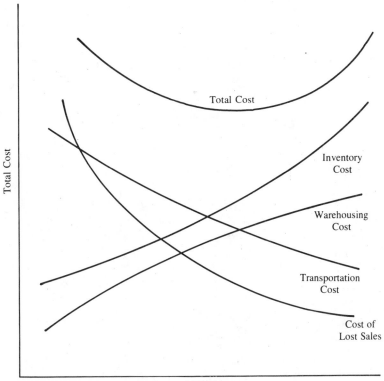

larger the product line the more likely total space requirements will be higher even at the same volume of sales as we increase the number of warehouses.

As indicated in Figure 5-9, as the number of warehouses increases total cost will generally decline over a certain range. Of course, there are differences among firms and their products which will cause differences in the slope of the total cost curve and the range of warehouses over which it will decline. The next section explores some of the factors which cause these differences. It should always be kept in mind that the company has to approach this decision also in a total cost framework and make the decision based on total cost.

Factors Affecting the Number of Warehouses

One of the most obvious factors affecting the number of warehouses is the need for customer service. There is usually a strong correlation, as stated previously, between the need for rapid customer service in local market areas which is caused by high substitutability of product. Obviously, if competitors are giving rapid service into a market area, a company can be adversely affected in sales volume if their service to customers in terms of lead time is inferior. Sales promotion and advertising efforts may be wasted if customers are not able to purchase the product when they want it.

Another closely related reason is lack of adequate transportation service. In other words, if rapid customer service is needed, i.e., low lead times, then fast transport service is a possible alternative. In the event that adequate transportation service is not available then another warehouse may be added. If it is felt that transportation service is deteriorating then warehouses are often investigated as an alternative.

An additional factor favoring decentralized warehousing is small quantity buyers, i.e., if the items are purchased in LCL or LTL quantities. The cost of shipping many LCL and LTL shipments from a centralized warehouse to customers would be much higher than shipping in CL or TL to decentralized warehouses and then shipping LCL or LTL to customers in the local market. As indicated previously, retailers and wholesalers are becoming increasingly conscious of the cost of maintaining inventory, and as a result they often wish to buy smaller quantities more frequently. If they desire the same approximate lead time, then warehousing may be necessary in a closer location. What is suggested here is the importance of the channel of distribution decision to warehousing requirements. In other words, if small retailers and wholesalers are a part of the channel, then the company can expect small orders with the possible need for more warehouses.

A final factor favoring decentralized warehousing would be instances when customers do not allow sufficient lead times before being stocked out. Also if demand is erratic and difficult to predict, then a decentralized approach to warehousing will be helpful in preventing stockouts.

SUMMARY

The warehousing decisions are very very important to the effective design of logistics decisions. In particular, the decision about ownership (private versus public) and the question of how many warehouses are central to logistics system design. Our focus in this chapter has been upon the ownership and number decision. However, the design and layout decisions were also treated. Subsequent chapters will add additional insight into warehousing decisions. In particular, the next chapter which considers packaging and materials handling touches upon warehousing and also the chapter discussing location.

Study Questions

1. Present an analysis of why warehousing is important to the logistics manager.

2. The logistics manager has a number of important decisions to make in the warehousing area. What are these decisions?

3. What are the basic types of space requirements in a warehouse? Briefly discuss each type.

4. Discuss the general principles used in warehouse layout.

5. Why do companies use public warehouses? What services are available from public warehouses?

6. What characteristics of companies favor a decentralized approach in warehousing?

Notes

1. Charles Taff, *Management of Physical Distribution and Transportation*, 5th ed. (Homewood, Illinois: Richard D. Irwin, 1972), p. 142.

2. *Ibid.*, p. 145.

3. L. P. Alford and John R. Bangs, Eds., *Production Handbook* (New York, New York: The Ronald Press Company, 1955).

4. J. C. Heskett, Robert M. Ivie, and Nicholas A. Glaskowsky, Business Logistics (New York, New York: The Ronald Press Company, 1973), pp. 16-17.

5. *Warehouse Operations*, General Services Administration (Washington, D.C.: U.S. Government Printing Office, 1964), p. 2.

6. *Public Warehouse Study* (Washington, D.C.: McKinsey and Company, Inc., 1970).

7. *Business Week*, (December 15, 1973), p. 28.

8. *Distribution Worldwide* (Radnor, Pennsylvania: Chilton Company, December, 1971, p. 83.

9. *Distribution Worldwide* (Radnor, Pennsylvania: Chilton Company, June, 1970), p. 60.

10. *Ibid.*, p. 62.

Case 5-1
High Strung, Inc.

The High Strung Corporation, a small manufacturer of tennis rackets located in central Pennsylvania, is faced with a problem that has grown from their ever-changing business environment. With the advent of indoor tennis courts and the increased popularity of the sport, High Strung is initiating a study of their present production capacity and warehouse requirements. Presently, because it is a small producer and is geared to meet a seasonal demand, High Strung is renting storage space from a local public warehouse. This situation arises also because of its lack of adequate logistics management personnel and its close personal association with the manager of the public warehouse.

The results of the study undertaken on the production and warehouse facilities have shown that High Strung has adequate facilities to slightly increase production and is able to rent additional space in the public warehouse. This is being done to keep up with rising demand and to gain market share in order to be able to market other tennis related items (e.g., tennis balls, clothes) in the future.

High Strung's planning department, however, has estimated that in ten years, by keeping up with demand and by widening its product line, the company's present warehouse policy will be insufficient and the construction of a private warehouse will be necessary. Employing your knowledge of inventory costs and controls and warehousing, explain fully under what circumstances, in this case, you would construct and fully utilize a private warehouse. What criteria would you set in making this decision? What problems would arise if you would remain using public warehouse space when industry conditions would warrant the use of a private warehouse? Under what conditions, if any, could you use a combination of both public and private warehouse space?

Case 5-2
Redwood, Inc.

The Redwood Corporation is a nationally known producer of wood products and furniture. The basic wood products manufactured and marketed by Redwood consist of construction materials and different grades of plywood and paneling. Redwood also holds a high position in the furniture market by offering full lines of high-quality home and office furnishings. Currently Redwood employs a centralized warehouse system consisting of two large warehouses, one for the basic wood products and the other for furniture, located adjacently in the northwestern section of the country. Although Redwood has attained national recognition for its products, it has not done so without encountering some logistics systems problems. According to Mike Larkin, president of Redwood: "Although our company is growing, it is not doing so at the rate we had planned for. Our five-year plan attempted to coordinate every department in the company in order to maximize our profits. However, somewhere in the plan, we goofed." After quite exhaustive deliberation over the five-year plan, the executive committee concluded that the problem seems to be based in the company's warehouse system. The logistics vice-president was asked to evaluate the present system and to present a solution to the executive committee in one week. His evaluation of the situation began with an assessment of the types of products his company was selling. The basic wood products are a bulky, relatively low-value commodity that competes in a highly competitive market. Because of this, these products cannot absorb high transportation charges, they incur low warehouse costs, and stockouts result in high amounts of lost sales. The furniture, on the other hand, is a light, rather expensive commodity that can stand higher transportation charges, which results in high warehouse costs and does not result in high amounts of lost sales because of a stockout. From this analysis, the vice-president of logistics concluded that the problem seems to be caused by the totally centralized distribution system. The next step in his analysis is going to assess the centralized-decentralized question.

If you were the vice-president of logistics, how would you approach this next step in the analysis? How would you conclude the analysis? How would you present your findings to the executive committee?

Chapter 6	# Materials Handling and Packaging

After studying this chapter, you should be able to:

- Explain the general nature and importance of materials handling and packaging in a logistics management context.

- Present the objectives of effective materials handling and packaging in a logistics system.

- Provide an explanation of how the logistics manager selects appropriate materials handling equipment and packaging.

- Present a description of the major types of equipment used for materials handling in a logistics system.

- Provide a view of packaging and its use in the logistics system.

In the preceding chapter, warehousing in the logistics system was considered in some detail and mention was made of the importance of the interior operating efficiency of the warehouse. Also, the importance of transferring goods efficiently from the link system (transportation carrier) into the warehouse was pointed out, as well as moving customer orders from the warehouse to the link system. A major factor contributing to the internal efficiency of the warehouse and the smooth transfer into and out of a plant or warehouse is the set of activities generally called materials handling. In addition, another factor which contributes importantly to the efficiency of warehouses is packaging. Both of these topics will be covered in this chapter.

It is worth noting at the outset that one could argue that materials handling and packaging could also be covered in the discussion of the link system which is treated in the next section of the book. This statement is made since one of their very important roles, particularly materials handling, is the transferability between the link and the node in the logistics system. Materials handling and packaging contribute not only to the efficient operation of the node in a logistics system but also to the efficiency of the link portion of the logistics system. Some individuals might argue that materials handling and packaging should really be treated under a separate heading, and perhaps it should be labeled "the interface" of the logistics system.

Since it is difficult to neatly classify materials handling and packaging into either node or link analysis and a separate section does not seem justified, a discussion of these two topics was "saved" for the interface chapter with link analysis. Also, it is most convenient for the approach of this particular text to discuss materials handling and packaging at this point in our analysis.

MATERIALS HANDLING

Definition

As indicated in the introductory comments, materials handling is quite important to the efficient operation of the warehouse and in transferring goods into and out of the warehouse and also in moving goods to various storage points in the warehouse. The term materials handling is somewhat difficult to define. Many individuals when they think about materials handling immediately picture elaborate equipment designed to move goods in a warehouse, e.g., forklift trucks or conveyor equipment. Other individuals when they think of materials handling visualize the actual handling of goods on a manual basis. Since the handling can either be performed by elaborate mechanical equipment or performed essentially by manual labor or both, it is most convenient to think of materials handling as short distance movement which usually takes place within the confines of a building such as a plant or a warehouse and between a building and a transportation agency. In a modern logistics system, the short distance movement thus described is most often performed by very specially designed equipment so

Movement

that it can be accomplished rapidly and efficiently, so it is not unusual to think of materials handling from an equipment perspective.

Some additional perspective can be gained about materials handling by reviewing the basic processes or procedures involved in materials handling.[1] First, as was indicated in the previous chapter on warehousing, materials handling involves movement. Raw materials, semi-finished goods, and finished products must be moved into and out of storage facilities or areas and usually moved within such facilities and storage areas. Therefore, materials handling can be thought of as a means of moving such items in an as efficient manner as possible.

Time

A second dimension of materials handling is time. Raw materials and semi-finished goods must be ready at a certain time, and materials handling plays an important role in reaching this objective. A third aspect of materials handling is quantity. The usage ratio of items in the warehouse varies, as does the delivery rate. Consequently, materials handling has a role to play in ensuring that items are moved and handled in the right quantity for manufacturing (physical supply) and for customers (physical distribution).

Quantity

Space

The fourth dimension of materials handling is space. In the warehouse, plant, or even the transport vehicle, space must be utilized effectively. The materials handling system greatly influences the proper use of space. Those four elements represent the basic aspects of materials handling. They must be considered not independently but rather in an integrated fashion.[2]

We should also note at the outset that the area of materials handling does not usually belong exclusively to the logistics manager. Materials handling activities can occur in a number of additional areas for a manufacturing firm, but most frequently materials handling occurs in the baliwick of the production or manufacturing manager. Here also, one finds short-distance movements of varying types occurring in conjunction with the manufacturing process. Once again this short-distance movement may occur both on a manual basis or be performed by equipment such as forklift trucks or overhead cranes.

Therefore, it should be noted that we are discussing materials handling from the perspective of a logistics manager. Most often the responsibility of the logistics manager for materials handling occurs in and around warehouses or the warehousing section of plants. Since other individuals in a company, such as the production manager, are concerned with materials handling, it may well be that some coordination will be required at least in terms of the purchase of equipment and perhaps maintenance. It might also be necessary in some instances for interchange of equipment to occur between manufacturing and logistics.

Objectives of Materials Handling

It is possible to gain some interesting perspectives about materials handling by discussing some of the general objectives of the area. We should note that the items discussed below are general objectives and consequently will have application to other areas besides logistics and will have varying degrees of importance for the logistics manager.

Increase Effective Capacity

One of the basic objectives of any materials handling system is to increase the usable capacity of the warehouse facility. A warehouse has fixed interior dimensions in terms of length, width, and height of the facility, i.e., the cube capacity. It is quite important in order to minimize the cost of operating the warehouse to utilize as much of this space as possible. There are usually two very important aspects of the use of warehouse space. One is the ability to use the height of the building as much as possible. There are many warehousing facilities where there is much wasted space because goods are not stored as high as possible. In extremely high buildings, this will usually require the use of such things as shelving and/or pallets but this is space that must be used (see Figure 6-1).

The second aspect of space utilization is to minimize aisle space as much as possible but at the same time not have aisles so narrow as to have inefficient movement in the warehouse facility. Quite obviously the type of materials handling equipment which is used will have an effect on the width of the aisles. Forklift trucks, for example, very often will require turning space and much wider aisles may be necessary than for some other types of materials handling equipment. But a very important objective of the materials handling area is to enable us to utilize the warehouse space as efficiently as possible (see Figure 6-2).

Improve Operating Efficiency

Another objective of a materials handling system is to reduce the amount or the number of times goods are handled. As noted in the previous discussion of warehousing, usually products are moved into the warehouse and then typically placed in a storage area; then they are moved to an order selection area to be "picked" and made up into orders; then moved and made ready for shipment to customers. This necessitates, quite obviously, a number of movements which cannot be avoided. However, there are instances in some warehouses where goods may be moved several times in each of the areas mentioned.

The additional handling and movement must be avoided if a warehouse is going to operate efficiently. Therefore, any materials handling system and the associated activities that go with it should be designed so as to insure that movements in a warehouse and from and to a warehouse are minimized as much as possible. At times, extra movement is unavoidable because of overcrowded conditions, i.e., any firm can face extenuating circumstances where products may have to be temporarily stored and then moved. However, an efficient design of a materials handling system should minimize the number of movements that take place and allow products to "flow through" the warehouse rapidly and efficiently. (See Figure 6-3.)

Effective Working Conditions

The objective of effective working conditions is very general but quite important to the logistics area. It has a number of important dimensions. One very obvious aspect is safety. All materials handling systems whether in connection with logistics or manufacturing have to give some consideration

FIGURE 6-1 Utilization of cube capacity of warehouse.

Source: From *Warehouse Operations*, General Services Administration, U.S. Government Printing Office, Washington, D.C., 1969.

FIGURE 6-2   Efficient use of aisle space.

Source: From *Warehouse Operations,* General Services Administration, U.S. Government Printing Office, Washington, D.C., 1969.

FIGURE 6-3 Efficient warehouse operations.

NOTE

1. Checking, sorting, and palletizing is performed as contents of car are unloaded.
2. Containers should be placed on conveyor so contents and sizes are readable by checkers and sorters.
3. Conveyor line may be set up on platform provided there is sufficient working space.

Source: From *Warehouse Operations,* General Services Administration, U.S. Government Printing Office, Washington, D.C., 1969.

to the area of safety and the system has to be designed so as to minimize the possibility of danger to people who are working around the area.

Another part of this objective is to eliminate as much as possible the monotonous and/or heavy manual labor aspects of short-distance movements in the warehouse. While it is difficult to completely eliminate all of the routine type of movements or seemingly boring aspects of working in a warehouse, as much as possible the materials handling system should be designed to perform this part of the work.

Taken to its logical conclusion, this objective suggests that warehouses should be automated as much as possible. Many firms for a variety of reasons including cost efficiencies have attempted to eliminate labor personnel from the warehouse. The area where most firms encounter difficulty in minimizing or eliminating personnel is in the order selection area. The frequency of numerous items ordered from the product line in small quantities almost defies automation. So while other areas that will be described are highly automated, the order selection area is not.

Improve Logistics Service

As indicated in several places in this chapter and the preceding chapter, materials handling as an activity center in logistics has a very important role to play in improving efficiency by making the logistics system respond quickly and effectively to plant and customer requirements. Materials handling plays a very key role in getting goods to customers on time and in the proper quantities. The efficient movement into the warehouse, location of stock, filling orders rapidly, and preparing orders for shipment to customers is a very important role of logistics. The same is also true of serving company plants.

The last objective is one that receives much attention from the logistics manager. He is constantly looking at his materials handling system, or should be, to make sure that it will respond quickly and efficiently to the customers' orders and the requirements of a production schedule. In some instances companies spend a lot of time and effort in trying to reduce transportation time by twelve or twenty-four hours. At the same time, their materials handling systems may be responsible for adding several days to the total elapsed time after a customer places an order. It is easy to overlook the potential for improved customer service that may be possible through improving the materials handling system.

Reduced Cost

Effective materials handling can contribute substantially to a cost minimization program. This objective can be achieved through increased productivity (more and faster throughput). Also, the more efficient utilization of space and cutting misplaced items will lead to decreased cost.

Another important perspective can be gained about materials handling by referring to Exhibit 6-1, which is a list of the twenty commonly accepted principles of materials handling. It would not be worthwhile to elaborate on each of these items individually since they are almost self-explanatory. It is a good idea to keep a copy of these principles and refer to them when involved in materials handling.

EXHIBIT 6-1   Principles of material handling.

1. *Planning Principle*. Plan all material handling and storage activities to obtain maximum overall operating efficiency.
2. *Systems Principle*. Integrate as many handling activities as is practical into a coordinated system of operations covering vendor, receiving, storage, production, inspection, packaging, warehousing, shipping, transportation, and customer.
3. *Material Flow Principle*. Provide an operation sequence and equipment layout optimizing material flow.
4. *Simplification Principle*. Simplify handling by reducing, eliminating, or combining unnecessary movements and/or equipment.
5. *Gravity Principle*. Utilize gravity to move material wherever practical.
6. *Space Utilization Principle*. Make optimum use of the building cube.
7. *Unit Size Principle*. Increase the quantity, size, or weight of unit loads or their flow rate.
8. *Mechanization Principle*. Mechanize handling operations.
9. *Automation Principle*. Provide automation that includes production, handling, and storage functions.
10. *Equipment Selection Principle*. In selecting handling equipment, consider all aspects of the material handled—the movement and the method to be used.
11. *Standardization Principle*. Standardize handling methods, as well as types and sizes of handling equipment.
12. *Adaptability Principle*. Use methods and equipment that adapt to the widest variety of tasks and applications except where special purpose equipment is justified.
13. *Deadweight Principle*. Reduce ratio of deadweight of mobile handling equipment to load carried.
14. *Utilization Principle*. Plan for optimum utilization of handling equipment and manpower.
15. *Maintenance Principle*. Plan for preventive maintenance and scheduled repairs of all handling equipment.
16. *Obsolescence Principle*. Replace obsolete handling methods and equipment when more efficient methods or equipment will improve operations.
17. *Control Principle*. Use material handling activities to improve control of production, inventory, and order handling.
18. *Capacity Principle*. Use handling equipment to help achieve desired production capacity.
19. *Performance Principle*. Determine effectiveness of handling performance in terms of expense per unit handled.
20. *Safety Principle*. Provide suitable methods and equipment for safe handling.

CATEGORIES OF EQUIPMENT

A discussion of materials handling would not be complete without reference to the various categories of equipment that could be used in a design of materials handling systems. There are many types of equipment available on the market today and each has certain general advantages and possible uses for particular types of products. It would not be in our best interest to discuss in great detail the engineering features of various types of materials handling equipment. The objective here is to provide a general exposure to the categories of equipment to develop some appreciation of how and when such equipment might be used in a logistics system.

Individually Powered and Controlled

One very important type of materials handling equipment is that which is individually powered and, therefore, not tied to a particular track or part of the warehouse. In other words, a piece of equipment that can move about freely. In some instances, this may be some type of a platform truck as illustrated which can be pushed manually from one location to another. Very often carts, as illustrated, are used in order selection areas or order pick areas which are pushed by individuals making up the orders.

Another type of individually powered equipment and one that is used frequently in many materials handling systems is the forklift truck (see Figure 6-4). The forklift truck is a very versatile piece of equipment which can be provided at a very reasonable cost; has the ability to perform a number of useful tasks in materials handling systems; and is available with various lift arrangements. Usually forklift trucks are used in conjunction with pallets but there are a number of different types of forklift trucks which do not really have to utilize pallets. The forklift truck operates very efficiently and can be used in a variety of different ways. The major disadvantage of a forklift truck is that it requires an operator and if the forklift is not being used then very often the operator may not be working. But all things considered, it is probably the most popular and most common type of materials handling equipment in existence. Even the smallest firm and the one with the simplest materials handling system can often afford to have a forklift truck available for use. Its biggest advantage is its versatility and the variety of ways it can be used in the warehouse in moving goods from one section to another or transferring goods into and out of the equipment of various transportation agencies. It is also possible to use the forklift truck for loading and unloading the equipment of many transportation companies.

Conveyor Systems

Conveyors are a very popular form of materials handling equipment particularly where an attempt is being made to automate a warehouse as much as possible. There are two basic types of conveyors. First, a roller conveyor which basically makes use of the gravity principle. In other words the conveyor is inclined and goods move down the conveyor by force of their own weight, typically at a slow pace depending on the incline of the conveyor. The other type is what might be called the wheel conveyor or belt conveyor which depends on power equipment and goods are moved either along level conveyors or up inclines to a section of the warehouse. Quite obviously companies will use a roller conveyor wherever possible to minimize their operating costs.

Conveyors are advantageous in terms of eliminating handling. Conveyor equipment with scanning devices and other automatic devices enable goods to be moved very efficiently and quickly from one area in the

FIGURE 6-4 Individually powered equipment.

Source: From *Warehouse Operations,* General Services Administration, U.S. Government Printing Office, Washington, D.C., 1969.

warehouse to another. It is quite obvious, however, that a modern conveyor system is something which is very expensive and requires a large capital investment. It is also fixed in location, i.e., it lacks versatility and much time and effort has to be put into the design of a conveyor system with particular reference to future needs.

If conditions change then it may be necessary to change the conveyor system and this, of course, often can only be done at very high cost. Organizations which invest in complex conveyor systems are usually the larger and more successful manufacturing firms. It should be noted, however, that there are some very simple kinds of conveyors that can be installed at a very reasonable cost. But when conveyors are used to automate a large distribution warehouse, for example, then this usually requires a significant investment of funds in a very complex and sophisticated conveyor system.

As suggested above, in analyzing the possibility of using conveyor systems in a warehouse, an organization highlights a basic issue in selecting materials handling equipment, viz., whether they will be capital intensive or labor intensive in their approach. Many large companies with sophisticated logistics requirements find capital intensive systems like elaborate conveyors to be extremely worthwhile because of reduced labor costs and possible improvements in distribution time. However, such approaches are not necessarily the right solution for all companies. Approaches which are more labor intensive may be much more appropriate. The analysis for finding the proper solution to this important question is analogous to that done for private versus public warehousing. In other words, conveyor systems have a very important segment of fixed costs which means that there must be sufficient volume of "throughput" to defray or spread the fixed costs. Labor intensive systems are highly variable in their cost structure like the public warehouse.

Cranes

There are a variety of cranes available which can be utilized in warehouses. The two basic types used in warehouses are so called bridge cranes and stacker cranes. The former are more common in physical supply warehouses or where heavy industrial type goods such as steel coils or generators have to be moved, stored, and loaded for shipment.

Stacker cranes have become increasingly popular in physical distribution warehouses because of their ability to function with narrow aisles and so effectively utilize the cube capacity of a warehouse. Also, such equipment is very adaptable to automation. There are stacker cranes on the market which are fully automated to put stock into and take it out of storage areas without an operator. The computer backup equipment with such systems is capable of selecting the best and also recalling where the stock was placed. We should also note that stacker cranes are usually used in conjunction with elaborate shelving systems.

While not as expensive usually as conveyor systems, cranes are also a capital intensive piece of equipment. Bridge cranes may be required because of very heavy items but stacker cranes should be justified on a cost basis. The advantages are the ability to lift heavy items quickly and efficiently with bridge cranes and with stacker cranes, the use of space effectively, and possible automation.

Other

There are a variety of other types of equipment including drag lines pulling carts in a continuous circle in a warehouse; elevators of various sorts; hoists; monorails; and other items which can be used. All these items are more specialized but can be used by companies to provide better materials handling.

Storage Equipment.   Our introductory comments in this section indicated that materials handling as an activity center also included storage equipment, which is often used in conjunction with particular types of equipment for moving products in warehouses. While there is much variety available in this area, we should note that most storage equipment has a primary role in trying to effectively use space in the warehouse. The three principal types are: (1) pallets and skids, (2) racks and shelves, and (3) containers. The possibilities are almost unlimited in what can be done in this area. The illustrations indicate how those items can be used and suggest their advantages. See Figures 6-5, 6-6, and 6-7.

Storage aids such as pallets or various types of "shelves" play an important role in the efficient use of the height of warehouses and are often used in conjunction with various types of materials handling systems. In highly automated warehouses of today, firms very often use a system of locating stock in a warehouse where materials handling equipment runs along fixed tracks (stacker cranes) and goods are automatically transferred into a shelving system on skids or pallets which makes possible the reduction of aisle widths and also the efficient use of height in a warehouse. Therefore, no discussion of categories of equipment would be complete without some consideration being given to what we might call storage aids. They have come to play an increasingly important role in the design of warehouses and are an important part of any overall materials handling system.

In design of the materials handling system, the above categories of equipment are quite obviously options which are available to the logistics manager. Some systems will incorporate all of the basic types of materials handling equipment; others may only employ one or two types. Also as we have seen, there are a variety of possibilities under each of the types indicated above.

Types of Materials Handling Equipment – A Design Perspective

Another perspective on materials handling equipment is often utilized in analyzing equipment needs. There are three categories using this approach. The first category is *flexible-path*, which includes manual hand trucks, all

FIGURE 6-5   Pallet stacking and shelving in warehouse.

Source: From *Warehouse Operations,* General Services Administration, U.S. Government Printing Office, Washington, D.C., 1969.

forklift trucks, and some order picking equipment. The design advantages are versatility and flexibility. However, it is customarily more labor intensive.

The second category would be *continuous flow-fixed path* equipment, which includes conveyors and drag lines. They are usually very efficient and highly automated. However, the investment is high; they are usually specialized to certain products (limited versatility); and they have limited flexibility. Where a company has volume flow and uniform size in their products, then this approach has many cost advantages.

A third type is *intermittent flow-fixed path* equipment. This category includes cranes, monorails, and stacker crane equipment. It offers the efficiency of continuous flow equipment with the possibility of stopping equipment if not needed.

There has been a virtual revolution in this whole area of materials handling as equipment manufacturers have seen the need and companies have seen the need for more efficient kinds of equipment being available for the movement of goods around the warehouse and into and out of the warehouse. The number of possible types of equipment available today

FIGURE 6-6   Pallet types.

Source: From *Warehouse Operations,* General Services Administration, U.S. Government Printing Office, Washington, D.C., 1969.

almost staggers the imagination. In a sense, it is overwhelming to the possible designer of a materials handling system. But on the other hand it represents an important challenge because of the possibilities which are available so as to enable the logistics system to operate more efficiently.

An interesting dimension of this discussion is whether the logistics manager should be an expert in the actual design of equipment for the materials handling area. It is very unlikely that this would be the case in

FIGURE 6-7   Standard pallet patters.

Source: From *Warehouse Operations,* General Services Administration, U.S. Government
Printing Office, Washington, D.C., 1969.

most instances. Usually the logistics manager would be dependent on a staff
of engineers available in the organization or upon the advice of various
equipment managers. It is important, however, that the logistics manager be
knowledgeable about his or her own system and its particular needs. This
enables him or her to establish the general parameters or limits for the
materials handling system that he or she is going to need. It will also provide
a framework for trying to decide what is going to be the best for the
particular company or firm. At this point, let us turn our attention to some of

the factors or criteria that will be used by the logistics manager in trying to decide what types of equipment should be selected.

Equipment Selection Factors

There are a number of different factors that affect the type of materials handling equipment that should be used by a company. Essentially those factors present a set of guidelines for the logistics manager to use in analyzing his or her requirements. Such an analysis has to be approached in a trade-off context measuring benefits against costs.

Physical Attributes of Product and Packaging

One does not have to have much imagination to realize that firms in the United States produce a vast array of different types of products. Even individual companies sometimes produce a vast array of individual products. If we are talking about a materials handling system that is going to move books in or around a warehouse this is quite distinct from storage of automobile tires or chainsaws of one sort or another. Therefore, the product or group of products that we are dealing with is going to have a bearing upon the type of materials handling equipment that we use.

For example, the weight of the item will obviously influence the design of a system. Large pieces of equipment that may have to be stored in a warehouse may negate any possibility of using something like a conveyor system and may require overhead bridge cranes. If the product is smaller and lighter in weight, then usually the option of using any one or several of the various categories of materials handling equipment exists. But the product, its weight, size, packaging, value, handling ability, susceptibility to damage, are all factors which are going to influence the type of equipment that can be used. Therefore, a consideration of the product and its various dimensions will be a very important first step in deciding which options are going to be available for possible selection of equipment and which will be most apropos for our materials handling system. The logistics manager, because of work with the transportation agencies and in the area of inventory, will be very knowledgeable about the product or products of the company and will know the factors which are going to influence the use of materials handling equipment.

Characteristics of Physical Facility

The physical characteristics of our warehouse(s) facility is also a factor that influences use of materials handling equipment. Very often in talking about warehousing one visualizes a large one-story facility, well lighted with very few obstacles, which will be conducive to the use of conveyors, forklift trucks, shelves, or any type of materials handling equipment that we have discussed. In some instances, it is not possible for us to have this type of facility and we may have to use a mobile storage facility where conveyors, for example, would not be feasible. We may be dealing with a facility which is old and has low ceilings and may negate the possibility of any type of shelving or containers. We may be dealing with a facility where the floors are such that a heavy duty forklift truck would not be possible. Firms do not always have the option of using the best type of facility and the facility itself will obviously have some important effect on the type of equipment that we can use.

If we are designing a brand new warehousing facility, then all the options that we have talked about are probably available to us in the selection of equipment. If we are dealing with a facility that is already in existence and in particular if it is an older facility, then this will place some constraints on the type of equipment possible to use.

Time Requirements   Time is a very important factor in a number of different ways for a logistics system, and as you would probably expect, it does have an effect upon the materials handling area. In a market or distribution warehouse where the firm is storing its finished goods which are very relatively high in value and where customers expect to receive their orders in a reasonable period of time after placing them, time is very often critical or should be. In these instances, companies will select materials handling equipment which will contribute to their ability to move goods into, around and out of the warehouse as fast as possible.

As we indicated in the previous chapter on warehousing, the distribution or transit warehouse is one which is noted for rapidity of movement. Therefore, one often finds the most sophisticated and largest variety of materials handling equipment in these types of facilities. These are the warehouses where consideration is usually given to automation and where we find the elaborate and sophisticated conveyor systems and the use of automatic storage placers and all the variety of materials handling equipment that we have discussed.

On the other hand, if we are talking about a storage warehouse or one that is used primarily in conjunction with the manufacturing facility for storage of semi-finished goods and perhaps basic materials, then time is not usually as critical. The type of equipment that would be used would be more basic and it might not be necessary to automate such a facility.

Because of the trade-off possibilities, a firm may be much more willing to invest large amounts of money in a sophisticated materials handling equipment if time is an important factor. It may be possible to increase sales or have savings in other areas by putting more into the materials handling system.

The three factors mentioned here will provide a basic framework for the logistics manager to begin to analyze his or her particular needs and the options that will be available to him or her in terms of materials handling equipment. Once this has been done then he or she will be in a position to look at what is available in each of these categories from the most likely equipment manufacturers. The logistics manager can always, of course, get additional engineering information from the company's own staff of people which will help further in designing the system that will best meet the company's particular needs. Quite obviously, there is a lot of detail that will be necessary in the final selection but the knowledge of what is generally

FIGURE 6-8 **Systems perspective of equipment selection.**

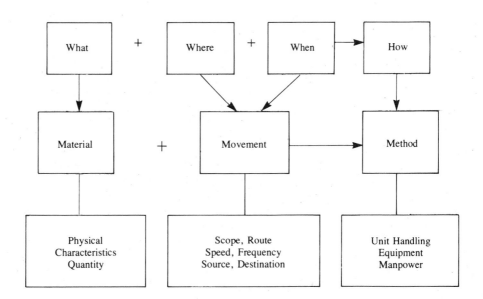

available and the factors that we have provide the very basis for the development of an efficient system for any organization.

Equipment Selection Factors—A Systems View

Materials handling equipment selection is usually made by applying some common sense along with some creativity. Such an approach will often solve the problem of equipment selection. Essentially the decision boils down to the material to be moved and the move itself.[3] See Figure 6-8.

The first step is to analyze the movement and examine whether it is necessary or whether it could be combined with another movement. The second step is to analyze the goods to be moved. What are the physical characteristics and what quantities are to be moved? The third step is to analyze the move. How frequently does it occur? What is the origin and destination? What speed is necessary?

Sources of Information

In evaluating and/or suggesting alternatives for materials handling equipment there are a number of important possibilities for possible help and insight.

Internal Staff

Many large companies and even smaller ones have staff engineers who are available to help the logistics manager analyze the situation. These are the individuals who can provide the detailed guidance once the initial analysis has been done by the logistics manager using the criteria suggested above.

Equipment Manufacturers

Equipment manufacturers maintain a staff of engineers who can provide cost data on possible alternatives from their company as well as the respective costs. Equipment has become so specialized today that this may be the best way to get detailed cost information.

Consultants

Another possibility is the use of consultants to provide a need analysis and select the best equipment. While such organizations are expensive, they often provide a very reasonable analysis based upon cost of using alternative resources.

Other

In addition to the sources cited above other possibilities include trade associations and self-study. It is usually only possible to get simplified data in either case. However, it is often a convenient place to start.

Summary

As we have indicated, materials handling is a very very important aspect of the logistics system. It contributes markedly to efficient operation and interacts quite importantly with other areas such as transportation and warehousing. It also interacts with our next area of discussion which is packaging. The size, the shape, the design of the package very often has to be done in conjunction with the selection of materials handling equipment. The type of packaging will, as we have indicated, affect what can be used as far as materials handling equipment and vice versa, the type of materials handling equipment will have some effect upon the packaging.

PACKAGING

Like materials handling, there are other individuals in addition to the logistics manager who may be concerned about packaging of the product. Also, packaging, like materials handling, in a sense is a nebulous concept and connotes a number of different things to different people. This may be attributable to the fact that there are a number of places in an organization where one might be concerned with packaging.

Before talking about the various dimensions of packaging from a logistics perspective, it would be a good idea to discuss the other areas of a company that are likely to be concerned about packaging and understand something about the interaction and coordination that might be necessary. One very obvious interest would be from the marketing area. In fact, packaging is a topic of interest when one discusses and delineates the various responsbilities of the marketing area. Packaging may be a way of selling a product or at least making available to the customer information about the product.

Packaging is also an area of concern to production managers since they are often responsible for placing goods into the package and the size and shape and type of package will very often have an effect upon labor efficiency. Production managers may look at a package from a somewhat different perspective than the marketing manager or even the logistics manager. Therefore, we can expect some interest to be expressed by the production manager in the types of packages. It may also be true that the legal section of the organization will be concerned about packaging. This is particularly true today when it is necessary to provide differing types of information about what is contained in the package. So some coordination may be necessary between logistics and the legal staff of a company. Packaging is, therefore, a concern to a number of different areas in a company which will require some coordination.

While we are discussing interest in the packaging area, mention should be made of why the importance to the logistics manager. As indicated in the introductory comments, the size, shape, and type of packaging will have an influence upon the materials handling as we have discussed it. Packaging will affect the operation of warehouses. Also, from a logistics manager's point of view packaging is quite important for effective damage protection. This is true not only in the warehouse but also in the use of various transportation agencies.

The size of the package may affect the ability of a company to use pallets or shelving or different types of materials handling equipment. So some consideration has to be given to the package in order to efficiently use the warehouse and the transportation agencies. There are many referenced examples of where packages were designed too wide or too high for efficient use of a transportation agency or for efficient use of a warehouse. So it is quite important to coordinate packaging with warehousing and with transportation. We have already noted in a number of different instances that if a good is delivered damaged it is likely to have a bad effect on future sales. So packing is quite important to the logistics manager to prevent goods arriving in a damaged fashion and therefore having a negative effect upon sales. It can also contribute to our handling costs if not done properly. So, overall packaging interacts with the logistics system in a number of different and important ways. With the above as background, we should discuss more explicitly the role of packaging in logistics.

The Role of Packaging

In the section on materials handling, we inferred some of the general aspects of packaging. In particular we alluded to how it can provide more efficiency in the logistics system.

*Identification of
Product and
Provision of
Information*

A very important part of packaging is the provision of information about what is stored in the package and helping to identify the product. It might be easiest to look at this from the perspective of a marketing manager that is trying to sell a product in competition with other products on a shelf in a store like a supermarket. The package should be designed so as to provide information about the product which would make it more appealing to the customer.

The logistics manager is usually not concerned about packaging from this perspective but provision of information is also important to people concerned about packaging from a logistics perspective. Goods have to be stored in a warehouse and they have to be identified properly so that they can be located easily and correctly so as to be able to get the right products for orders. A lot of time and effort may be spent by firms when they design a package to make sure that it provides information to people working in the warehouse.

It is also important that a customer be able to get information from the package. For example, if it is easily damaged, this is information that is usually provided on the package; or if it should be set in only one position, this is information that should be provided on the package. Sometimes color codes are used so that goods will be stored in certain areas of a warehouse according to color. Sometimes it is important that weight be noted on the package because this will affect people who might have to lift the package or what can be set on top of the item. Therefore, providing information is an important role of the packaging area, i.e., to provide the right information correctly and easily to people who are going to have to deal with the packages.

The techniques for providing information include color coding, computer-readable tables, symbols, and number codes. The technique or combination of techniques used will depend on the particular circumstances in the organization. However, as stated above, provision of the information is very important.

*Improvement of
Efficiency in
Handling and
Distributing
Packages*

An aspect of major concern in dealing with packaging is the ease of handling in conjunction with materials handling and transportation. Large packages, for example, may be desirable from a production perspective but size and weight of the contents might be such as to cause problems for materials handling equipment or also for the transfer into and out of the equipment of a transportation agency. So one of the objectives of any design of a package is to give some consideration to maximizing ease of handling in the warehouse and also for transfer from the warehouse. This obviously is also quite important as far as the production manager is concerned who is going to have to put the goods into the box which is selected.

The important considerations fall into three areas. The first is the physical dimensions of the package. Consideration would have to be given to space utilization in terms of the warehouse, transport vehicle, and pallets. The materials handling equipment would also have to be considered in terms of the physical dimension of the products. The second consideration would be strength of the package with a need to analyze the height of the package, the nature of the handling, and the type of materials handling equipment to be used. The final consideration would be shape.

Protection   An item of major concern to the logistics manager is protection of the goods which are in the package. This is important in the warehouse where goods are going to be moved around and could drop from the conveyor or be hit with a forklift truck. So the package must be designed to provide adequate protection for the product in the warehouse. Protection through logistics is also going to be important when it is moving by a transportation agency. The type of transportation agency, as shall be pointed out in the next section on link analysis, will influence the packaging which is going to be required. Some agencies are noted for minimizing packaging requirements because the damage susceptibility is not nearly as great. So the type of transportation agency that we use will have an effect on the kind of packaging required to protect it from damage. Therefore, one very important objective is to minimize the probability of damage to goods.

In analyzing the protection consideration attention must be given to what we have to protect against. These possibilities would include, as suggested, shocks in handling and transport, water damage, pilferage, and temperature changes.

There are a number of ways the protection needs could be analyzed. These would include trial runs through the logistics system, mechanical simulation, and general information.

What Is Packaging?

There are two types of packaging generally discussed. One is called consumer packaging or interior packaging and the other is called exterior or industrial packaging. The marketing manager is most usually concerned about the former because the consumer or interior packaging provides information important in selling the product or motivating the customer to buy the product or giving maximum visibility to the product when it is on the retail shelf in competition with others. So consumer packaging has to be appealing to the customer. In fact, it is often referred to as a silent salesman.

On the other hand, industrial or exterior packaging is of primary concern to the logistics manager. This is the area that provides protection to the goods which are going to have to be moved and stored in the warehouse and also in effectively using the space which is available from transportation companies in their vehicles. It also has to provide information and ease of handling as we have indicated in the discussion of the role of packaging.

While it is convenient to talk about the types of packaging in this dichotomous fashion and quite often we can slice packaging in this way, it should be noted that there is obviously some overlap between these two areas. One cannot design interior (consumer) packaging without some consideration being given to the exterior or industrial packaging which is going to be moved. It does not make sense to spend a lot of time and effort in trying to minimize damage as far as the exterior package is concerned if some consideration is not given to interior protection also.

Therefore, there has to be interaction or coordination between the marketing and logistics area as far as the consumer and industrial dimensions of packaging are concerned. It is also quite important that there be interaction with the people in the production area as far as both consumer and industrial packaging are concerned since they are the ones typically that are going to have to join the two.

Packaging Materials

There are a variety of different types of exterior packaging materials available to the logistics manager. In fact, as has been the case with materials handling, there has been a virtual revolution in the last decade as far as packaging materials are concerned. At one time there was much affection for the harder materials such as wood or metal containers for protection. But these added considerable weight for shipping which increased transport costs since customers are billed for total weight including package.

In more recent years, there has been a definite trend toward softer materials for packaging. To a large extent this has been accomplished with the use of corrugated materials for protection, particularly with respect to the outside of the package, and also to some extent with the interior materials which are used in the package. However, maybe the type of soft goods that has created the most revolutionary aspects in packaging has been the plasticized materials which are now available which enable manufacturers to automate highly the packaging area and to maximize protection as well as minimize costs.

The new materials have been cheap and highly protective. In addition, their light weight helps to minimize transportation costs. So if there has been a revolution in the packaging area, it has been probably attributable to the development of these types of materials.

Package Selection

The packaging area has two important questions that must be answered from a logistics perspective. First, the physical dimensions are of concern, i.e., the size and shape. Second, the type of material will be important. We will look at these two aspects in the order presented. Before doing this, it should be noted that these factors or criteria are guidelines for the logistics manager.

Physical Dimensions

One of the most important factors is the characteristics of the product, i.e., size, shape, weight, etc. Shoes which are relatively uniform in size and shape are much different than glassware, which can vary considerably.

Materials

Another factor is the characteristics of the logistics system, i.e., mode, number of handlings, materials handling equipment, length of storage. These are all factors which will affect the physical dimensions of the package.

Finally, the logistics-marketing interface will have an impact. The coordination factor previously alluded to will influence the size and shape of the package.

The physical dimension of the product will affect materials that can be used. Small consumer products like glassware are much different than computers or auto tires.

The mode of transportation will have an effect. Airlines and motor carriers often require much less packaging than rail or water. Time to be stored is another factor affecting type of materials. Usually the longer the period, the better the packaging. Finally, the production interface is important to materials selection.

Containerization

No discussion of packaging would be complete without giving consideration to containerization. Containers are physical equipment used for unification of small shipments which can be moved on an intermodal basis as one shipment since they are loaded into a container.

The cargo container is a shipping container which is usually of weatherproof construction. It can, therefore, be stored outside or can be transported in open cars or on the dock of a ship. Typically, the cargo container is of rugged construction for movement by mechanical means (forklift, crane, etc.) and as indicated, it is feasible to interchange between or among modes.

Containers are attractive to users very simply because of reduced cost. Such savings are the result of lower transportation cost, reduced handling cost, reduced loss and damage, reduced inventory costs, reduced paper-work, and reduced packaging cost.

Summary

As was the case in our analysis of materials handling, it should be noted that there are some strict engineering dimensions to packaging. The strength of materials or the protective ability of materials is something very often that would not be well known to the logistics manager. Typically, however, the logistics manager would have a staff of engineers that could be called upon for this type of information. Also, it could be provided external to the firm by consulting firms or the manufacturers of the materials. But the logistics manager is in a good position to analyze the product, the kind of transportation agencies used, the materials handling system, and come up with some type of general framework for analyzing packaging requirements.

All these factors will have an effect upon the type of packaging that can be used. Once this has been analyzed and the usable options delineated, then the next step is to get the engineering information from internal or external sources and make a decision on what is best for the organization.

CONCLUDING COMMENTS

Both materials handling and packaging interface with the link and node systems have been discussed in this section dealing with nodal analysis because they are very important in nodal activities. But as we have indicated they also have an effect in the link part of our system. Overall they are areas of great concern to the logistics manager and represent areas where there will have to be a lot of coordination with other people in the organization. There have been many exciting developments in terms of availability of materials handling equipment and packaging materials which makes the decisions in a sense more difficult but at the same time more challenging than they were before. The logistics manager may be able to realize some important economies and trade-offs in this area which will save the company money or contribute to the overall efficiency of the logistics system with a consequent impact upon the profts of the organization.

Study Questions

1. Discuss the general relationships of materials handling and packaging in the logistics system.
2. What is the role of materials handling for a logistics system?
3. Discuss the advantages and disadvantages of different types of materials handling equipment.
4. How does the logistics manager decide what type of materials handling equipment he needs?

Notes

1. *Basics of Material Handling*, (Pittsburgh, Pennsylvania: The Materials Handling Institute, 1973), pp. 4-6.
2. *Ibid.*, pp. 8-10.
3. *Ibid.*, pp. 12-14.

Case 6-1
The Oberlin Distribution Company

Oberlin Distribution Company is located in St. Louis and is the major distribution center for Halifax Piper, Inc., its parent company.

At present, Oberlin uses individually powered and controlled manual equipment, along with a fairly large labor force. Although Oberlin has provided efficient service in the past, due to increasing labor costs and the automation of many of its competitors, Oberlin's service level has fallen substantially.

You have just been contracted by Oberlin to conduct a study and analyze their warehouse operations. As you progress with the study you find that the building in which Oberlin conducts its warehousing operations is underutilized and that the materials handling equipment is old and needs to be replaced. There is a very high level of throughput in the warehouse, and because of the interior design and use of obsolete equipment, many orders are backed up, taking from one to three additional days to be filled.

Questions

1. As a logistics consultant, discuss the objectives of a materials handling system and relate them to the Oberlin warehouse.

2. Because the distribution center building used by Oberlin is underutilized and fairly new, discuss the various categories of equipment that Oberlin could use in order to improve its present system. (Be sure to discuss equipment selection factors).

3. Make final conclusions and make specific recommendations for Oberlin to follow.

SELECTED BIBLIOGRAPHY FOR PART II

ALFORD L. P., and JOHN R. BANGS, Editors, *Production Handbook*. New York: The Ronald Press Company, 1955.

AMMER, DEAN S., *Materials Management*, 3rd Edition. Homewood, Illinois: Richard D. Irwin, Inc., 1968.

BALLOU, RONALD H., *Business Logistics Management*, 2nd Edition. Englewood Cliffs, New Jersey: Prentice-Hall, Inc., 1973, Chapters 7, 9, and 11.

BUFFA, ELWOOD S., *Production-Inventory Systems*: *Planning and Control*. Homewood, Illinois: Richard D. Irwin, Inc., 1968.

Department of Commerce, Bureau of the Census, *1967 Census of Business, Public Warehousing*. Washington, D.C.: U.S. Government Printing Office, 1970.

General Services Administration, *Warehouse Operations*. Washington, D.C.: U.S. Government Printing Office, 1964.

HERRON, DAVID P., "ABC Data Correlation," Reprinted in: *Business Logistics in American Industry*. Karl Ruppenthal and Henry A. McKinnel, Jr., Editors. Stanford, California: Stanford University, 1968, pp. 87-90.

HESKETT, JAMES L., NICHOLAS A. GLASKOWSKY, JR., and ROBERT M. IVIE, *Business Logistics*, 2nd Edition. New York: The Ronald Press Company, 1973, Chapters 3, 10, 11, 14, 17, and 18.

JENKINS, CREED, *Modern Warehouse Management*. New York: McGraw-Hill Book Company, 1968.

MAGEE, JOHN F., *Industrial Logistics*. New York: McGraw-Hill Book Company, 1968, Chapters 4, 5, and 7.

MARKS, NORTON E., and ROBERT M. TAYLOR, Editors, *Marketing Logistics*: *Perspectives and Viewpoints*. New York: John Wiley and Sons, Inc., 1967, Sections IV and V.

McELHINEY, PAUL T., and ROBERT I. COOK, Editors, *The Logistics of Materials Management*. Boston: Houghton Mifflin Company, 1969.

MEAN, HARLAN, "Policy Conflict and Inventory Control," *Financial Executive*, December 1963, pp. 13-17.

TAFF, CHARLES A, *Management of Physical Distribution and Transportation*, 6th Edition. Homewood, Illinois: Richard D. Irwin, Inc., 1972, Chapters 6, 7, 10 and 11.

Part III

The purpose of this section is to acquaint the reader with the economic and operational characteristics of the transportation system and with the decision making areas necessary for effective control of the link function. Transportation, usually the most significant logistics cost element in the firm, is an area requiring daily decision making. The management of the transportation function necessitates a thorough understanding of: the interrelationship of the link and node; the economic and service characteristics of the various suppliers of link service; the pragmatics of transportation pricing; and the impact of transportation regulation upon the utilization of carrier services and logistics control.

In the first chapter, a carrier selection framework is established followed by a discussion of the economic and operational characteristics of the various modes in light of the carrier selection determinants. In the second chapter, attention is directed to transportation pricing and services offered. The third chapter considers the functions involved in traffic management. Throughout the chapters emphasis is placed upon the pragmatics of the transportation system.

| Chapter 7 | The Network System |

After studying this chapter, you should be able to:

- Explain the role and importance of transportation to logistics systems and the relationship between the link and the node in logistics systems.

- Discuss the variables used in selecting modes of transportation and particular carriers within the modes.

- Present an overview of the transport system, including the basic modes of transportation, coordinated transportation systems, indirect agencies, and special carriers.

As pointed out in an earlier chapter, logistics can be viewed as a series of links and nodes. The nodes are fixed points in the system where some activity occurs which temporarily halts the flow of goods in the logistics pipeline. Connecting these nodes are links which are the transportation networks that exist between the various nodes.

In this section we are concerned with the transportation network—link—in the logistics system. Attention is given to the fundamental relationship existing between the link and the node, the link selection decision, and the nature of the transportation system. In the latter area, attention is focused upon the modes of transportation and upon transportation rates and services. Transportation rates and services are considered in the next chapter.

THE ROLE OF TRANSPORTATION IN LOGISTICS

A college student, Joe College, home for summer vacation, was having a friendly discussion with a friend, Fred Unfamiliar, who asked Joe what he was majoring in at college. Joe responded quite excitedly, "Logistics and Transportation!" Fred thought a moment and then asked, "Why are you studying transportation and logistics? All a firm does is give the freight to a carrier, signs some pieces of paper, and the task is completed." But, unfortunately, the transportation function of logistics is not this simple. There is much more to transportation than merely calling a carrier to transport a firm's goods.

The transportation area is a highly complex arena that requires a highly qualified individual to operate. The area is filled with such complexities as many modes from which to choose, a multiplicity of carriers within each mode, varied combinations of modes and carriers to serve given links, a regulatory structure that affects the carrier operations, and a system of transportation pricing that defies all laws of logic. To the neophyte, transportation is one of the major stumbling blocks to fully understanding the operation of a logistics system, that is, transportation appears to be a thicket of throny bushes with the many thorns creating an equal number of problems.

Therefore, knowledge of the transportation system is fundamental to the efficient and economical operation of the logistics function in the firm. Transportation is the basic link among a firm's plants, warehouses, and raw material sources—the nodes. More specifically transportation creates time and place utility in goods, that is, transportation enables the firm to physically move goods to the place desired and at the time desired.

It is virtually inconceivable in today's economy for a firm to function without the aid of transportation. Most firms are geographically divorced from their raw material sources and/or their market areas. Production economies gained from specialization of labor result in a concentration of manufactured goods in a location which normally does not coincide with the location of demand for the goods. Therefore, transportation is necessary to bridge the gap existing between production and consumption—the producer-consumer gap.[1]

At the outset of this chapter it is necessary to provide a word of caution regarding the misconception of transportation and logistics as being one and the same. True, transportation is a major aspect of logistics, but it is not the exclusive function. Transportation must be viewed as being a logistics sub-function, along with storage, materials handling, inventory control, etc. Application of the systems approach requires viewing transportation as a subfunction. Viewed yet another way, optimizing the transportation function does not necessarily result in optimizing the logistics function as a whole.

To say that transportation is logistics implies that it, transportation, operates independently of other logistics functions. Nothing could be further from the truth, for transportation has a direct impact upon nodal operations. The quality of link service provided over a link has a direct bearing upon inventory costs and/or stockout costs at a node as well as the cost of operating the node. More will be said on this subject at a later point in this chapter.

The above statements are not to be construed to imply that transportation is a rather minor logistics function not deserving attention. This by all means is a false interpretation. Transportation decisions interact directly with other logistics elements as well as causing an impact among other elements. For example, if a firm decided to switch from rail to air transport to serve a given raw material source-plant link, the increased speed, lower transit time, of the air service requires the holding of lower inventories to meet anticipated usage, less warehousing space, and less stringent product packaging resulting from a smoother movement by air. The lower inventory levels will reduce inventory insurance requirements and capital tied up in inventory, thereby reducing inventory carrying costs. These advantages, effects upon other logistics function, are realized, however, at the cost of higher transportation costs. Thus, the transport decision cannot be made in a vacuum; attention must be given to effect of the transport decision upon other elements in the logistics system— the application of the total cost or systems approach.

In addition, one can see the importance of transportation by reviewing the impact of transportation upon the nation's economy. In 1977, it is estimated that U.S. firms spent $172.2 billion for moving freight. This includes the $170.2 billion for for-hire and private transportation plus shipper costs of $2.0 billion for loading and unloading freight and for operating and controlling the transportation function.[2] This represented 9 percent of the G.N.P.

In summary, transportation is a vital part of the logistics system, but it is not the only function in logistics. Transportation permits the firm to bridge the producer-consumer gap and thereby create time and place utility in goods. Transportation pervades all other functions of logistics. In the next section, attention is given to the transport selection decision.

THE TRANSPORT SELECTION DECISION

Conceptually, the logistics system of a firm is a series of nodes—raw material sources, production and demand centers, and commodity storage points—and links—transportation methods. The transportation link occasions the flow of goods between the various nodes, i.e., it bridges the producer-consumer gap. The transportation firm utilized to link the nodes is a decisive factor in the efficient performance of the nodal tasks and, in part, determines the "extent of the market or volume of demand for particular goods."[3] Selection of the transport firm enables the transport user to exercise control over the quality of link service provided.

This section considers the carrier selection decision for situations in which the link has already been determined. This implies that a previous decision has been made regarding the various nodes in the system that are to be linked. More specifically, we are not considering at this time the decision concerning which node will be linked with another. The purpose of this section is to concentrate upon the factors that are relevant to the carrier selection decision regardless of what nodes are involved.

The Link-Node Relationship

The carrier selection decision is a specialized purchasing process whereby a firm purchases the services of a carrier to provide the necessary and vital link among logistics nodes. The carrier selected to provide the link service has a direct bearing upon the operation of the logistics node and other functions in the logistics system. As DeHayes points out:

> The choice of transport mode directly affects all other elements of the logistics system (e.g., packaging, production, planning, warehousing, facility location, information processing, and inventory control). Consequently, the transport method must be selected to provide for efficient operation of the entire system.[4]

Scope of Transport Selection Decision
The carrier selection decision, then, entails more than a mere evaluation of the prices charged by different methods of transportation. The prices charged by a method of transport is but one factor that must be considered in the decision. The other costs are those associated with the effect of the transport method's service upon the nodal operation. The transit time incurred by different methods will have varying effects upon the inventory level required at the nodes, that is, the longer the transit time the greater the required inventory level to protect the node against stockouts until the next shipment arrives. The dependability of the transport method and the degree of safe delivery also affect the inventory levels held at a node, the utilization of materials handling equipment and labor, and the time and cost associated with carrier communications to determine the status of the shipment or to seek reparations for damage caused while the goods are in transit.

Much has been done with respect to carrier prices and pricing practices in the carrier selection decision. Measurement and evaluation of the logistical implication of the carrier cost determinant is much easier than that of carrier service performances; carrier rates are published and the direct transportation cost via alternatives is easily computed. However, selection of the transport method based upon lowest transport costs, direct link costs, does not guarantee the least cost decision for the logistics system as a whole. The selection of the lowest direct transport cost alternative to serve the link quite often results in elevated costs for other logistics elements.[5]

The Carrier Selection Decision

As was mentioned earlier, the carrier selection decision is a specialized purchasing process whereby a firm selects a carrier to provide the necessary and vital link among logistics nodes. To conceive of this decision as merely requiring an evaluation of transportation rates (prices) to be assessed by alternative transport methods is to miss the major impact of the logistic approach. True, the transport rate is a factor in the decision but it is not the sole factor; consideration must be given to the quality of the link service and the effect of this service upon the cost of nodal operations.

Two-part Decision   The carrier selection decision is a twofold decision. First, a mode of transport (rail, motor, air, water, pipeline) is selected and second, a particular carrier (s) from within this mode must be chosen. A great deal of attention has been given to the evaluation of the first aspect of the decision—the selection of a mode of transport to serve the link. This usually involves the evaluation of the rates and service levels via alternative modes. For example, in a decision regarding use of air or rail carriers, consideration would be given to advantages of low transit time by air (causing lower inventory levels, lower inventory costs and reduced costs of stockouts) and the low rates (direct link costs) by rail. A decision is then reached by selecting the mode that occasions the lowest logistics costs, both nodal and link costs. The analysis is not continued beyond the modal selection decision and it is assumed that once this decision is made the selection of a specific carrier is merely child's play, that is, it is implicitly assumed that all carriers in a given mode provide the same level of service and, therefore, will have the same impact upon nodal costs.

It is not intended here to discount the importance of the modal decision in the carrier selection process, but rather to point out the importance of continuing the process to include the evaluation of the specific carrier(s) within the mode. True, most carriers in a given mode have the technical characteristics that would enable each to provide the same level of link service, but, in fact, these service levels can vary greatly from one carrier to another. Also since most interstate common carriers* in a given mode participate in rate bureau publication of rates, the rates via alternative

* See pages 215-220 for a discussion of the legal classification of carriers.

carriers in a mode are usually the same for a given movement. Thus, allowing for slight rate disparities, the transport rate is not an important criterion in selecting a specific carrier, but the rate is important in modal selection. Carrier service performance, then, becomes the relevant carrier selection determinant for selecting a specific carrier from one mode.

What, then, are the criteria used to evaluate the alternative modes and carriers? The carrier selection works dealing with general commodity movements or specific commodity movements have delineated the salient selection determinants to be carrier costs and service performance. The relevant service performance determinants are: transit time, reliability, capability, accessibility, and security. The interaction of the carrier cost and service determinants in the logistics function of the firm is discussed below.

Transportation Cost

Transportation cost was the predominant carrier selection determinant in early carrier selection works. Farris and McElhiney[6] point out that in the early stages of carrier and industrial development, the carrier selection decision was basically choosing the carrier occasioning the lowest transportation costs. Flood[7] identifies the transportation cost areas as: rates, minimum weights, loading and unloading facilities, packaging and blocking, damage-in-transit, and special services available from a carrier, e.g., stopping-in-transit, reconsignment, etc.

Again one can see that this type of analysis is oriented toward the evaluation of alternative modes. The rates, minimum weights, loading and unloading facilities, packaging and blocking will vary from one mode to another. However, the importance of transportation costs receded somewhat with the advent of the business logistics concept. Attention is now focused upon the cost trade-offs existing between the service provided by a carrier and the cost of nodal operations. But, the transportation cost disparities prevalent among alternative modes remains an important criterion in the carrier selection decision for the modal decision in the carrier selection process.

Transit Time and Reliability

Transit time is the total time that elapses from the time the consignor makes the goods available for dispatch until the carrier delivers same to the consignee. This includes the time required for pick-up and delivery, for terminal handling and for movement between origin and destination terminals. Reliability refers to the consistency of the transit time provided by a carrier, i.e., reliability is a measure of variation in the transit time provided by the link supplier.

Transit time and reliability affect the nodal costs of inventory and stockouts (lost sales or foregone productivity). Lower transit times result in lower inventories, while less dependability causes higher inventory levels or costs of stockouts.

In a study of intermodal transportation, Roberts and Associates[8] indicate that transit time and reliability are generally the important carrier service dimensions given consideration by a firm; transit time alone offers little or no benefit with poor reliability. Inventories and consequently inventory carrying costs can be minimized at a node with a given level of lead time. (As noted in an earlier section carrier transit time is one of the factors that determines lead time.) But, if the transit time varies greatly, i.e., transit time is not consistent, this minimization process cannot be accomplished at the node without increasing inventories above the level that would be required if the transit time were consistent. More specifically, the node is now required to hold larger amounts of inventory as a safety factor against stockouts that could arise from inconsistent link service.

The marketing implication of transit time and reliability is that a seller can gain a competitive advantage in the market place by utilizing a carrier that provides dependable service.[9] Thus if your firm can provide a customer with a lower and more dependable transit time than your competitor, the customer can reduce his cost of inventories or stockout and your firm can increase sales. Sales are quite sensitive to consistent service[10] and the logistics manager must place greater attention upon carrier transit time and reliability. Logistics service can be utilized to differentiate a firm's product in the market place, thereby increasing the marketability (the creation of possession utility) of the product.

Capability and Accessibility

Capability and accessibility determine whether a particular carrier can physically perform the transport service desired over a link. Capability refers to the ability of the carrier to provide the equipment and facilities required for the movement of a particular commodity. Such requirements as equipment that can provide controlled temperatures or humidity and facilities for special handling are examples of capability factors. Accessibility considers the ability of the carrier to provide service over the link in question, i.e., the availability of carrier routes and terminals in the proximity of the shipping locations. Accessibility refers to the ability of a carrier to physically approach (have access to) the nodes. The accessibility of a carrier is constrained by the geographic limits of its route network (rail lines or waterways) and/or the operating scope authorized by regulatory agencies. The inability of a carrier to provide the desired capability and availability service requirements can eliminate the carrier from consideration in the carrier selection decision.

Security

Security is concerned with the arrival of the goods in the same condition as they were in when tendered to the carrier. Although the common carrier is held liable for all loss and damage, with limited exceptions (the exceptions are: Acts of God, Acts of Public Enemy, Acts or Default of the Shipper, Inherent Nature of the Commodity, and Acts of a Public Authority), the firm does incur nodal costs when goods are delivered in a damaged condition or when lost. The provision of unsafe link service results in opportunity costs of foregone profits or productivity as a consequence of the goods arriving in a damaged condition and not available for sale or use. To guard against these opportunity costs, a firm will increase inventory levels with resulting increased inventory costs. The continued use of a carrier that provides unsafe link service will have adverse effects upon customer satisfaction and consequently an adverse effect upon sales.

If the firm uses a common carrier, the carrier is held liable for the damage to the lading. For the shipping firm to recover the damage value, a claim must be filed with the carrier. This entails a cost for preparation and documentation of the claim as well as the possibility of legal fees to have the claim settled through the courts. Therefore the nodal cost associated with claim settlement also is aggravated by frequent damage to the commodities.

Relative Importance of the Determinants*

It has been found that carrier service performance is the important selection determinant area when selecting a carrier from one mode. Transportation cost is of lesser importance in such a situation. The interaction of the link service quality and nodal costs is the logistics area given greatest attention in the carrier selection decision when selecting a carrier from within one mode.

The lesser importance of the transportation cost determinant in the carrier selection decision made from one mode is to be expected. Most interstate common carriers in a given mode participate in joint publication of rates. This joint publication of rates results in equal rates, with some minor variations, charged by alternative transport suppliers and precludes the shipper from differentiating the potential carriers with respect to the carrier's link cost impact upon the overall logistics objectives.

The relative unimportance of transportation cost in the carrier selection decision from one mode does not mean that shipper demand is price inelastic. The rates and charges by carriers in one mode are relative to the cost to be occasioned by carriers in other modes and by private transportation. That is, the rates charged by carriers in a given mode are relatively unimportant as an evaluative criterion in selecting a carrier from that mode, but if the rates in this mode are increased such that the total logistics cost of the presently used mode are higher than that of other modes, it would become advantageous for the shipper to utilize the services of carriers in another mode. Thus, the transportation cost factor is relatively unimportant in the selection of a carrier from within one mode, but it is important in the modal selection decision.

As pointed out above, transit time and reliability are generally the important carrier selection determinants, with reliability being the more important. In the selection of a carrier from one mode it was found that reliability is the most important determinant. But transit time is not as equally important: security and certain accessibility and capability determinants are more important than transit time. The reason for the relatively lesser importance of transit time in selecting a carrier from one mode is that the technical capabilities of the alternative carriers enable the potential vendors to provide essentially the same transit time over a link. With transit time being potentially equal, if not the same, for the carriers considered, the logistics cost impact of transit time is the same for the alternative suppliers, which precludes the transport buyer from differentiating the carriers upon

---

* The material in this section is based upon: Edward J. Bardi, "Carrier Selection from One Mode," *Transportation Journal*, Vol. 13, No. 1 (Fall 1973), pp. 23-29.

this selection determinant. However, if carriers in one mode provided different transit time over a given link, transit time would permit differentiation of the carriers and would be of greater importance, as it is in the modal selection decision.

Summary

The carrier selection decision is a specialized purchasing process whereby a firm selects a carrier to provide the necessary and vital link among logistics modes. The carrier selection decision is twofold, the selection of a mode of transport and then the selection of the carrier(s) from the mode. The criteria used in selecting a carrier are: transport cost, transit time, reliability, accessibility, capability, and security. The importance of these criteria varies from the modal decision to the specific carrier decision. The dominating influence of transportation cost in the carrier selection decision has receded, but transportation cost remains an important determinant in the modal decision. Reliability of the transit time provided is the most important determinant in the carrier selection decision.

THE TRANSPORT SYSTEM

The preceding sections provide a framework for analyzing the carrier selection decision. Our attention is now directed toward the transportation system per se, i.e., consideration is given to the types of link suppliers available. The transport system is examined from four different bases: (1) the basic modes of transportation; (2) the legal classification of carriers; (3) the coordinated transport service systems; (4) the indirect and special modal suppliers. In each area the operational and service characteristics are considered; knowledge of these characteristics is fundamental to the link service decision.

The Basic Modes of Transportation

The basic modes of transportation available to the logistics manager are: rail, motor, water, pipeline, and air. Each mode has different economic and technical structures and each can provide different qualities of link service. In this section we will examine the structure of each mode as it relates to the cost and quality of link service possible via the basic modes—the basis for the modal selection analysis.

The relative importance of each mode is evidenced in the distribution of ton-miles (an output measurement combining weight and distance, tonnage multiplied by miles transported) of traffic moved by each; this distribution is given in Table 7-1. These data suggest that the relative importance of rail

TABLE 7-1

Distribution of Intercity Freight by Modes (For-hire and Private)
(billions of ton-miles)

	Rail		Motor		Pipeline		Water			
	Amt	%	Amt	%	Amt	%	Amt	%	Amt	%
1940	379	61.3	62	10.0	59	9.5	118	19.1	.02	.00
1960	579	44.1	285	21.8	229	17.4	220	16.7	.89	.07
1965	709	43.3	359	21.9	306	18.7	262	16.0	1.91	.12
1970	768	39.7	412	21.3	431	22.3	319	16.6	3.4	.18
1973	858	38.5	505	22.6	507	22.7	358	16.0	3.94	.18
1977	831	35.6	561	24.1	560	24.0	375	16.1	4.18	.18

Source: Transportation Facts and Trends, 14th ed., Transportation Association of America, 1978, p. 8.

transport has lessened and that of motor and pipeline has made a substantial increase. Air transport has continued to advance in the movement of property. On the surface these data suggest the increased use of "premium" transportation—motor and air—by shipping firms attempting to provide the level of customer service desired by trading off higher transportation costs (by motor and air as compared to rail and water) for lower nodal costs. In 1976 the regulated (common and contract) for-hire carriers received the following freight revenues: rail, $18.0 billion; motor, $26.0 billion; oil pipeline, $2.1 billion; water, $.9 billion; and air, $1.3 billion.[11]

Railroads. All railroads in the United States are classified as common carriers* and are thus subjected to the legal service obligations to be discussed later. Since no legal restraints (ICC regulations regarding operating authority) are imposed upon railroads regarding the types of commodities to be transported, railroads have a distinct advantage as to availability and capability of providing service to "all" shippers. This is not to imply that railroads can transport any product anywhere for there are limitations upon the accessibility of rail transportation. But with respect to the ability to transport a wide variety of goods, the railroads have a distinct advantage over other common carriers in the different modes. For example, the railroads are capable of transporting dry cargo, liquid cargo, frozen foods, fresh fruits and vegetables requiring controlled temperatures, odd-shaped and -sized equipment, etc. The major point is that the railroads are not restricted as to the type of cargo to be transported; rather, all railroads are

---

* The ICC recently exempted from economic regulation the movement of fruit by railroads. This authority was given to the ICC by the 4-R Act of 1976.

Number of Companies

Market Structure

Distance and Volume

legally, as well as physically, capable of transporting all commodities tendered for transportation. This is not always the case with the other modes.

The railroad industry may be classified as consisting of a small number of large firms. In 1978, there were 42 Class I carriers (railroads with $50 million or more annual gross operating income), 64 Class II carriers (railroads with $10-$50 million annual gross operating revenue) and 215 Class III carriers (railroads with less than $10 million annual gross operating income).[12] This is a rather limited number of carriers and may suggest something as to the availability of rail carrier service. However, it needs to be pointed out that the railroads are required to provide through service and in some cases publish joint rates (one rate applying when more than one carrier is involved in the movement); the result of this regulatory require- ment is to make rail service available to points beyond the geographic limits of a particular carrier.

In part the limited number of rail carriers is attributed to the economic structure of this mode. Railroads fall within that infamous group of business undertakings labeled as "natural monopolies"; that is, a large investment (in terminals, equipment, and trackage) is necessary to begin operation and the accompanying huge capacity capable with this investment results in the railroads being a decreasing cost industry. As output (ton-miles) is in- creased, the average per unit cost of production decreases. Thus, it is economical and beneficial to society to have fewer railroads in operation in a given area and to permit these few firms to realize the economies inherent with large-scale output. To assure that the railroads do not abuse this monopolistic situation by charging very high prices (rates), all railroads are regulated as common carriers and are required to charge reasonable rates.

Railroads are primarily long-distance, large-volume movers of low- value, high-density goods. The average length of haul in 1975 was 518 miles as compared to 287 miles by truck.[13] The average size shipment is also quite high for rail transport, as evidenced by the average load of 61.7 tons for the movement of agriculture, forest, and mine products and 36.3 tons for manufactured goods.[14] The reason for these long-distance, large-volume movement characteristics for rail movement is ingrained in the economic and technical characteristics of the mode. The decreasing cost structure of railroads suggests that large-volume, long-distance movements lower the average cost of production by increasing output (ton-miles) and thereby spreading the fixed costs over a greater output base.

A major advantage of using railroad transportation is the long-distance movement of commodities in large quantities at relatively low rates. Products of forests, mines, and agriculture are the major products trans- ported by railroads. These products are characterized by low value and high density; transportation costs account for a substantial portion of the selling price of such products. As can be seen from Table 7-2, rail transportation has one of the lowest levels of revenue per ton-mile of all modes, with the rail revenue per ton-mile being the lowest of those modes capable of transporting general commodities domestically—rail, motor, and air.

TABLE 7-2

Average Revenue Per Ton-Mile

(in cents)

Year	Rail*	Motor*	Water†	Oil Pipeline	Air
1970	1.43	7.46	.303	.271	21.91
1972	1.62	8.00	.328	.285	22.75
1975	2.04	9.20	.518	.368	28.22
1977	2.29	10.47	.510	-	34.21

*Class 1 rail and motor carrier.
†Barge lines.
Source: Transportation Facts and Trends, 14th ed. (Washington: Transportation Association of America, 1978), p. 7.

*Service
Characteristics*

Low accessibility is one of the primary disadvantages of rail transport. Accessibility refers to the ability of the carrier to provide service to and from the nodes in a particular situation. Once the rail trackage is laid the rail carrier cannot deviate from this route. Therefore, if a shipper or consignee is not adjacent to the rail right of way, rail transport is not easily accessible. To use rail service when the shipper or consignee is not adjacent to the track, the shipper must utilize the services of another mode of transport, namely truck, to gain access to the rail service. Thus rail service may not be advantageous in such logistics situations as the ultimate delivery of consumer goods to retail outlets.*

Rather long transport times is another area where rail transport stands at a disadvantage. The average speed of a box car is approximately 20 miles per hour,[15] even though speeds of 50-60 miles per hour are attainable on the "open" road. The problem occurs in the classification yard where box cars are "consolidated" or marshalled into train units. This huge physical task requires the consolidating of box cars going in a similar direction and the breaking out of cars that have reached destination or that must be transferred to another train unit going toward ultimate destination of the shipment(s). This function adds to the overall slow speed of rail transport.

Other service qualities of importance to the logistics manager—reliability and safety—are rather favorably provided by railroads. Weather conditions are not as disruptive to rail service as to other modes and thereby

---

* Many railroads are making use of "piggyback" (trailer-on-flatcar) service to overcome this inherent accessibility problem. A motor truck trailer is moved on a rail flatcar between origin and destination terminals, but the trailer is transported over the highways to gain access to the consignor and consignee. Piggyback service is discussed in greater detail in the Coordinated Transportation section of this chapter.

cause minor fluctuations in transit time reliability. The movement of goods by rail transport requires considerable packaging and resultant packaging costs. This stems from the car classification operation where cars are coupled at impacts ranging from one to ten miles per hour and the rather rough ride occasioned by the steel wheels riding on steel rails. But these service qualities will differ among the carriers and must be researched with regard to particular carriers.

Motor Carriers.   The motor carrier is very much a part of any firm's logistics system; the motor truck, from the small pick-up truck to the largest tractor/semi-trailer combinations, is utilized in some capacity in almost every logistics operation. Our nation's sophisticated network of highways permits the motor carrier to reach all points of the country and therefore the motor carrier is capable of providing transportation service to virtually all shippers. Table 7-1 points out that from 1940 to 1977 the motor carriers have made great inroads into the number of ton-miles transported in the U.S.

Types of Legal Carriers

Unlike the railroads, the regulated for-hire portion of the motor carrier industry consists of both common and contract carriers. In addition, there are exempt for-hire carriers as well as private carriers. Approximately 40 percent of the intercity ton-miles of freight transported by truck is via regulated carrier—common and contract carriers; exempt and private carriers transport the remaining 60 percent of the intercity ton-miles. This is compared to the 100 percent of the intercity ton-miles transported by regulated carriers in the railroad industry, which results from all railroads being common carriers.

Exempt and private carriage in motor transportation is quite substantial. The exempt carrier primarily transports agricultural, fish, and horticultural products—the exempt commodities referred to in the next section. The private carriers have found it advantageous to transport a variety of products, but the products most commonly moved by private truck transportation are high value-high rated traffic as well as commodities that require "personalized" service such as driver-salesman operations.

Market Characteristics

The regulated motor carriers consist of a large number of relatively U.S. Coastwise carriers operate along the coast, that is, between points on is maintained through public expenditures, which reduces the entry capital Class I carriers (annual operating revenue of $3 million or more), 2,929 Class II carriers (annual operating revenue of $500,000 to $3 million) and 12,900 Class III carriers (annual operating revenue of less than $500,000).[16]

This large number of carriers is due in part to the low capital requirements for entry into the trucking business. The cost structure is characterized by high variable, low fixed costs. The motor carrier does not require extensive investment in terminals and equipment and does not invest in its own highway. The highway is built and maintained by government with the motor carrier paying for this on a use basis—highway use taxes, licenses fees, etc.; these expenses are variable and thus contribute to the high variable cost structure.

The large number of motor carriers is suggestive of a high degree of availability, i.e., there are many more motor carriers available in an area than railroads, for example, and this greater number of producers of motor transport service suggests a greater availability of motor service. However, the availability of the motor carrier is somewhat restricted by the operating authorities granted particular carriers. These operating grants place limits upon the type of commodity transported by a carrier and the area within which the carrier is permitted to provide service. A common motor carrier of property may have operating authority to transport general commodities, household goods, heavy machinery, liquid petroleum products, building materials, explosives, etc.; as a common carrier of a specific commodity a motor carrier is precluded by regulation from transporting any other commodity, except if specific authorization is given by the ICC. The area the carrier is authorized to serve may be a broad regional area, particular states, or particular cities and the authorization may restrict the carrier's provision of service over regular routes or irregular routes. The point is, the availability of regulated motor carriers is not entirely determined by the number of carriers serving an area, but rather the ability, as defined by ICC operating authority of the carriers, to transport given commodities between particular points.

Service Characteristics

The regulatory controls regarding the commodities transported and the areas served have a direct bearing upon the accessibility of particular carriers. But, the major advantage of motor transport over other modes is its inherent ability to provide service to any location. Truck transportation is not restricted to providing service to customers located adjacent to a track, waterway or airport. The truck is capable of reaching virtually all shippers since our highway system provides access to all plants, warehouses, etc. For the logistics manager the motor carrier is the most accessible mode of transportation that exists today.

Motor carrier operations do not necessitate the trailers being coupled together to form long "train" units, because each cargo unit (trailer) has its own power unit and can be operated independently. Thus on truck load movements, the shipment goes directly from the shipper to the consignee, bypassing the terminal area and the time required for consolidation. Such technical and operational characteristics enable the motor carrier to provide relatively low transit times, lower than rail and water, but higher than air.

Weather conditions and traffic conditions existing on the highways can cause disruptions in motor service and thus affect transit time reliability. These factors affect the dependability of all motor carriers, but the reliability of a specific carrier is related to the degree of operating efficiency achieved for a given link and may vary among links for a given carrier.

Motor carriers transport primarily manufactured commodities relatively short distances. Manufactured commodities are characterized by high value and include such commodity groups as: textile and leather products, rubber and plastic products, fabricated metal products, communication products and parts, photographic equipment. The average length of haul for Class I intercity carriers is approximately 277 miles. However, it should be pointed out that the motor carriers do transport low value products (coal, grain) and do move products long distances (transcontinental movements).

The physical and legal constraints as to carrying capacity make motor transport somewhat amenable to small size shipments. This has a direct impact upon inventory levels held as well as the shipment quantity necessary for gaining the lower truckload (volume discount) rate. The smaller shipment size coupled with lower transit times enable the logistics manager to reduce inventory carrying costs while maintaining or improving upon customer service levels.

The other relevant service attribute, safety, is difficult to generalize upon. The packaging required for motor carrier movements is less stringent than that required for rail or water; this results from the use of pneumatic tires and improved suspension systems that make the motor carrier ride quite smooth. Again, the actual degree of safety occasioned by a particular carrier for a given link is dependent upon the actual operations of individual carriers.

Lastly, the relatively high cost by motor carrier must be considered. As pointed out in Table 7-2, p. 208, the average revenue per ton-mile by truck is approximately five times that by rail and 20 times that by water. This again suggests that commodities moved by truck must be of high value to sustain the transportation costs or that the costs trade-offs (savings) of inventory, packaging, warehousing, and/or customer service costs warrant the use of this higher cost mode.

Water Carriers. * Water transportation has been a major factor in the development of the U.S. and remains as an important factor in today's economy. The location of many of our major cities has been influenced by water transportation, for in the early stages of the U.S. development water transportation served as the only means of connecting the U.S. to Europe which was the market area for U.S. agriculture production and the source of manufactured goods. Thus, many of the larger, industrial cities are located along major water transport routes.

Scope of Service   Domestic commodity movements take place along the Atlantic, Gulf, and Pacific coasts as well as inland via the internal navigable waterways (Mississippi, Ohio, Missouri, etc.) and the Great Lakes. Water carriers are classified as internal water carriers, Great Lakes carriers and coastwise and intercoastal carriers. Internal water carriers operate on the internal navigable waterways (Mississippi, Ohio, etc.). Great Lakes carriers operate on the Great Lakes and provide service to shippers along the northern border of the U.S. Coastwise carriers operate along the coast, that is, between point on the Atlantic, while Intercoastal carriers operate between points on the Atlantic and the Pacific via the Panama Canal.

---

* The material in this section pertains to domestic water transportation, not international.

All four legal classifications of carriers exist in water transportation. The regulated for-hire carriers (common and contract) account for a small portion of the intercity ton-miles of freight transported by water carriers. Approximately 7 percent of the ton-miles are transported by regulated carriers and the remaining 93 percent by exempt and private carriers. Of the 181 regulated carriers, there are approximately 81 carriers that earn more than $100,000 per year and the remaining 100 carriers have annual revenues that are less than this.[17]

Part of the reason for the large portion of unregulated traffic being transported in water transport is attributable to the rather low capital restraint for entry and the type of operations exempt from federal economic regulation. To begin operation as a water carrier, no investment is required for the right of way, i.e., the highway is provided by nature and the facility is maintained through public expenditures, which reduces the entry capital required to that necessary for equipment. Thus, private water transport is not precluded by the invenstment as it is for private rail transport. The exemption exists for the transportation of bulk commodities or for the transportation of bulk oil products and these types of goods are the major commodities transported by water.

The preceding discussion indicates that the cost structure of the water carrier is one of high variable costs and low fixed costs. This is similar to that found for motor transport and is attributable to the public investment for the water carrier's highway—the waterway.

Water carriers are primarily long distance movers of low value, high density cargoes that are easily loaded and unloaded by mechanical devices. Mineral, agriculture and forest products are the major commodities transported. These products are shipped in large quantities as evidenced by one barge being capable of transporting about 1,500 tons. The average length of haul is 376 miles for internal water carriers, 535 miles for Great Lakes carriers and 1,367 miles for the coastwise and intercoastal carriers.[18]

The principal advantage of using water transport is its low cost. Table 7-2, p. 208 shows that average revenue per ton-mile via water carriage is lower than that for rail, motor, and air. Thus, water transport is most advantageous for those commodities with a low value to weight relationship, or stated alternatively, for commodities in which the transportation cost is a significant portion of the selling price.

In return for this low rate, the shipper receives a slow method of movement. Possibly water transport provides the highest transit time of all modes. Internal and Great Lakes operations are affected by weather conditions—ice and low water levels cause disruption in service. In addition, the accessibility of water transport is greatly restrained. Only shippers adjacent to the waterway can use water transport directly. In other situations, the use of water carriage requires a prior or subsequent movement by land transport. Thus, the major disadvantages of water transport are long transit times and low accessibility.

Air Carriers.   Passenger movement is the principal business of the air carrier; passenger revenue accounts for the majority of air carrier business. In the movement of freight, air transport is in somewhat of an infancy stage ; air transport accounts for less than one percent of the total intercity ton-miles of freight.

Market Characteristics   The air carrier industry is made up of a small number of carriers and all major commercial air carriers are regulated by the Civil Aeronautics Board (CAB) as common carriers. The CAB economic regulation is similar to that exercised over land carriers by the ICC; rates and fares as well as levels of service are regulated. The air regulation is definitely promotional in nature and is directed toward providing a stable supply of air transport. As of 1978, air cargo operations have been deregulated, i.e., air cargo is exempt.

Reference to the type of air carrier takes somewhat of a different form than the common, contract, etc. Air carriers are classified as a) domestic trunk lines—carriers operating between principal population centers; b) feeder or local service—carriers operating between lesser populated centers "feeding" into the major population centers; c) intra-Hawaiian—carriers operating within the State of Hawaii; d) Alaskan—carriers operating with the State of Alaska and between Alaska and the continental U.S.; e) international and overseas—carriers operating between the U.S. and foreign countries; f) helicopter—carriers using helicopters to provide pick-up and delivery service between airports and downtowns; g) all cargo—carriers carrying freight only, not passengers; h) supplemental—carriers providing charter service primarily; and i) air taxi—carriers operating exempt from CAB economic regulation.*

Cost Characteristics   The cost structure of the air carrier consists of high variable costs in proportion to fixed costs, somewhat akin to the motor carrier cost structure. Like motor and water carriers, the air carriers do not invest in the highway-airway. Terminals are built by government and lease payments and landing fees are paid for their use; these costs are variable. However, the equipment cost is quite high, but it is still a small part of the total costs.

Freight movement by the major commercial air carriers started as a by-product of the passenger business. Excess capacity existed in the "belly" of the plane and thereby offered potential for the movement of freight. Cargo was moved as incidental to the primary movement of passengers, but as cargo demand grew the carriers began to give serious consideration to this business arena. Now, the domestic trunk line and international and overseas carriers have dedicated equipment specifically to freight movement and have developed and operated freight service to meet the evergrowing needs of freight shippers. The all-cargo lines have always concentrated upon cargo transportation.

---

*   For additional discussion of the types of air carriers, see: Ray J. Sampson and Martin T. Farris, *Domestic Transportation*, 4th ed. (Boston: Houghton Mifflin Co., 1979), pp. 79-83.

The major advantage of using air transportation is speed. Air transport affords a distinct advantage in low transit time over large distances. Thus, air transport is a necessary means of movement for emergency shipments or shipments that have a high degree of perishability both in the physical sense of spoilage and in the service realm of lost sales or productivity.

Cost is the major disadvantage of using air transportation and precludes many shippers from utilizing this mode. The average revenue per ton-mile for air carriers is approximately 20 times that of rail and three times that by motor. (See Table 7-2) This suggests that commodities with high value to weight relationships can sustain this high transport cost. For such commodities air transport is a viable transport method; transportation is a smaller portion of the selling price than is inventory holding costs. In this shipping situation the logistics manager can reduce inventory levels and inventory costs and rely upon the speed of air transport to meet nodal demand.

Accessibility of air transport is somewhat limited. Most firms using air carriers must rely upon land carriers to make the freight available at the airport. The most common and most feasible mode used is the motor carrier; both local for-hire and private motor carriage are utilized to overcome the air carrier accessibility problem.

The reliability of air transport is also somewhat of a disadvantage. Air service is definitely subject to interruptions caused by weather conditions. These conditions result in increased transit time and adjusted higher inventory levels. But with the advent of instrument flying and the adoption of these devices at a greater number of airports this interruption in service is decreasing.

Air transport has become a very viable alternative to water (ocean) transport for international shipments. The reduced transit time by air plus the reductions in tie-ups and handling costs at ports enable exporters and importers to reduce overall logistics costs and improve upon customer service. Again, the high rate via air must be traded off against reductions in other logistics costs in order to justify use of this method of transport.

Pipelines. The pipeline industry refers to oil pipelines and not natural gas pipelines. All oil pipelines are regulated as common carriers and there are approximately 100 such carriers; natural gas pipelines are regulated by the Federal Power Commission, the same as any public utility.

The pipeline is not an acceptable method for moving general commodities, rather its use is restricted to the movement of liquid petroleum products. Some attempts have been made to move commodities such as coal in a slurry form; the movement of such commodities by pipeline has not been a viable alternative to other modes, namely water and rail. Pipeline transportation is not a suitable form for general commodity transportation.

The pipeline cost structure is one of high fixed costs and low variable costs, quite similar to that existing for the railroads. The investment in the line, terminals and pumping stations is the major factor contributing to this cost structure.

EXHIBIT 7-1

Performance rating of modes by selection determinant

Selection Determinants	MODES				
	Railroad	Motor	Water	Air	Pipeline
Cost	3	4	2	5	1
Transit Time	3	2	4	1	-
Reliability	2	1	4	3	-
Capability	1	2	4	3	5
Accessibility	2	1	4	3	-
Security	3	2	4	1	-

1 = best, lowest; 5 = worst, highest

Low cost, as compared to other modes, is the major advantage to using oil pipelines. However, the inability to transport solids limits its usefulness in the logistics system of a firm manufacturing durable goods.

Summary. The logistics manager's decision as to the mode of transportation to utilize is based upon cost and service characteristics. The relative advantages and disadvantages of each mode are summarized in Exhibit 7-1. The reader must recognize that the ratings are generalizations; the exact relationship among specific carriers of different modes may vary.

Legal Classifications of Carriers

Transportation firms engaged in interstate transportation of property are classified into four categories: (1) common, (2) contract, (3) exempt, and (4) private. The first three are for-hire carriers while the latter is not a for-hire carrier, that is, private transportation is provided by the firm desiring movement of its goods and the service of a private carrier is not made available (sold) to other shippers.

Common Carrier. The common carrier is a for-hire carrier that holds itself out to serve the general public at reasonable charges and without discrimination. The common carrier is the most highly regulated (from the standpoint of economic matters) of all the legal types of carriers. The economic regulation imposed upon these carriers is directed toward protecting the shipping public and insuring sufficient supply, within normal limits, of transport service. Thus, use of a common carrier in the logistics system requires the logistics manager to have knowledge of these regulations as to the effect of same upon the type and quality of transport possible by common carriers. A thorough discussion of transportation regulation is not intended here, rather, the implications of these regulations upon the quality

*Service
Requirements*

and cost of common carrier link service is of primary concern. The distinguishing facets of the common carrier are rooted in the level of economic regulation imposed upon the carriers.

The essence of this regulation is found in the legal service requirements imposed upon the common carrier. These requirements are: to serve, to deliver, to non-discriminate, and to charge reasonable rates. Embedded within these service requirements is the underlying principle of public protection, for the common carrier is recognized as being a business enterprise affecting public interest. To guarantee the continued provision of the level and quality of transportation service required for the economy to function, the federal government has resorted to regulatory controls to achieve these objectives. These legal service requirements are not imposed upon the other types of carriage.

Duty of Service

The requirement that the common carrier serve the public entails the carrier's transporting all commodities offered to it. The common carrier cannot refuse to carry a particular commodity or to serve a particular point within the carrier's scope of operation. This suggests that the logistics manager is assured a supply of transport service since the common carrier cannot refuse to transport the firm's commodities, even if the movement is not the most profitable for the carrier. There are, however, two qualifications upon this requirement to serve: one, the carrier is required to provide service up to the limits of its physical capacity, where capacity is determined by the level of plant necessary to meet normal carrier demand, and second, the common carrier is required to serve those shippers within the carrier's shipping public. For example, a common carrier motor carrier of household goods is not required to serve a shipper of bulk oils; the bulk oil shipper is not within the carrier's public.

Entry into the common carrier sector of transportation is regulated by the Interstate Commerce Commission (ICC) for rail, motor, and water and by the Civil Aeronautics Board (CAB) for air. A common carrier must prove to the regulatory agency that a public necessity exists for the proposed service and that the provision of the proposed service will be a public convenience. It may be argued that this regulatory constraint upon entry is a protective device for the sole benefit of the carrier, but in the long run, protection of the carrier is also protection of the public. Entry control protects the common carrier from excessive amounts of ruinous competition and thereby assures a continuous and stable supply of transportation to the public.

*Duty of Safe
Delivery*

The delivery requirement refers to the common carrier's liability for the goods entrusted into the carrier's care. The common carrier is required to deliver the goods in the same condition as they were when tendered to the carrier at origin of the shipment, or more specifically, the common carrier is liable for all loss and damage or delay resulting to goods while in the care of the carrier. There are limited exceptions to this absolute level of liability; they are Acts of God, Acts of Public Enemy, Acts of Public Authority, Acts of the Shipper, and the Inherent Defects of the Goods. The logistics manager, then, is able to transfer the risk of cargo damage, or the bearing of this risk, to the carrier when the common carrier is used over the link. The ICC assures the shipping public that the common carrier is capable of paying such cargo liability claims by either controlling the financial stability of the carrier or requiring the common carrier to purchase cargo liability insurance. It should be pointed out that the shipper indirectly pays for this transfer of cargo damage risk to the carrier through the carrier's building this factor into its pricing structure.

*Duty to Not
Discriminate*

Additional protection for the shipping public is found in the requirement that the common carrier not discriminate among shippers, commodities, or places. Discrimination is the charging of different rates and/or the providing of different types of service for essentially similar movements of similar goods. It should be recognized, however, that there are forms of permissible discrimination. For example, the charging of lower rates for volume movements and higher rates for less than volume movements is discriminating in favor of the larger volume shipper. But, the volume rates must be the same for all shippers shipping a given commodity between two given points and vice versa for the less-than-volume rate. Cost difference also justifies quoting different rates for volume, and less-than-volume movements.

*Duty to Charge
Reasonable Rates*

Finally, the duty to charge reasonable rates constrains the carrier from charging excessively high rates which is entirely possible with controlled entry. The regulatory bodies are conferred the responsibility of protecting the shipping public from excessive rates that result in excessively high profits, profits that are above those considered reasonable for the industry. At the same time the regulatory bodies are intrusted with the responsibility of assuring that the carrier rates are high enough to insure the survival of the carrier and consequently the continued supply of service to the public. Therefore, this requirement has two protective dimensions: protection of the shipping public from rates that are too high and protection of the carrier from charging rates that are too low, with the latter ultimately resulting in the protection of the public through the assurance of the continued supply of transportation service.

An unusual pricing procedure exists in the common carrier sector, the joint publication of rates by carriers. The carriers get together and publish rates through rate bureaus which results in the equality of rates charged by competing carriers in one mode. This form of collective pricing is permitted under the Reed-Bulwinkle Act of 1948. The ICC still oversees the reasonableness of the rates and the carriers have the ability to take independent action—to charge a rate that is different from its competitors.

In summary, the common carrier might be considered the backbone of the transportation industry. The common carrier makes itself available to the public, without providing special treatment to any one party, and is regulated as to the rates charged, the liability assumed, and the service provided. The common carrier is used quite extensively in most logistics systems.

Definition

Contract Carrier. The contract carrier is a for-hire carrier that does not hold itself out to serve the general public, but rather serves one or a limited number of shippers under specific contract with these shippers. The contract carrier is also regulated with respect to economic matters but there are no legal service obligations imposed upon the contract carrier. The terms of the contract contain provision pertaining to the rates to be charged, liability, type of service, equipment, etc., that is to be provided by the carrier. Usually the rates via contract carrier are lower than by common carriers. The regulatory bodies do control entry into this sector of transportation, but the requirement of proving public convenience and necessity is eliminated for securing contract carrier authority.

Service

The contract carrier provides a specialized type of service to the shipper. The carrier does not serve the public in general and therefore can tailor its services to meet the needs of the specific shipper(s). Since the contract carrier does not serve the public and therefore does not have general purpose equipment, it is possible for the carrier to utilize special equipment and to arrange pick-ups and deliveries to satisfy the few shippers with whom the carrier is contracted. In general it may be assumed that contract carriage is essentially similar to that possible with private transportation, at least in terms of the level of service provided.

Scope of Operations

One serious problem exists in the use of a contract carrier and that pertains to the availability of same. Unlike the common carrier that is required to be available to all, the contract carrier is available only to those shippers with whom the carrier has signed a contract and to those shippers for whom the contract carrier has secured a permit from the ICC or CAB to serve. Thus, the contract carrier is not as readily available as the common carrier and the establishment of a contract carrier to serve a firm will entail the logistics manager's intervention and assistance in the carrier's obtaining a contract authority to operate as a contract carrier.

Definition

Exempt Carriers. The exempt carrier is a for-hire carrier that is not regulated with respect to economic matters, i.e., this carrier is exempt from economic regulation. There are no regulations governing rates charged or services provided by the exempt carrier. The laws of the market place determine the rates, services and supply of such carriers. The only controls to entry into this sector of the transport industry are those pertaining to capital requirements, which are not seriously restrictive for some modes.

Service

An exempt carrier gains this status by the type of commodity hauled or by the nature of its operation. For example, a motor carrier is classified as an exempt carrier when exclusively transporting agricultural products, newspapers, livestock and fish. With respect to the type of operation, examples would include motor carriers whose operations are primarily local, water carriers that transport bulk commodities (e.g. coal, ore, grain, etc.) or water carriers that haul bulk liquid in tank vessels.

By reason of the limited amount of exempt carriers, that is the limited number of areas where exempt carriers are possible, the availability of such carriers is restrictive. But for those commodities movements, such as agricultural products, for example, where exempt carriage is possible, such firms make significant use of these carriers. The primary reason for using an exempt carrier is that of lower transport rates. For the movement of industrial commodities, the exempt carrier is not a viable means of link service.

Definition

Private Carrier. Private carriage essentially is a firm that provides its own transportation. The private carrier is not for-hire and not subject to federal economic regulations. More specifically, private carriage is any person who transports in interstate or foreign commerce property of which such person is the owner, lessee, or bailee, when such transportation is for the purpose of sale, lease, rent or bailment, or in furtherance of any commercial enterprise.[19] The crucial aspect of the legal distinction of a private carrier is that the transportation function must not be the primary business of the controlling firm, or stated differently, the primary business of the owner of the carrier must be some commercial endeavor other than transportation.

The most prevalent type of private transportation is via motor vehicle; the preponderance of private motor vehicle fleets has made private carrier synonymous with private motor carrier. One estimate on the importance of private trucking is that in 1967, 75 percent of the trucks were involved in private transportation [20] The relative ease of capital requirement for entry into motor transport and the high degree of accessibility via motor vehicle has made this mode most advantageous to shippers desirous of providing their own transportation. It should be pointed out that private transportation by water does exist primarily for the movement of bulk raw materials. To a much lesser extent private rail carriers prevail in the movement of bulk products short distances, e.g., within a plant, between plants, or from plants to rail sidings. Private aircraft has made substantial inroads in the movement of company personnel and to a lesser degree the movement of emergency shipments of property for a firm.

Rationale

The basic reasons for a firm to enter into private transportation are cost and service. With the trend of for-hire carrier rates on the increase, many firms have found private transport a means of controlling transportation costs. Basically, transport costs can be reduced by private transportation if the private carrier operation is conducted as efficiently as for-hire operations. If this same degree of efficiency is possible, private transport theoretically should be lower in cost since the for-hire carrier profit is eliminated. However, one major operational problem, the empty back haul,* has resulted in elevated costs.

The increased customer demand for "good" service can be realized by private carriage. George W. Wilson has pointed out the service advantage as follows:

---

* The empty back haul refers to a vehicle going from origin to destination loaded and returning empty.

Advantages
Normally a shipper can obtain more rapid delivery or expedited movement to a particular buyer in cases of urgent demand, assuming some spare transportation capacity. This enhances customer good will. There is also greater assurance of the safe delivery of goods not mixed with those of other shippers where LTL shipments are involved. There is a certain value in terms of advertising and perhaps prestige in having the shippers name on transport facilities. There is also an increased ability to reduce congestion at the loading dock, since one can schedule pickups to suit one's convenience to a greater extent than is possible through reliance upon common carriage.[21]

Disadvantages
Private transportation does contain some disadvantages. The main disadvantages are large capital investments required as well as labor and management problems. The capital invested in the transport fleet has alternative uses in other operations of the firm and this capital must provide a return that is at least equal to other investment opportunities. The labor problems are those associated with the firm's dealing with a new labor union. Also, administrative problems may arise when existing managers are utilized in the management of a private transport operation.

The use of private transportation is a viable and an increasingly important component of a logistics system. The cost and service benefits afforded to a firm make this a serious alternative to for-hire transportation.

Summary

The logistics manager must make the decision as to what legal type of carriers to use in the provision of link service. There are four legal types of carriers: common, contract, exempt, and private. Federal economic regulations impose certain restrictions upon the operation of the common and contract carrier, whereas no such economic regulation is imposed upon the exempt and private carrier. The common carrier is the most highly regulated of all carrier types, with controls established to deal with the rates and services provided.

Coordinated Transportation

Definition
Coordinated transport services refer to the use of two or more carriers of different modes in the through movement of the shipment. Such services are offered to the public by the carriers via the publication of one rate from origin to destination by carriers of different modes. In other situations the logistics manager, through routing, makes use of different modes in getting a product to final destination.

Rationale
It is often necessary for the logistics manager to utilize different modes of transport to service a given link. Numerous reasons could be put forth as to why coordinated services are necessary, but basically the reasons are the

service characteristics and costs of the various modes. For example, the limited accessibility of air transport requires coordination with some land carrier to make the pick-up and delivery movements. Similar examples of accessibility restraints could be given for rail, water and pipeline, but not for motor which has a definite advantage in this area. By manipulating the modes a logistics manager can overcome rather disadvantageous service qualities of a given mode and yet retain the mode's basic advantage, usually low costs. This is the primary motivation in the combination of rail and water in the movement of coal or grain; the rail segment improves upon the accessibility of water transport and the water portion permits savings in the low cost service for the long distance portion of the move.

The result of coordinated services is the maximization of the primary advantages inherent in the modes and the minimization of the disadvantages, but the combined services will have both the good and bad aspects of the modes utilized. For example, the coordination of rail and water will have a lower total cost than an all rail movement, but a higher cost than all water. Likewise, the transit time via the combined system will be lower than all water, but higher than all rail. The decision to use combined modes must rest with the impact upon total cost of the logistics function.

Types

Various types of coordinated services exist. These are shown in Figure 7-1. The most prevalent forms have been the truck-rail, truck-water and truck-air. However, rail-water, pipeline-water, and pipeline-truck also are found.

The rather extensive use of the motor carrier in coordinated service is attributable to the extremely high degree of accessibility afforded by motor transport. The services labeled as birdyback, fishyback, and piggyback are examples of coordination in which the motor carrier trailer, with the cargo intact, is physically transferred to another mode. In the case of birdyback the accessibility of motor is combined with the speed of the airline; in fishyback, motor accessibility is coupled with the low cost water carriage; and in piggyback, the accessibility of the truck is added to the low cost rail service. However, in each case the combined service shows traces of the disadvantages of one of the other modes involved, e.g., birdyback has the disadvantage of the high cost inherent to air transport.

Limitations

One substantial stumbling block to coordinated service is the reluctance of the carriers to participate. The ICC has the power to require rail and water carriers to cooperate, but this power does not exist for other modal pairs. The carriers are willing, even eager, to coordinate in situations where the participating carriers enjoy movements that normally could not be transported in its entirety by any one of the carriers coordinating. But, for situations in which a carrier can transport the commodity the entire distance over its own lines, the carriers are hesitant to coordinate with other carriers.

Another problem that exists with coordinated services is the rehandling of freight from one mode to another. This creates time delays and adds to the cost of transporting the freight. This problem has been eliminated in some forms of coordination in which the motor carrier trailer is transferred to

FIGURE 7-1   Types of coordinated services.

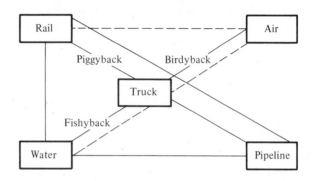

another mode of transport. But, for situations in which a carrier can transport the commodity the entire distance over its own lines, the carriers are hesitant to coordinate with other carriers.

Another problem that exists with coordinated services is the rehandling of freight from one mode to another. This creates time delays and adds to the cost of transporting the freight. This problem has been eliminated in some forms of coordination in which the motor carrier trailer is transferred to another mode of transport. But, the transferability of the motor carrier trailer is a special form of coordination termed containerization, the trailer being a container.

Simply stated, a container is a big box into which is placed the commodities to be shipped. After initial loading, the commodities per se are not rehandled in shipment until they are unloaded at destination. Through the course of the movement, the container is handled and not the commodities. The container can be transferred from one mode to another mode eliminating the need to handle the commodities each time. The reduction in handling of the commodity reduces handling costs, the cost of damage, theft and pilferage and the time required to complete the modal transfer.

Containerization   Containerization changes the materials handling function from a labor intensive to a capital intensive operation. Less labor is required to handle containerized freight because the container is too large and too heavy to be manually moved. The materials handling system is modified to include cranes and forklift trucks—equipment capable of handling the large, heavy container. Many firms have found this to be a desirable avenue for increasing productivity and controlling materials handling costs, especially in periods of continual labor cost increases.

Notable acceptance of containerization has been gained in international distribution. The time and cost associated with shipment handling at the ports are reduced as well as damage and theft. Some firms have found that containerizing shipments to foreign markets has resulted in 10-20 percent reductions in costs and has increased the level of service provided to foreign markets.

Two major problems have plagued general adoption of containers for international movements—the lack of suitable container standards and the reluctance of shippers and carriers to invest in the container. The International Standards Organization has been working toward the development of international standards, but the multiplicity of constraints imposed by the physical (modal equipment, street widths, etc.) limitations of various countries have placed barriers to the transferability of the container among transport facilities of various nations. The question of who will invest in the container is directly related to the unbalanced movements among nations and the resultant question of who is to incur the cost of moving the empty container back to origin.

Piggyback.   Piggyback or Trailer on Flatcar (TOFC) is a specialized form of containerization in which rail and motor transport coordinate. In piggyback, the motor carrier trailer is placed on a rail flatcar and moved the long distance portion by rail and the short pick-up and delivery portions by motor truck. This service combines the long haul, low cost advantage of rail with the accessibility of motor.

There are five basic plans of piggyback available. The plans are restricted as to the groups that can utilize each. The plans and their availability are as follows:

Plan I: This plan is available to for-hire motor carriers (common and contract). The railroad provides the motive power, flatcar and right of way. The railroad does not participate in the origination of the commodity inside the trailer; the for-hire motor carrier originates the shipment and has all shipper responsibility.

Plan II: This is an all rail plan in which the railroad offers piggyback service to the shipping public. The railroad provides the trailer and pick-up and delivery service—door-to-door service. The railroad originates the shipment and has all shipper responsibility.

Plan II¼: Plan II¼ is a modification of Plan II in which the railroad continues to provide the trailer but offers either pick-up or delivery, but not both. This is useful when the shipper of consignee owns or leases a truck. A lower rate is charged for Plan II¼ than for Plan II.

Plan II½: This is another hybrid of Plan II. The trailer is still provided by the railroad but neither pick-up nor delivery is provided. This is a ramp-to-ramp service and a lower charge is assessed than that for either Plans II or II¼.

Plan III: The railroad furnishes the flatcar, motive power and right of way, but the shipper provides the trailer. Under this plan the shipper is incurring the cost of the trailer ownership and the rates for Plan III are lower than Plan II rates.

Plan IV: Under this plan the railroad provides ramp-to-ramp service of the shipper's trailer and flatcar. The shipper makes a greater investment (trailer and flatcar) in the transportation equipment and a rate lower than both Plans II and III is charged.

Plan V: This is a truly coordinated plan offered by cooperating railroads and for-hire motor carriers. The two modes publish joint rates (one rate) for an origin-destination link and each participates in the movement and revenue.

The vast majority of the piggyback shipments move under Plans II, II¼ and II½. Since Plans III and IV require an investment or lease of equipment, these plans are not used to any great extent by shippers. Plan I has been used by motor carriers to reduce the imbalance in load patterns. Lastly, Plan V generates very little volume since it requires the joint efforts of a railroad and motor carrier and, without required coordination, this will occur when it is mutually beneficial to both parties.

Indirect and Special Carriers

The transport methods grouped under this category offer specialized or intermediary type transportation service. In some cases these carriers have line haul equipment and in others these carriers merely provide pick-up and delivery movements and perform the consolidation function.

The movement of small shipments (less than 500 lbs.) creates serious operational problems for the major modes. The small shipments must be consolidated into larger size shipments in order for the move to be economical for the carrier. Added time and costs are occasioned by the carrier resulting in extended transit times and transportation charges for the small shipments.

A number of transportation companies, namely bus, express and package carriers, have concentrated upon such freight movements. The bus lines are moving small packages in the luggage compartments of the vehicle. These carriers have small cargo carrying capacity, the space not required for passenger luggage, and therefore do not require large size shipments to make this service economical for the bus lines. Coupled with the frequent schedules, the bus lines offer a viable alternative to the logistics manager faced with the distribution of many small package shipments.

United Parcel Service

A common carrier motor carrier, United Parcel Service (UPS) has made great strides in the efficient movement of small shipments. UPS has been an innovator in terminal handling and scheduling of pick-up and delivery movements and has been able to profitably transport the small shipment while providing better service and lower transit time than other major modes. There are regulatory limitations as to the type of package that can be transported by UPS; presently these restrictions are: (1) a maximum weight of 50 pounds per package and, (2) a maximum length and girth of 108 inches.

Other express companies exist for air transportation. These agencies provide excellent care and speed in the movement of air freight. But the cost of such service is quite high and prohibitive for low-value, high-density commodities. The major advantage of using an express company is the low transit time offered which is extremely important for emergency shipments.

Freight Forwarders   Domestic surface freight forwarders are regulated as common carriers although such transport companies do not provide intercity transportation in their own intercity (line haul) equipment. The freight forwarder collects small shipments from shippers, consolidates these shipments into large loads, and presents the consolidated shipments to railroads or motor carriers for the intercity movement. At destination the freight forwarder breaks down the individual shipments and delivers same to the correct consignee. The freight forwarder realizes its revenue from the difference between the high less-than-volume rate paid by the shipper and the lower volume rate assessed by the for-hire carrier the freight forwarder uses. The main advantage of using a freight forwarder is lower transit time for small shipments. The freight forwarder has the same legal service obligations imposed upon it than does any common carrier railroad, motor carrier or water carrier subject to ICC regulations.

International freight forwarders also exist and provide, in addition to that described above, clerical assistance in the voluminous documentation associated with international movements. The international freight forwarder is an essential element in an international logistics system when the international portion of the firm's business is small and the firm cannot economically justify hiring the expertise necessary to control international moves.

Lastly, an indirect form of transportation known as the shippers association has developed for the movement of small shipments for shippers. The shippers association performs the consolidation function for its members, presents the larger loads to for-hire carriers and pays a lower rate for the larger volume movement. The association passes on the lower volume rate to the members, thus benefiting the shipper members.

SUMMARY

In this chapter consideration was given to the carrier selection decision for the provision of the link service in the logistics system. The determinant used to evaluate potential link suppliers consists of the direct link cost plus the link service qualities that have a direct bearing upon the cost of nodal operations. The characteristics of the transportation suppliers was given in light of the carrier selection framework.

In the next chapter, the nature of the rates and services afforded by the transportation companies is considered. Knowledge of these facets of the transportation system is fundamental to the operation and control of the logistics link.

Study Questions

1. What criteria should be used to evaluate alternative modes and carriers? Why?
2. Compare and contrast the important characteristics of the four legal classes of carriers.
3. Of what importance are the legal service requirements that are imposed upon a common carrier?
4. Define discrimination.
5. Compare and contrast the advantages and disadvantages of the five basic modes.
6. What caused the railroads to become primarily long distance, large volume movers of low-value, high-density goods?
7. Why do regulated motor carriers primarily consist of a large number of relatively small firms?
8. Define coordinated transportation and describe the most used forms.
9. What are the advantages and disadvantages of using coordinated transportation compared to using one of the five basic modes?
10. Explain the effect of containerization on the logistics function.
11. What are the indirect and special carriers? Explain why their services are needed.

Notes

1. A. M. Milne and J. C. Laight, *The Economics of Inland Transportation,* 2nd ed. (London: Sir Isaac Pittman & Sons, 1963), pp. 11-17.
2. Transportation Association of America, *Transportation Facts and Trends*, 14th ed. (Washington, D.C.: Transportation Association of America, 1974), p. 4, and January 1979 supplement.
3. Milne and Laight, *loc. cit.*.
4. D. W. DeHayes, Jr., "Industrial Transportation Planning: Estimating Transit Time for Rail Carload Shipments," *Transportation Research Forum Papers,* 1969, p. 101.
5. Donald J. Bowersox, Edward W. Smykay, and Bernard J. LaLonde, *Physical Distribution Management,* rev. ed. (New York; Macmillan Co., 1968), p. 144.
6. Martin T. Farris and Paul T. McElhiney, eds., *Modern Transportation: Selected Readings* (Boston: Houghton Mifflin Co., 1967), p. 209.
7. Kenneth U. Flood, *Traffic Management*, 3rd ed. (Dubuque, Iowa: Wm. C. Brown Co., 1975), pp. 15-19.
8. M. J. Roberts and Associates, "Intermodal Freight Transportation Coordination: Problems and Potential" (University of Pittsburgh: Graduate School of Business, 1966), p. 126.

9. R. H. Ballou and D. W. DeHayes Jr., "Transport Selection by Interfirm Analysis," *Transportation and Distribition Management,* 7, No.6 (June 1967), pp. 33-37.

10. See for example: P. Ronald Stephenson and Ronald P. Willet, "Selling with Physical Distribution Services," *Business Horizons,* XI, No. 6 (December 1968), pp. 75-85

11. *Transportation Facts and Trends, op. cit.,* p. 6.

12. Interstate Commerce Commission, 92nd *Annual Report* (Washington: Government Printing Office, 1978), p. 132.

13. *Transportation Facts and Trends, op. cit.,* p. 14.

14. Dudley, F. Pegrum, *Transportation: Economics and Public Policy,* 3rd ed. (Homewood, Illinois; Richard D. Irwin, Inc., 1973), p. 28.

15. Association of American Railroads, "Railroad Facts," 1974 ed. (Washington: Association of American Railroads, 1974), p. 45.

16. Interstate Commerce Commission, *loc. cit.*

17. Interstate Commerce Commission, *ibid.*

18. *Transportation Facts and Trends, loc. cit.*

19. *Interstate Commerce Act,* Section 203(17) (Washington: Government Printing Office, 1958), p. 123.

20. "The Elements of Private Carriage" (Washington: The Traffic Service Corporation, no date), Monograph, p. 1.

21. George W. Wilson, *Essays on Some Unsettled Questions in the Economics of Transportation.* (Indiana University Business Report, No. 42, 1962), pp. 173-74.

Case 7-1
American Products, Ltd.

American Products, Ltd., is a newly formed conglomerate that produces a wide variety of household products, from toaster ovens to refrigerators to television sets.

American Products is located in Denver, Colorado. The production facilities consist of 23 buildings on a 200 acre lot. The entire product line is manufactured and warehoused at the Denver location.

The raw materials used in the production of American's products come from throughout the United States. The majority of these products are transported by rail with the remaining supplies coming in by truck common carrier.

The American complex at Denver has extensive rail sidings and truck bays, and there are very few problems with the coordination of incoming supplies to the plant.

Although there are no problems encountered with the inbound logistics activities (those of physical supply to the manufacturing complex), this is not quite the case for the outbound logistics activities (the physical distribution of the finished products to the consignees).

Because of the extensive rail sidings at the American Complex, rail common carriage is the predominant means of transport for the commodities leaving Denver bound for the a destination greater than 200 miles from the plant. The commodities that are shipped 200 miles or less go by motor common carrier.

American's traffic department is very efficient, and periodically, an analysis of the logistics activities takes place.

A checklist of specific variables has been developed by the traffic department, and the analysis focuses on these variables and their relation or possible relation to American's logistics activities.

Checklist

1. Transport mode selection
2. The carrier selection decision
   a. transport cost
   b. transit time and reliability
   c. capability and accessibility
   d. security
3. The type of transport system used
   a. rail common carrier vs. a rail private fleet
   b. motor common carrier vs. private motor fleet

Use the checklist provided and analyze American's present operations from a transport perspective.

1. List criteria both pro and con for the two types of transport systems presently used by American. (Analyze the systems using the data provided in section 2 in the above checklist.)
2. Make any conclusions or recommendations which you feel will improve American's logistics sytems.

| Chapter 8 | Transportation Rates and Services |

After studying this chapter, you should be able to:

- Present an overview of the regulation, controls, and policy that affect the rates of transportation agencies that may be utilized by the logistics manager.

- Discuss the basic factors that affect the rates charged by transportation services.

- Explain the basic types of rates and demonstrate how to determine the appropriate transportation charges.

- Discuss some of the special rates offered by carriers and explain why they are utilized.

- Explain some of the special services offered by carriers.

The preceding chapter analyzed the various modes of transportation within the link selection decision framework. In this chapter our attention is directed toward that murky quagmire of transportation rates and services. Specifically, we will examine the somewhat unique characteristics of the transportation pricing system, the services offered by common carriers, and the controls applicable to this almost alien field. Before the actual rate structures are considered, a brief review of Federal rate regulation is given.

RATE REGULATION*

Federal regulation of transportation and transportation rates has been with us since passage of the Act to Regulate Commerce of 1887. The years immediately preceding the enactment of this law were full of turmoil, both for the shippers and the carriers. Inland transportation was basically railroad and the carriers were charging high rates when possible and discriminating against small shippers. The need to exercise control over transportation industry was important to the growth of our economy and to the assurance of a stable supply of transportation services compatible with the needs of an expanding society.

Initial Period   The original act required carriers (railroads) to charge "reasonable" rates and to publish their rates in tariffs which were to be made available to the public and filed with the Interstate Commerce Commission (ICC). Also, the act precluded personal discrimination, undue preference or prejudice, and long and short haul discrimination (charging more for a shorter haul than a longer haul when the shorter is included within the longer). From 1887 to 1920, amendments were made to the original act, but these amendments were directed toward increasing ICC control and enforcement powers. This period of regulation is best characterized as being negative, restricting the carrier from providing rates and services that were not in the best interest of society, and is best exemplified by the ICC's power to regulate the maximum level of rates.

Post-World War I Period   The period after 1920 witnessed a change in regulatory policy—from being very restrictive to being more carrier promotional. This emanated from the financial chaos experienced by the railroads as a result of severe intramodal competition and intermodal competition of the emerging motor carrier; the regulations were directed toward promoting the viability of the carrier. Power was given to the ICC to control the minimum level of rates, i.e., the concept of "reasonable rates" assumed the dimension of being compensatory to the carrier. The rates charged by carriers must be high enough to compensate the carrier for the costs incurred in the provision of the service. This protective nature of transportation regulation is indirectly the protection of the public through providing some assurance of carrier

---

* For a thorough discussion of Transportation Regulation see: Robert C. Lieb, *Transportation: The Domestic System* (Reston, Va.: Reston Publishing Co., 1978), chapters 11-14.

Current Period

*Nature of Rate
Regulation*

Procedures

Rate Bureaus

viability and, thereby, a degree of stability of transportation supply for the shipping public.

Today, the ICC administers the Federal economic regulations for railroads, motor carriers, water carriers (domestic as opposed to international water carriers), pipelines, and freight forwarders. Federal economic controls for air carriers are administered by the Civil Aeronautic Board (CAB). Basically the rate (economic) regulation for all modes is the same, and characteristic of that found in the original act.

A common misconception of the Federal transport rate regulation is that the regulatory commissions establish the rates that are charged by the common and contract carriers. This most definitely is not the case. The carriers develop the rates they will charge and file same with the regulatory agencies. The agencies, upon receiving complaints from shippers or carriers or upon their own initiative, may undertake a study of the reasonableness of the proposed rate; if the rate is found to be unreasonable, the agencies have the power to set aside the proposed rate. The carrier, not the regulatory commissions, initiates the rates which are then subject to regulatory scrutiny.

Rate changes proposed by carriers do not take effect immediately. A rate change does not become effective until 30 days after the rate proposal is made. This "waiting" period provides time for shippers and other carriers to examine and determine the impact of such carrier rate action and permits such interested parties to file protests with the regulatory agencies. The protest then sets in motion the commissions' examination of the reasonableness of the rate. If no protests are filed and the commissions do not exercise the power to examine the rate without protest, the rate change becomes effective within 30 days.

Common rail and motor carriers establish rates on a cooperative basis, i.e., the carriers within one mode get together to determine the rates to be charged the shipping public. This practice is grounded in the rate bureau concept. The rate bureau acts as the rate publication agent for participating carriers. The effect of rate bureau publication of rates is the minimization of price competition among the transportation companies. However, this collective pricing procedure was legalized by the Reed-Bulwinkle Act of 1948 which excluded such practices from antitrust laws. Such collective prices (rates) still must pass the ICC requirement for reasonableness which precludes the possibility of monopolistic profits being realized by the cooperating carriers.

Collective pricing in transportation is necessitated by the interchange of traffic between and among carriers so as to permit the efficient and economical movement of commodities beyond the operating scope (both in terms of physical facilities and regulatory sanction) of the originating carrier. Such practices also reduce carrier costs associated with the publication of tariffs and at the same time reduce the complexity, in terms of the number of tariffs to be reviewed to determine the appropriate rate, of the carrier pricing mechanism.

EXHIBIT 8-1   Rate bureau rate-making procedures.

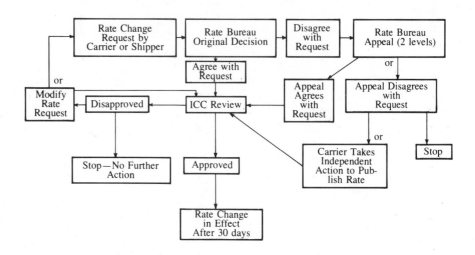

Essentially, the use of rate bureaus results in all participating carriers charging the same rate for a given commodity movement, as alluded to in the previous chapter. However, each participating carrier in the bureau has the right of independent action: this permits the carrier to establish a rate that is higher or lower than the one ascribed by the bureau. Such independent action does occur and this adds some degree of competitiveness to the rate, but generally not a great deal. Thus, common carriers are not usually price competitive, but rather they are service competitive.

Exhibit 8-1 describes the rate bureau rate-making procedure. After the rate bureau reviews the carrier or shipper rate request, a carrier may appeal an unfavorable decision to the bureau or the carrier may publish the rate independent of the bureau as indicated in Exhibit 8-1. All rates are subject to ICC review.

Summary

The rate regulations exercised by the regulatory agencies can be grouped into two areas: rate criteria and rate controls. The rate criteria are:

1. rates must be just and reasonable;
2. rates shall not result in undue preference or prejudices or personal discrimination; and,
3. rates shall not result in long and short haul discrimination (for railroads).

The rate controls are:

1. rates must be published in a tariff;
2. thirty days notice must be given before implementation of a rate change; and
3. limits can be established for both the minimum and maximum rate.

BASES FOR RATES

As pointed out previously, the carriers establish the rates to be charged, not the regulatory agency. In this section attention is directed toward the basis used or the factors considered by carriers in determining the rates. Consideration is given to (1) cost of service and value of service which affect the different rates established for different commodities, (2) distance and (3) volume or the weight of the shipment. In other words, the rate paid by a shipper will usually be affected by all three of the aforementioned factors, i.e., the commodity being shipped, the distance from origin to destination, and the weight tendered for shipment.

Commodity – Cost of Service

Definition

Basing rates upon the cost of providing the transport service considers the supply side of the pricing coin. The cost of supplying the service establishes the floor for a rate, i.e., the supply cost is the lower limit for the rate so as to permit the viability of the carrier.

Cost Concepts

A continual problem of what cost basis is to be used has plagued this area. Fully allocated (average total) costs have been used as well as average variable costs and out-of-pocket (marginal) costs. In essence this problem set up subfloors to the lower limit of rates—the higher limit will be that based upon full allocated costs and the lower limit upon out-of-pocket costs. The ICC use of these bases had varied and is dependent upon the particular citcumstances surrounding the case in question.*

In addition to the above, the problem of cost of service as a basis for rates is increased by the existence of common and joint costs. Common and joint costs are incurred for the production of more than one unit of output; such costs cannot be directly allocated to a particular production unit. (Joint cost is a particular type of common costs in which the costs incurred in the production of one unit unavoidably results in the production of another product. For example, the movement of a commodity from A to B unavoidably results in the production of the movement capacity and cost from B to A —more commonly known as the back haul.) The procedure used

---

* See: John J. Coyle, "The Compatibility of the Rule of Ratemaking and the National Transportation Policy," *ICC Practitioners' Journal*, March-April 1971, pp. 340-353.

FIGURE 8-1   Example of value of service pricing.

Maximum rate = 50¢

A _____ B

A production Cost = $2.00   B production cost = $2.50

to assign these costs determines the cost basis and permits latitude for cost variations and, consequently, rate variations.

Commodity–Value of Service

Definition

Value of service pricing considers the demand side of the pricing coin. One may define value of service pricing as "charging what the traffic will bear." This basis considers the ability of the transported product to withstand transportation costs. For example in Figure 8-1, the highest rate that can be charged to move producer A's product into point B is 50 cents per unit. If a higher rate is assessed, producer A's product will not be competitive in the B market area. Thus, value of service pricing places the upper limit upon the rate.

Generally, rates vary by product transported. One explanation for this is the difference in cost associated with various commodity movements, but the value of service pricing concept is also ingrained in this difference. For commodities with a higher value, transportation charges are a small portion of the total selling price. Table 8-1 points out that the rate, for a given distance and weight, on diamonds is 100 times greater than that for coal, but transportation charges for diamonds amount to only 0.01 percent of the selling price for diamonds but 25 percent for coal. Thus, high value commodities can sustain higher transportation charges and the transport services are priced accordingly—a specific application of demand pricing.*

Distance

Rates usually vary with respect to distance, i.e., the greater the distance the commodity moves the greater the cost to the carrier and the greater the transportation rate. However, there are certain rates that do not bear a relationship to distance. An example of this is a blanket rate.

Exceptions

Blanket rates do not increase as distance increases: the rate remains the same for all points in the blanket area as designated by the carrier. The

---

*   It could be argued that for high valued goods the carrier bears a higher cost associated with the increased risk of liability in case of damage.

TABLE 8-1
Transportation Rates and Commodity Value

	Coal	Diamonds
Production value per ton[*]	$30.00	$1,000,000.00
Transportation charge per ton[*]	10.00	1,000.00
Total selling price	$40.00	$1,001,000.00
% transportation cost of selling price	25%	.01%

[*]Assumed.

postage stamp rate is a good example of a blanket rate. No matter what distance you ship a letter the cost to the shipper (sender) is the same. Examples in transportation where blanket rates have been employed include the commercial zone* of a city, a given region of a state, or a number of states. In each case the rate into or out of the blanket area will be the same no matter where the origin or destination is located in the blanket area.

Rationale   The reason for such rates is the simplification of rate quotation and the assurance of a demand for transportation of the commodity. In the case of commercial zones, the carrier's tariffs are made simpler by quoting one rate to the commercial zone and then stating that points included in the commercial zone will take the same rate. If this was not done, the carrier would be required to publish rates to and from all suburbs surrounding the city and this would add to the carrier's cost of publishing tariffs and certainly make the logistics manager's job much more complex. The use of wide geographic blanket areas is an attempt by the carrier to assure a demand, marketability, of the product to be transported in a given market area; the blanket rate reduces or eliminates a producer's geographic disadvantage resulting from the higher transport costs associated with being located a greater distance from the market. Thus, all producers (consumers) in the blanket area will be assessed the same rate, no matter what the distance from origin or destination, thereby eliminating any transportation cost burden upon the demand for a product. This, then, makes possible the demand for transportation of a product because there is a demand for the product in the market area.

The majority of transportation rates, however, do increase as distance increases, but the increase is not in direct porportion to distance. This relationship of rates to distance is known as the tapering rate principle. As shown in Figure 8-2, the rate increases as distance increases but not linearly.

---

*   The commercial zone is defined as the city proper plus surrounding points, determined by population, and all rates published to the city are applicable to the surrounding points within this limit.

FIGURE 8-2   Example of tapering rate principle.

The reason for the tapering rate structure is the spreading of terminal costs (cargo handling, clerical and billing) over a greater mileage base. These terminal costs do not vary with distance; as the distance the shipment moves is increased, the lower the terminal cost per mile. The intercept point in Figure 8-2 corresponds to the terminal costs.

Weight of Shipment

Freight rates are quoted in cents per hundredweight (actual weight in pounds divided by 100 = hundredweight, cwt) and the total transportation charge is determined by total weight of the shipment, in cwt, and the appropriate rate per cwt. The rate per cwt bears a relationship to the volume being shipped; a lower rate is charged for volume shipments and a higher rate for a less-than-volume quantity. This, in essence, is a quantity discount offered by carriers for shipping large volumes (buying link service in a large quantity).

These quantity discounts are termed carload (CL) and less-than-carload (LCL) by railroads and truckload (TL) and less-than-truckload (LTL) by motor carriers. The CL and TL rates represent the lower, volume rates and the LCL and LTL rates denote the higher, less-than-volume rates.

One noteworthy exception to the rate-volume relationship is the any quantity (AQ) rate. The AQ rate bears no relationship to volume shipped; the rate per cwt remains constant regardless of the volume tendered to the carrier for shipment.

THE TRANSPORTATION PRICING SYSTEM

As a logistics manager one of the most difficult and confusing areas of your responsibility will be the determination of prices of various transportation services which are available for use as part of a logistics system. It is not always easy to determine how much it will cost to move a barrel of pickles from Toledo, Ohio, to New York City.

For an appreciation of the problem let's examine the nature of a transportation service. It would be simple if all transportation service were sold on the basis of ton-miles, that is, we would have to pay X dollars to move one ton, one mile. But, in fact, transportation services are not sold in ton miles. Transportation services are sold for moving a specific commodity, pickles, between two specific points, Toledo and New York City. This fact gives some insight into the enormous magnitude of the transportation pricing problem. There are over 33,000 important shipping and receiving points in the United States. Theoretically, the number of different possible routes would be all the permutations of the 33,000 points. The result is in the trillions of trillions. In addition, it is necessary to consider the thousands and thousands of different commodites and products which might be shipped over any of these routes. On top of that there are the different modes to consider and different companies within each mode. It also may be necessary to give consideration to the specific supply and demand situation for each commodity over each route.

Class Rates

Since it is obviously impossible to quote trillions and trillions of rates, the transportation industry has taken two major steps toward simplification.

Shipping Points

The first was to consolidate the 33,000 shipping points into groups. The nation was divided into geographic squares and the most important shipping point (based on tonnage) in each square serves as the *rate base point* for all other shipping points in the square. The purpose of this is to reduce the potential number of distance variations for rate making purposes. The distance from each base point to every other base point was determined by the railroads and placed on file with the ICC and published in the National Rate Basis Tariff. The distance between any two base points is referred to as the Rate Basis Number. The first simplifying step has reduced the number of possible origins and destinations for pricing purposes.

Items

The second step deals with the thousands and thousands of different items which might be shipped between any two base points. The railroads have established a national scale of rates which has been placed on file with the ICC and gives a rate in dollars per hundredweight (cwt) for each Rate Basis Number. These rate scales are the basis for a simplified product classification system.

Classification simply means grouping together products with similar transportation characteristics so that one rating can be applied to the whole group. Items which are of high demand and high value might be placed in Class 100, which means they will be charged 100% of the First Class Rate. Items of low value such as coal, might be placed in Class 20, which means it will be charged 20% of the First Class Rate. This percentage number for the appropriate classification is called a *class rating* and is the group into which a commodity is placed for rate-making purposes.

Now the number of possible pricing situations has been sufficiently reduced to allow the formation of a transportation pricing system. The price of moving a particular item between two particular points is determined as follows: *First*, look up the rate basis point for the origin and for the destination then determine the *rate basis number* between the two base points. Next, determine the classification rating (*class rating*) for the particular product to be shipped. Finally, find the rate in the proper class rate tariff that corresponds to the appropriate *rate basis number and class rating*. Then multiply this rate, which is in cents per cwt, by the total shipment weight in cwt to determine the cost to move that specific product between those two points.

The word tariff is commonly used to mean almost any publication put out by a carrier or a tariff publishing agency which concerns itself with the pricing or service performed by the carrier. All the information needed to determine the cost of a move is in one or more tariffs.

Example

It is now time to give an example of the mechanics involved in determining the class rate charges for a motor carrier movement. Assume we are shipping wine in bulk from Baltimore to Philadelphia, What would be correct class rate charges for shipping (1) 40,000 pounds, (2) 15,000 pounds, and (3) 35,000 pounds?

(1) A 40,000-pound shipment of wine in bulk.

    a. The rate basis number found in Middle Atlantic Conference (MAC) Tariff 41-A, page 241, is 66 (at the intersection of Rate Groups Philadelphia and Baltimore in the vertical and horizontal portions of the tariff respectively). (Exhibit 8-2.)

    b. The class ratings and minimum weight, found in the National Motor Freight Classification A-9, page 242., for wine in bulk, item #111510, are LTL = 100, TL = 50 and minimum weight = 40,000 lbs., 40.(2) Since our shipment weighs 40,000 lbs., the TL rating of 50 is used—the lower, volume rating. (Exhibit 8-3.)

    c. The applicable rate is given in MAC Tariff 41-A, page 243, and is determined by the intersection of the horizontal line of rate basis number 66, D30M, and the vertical line of class 50. This gives the class rate of $.84 per cwt. (Exhibit 8-4.)

    d. The transportation charge is found by multiplying the rate per cwt times the number of cwt's in the shipment, or:

$$40,000 \text{ lbs.} = \frac{40,000}{100} = 400 \text{ cwt.}$$

$$400 \text{ cwt @ \$.84 per cwt} = \textbf{\$336.00}$$

(2) A 15,000-pound shipment of wine in bulk.
  a. The rate basis number is again 66, but the rating used is 100 because the weight of the shipment is less than 40,000 lbs., the weight required to use class 50.
  b. From MAC Tariff 41-A, the rate for class 100 at the rate basis number 66, C, is $1.80 per cwt.
  c. The transportation charge is $270.00 and is determined as follows:

$$15,000 \text{ lbs.} = 150 \text{ cwt}$$

$$150 \text{ cwt @ \$1.80 per cwt} = \textbf{\$270.00}$$

(3) A 35,000-pound shipment of wine in bulk.
  a. The shipper has the option of shipping the shipment at TL or LTL when the weight of the shipment is less than the minimum weight specified in the tariff, but the shipper will be charged for at least the minimum weight specified to get the lower volume rate. *The shipper has the option of utilizing the rate that results in the lowest charge.*
  b. In this case the 35,000 lbs. is less than the 40,000 lbs. minimum, but it is cheaper to ship this as 40,000 lbs. (the basis of determining the transportation charge) at $.84 per cwt than as the actual weight of 35,000 lbs. at $1.80 per cwt; or

$$350 \text{ cwt @ \$1.80 per cwt} = \$630.00, \text{ or}$$

$$400 \text{ cwt @ \$.84 per cwt} = \textbf{\$336.00}$$

In this case the shipper would elect to ship the 35,000 lbs. as 40,000 lbs. and pay $336.00, rather than $630.00.

The latter example points out the need for the logistics manager to analyze at what volume it becomes profitable (lower cost) to ship a LTL size shipment as a TL shipment at the TL *minimum weight* and lower *TL rate*. This can be accomplished by determining the weight break—volume at which the LTL charges equal the TL charges at the TL minimum weight.

That is:

$$\text{LTL rate} \times (WB) = \text{TL rate} \times \text{Minimum weight}$$

$$\text{where } WB = \text{the weight break volume.}$$

Plugging in the numbers from part (c) of the above example we find the weight break to be:

$$\$1.80 \ (WB) = \$.84 \ (400)$$

$$WB = 187 \text{ cwt (rounded off)}$$

Next, a rather simple decision rule can be established for use by shipping clerks to determine when it is economical to ship a LTL shipment as a TL shipment. In this example the decision rules are as follows:

1. If the shipment weighs less than 187 cwt (WB), ship actual weight at LTL rate ($1.80 per cwt):
2. If the shipment weighs between 187 cwt (WB) and 400 cwt (minimum weight), ship as 400 cwt (minimum weight) as the TL rate ($.84 per cwt); and
3. If the shipment weighs more than 400 cwt, ship actual weight at TL rate ($.84 per cwt).

Exception Ratings (Rates)

Now that it all seems so simple it is time to complicate things again. Although the classification and class rate system are the backbone of the transportation pricing system, in reality only about 10 percent of all volume (CL to TL) freight moves under this pricing system. The remaining 90 percent moves either under an exception rating (rate) or commodity rate. These two rate types complicate the simplification inherent in the class rate structure.

Exception ratings are published when the transportation characteristics of an item in a particular area differ from those of the same article in other areas. For example, large volume movements or intensive competition in one area may require the publication of an exception rating; the exception rating applies rather than the classification when an exception rating is published. The same procedures described above apply to determining the exception rate, except now the exception rating (class) is used instead of the classification rating. An example of an exception tariff is the MAC Tariff 10 R shown on page 244. (Exhibit 8-5)

Continuing with our earlier example of moving wine in bulk from Baltimore to Philadelphia we find that item #9540, Liquors, Beverages:

EXHIBIT 8-2 Table of rate basis numbers.

COMPOSITE PAGE

MAC TARIFF 41-A

TABLE OF RATE BASIS NUMBERS

AND RATE GROUPS (Note 5)	Aberdeen....Md.	Abingdon....Md.	Alexandria...Va.	Annapolis...Md.	Baltimore...Md.	Bel Air....Md.	Bradshaw...Md.	Cabin John...Md.	Carderock...Md.	Cedarhurst...Md.	Clarksville...Md.	College Park...Md.	Conowingo....Md.	Sykesville...Md.	Washington...D.C.	Woodstock.....Md.
							BETWEEN RATE GROUPS(Note 5)									
						APPLY RATE BASIS NUMBERS (For Rates, see SECTION 1)										
Camden............N.J.	58	58	73	79	66	70	58	80	86	70	70	70	59	58	70	70
Chester............Pa.	50	53	68	74	62	66	53	78	83	66	66	68	54	66	68	66
Clementon..........N.J.	59	64	76	81	70	74	68	84	89	74	76	76	64	74	74	74
Hempstead..........N.Y.	92	93	103	114	100	103	93	113	118	106	102	103	93	102	103	102
Hicksville.........N.Y.	99	99	109	120	106	109	99	118	124	98	108	109	99	108	109	108
Hightstown.........N.J.	66	68	79	88	74	77	68	87	92	77	77	77	68	77	77	77
Hopewell...........N.J.	64	66	79	88	74	77	66	87	92	77	76	77	68	77	77	77
Jamesburg..........N.J.	68	70	80	88	74	79	70	89	94	79	79	79	70	79	79	79
Jersey City........N.J.	76	77	87	99	84	87	77	97	102	86	86	87	77	86	87	86
Lansdale...........Pa.	61	64	76	83	70	74	64	86	91	73	74	76	64	74	76	74
Malvern............Pa.	57	58	74	81	68	74	59	83	88	68	73	73	57	73	73	73
Manville...........N.J.	68	70	80	89	76	79	70	90	95	79	99	80	70	79	80	79
Morristown......N.J. *C	86	87	97	108	94	97	87	107	112	96	96	97	87	96	97	96
Morristown......N.J. ¶D	77	79	90	99	86	87	79	100	105	87	87	90	76	87	90	87
Mount Holly........N.J.	62	64	77	83	70	76	64	86	91	74	74	76	64	74	76	74
Mount Kisco....N.Y. #A	111	101	111	122	108	111	101	121	126	110	110	111	101	110	111	110
Mount Kisco....N.Y. ¢B	88	89	99	110	96	99	89	109	114	98	98	99	89	98	99	98
Newark.............Del.	41	44	64	68	56	61	44	72	77	59	59	62	47	59	62	59
Newark.............N.J.	76	77	87	98	84	87	77	97	102	86	86	87	77	86	87	86
New Brunswick......N.J.	68	70	80	89	76	80	70	90	95	79	79	80	70	79	80	79
New Castle.........Del.	46	50	66	73	61	66	50	76	81	66	64	66	53	64	66	64
New York(Note 1)...N.Y.	76	77	87	98	84	87	77	97	102	86	86	87	77	86	87	86
Norristown.........Pa.	58	61	74	81	68	73	61	83	88	70	73	73	59	73	73	73
Nyack..............N.Y.	84	86	96	105	90	92	86	102	107	90	92	92	84	92	92	92
Penns Grove........N.J.	53	57	70	79	64	77	57	80	85	74	68	70	58	68	70	68
Perth Amboy........N.J.	76	77	87	98	84	87	77	97	102	86	86	87	77	86	87	86
Philadelphia.......Pa.	56	58	73	79	66	70	58	80	85	70	70	70	59	70	70	70
Phoenixville.......Pa.	58	59	74	83	70	74	59	84	89	70	73	74	59	73	74	73
Piermont...........N.Y.	84	86	96	105	90	92	86	102	107	87	92	92	84	92	92	92
Plainfield.........N.J.	70	73	83	91	77	80	73	93	99	80	80	83	73	80	83	80
Plymouth Meeting......Pa.	58	62	76	83	70	74	62	84	89	73	73	74	61	73	74	73
Port Chester....N.Y. #A	88	90	99	110	96	99	90	109	114	98	98	99	90	98	99	98
Port Chester....N.Y. ¢B	86	90	98	107	92	96	90	106	111	96	96	96	90	96	96	96
Riverhead..........N.Y.	111	112	122	133	119	122	112	132	137	109	121	122	112	121	122	121
Riverside..........N.J.	59	66	76	83	70	74	64	84	89	74	74	74	64	74	74	74
Trenton............N.J.	62	66	77	85	73	76	66	86	91	76	76	76	66	68	73	73
Westwood........N.J. *C	82	85	95	103	88	89	85	102	107	90	92	92	84	92	92	92
Westwood........N.J. ¶D	72	80	90	98	83	83	80	100	105	90	90	90	80	90	90	90
Wharton.........N.J. *C	86	87	97	108	94	97	87	107	112	96	96	96	87	87	97	96
Wharton.........N.J. ¶D	76	79	90	98	84	84	79	97	102	83	86	87	76	87	87	87
White Plains....N.Y. #A	88	90	99	110	96	99	90	109	114	98	98	99	90	98	99	98
White Plains....N.Y. ¢B	86	90	98	107	92	96	90	106	111	96	96	96	90	96	96	96
Wilmington.........Del.	44	50	66	72	59	64	50	74	79	64	64	64	51	64	64	64
Woodbury...........N.J.	59	64	76	81	70	74	64	84	89	74	74	74	64	74	74	74
Yonkers........N.Y. #A	88	90	99	110	96	99	90	109	114	98	98	99	90	98	99	98
Yonkers........N.Y. ¢B	86	90	98	107	92	96	90	106	111	92	96	96	90	96	96	96

For explanation of Reference Marks not explained on this page, see last page(s) of this Tariff.

Source: Middle Atlantic Conference Tariff 41-A, Washington, D.C.

EXHIBIT 8-3   National motor freight classification.

Item	ARTICLES	CLASSES		
		LTL	TL	Ⓜ
111400	**LIQUORS, BEVERAGE:**			
111420	**Beverages,** alcoholic, carbonated, containing not exceeding 6 percent of alcohol by volume, in glass containers or metal cans in boxes..	65	35	30.2
111450	**Liquors,** alcoholic, NOI, in glass or in metal cans in barrels or boxes, see Note, item 111452; in Package 1352; or in bulk in barrels; also TL, in tank trucks, see Rule 370.................	100	50	40.2
111452	**Note**—Wooden boxes must be nailed with cement-coated nails; or must be encircled by two or more continuous metal or wooden straps; or must be encircled by one wire or metal strap around the center or by one wire or metal strap around each end, securely fastened to prevent removal; or all side joints must be sealed with metal seals and ends nailed.			
111470	**Liquors, Malt: Ale, Beers, Beer Tonic, Porter, Stout or non-intoxicating Cereal Beverage,** in glass in bottle carriers with tops securely fastened, see Note, item 111473, in glass or metal cans in barrels or boxes, in metal dispensing containers less than 5 gallons capacity in carriers made of 500 pound test solid fibreboard, in boxes enclosed in crates, or in bulk in barrels; also TL, in open top carriers, or in metal cans in fibre boxes, not sealed, or in Packages 174, 186, 238, 788, 966, 1145, 1155, 1162, 1257, 1261, 1360 or 1376......................	65	35	50.2
111473	**Note**—Bottle carrier containers made of fibreboard need not meet the certificate requirements of Rule 220 and Rule 290 but must be equipped with partitions full shoulder height of the bottles loaded therein. Such partitions must touch all four sides of the carrier. Inner packaging must comply with Rule 290 or Package 174.			
111490	**Vermouth,** in containers in barrels or boxes, or in bulk in barrels..........................	100	50	40.2
111510	**Wine, NOI:**			
Sub 1	In glass in wicker baskets, covers sealed...	150	50	40.2
Sub 2	In containers in barrels or boxes, see Note, item 111452; in Package 1342; or in bulk in barrels; also TL, in tank trucks, see Rule 370...	100	50	40.2
114000	**MACHINERY GROUP:** Articles consist of Machinery or Machines, or Parts Named, see Notes, items 114012 to 114024, inclusive, as described in items subject to this grouping.			
114012	**Note**—LTL shipments of machinery or machines, loose or on skids, must have small detachable parts removed and shipped in barrels or boxes. Such barrels or boxes must be specified on shipping orders and bills of lading. Fragile parts not detached must be protected.			
114014	**Note**—Unless otherwise provided, parts or pieces weighing 50 pounds or over of KD machinery and machines may be accepted loose or on skids and classed as in packages when such parts or pieces are shipped with the articles of which they form a part and classes are provided for such KD machinery or machines in packages.			
114016	**Note**—The following fittings, power equipment or power transmission appliances for machinery or machines, will, if shipped in mixed TL with such machinery or machines, be taken at the TL class and at not less than the TL minimum weight applicable on such machinery or machines: air compressors; belts; boilers, including fire brick and fire clay for setting; boiler parts, boiler fronts and grate bars; clutches; cog, gear, pulley or sprocket wheels; electric generators; engines; exhaust fans or rotary blowers; feed water heaters; foundation anchors or rods; fuel economizers; motors; pipe or pipe fittings; power pumps; power control switchboards; shafts or shafting; shaft collars, couplings, hangers or pillow blocks; smoke flues, smoke stacks or turbine water wheels, in packages, loose or on skids, as provided in separate description of articles for TL quantities.			
114090	**Air Cleaners or Air Filtering Machines,** electrostatic or mechanical, without blowers or fans, LTL, in boxes, crates or if weighing each 500 pounds or more, on skids; also TL, loose or in packages...	85	55	24.2
114110	**Air Cleaners, Coolers** other than water evaporative type, **Dehumidifiers, Heaters** other than portable, **Humidifiers or Washers,** with blowers or fans, see Note, item 114112............	85	45	24.2
114112	**Note**—Also applies on accompanying wrought iron or steel pipe parts.			
114130	**Air Coolers,** water evaporative type, with blowers or fans, with or without heating action, in boxes or crates:			
Sub 1	Portable, without stands, see Note, item 114132...	85	45	24.2
Sub 2	NOI...	110	{ 70	14.2
			85	10.2
114132	**Note**—Applies only on coolers of the hand portable type, without wheels or casters, net weight not in excess of 50 pounds each.			
150600	**PAPER:**			
150620	**Absorbent Base for Impregnation and Making Laminated Plastics,** in packages............	65	35	36.2
150640	**Artists' Board,** pulpboard or fibreboard, cloth covered, painted or coated, in packages........	70	45	24.2
150650	**Autographic Register, Cash Register, Computing Machine or Ticket Issuing Machine,** other than forms, cards, checks or tickets, see Note, item 150652, plain, or ruled, not otherwise printed, see Note, item 150654, in boxes...	55	35	36.2
150652	**Note**—Also applies when interleaved with carbon paper or backed with carbon.			
150654	**Note**—Also applies when the articles bear marginal lettering or numbering for identification purposes.			
151010	**Ground Wood Paper,** other than newsprint and unfinished blank wall paper, fibre content consisting of not less than 60 percent ground wood, including such papers as catalog, directory, drawing, manila, novel, poster, printing, tablet or writing paper (will not include paper which has been further processed after its original manufacture), see Note, item 151012, in packages:			
Sub 1	In rolls 16 inches or more in diameter, or in sheets measuring 336 square inches or more......	55	35	40.2
Sub 2	In rolls less than 16 inches in diameter, or in sheets measuring less than 336 square inches....	55	35	36.2
151012	**Note**—Bills of lading and shipping orders must contain notations reading: "Ground wood papers, other than newsprint and unfinished blank wall paper, fibre content consisting of not less than 60 percent ground wood."			
151192	**Note**—Applies on chemically treated paper such as used for manufacturing washers, gaskets or packing shapes.			
151210	**Paper,** dusting or polishing, in boxes..	70	40	36.2
151230	**Paper or Paperboard,** surface coated with flock, NOI, in packages........................	100	50	30.2
151250	**Paper,** NOI, not printed, in packages...	70	40	36.2
151270	**Pari-mutuel Ticket Issuing Machine Paper,** printed, requiring further printing, in rolls in boxes...	70	35	36.2

For explanation of abbreviations and reference marks, see last page of this tariff.

Source: National Motor Freight Classification A-9. Washington, D.C.

EXHIBIT 8-4 Class tariff.

COMPOSITE PAGE

MAC TARIFF 41-A

SECTION 1
TABLE OF CLASS RATES FOR CLASSES 100 AND LOWER

APPLICATION OF WEIGHT GROUPS:

A – Applies on LTL or AQ shipments weighing each less than 2,000 pounds.
B – Applies on LTL or AQ shipments weighing each 2,000 pounds or more but less than 6,000 pounds.
C – Applies on LTL or AQ shipments weighing each 6,000 pounds or more.
D – Applies on TL shipments (See Note A).
D30M–Applies on TL shipments, minimum weight 30,000 pounds (See Note A).
NOTE A: Where the charge under the rates in Line D30M is lower than the charge under the rates in Line D on the same shipment via the same route, such lower charge will apply.

RATE BASIS NUMBER	WEIGHT GROUP	100	92½	85	77½	70	65	60E	60	57	55	50	50K	47½	45	42½	40	37½	35	32½	30	27½
													RATES IN CENTS PER 100 POUNDS									
33	A	181	171	161	153	143	134	135	126	120	117	110										
	B	121	114	106	98	89	85	87	80	76	73	68										
	C	88	82	75	69	62	58	60	54	52	49	46										
	D	77	72	66	61	55	51	54	48	46	44	41	41	40	38	36	34	33	31	29	27	25
	D30M	75	70	64	59	53	49	52	46	44	42	39	37	37	35	33	31	29	28	26	24	22
65 66	A	277	261	244	229	213	200	196	186	177	173	160										
	B	216	202	187	172	157	148	145	138	131	127	116										
	C	180	167	153	140	127	118	115	109	103	100	91										
	D	168	156	143	131	119	111	108	102	97	94	86	86	86	81	77	73	69	64	60	56	51
	D30M	166	154	141	129	117	109	106	100	95	92	84	81	80	76	72	68	64	59	55	51	47
67 68	A	286	269	252	235	218	205	201	191	183	178	164										
	B	225	210	195	178	162	154	151	143	137	132	120										
	C	188	174	160	146	132	124	120	114	109	105	96										
	D	176	163	150	137	124	116	113	107	102	99	90	90	89	85	80	76	71	67	62	58	53
	D30M	174	161	148	135	122	114	111	105	100	97	88	84	84	79	75	71	67	62	58	54	49
69 70	A	289	272	255	239	221	207	203	194	185	180	167										
	B	228	213	198	182	166	156	153	145	139	133	123										
	C	191	177	163	149	135	126	123	116	111	106	98										
	D	179	166	153	140	127	118	115	109	104	100	92	91	91	86	82	77	73	68	63	59	54
	D30M	177	162	151	138	125	116	113	107	102	98	90	86	85	81	76	72	68	63	59	55	50
71 72 73	A	295	277	259	243	225	211	206	197	188	183	169										
	B	233	218	202	186	169	159	156	148	142	137	125										
	C	197	183	168	154	139	129	126	119	114	110	100										
	D	184	171	157	144	130	121	118	112	107	103	94	94	94	89	84	80	75	70	65	61	56
	D30M	182	169	155	142	128	119	116	110	105	101	92	88	88	83	79	74	70	65	61	56	52
74	A	299	281	262	246	228	214	209	199	190	185	171										
	B	238	221	205	189	172	162	158	151	144	139	127										
	C	201	186	171	157	142	132	128	121	116	112	102										
	D	188	174	160	147	133	124	120	114	109	105	96	96	95	90	86	81	76	71	66	62	57
	D30M	186	172	158	145	131	122	118	112	107	103	94	90	89	85	80	76	71	66	62	57	53
75 76	A	305	287	269	250	232	218	213	203	194	189	174										
	B	244	228	212	194	176	167	162	155	147	143	130										
	C	207	192	177	161	146	137	132	126	119	116	105										
	D	194	180	166	151	137	128	124	118	112	109	99	99	99	94	89	84	79	74	69	64	59
	D30M	192	178	164	149	135	126	122	116	110	107	97	93	92	88	83	78	73	69	64	59	54
77	A	309	290	271	254	234	219	215	205	196	190	176										
	B	247	231	214	197	178	168	164	157	149	144	132										
	C	211	196	180	164	148	138	134	128	121	117	108										
	D	197	183	168	154	139	129	126	120	114	110	101	101	100	95	90	85	80	75	70	65	60
	D30M	195	181	166	152	137	127	124	118	112	108	99	94	94	89	84	79	74	70	65	60	55
84	A	328	307	287	269	248	232	227	217	206	201	186										
	B	267	248	230	212	192	181	176	169	160	155	142										
	C	230	213	196	180	162	152	141	137	131	124	120										
	D	215	199	183	168	151	141	137	131	124	120	110	110	109	103	98	92	87	81	76	70	65
	D30M	213	197	181	166	150	139	135	129	122	118	108	103	102	97	92	86	83	76	71	65	60
87	A	336	316	295	275	254	238	231	221	212	205	190										
	B	275	257	238	218	198	186	181	173	166	159	146										
	C	239	221	203	186	168	156	151	144	138	132	121										
	D	223	207	190	174	157	146	141	135	129	124	114	113	113	107	101	96	90	84	78	73	67
	D30M	221	205	188	172	155	144	139	133	127	122	112	107	106	101	95	90	84	79	73	68	62
88 89 90	A	346	325	303	283	261	244	238	228	217	211	195										
	B	285	266	246	226	205	192	187	180	171	164	151										
	C	248	230	212	194	175	162	157	151	143	138	126										
	D	232	215	198	181	164	152	147	141	134	129	118	118	118	112	106	100	94	88	82	76	70
	D30M	230	213	196	179	162	150	145	139	132	127	116	111	110	105	99	93	88	82	76	70	65

Source: Middle Atlantic Conference Tariff 41-A. Washington, D.C.

EXHIBIT 8-5   Exception tariff.

COMPOSITE PAGE

MAC TARIFF 10-R

SECTION 4
EXCEPTIONS TO NATIONAL MOTOR FREIGHT CLASSIFICATION
(See Item 380)

ITEM	ARTICLES	CLASSES (Ratings)		
		AQ	LTL	TL
9400	LAMPS OR LIGHTING GROUP: Lighting Fixtures, electric or gas, NOI, other than cast iron,with or with- out globes or shades; or Parts,NOI,other than cast iron or other than glass, in barrels, boxes or crates....................................... APPLICABLE ONLY for local or joint hauls via Byrnes,L.I. Motor Cargo,Inc.	200	..	..
9420	LAMPS OR LIGHTING GROUP: Lighting Fixtures,fluorescent(Note A),with equipment of electrical apparatus, with or without equipment of lamps(Note B) or Parts,NOI,in boxes or crates... NOTE A: Applies only on lighting devices designed for permanent wiring to walls, ceilings, floors or posts or other similar mountings. NOTE B: Accompanying equipment of iron or steel or plastic reflectors may be in packages. APPLICABLE ONLY for local or joint hauls via Rupp-Southern Tier Freight Lines,Inc. (File R-261)	200	..	..
9440	LEATHER OR LEATHERBOARD: (File R264) Leather, NOI, or Enameled or Patent Leather................................	..	..	45
9460	LICORICE MASS, in packages..	..	..	37½
9480	LIQUORS, BEVERAGE: (Files R198;D5152) Liquors, alcoholic, NOI: In glass in cases or in bulk in barrels..................................... In bulk in barrels in bond (Note A)... NOTE A: This item shall be understood to embrace goods on which the Internal Revenue Tax has not been paid but does NOT include goods moving under U.S. Customs Bond.	..	..	Ⓛ 45 Ⓝ 70 Ⓡ 50 Ⓣ 40
9500	LIQUORS, BEVERAGE: Liquors, malt: Ale, Beer, Beer Tonic, Porter, Stout or non-intoxicating Cereal Beverages; In glass in bottle carriers with or without tops securely fastened or without tops; or in glass or metal cans in barrels or boxes; in boxes enclosed in crates; or in bulk in barrels, Min. Wt. 10,000 lbs........... APPLICABLE ONLY on traffic moving under rates shown in Tariff 8-R,MF-ICC A-1458 and Tariff NY-1-J,PSC-NY-MT A-120. (File R205) NOT APPLICABLE for local hauls via Apex Express,Inc.,Eastern Freight Ways,Inc., Royal Motor Lines, Inc., nor Victor Lynn Lines, Inc., nor for joint hauls via these carriers and their connections.	..	..	32½
9540	LIQUORS,BEVERAGE: (Files R198;D5152) Wine,in containers in barrels or boxes,or in bulk in barrels...............	..	..	45
9760	MACHINERY, APPLIANCES AND SUPPLIES, electrical: As enumerated in List No. 11, Section 2, in straight or mixed truckloads(except as otherwise provided).. As enumerated in List No. 12, Section 2, in straight or mixed truckloads(except as otherwise provided)..	..	.. ..	40 55
9780	MACHINERY GROUP: (Files D918;E6568) Air Coolers, Coolers, other than water evaporative type,Dehumidifiers,Heaters, other than portable,Humidifiers or Washers,with blowers or fans,with or without air filters (Note A): Weighing each less than 600 lbs., TL Min. Wt. 24,000 lbs.(Note B)........... Weighing each 600 lbs. or more, TL Min. Wt. 20,000 lbs.................... NOTE A: Ratings also apply on Wrought Iron or Steel Pipe Parts. NOTE B: When from Buffalo,Dunkirk,New York and Syracuse,N.Y.,or Avenel(Middlesex Cy.),Jersey City, Newark or Trenton,N.J.,truckload minimum weight shall be 23,000 lbs.	..	.. ..	40 40

Ⓡ - APPLICABLE ONLY for local hauls via Newburgh Transfer,Inc.,or for joint hauls via this carrier in
      connection with The Davidson Transfer & Storage Co.
Ⓛ - NOT APPLICABLE for local or joint hauls via Fleet Motor Lines,Inc., or carriers shown in Notes 11
      and 12, except Feuer Transportation,Inc.,Long Transportation Company,or Perkins Trucking Co.,
      Inc.
Ⓣ - NOT APPLICABLE for local or joint hauls via Fleet Motor Lines, Inc., or carriers shown in Notes 11
      and 12.
Ⓝ - APPLICABLE ONLY for joint hauls via Newburgh Transfer,Inc.,and its connections, except as noted.
For explanation of Reference Marks not explained on this page,see last page(s)of this Tariff.

Source: Middle Atlantic Conference Tariff 10-R. Washington, D.C.

Wine, etc., makes an exception to the TL rating found in the National Motor Freight Classification A-9. The classification rating was 50, while the exception rating is 45. For a shipment of 40,000 lbs. of wine in bulk and using the same procedure outlined for determining class rates (the intersection of the horizontal line of rate basis number 66, D30M, and the vertical line of class 45 in MAC tariff 41-A, page 243 (Exhibit 8-4), the exception rate is $.76 per cwt. The transportation charges then become: 400 cwt @ $.76 per cwt = $304.00, a savings of $32.00 over the class rate charges.

Commodity Rates

A commodity rate can be constructed on a variety of bases but the most common is a specific rate published on a specific commodity or group of related commodities between specific points and generally via specific routes. Commodity rates are complete in themselves and are not part of the classification system. If the commodity you are shipping is not specifically stated or if the origin-destination is not that specifically spelled out in the commodity rate, then the commodity rate for your particular movement is not applicable. When a commodity rate is published it takes precedence over the class rate or exception rate on the same article between the specific points.

This type of rate is offered to those commodities that are moved in large quantities with regularity. But, such a pricing system completely undermines the attempts to simplify transportation pricing through the class rate structure. It has caused transportation pricing to revert to the publication of a multiplicity of rates and adds greatly to the complexity of the pricing system.

An example of a commodity tariff, MAC Tariff 41-A is given in Exhibit 8-6. Again continuing with our example of shipping 40,000 lbs. of wine in bulk from Baltimore to Philadelphia, we find that item #28450 of MAC Tariff 41-A contains a commodity rate of $.57 per cwt with a minimum weight of 23,000 lbs. for the movement of wine in bulk from Baltimore to Philadelphia. (Note: This rate does not apply on the movement of wine in bulk from Philadelphia to Baltimore.) Notes 2 and 3 refer to surrounding points to which the commodity rate also applies—the blanket area concept referred to earlier. For the movement of 40,000 lbs. of wine using the commodity rate, the transportation charges are $228.00 (400 cwt @ $.57 per cwt). The commodity rate results in the lowest charge of the three types of rates, which is the general case.

Rate Constructs

A transportation rate has another dimension, the rate construct, in addition to being either a class, exception or commodity rate. The rate construct

EXHIBIT 8-6   Commodity rate tariff.

MAC TARIFF 41-A

SECTION 3
COMMODITY RATES IN CENTS PER 100 POUNDS UNLESS OTHERWISE SPECIFICALLY PROVIDED

ITEM 28350:   (File B4700)
  LIQUORS, BEVERAGE:
    Liquors, Malt:
      Beer, in bottles or cans in boxes, or in bulk in barrels.

FROM	TO	TL RATE	MIN. WT.
New York(Note 1),N.Y.:			
Zone 1..................	Points named in Note A.....	60	28M
Zone 2..................	Points named in Note A.....	62	28M

NOTE A: Rates apply TO:
  Aberdeen......Md.   Chesapeake City..Md.   Elkton........Md.   Havre De Grace....Md. Rising Sun......Md.
  Bel Air......Md.   Conowingo........Md.   Forest Hill..Md.   Perryman.........Md.
NOT APPLICABLE for local or joint hauls via Service Trucking Co., Inc.

ITEM	COMMODITY	FROM	TO	TL RATE	MIN. WT.
28400	LIQUORS,BEVERAGE: Vermouth,in containers in barrels or boxes or in bulk in barrels. (File IR1698)	New York(Note 1),N.Y.: Zone 1.............	Baltimore(Note 3)......Md.	79 70	23M 30M
			Washington(Note 4)....D.C.	81 73	23M 30M
		Zone 2.............	Baltimore(Note 3)......Md.	81 72	23M 30M
			Washington(Note 4)....D.C.	83 75	23M 30M
		Pennington........N.J.	Baltimore(Note 3)......Md.	67	23M
		Philadelphia.......Pa.	Washington(Note 4)....D.C.	69 57	23M 30M
28450	LIQUORS,BEVERAGE: Wine, NOI,in containers in barrels or boxes or in bulk in barrels. (Files P3583;A198)	Baltimore(Note 3)..Md.	Philadelphia(Note 2)...Pa.	57	23M
		Philadelphia(Note 2) ....Pa.	Washington(Note 4)....D.C.	69 57	23M 30M
28475	LIQUORS,BEVERAGE: Wine,NOI,actual value not exceeding $3.00 per gallon, in containers in barrels or boxes.	②⑤ Newark........N.J. (File E3366)	Baltimore(Note 3)......Md.	80 71 ⓒⓛⓜ 64	23M 30M 80M
			Washington(Note 4)....D.C.	82 74 ⓒⓛⓜ 64	23M 30M 80M
28500	LIQUORS, BEVERAGE: Wine, NOI,in containers in barrels or boxes. (File E3366)	New York(Note 1),N.Y.: ②⑤ Zone 1.........	Baltimore(Note 3)......Md.	79 70 63	23M 30M (Note A)
			Washington(Note 4)....D.C.	81 73 63	23M 30M (Note A)
		②⑤ Zone 2........	Baltimore(Note 3)......Md.	81 72 65	23M 30M (Note A)
			Washington(Note 4)....D.C.	83 75 65	23M 30M (Note A)

(Concluded on next page)

ⓒ - Where the weight of a single shipment is in excess of the weight that can be transported in a single
       vehicle (truck or trailer), the following provisions will govern:
       (1) The entire shipment must be available for receipt and movement by the carrier at one time and
           place on one bill of lading.
       (2) Rate will NOT apply on shipments requiring more than two vehicles. The excess over the quantity
           that can be loaded in two vehicles will be treated as a separate shipment.
For explanation of Reference Marks not explained on this page, see last page(s)of this Tariff.

Source: *Middle Atlantic Conference Tariff 41-A*, Washington, D.C.

FIGURE 8-3 Rate constructs.

$$X$$

$$N_1 \text{————————} N_2$$

(a)

$$\$1.00$$

$$N_1 \text{————————} N_2$$

(c)

$$X \qquad\qquad Y$$

$$N_1 \text{————————} N_2$$

(b)

$$\$.30 \qquad \$.40 \qquad \$.30$$

$$N_1 \text{—} I_1 \text{———} I_2 \text{———} N_2$$

(d)

refers to rates having the characteristics of (1) the number of carriers participating in the move and (2) the number of rates required to determine the actual rate between a particular origin-destination (nodal) pair. Under the first characteristic, the rate can be either local or joint, while in the second, the rate can be either through or combination.

Local vs. Joint

A local rate is one in which only one carrier participates in the link service provided. A joint rate requires more than one carrier to complete the desired service. Parts (a) and (b) of Figure 8-3 depict a local and joint rate, respectively; in (a) carrier X provides the link service between nodes N_1 and N_2 and the construct of this rate is local. In part (b), carriers X and Y participate in providing the link service and the construct of this rate is joint.

Through Rate

A through rate is one that is quoted between the specific nodal pair to be linked. The combination rate requires the combining of several intermediate rates to determine the appropriate rate between a nodal pair because the carrier(s) does (do) not have one through rate in effect between this pair. Parts (c) and (d) of Figure 8-3 are examples of through and combination rates, respectively. In part (c) the through rate is given specifically to be $\$1.00$ between N_1 and N_2, but in part (d) the rate of $\$1.00$ is derived from the combination of intermediate rates of $\$.30$, $\$.40$ and $\$.30$, from N_1 to I_1, I_1 to I_2 and I_2 to N_2, respectively.

As stated above a rate has two construct characteristics. Thus, if one rate is published between a nodal pair, but two carriers participate, this is an example of a joint, through rate. If two or more rates must be combined to get the rate between a nodal pair and only one carrier is involved, this would be a local, combination rate. Diagram the situation representing a joint, combination rate and one describing a local, through rate.

The order of priority for rates states that a through rate takes precedence over a combination of rates. But for situations in which the combination rate is lower than the through rate, the aggregate of the intermediates rule permits the shipper to use the lower combination rate. Thus, if in part (d) of Figure 8-3 the combination rate was $\$.90$ rather than $\$1.00$ (through rate), the shipper would have the right to use the lower combination rate.

Other Rates

In addition to class rates, exception rates, and commodity rates there are many special rates which have developed over the years to meet very specific situations. The most prevalent and most important of these special rates are: all-commodity rates, released value rates, actual value rates, deferred rates, multiple vehicle rates, and incentive rates.

All Commodity Rates

All commodity rates, also known as freight-all-kinds or FAK rates, are a recent development in which the carrier specifies the rate per shipment either in dollars per hundredweight or in total dollars per shipment with a specified minimum weight. The commodity or commodities being shipped is not important. These rates tend to price transportation services on the basis of cost rather than the value of service and are used mostly by shippers who send mixed commodity shipments to a single destination.

Released Value Rates

Released value rates and actual value rates are the two most important of a whole host of value rates; these rates are based upon the degree of liability (commodity value) the carrier assumes. Generally, a common carrier is liable to the extent of the value of any goods lost or damaged while in its custody. A released value rate is a rate which is based on the carrier's assumption of a certain fixed liability, usually stated in cents per pound. Usually this fixed liability is considerably less than the actual value of the goods. As a result of this limited liability the shipper is given a lower rate. Released value rates are used extensively in the shipment of household goods. Actual value rates are used when there is a great variation in the values of goods considered to be the same commodity. In these cases one rate is not desirable because some shipments have a high liability potential while other shipments have a low liability potential. The actual value rates make allowances for this potential difference and the liability difference is reflected in the rate charged.

Deferred Rates

Deferred rates are most common in air transportation and, in general, allow the carrier to charge a lower rate for the privilege of deferring the arrival time of a shipment. A deferred rate allows the carrier to move shipments at the carrier's convenience as long as the shipment arrives within a reasonable time or by the scheduled deferred delivery date. This allows the carrier to use the deferred rate shipments as "filler freight" to achieve fuller loading of its vehicles.

Multiple Vehicle Rates

Multiple vehicle rates are actually a special type of incentive rate offered to shippers who ship more than one vehicle load of a particular commodity at one time to a single destination. These rates were first used by motor carriers to overcome the fact that a rail car holds more than a truck. By publishing lower multiple vehicle rates they were able to more effectively compete with the railroads. Another rationale for multiple vehicle rates is to reduce the transportation costs for commodities and thus allow these commodities to move to more distant markets. The justification for lower rates is the savings achieved by economics of scale. The railroads can often demonstrate savings in multiple vehicle pick-ups. Multiple vehicle rates have progressed to the unit train rates given for whole trainloads of commodities such as coal, ore and grain.

Incentive rates, or in-excess rates, are published by a carrier to encourage heavier loading of individual vehicles so the carrier can improve its equipment utilization. One rate is charged on all cargo up to a certain minimum weight and a lower rate is charged on all cargo in excess of the minimum weight.

TRANSPORTATION SERVICES

The preceding material on transportation rates did not specifically delineate in its entirety the nature of the transportation service. One may have the misconception that carriers merely provide commodity movement service between two nodes; in reality the carrier provides the basic link service and more. The additional services are contained within the areas of terminal and line haul services offered by the carriers. For some services, no additional fee is charged above the transportation rate while extra charges are assessed for other services. The logistics manager must be cognizant of these "extra" services so as to take advantage of same in the achievement of overall logistics objectives.

Terminal Services

Terminal Functions
Although carrier terminal operations fall outside the realm of the logistics manager's direct control, it is worthwhile to explore the nature of this operation so as to provide the logistics manager with some knowledge of the constraints or problems imposed by carrier terminals upon the provision of link service. Essentially, the carrier's terminal performs five basic functions: concentration, dispersion, shipment service, vehicle service, and interchange.[1] The performance of these functions requires time and therefore has an impact upon the total transit time provided by a carrier. The concentration function is the consolidation of many less-than-volume size shipments into one large shipment that is economical for the carrier to transport. Thus if a shipper tenders a 2,000 lb. shipment to a carrier, this shipment will be combined with other small shipments before being dispatched on toward destination. The dispersion function is just the opposite; when a consolidated shipment arrives at the destination terminal the many shipments in the vehicle must be broken down (breakbulk) for dispatch to the individual consignees. Shipment service is the provision of freight handling services for the consolidation and dispersion functions as well as the performance of the clerical, billing, routing, and other functions for the shipment. Vehicle service essentially is the maintenance of a supply of vehicles to meet demand. This latter function requires the carrier to constantly review the distribution of vehicles among terminals so that sufficient supply is available

to provide the transport service demanded by the shipping public and by regulatory requirements. Finally, the interchange function provides the facilities for the exchange of freight between carriers coordinating to provide through service.

In addition to the above functions performed at the carrier's terminal, pick-up and delivery service is provided. Pick-up and delivery involve the actual going out to the shipper's plant to pick up freight ready for movement or to make ultimate delivery of the shipment at the consignee's plant. There may or may not be a charge for this service. Some carriers include the charge for pick-up and delivery in the line-haul rate; for example, the motor carrier LTL rates include the pick-up and delivery service. The carrier's tariff must be consulted to determine if such charges are applicable for the provision of this service.

Embraced within the concentration function is the carrier performance of the loading and unloading of small, LTL, or LCL shipments into the vehicle. But for TL and CL size shipments the shipper is required to load the vehicle and the consignee is to unload it. Normally this task is performed by the logistics department, but, if a firm wishes, the carrier will perform these services at an added cost. Notable exceptions exist to the above generalizations regarding loading and unloading, especially for motor transport. Again, the carrier's tariff must be consulted to determine the shipper (consignee) loading (unloading) requirements.

Demurrage and Detention

The shipper or consignee does not have unlimited time to load or unload a vehicle. The carrier grants the firm a specified amount of free time to accomplish these tasks. Charges are assessed for holding the vehicle beyond the free time; these are known as demurrage (rail) and detention (motor). For railroads, the free time for loading or unloading a boxcar is 24-48 hours, Saturdays, Sundays, and holidays excluded. If the vehicle has not been released after this time has elapsed, the shipper or consignee is charged $20 per day for the first four days the vehicle is held beyond the free time, $30 per day for the next two days the vehicle is held beyond the free time, and $60 per day thereafter.

For motor carriers, the free time when tractor and trailer are detained is based upon the weight of the shipment; the maximum free time is seven hours for 44,000 pounds or more. Detention charges when the tractor and trailer are detained beyond the free time are based upon $9 per 30 minute increments. When only the trailer is detained, free time is 24 hours with detention charges of $25 per day for the first two days after the free time, $35 per day for the next two days, and $50 for each day thereafter.

Demurrage and detention charges are directed toward reducing the amount of use made of the carrier's vehicle as a short term warehouse. Many consignees find advantageous the use of these vehicles as temporary storage facilities when permanent storage capacity is fully utilized. However, the logistics manager must weigh the demurrage and detention charges against the cost of short term warehousing and in addition one must consider the implications of holding vehicles for short term warehousing upon the vehicle shortage problem.

As noted in an earlier section, transportation rates are quoted in terms of cents per cwt. Thus, it is imperative that the exact weight of the shipment is determined so that the carrier realizes the appropriate revenue and the shipper pays the correct charges. The carriers maintain weighing devices which are controlled by the regulatory commissions. Upon request, the carrier will have the vehicle and contents reweighed if the original weight is felt to be in error. For some commodities that have a homogeneous weight per package, an agreed weight per package, case, carton, etc., is specified in the carrier's tariff; this weight is determined jointly by the carrier and shipper and subject to regulatory scrutiny. If an agreed weight is in effect, the total weight of the shipment is determined by the number of packages being shipped times the agreed weight.

It is imperative in many situations for the logistics manager to know where a shipment is and/or when it will arive at destination. Such information is needed to advise customers, production departments, or company warehouses so as to eliminate customer ill will and stockouts, and to improve the utilization of materials handling equipment and labor. Carriers provide this monitoring function known as tracing and expediting. Tracing is tracking the movement of a shipment to determine its location in the link pipeline. Expediting utilizes the same procedure as tracing but with the objective of getting the shipment to destination quicker than normal. The provision of such services by the carrier enables the logistics manager to assure a certain level of link service with a low cost carrier rather than utilize high-cost premium transport.*

Line-Haul Services

Carriers also provide line-haul services that permit the logistics manager to effect changes in the original shipping order and to realize savings in transportation costs. The line-haul services to be discussed are reconsignment and diversion, pool car (truck) service, stopping in transit, and transit privilege.

Reconsignment and Diversion

Reconsignment and diversion are used interchangeably to mean the changing of the destination and/or consignee of the shipment while paying the through rate from origin to final destination; but there is a technical difference between the two. Reconsignment permits the shipper to change the destination and/or consignee after the shipment has reached its original destination, but before it has been delivered to the original consignee. Diversion enables the shipper to effect the same changes while the shipment is enroute and prior to reaching the original destination.

Figure 8-4 depicts these services. Part (a) is an example of reconsignment. Here the shipper reconsigns the shipment from N_2 to N_3 and would pay the N_1 to N_3 rate of $1.10 rather than the combination rate (N_1 to N_2 plus N_2

---

* For additional information see: R. C. Colton and E. S. Ward, *Industrial Traffic Management*, 4th ed. (Washington: The Traffic Service Corporation, 1956), chapter 12.

FIGURE 8-4 Example of reconsignment and diversion.

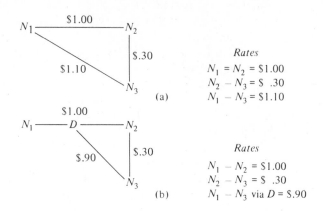

(a)

Rates

$N_1 = N_2 = \$1.00$
$N_2 - N_3 = \$ .30$
$N_1 - N_3 = \$1.10$

(b)

Rates

$N_1 - N_2 = \$1.00$
$N_2 - N_3 = \$ .30$
$N_1 - N_3$ via $D = \$.90$

to N_3) of $1.30. In Part (b) the shipper diverts the shipment at D for a new destination at N_3 and pays the through rate from N_1 to N_3 via D of $.90 rather than the combination rate (N_1 to N_2 plus N_2 to N_3) of $1.30. In both cases the shipper would be assessed a nominal fee for the reconsignment and diversion service.

Rather extensive use of reconsignment and diversion services are made in the movement of perishable products (fruits, etc.) and for movement in which the original consignee refuses the shipment or cancels the order. In the case of perishable products the goods may be started in movement prior to having a buyer, using the time in transit to obtain a buyer; once the buyer is found for the products in transit, a reconsignment or diversion order is issued with the buyer named as consignee. In situations where the original buyer decides not to accept the order, the reconsignment or diversion order can be utilized to change the destination of the shipment to a new buyer location or to have the shipment stopped and returned to the seller's location. These services permit the shipper to amend the original contract (bill of lading) with the carrier and to realize the benefits of the lower through rate (tapering rate principle) from origin to new destination.

Pooling

Pool car or pool truck service permits the shipper to combine many LCL or LTL shipments into one CL or TL shipment and to send same to one destination and one consignee. The lower CL or TL rate applies to the combined shipments and, thus, effecting savings for the shipper. Since the service requires one destination and one consignee, the shipment is usually sent to a warehouseman or drayage firm* which breaks down the consolidated shipment (the dispersion function) into the individual shipments and delivers same to appropriate consignee. The warehouseman or drayage firm

---

* A drayage firm is a motor carrier specializing in providing pick-up and delivery service.

FIGURE 8-5   Example of stopping in transit service.

N_1 ————————————— N_2 ————————————— N_3

30,000 lbs.   15,000 lbs.   15,000 lbs.
(total shipment)

Rates/cwt

	LTL	TL	Minimum Weight
N_1 to N_2	3.00	2.00	30,000
N_1 to N_3	4.00	2.50	30,000

Stop-off charge = $15.00 per stop-off.

assesses a fee for this service. The opposite for inbound movements is possible, i.e., the warehouseman combines small shipments from a firm's suppliers, presents them to a carrier who delivers them to the firm's plant, with the lower, volume rate applying.

In Transit Services   Another service, stopping in transit, offers the shipper the opportunity to stop the vehicle in transit to complete loading or to partially unload freight and to pay the lower TL or CL rate between the most distant origin-destination nodal pair on the highest weight in the vehicle at any time. A stop-off charge is assessed for each intermediate stop but not the final destination. Figure 8-5 is an example of the use of the stopping in transit service. The shipper at N_1 has two customers located at N_2 and N_3 that have purchased 15,000 lbs. each. If the shipper sent this out as two LTL shipments, the total charge would be $1,050.00 (150 cwt @ $3.00/cwt + 150 cwt @ $4.00/cwt). Utilizing the stopping in transit service, the firm would incur $765.00 (300 cwt @ $2.50/cwt, the TL rate between N_1 and N_3 which is the most distant nodal pair, plus $15.00 for the stop-off at N_2 to partially unload). The same procedure would hold for the opposite situation, i.e., picking up 15,000 lbs. at N_3, stopping at N_2 to load an additional 15,000 lbs. and delivering 30,000 lbs. at N_1.

The final line-haul service is the transit privilege. The transit privilege permits the shipper to stop the shipment in transit and to perform some function that physically changes the characteristic of the product. The lower through rate applies from origin to final destination rather than the combination of rates from origin to transit point and from transit point to final destination. The transit privilege has been established for the milling of grain, fabrication of steel, processing of lumber, and the storage of various commodities for aging, etc.

In essence, the transit privilege eliminates any geographic disadvantage associated with processor's location. For example, in Figure 8-6, the miller of grain, M_1, would pay the 90-cent rate rather than the combination rate of

FIGURE 8-6   Example of transit privilege.

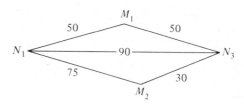

Both millers M_1 and M_2 would pay the same 90¢ rate.

$1.00. Likewise, miller M_2 would pay the 90-cent rate. If the rates on grain or flour, for example, differ, the one generating the highest revenue for the carrier is the one that is applicable. The transit privilege is not available at all points, only those points specified by the carrier with ICC scrutiny.

SUMMARY

In this chapter an attempt was made to acquaint the reader with the intricacies of transportation rates and services. Such knowledge is fundamental to the operation and control of the logistics system and more specifically to the operation and control of the link activities. The transportation activity is a daily operation in any logistics system and it requires considerable expertise with carrier tariffs, regulation and service for efficient and economical operation of the most vital logistics function.

Study Questions

1. Outline the procedure used to determine transportation rates.
2. Determine the lowest possible charges for a shipment of 30,000 lbs. of air coolers from Jersey City, New Jersey, to Baltimore. Note: Each item weighs 379 lbs.
3. Determine the lowest possible transportation charges for a shipment of 35,000 lbs. of wine in barrels from Washington, D.C., to Philadelphia.
4. Determine the weight break and establish the decision rules for the movement of vermouth in containers from Annapolis, Maryland, to Phoenixville, Pennsylvania. Use the class rates only.
5. Compare and contrast the cost of service with the value of service as a basis for determining rates.
6. What is the tapering principle and why is it important?
7. Define the rate basis number and the class rating. Explain how they are used to determine a rate.

8. What are the various pricing systems and why are they used?
9. Describe rate constructs.
10. Relate the difference between release value and actual value rates.
11. Terminal services are important for what reasons?
12. What is the effect on the consignee of demurrage and detention charges?
13. List the various line-haul services and describe when the services would be used by shippers.

Notes

1. Roy J. Sampson and Martin T. Farris, *Domestic Transportation*, 4th ed. (Boston: Houghton Mifflin Company, 1979), p. 124.

Case 8-1
Prentice Industries

Prentice Industries is a large multinational firm which operates in 15 countries internationally and 35 cities in the continental United States.

Prentice's product line, basically power-type commodities, ranges from large multiton transformers to computer tie-in circuits to dry cell batteries.

The international branches do not perform the logistics functions associated with the transfer of commodities and raw materials. The majority of the logistics activities are carried out by an international freight forwarder based in the port of New York City.

Large to midrange power transformers are moved by special motor carriers for Prentice and no real problems are incurred by the logistics department.

The majority of the logistics activities center on the movement and storage of dry cell batteries. In a recent cost study undertaken by Prentice, it was shown that the total logistics costs for the transfer of the dry cell batteries from the Williamsport, Pennsylvania, plant to a major distributor in New York City was much higher than previously forecasted.

At present, the dry cell batteries are shipped, not spent, in boxes to the distributor in New York City (Zone 1). Prentice ships in quantities of 35,000 pounds per shipment.

Questions

1. What rates are applicable on the shipments of batteries?
2. Which type of rate should be used?
3. What will the total charge be?

Class   *Exception*
Applicable?____ Yes ____ No   ____ Yes ____ No
Item # _____   _____
Class rating: LTL _____   :
                    TL _____   _____
Minimum weight _____   _____
R.B.N. _____   _____
Weight group _____   _____
Rate _____   _____
Total charge _____   _____

Commodity   *Rate Which Should be Used*
Applicable ____ Yes ____ No   Rate type _____
Item # _____   Total charge _____
Minimum weight _____
Rate _____
Total charge _____

Chapter 9	Traffic Management

After studying this chapter, you should be able to:

- Present an overview of the important daily or tactical activities of the traffic management function in a logistics system.

- Understand the function, role, and importance of the bill of lading document.

- Discuss the various types of claims that can be filed with carriers and the procedures for filing.

- Discuss and analyze the opportunity of private trucking as an option in the transportation area of the logistics system.

- Explore the special area of international logistics with a particular emphasis upon the transportation aspect of international operations.

Traffic management is the actual day-to-day operation of the transportation system utilized in the provision of link service among the firm's nodes. Attention in this chapter is directed to the daily activities of traffic management, including documentation (the bill of lading), payment of the freight bill, filing claims, the operation of a private truck fleet, and international logistics. Within each activity, emphasis is placed upon the specific operating requirements and decision-making areas that afford opportunities for improved efficiencies.

THE BILL OF LADING

The bill of lading is probably the single most important transportation document; it originates the shipment, provides all the information for the carrier to accomplish the move, stipulates the transportation contract terms, acts as a receipt for the goods tendered to the carrier, and in some cases, shows certificate of title to the goods. Exhibit 9-1 shows a copy of a motor carrier bill of lading.

Scope

All interstate shipments via common carriers begin with the issuance of a properly completed bill of lading. The information on the bill specifies the name and address of the consignor and consignee as well as routing instructions for the carrier to follow. A description of the commodities in the shipment, the number of items in each commodity description, and the class or rate for the commodity also are inserted on the bill. Many shippers provide their own bills of lading that have preprinted on the bill the shipper's name and a description of the commodities most commonly shipped. This reduces the time required for filling out the bill, thereby eliminating delays at the shipper's loading facilities.

Straight Bill of Lading

The straight bill of lading is a nonnegotiable instrument, which means that possession of the original copy of the straight bill does not show certificate of title to the goods. The terms of sale agreed upon by the buyer and seller generally dictate where title passes when the straight bill of lading is used. The carrier does not require presentation of the original copy of the straight bill to effect delivery; the carrier merely is required to deliver the goods to the person or firm named as consignee on the straight bill of lading.

The order bill of lading is a negotiable instrument and shows certificate of title to the goods named on the order bill. Use of the order bill of lading enables the consignor to retain security interest in the goods; i.e., payment of the invoice value of the goods must be made prior to delivery of the goods to the consignee. The carrier cannot deliver the goods until the consignee, or rightful owner, presents the original copy of the order bill of lading to the carrier.

Order Bill of Lading

The procedural use of the order bill of lading is as follows. The order bill of lading is completed and a copy is given to the carrier. The original copy is forwarded to the consignor's bank, where a sight draft in the amount of the invoice price of the shipment is attached. This is then sent to the

EXHIBIT 9-1   Bill of lading.

NATIONAL MOTOR FREIGHT CLASSIFICATION A-10

RULES—Continued

(To be Printed on White Paper)

UNIFORM STRAIGHT BILL OF LADING

Shipper's No. ....

Agent's No. ....

Original—Not Negotiable—Domestic

.... Carrier.

RECEIVED, subject to the classifications and tariffs in effect on the date of the issue of this bill of lading,

From ...., Date ...., 19 ....,

At .... Street, ... City, ... County, ... State,

the property described below, in apparent good order, except as noted (contents and condition of contents of packages unknown) marked, consigned, and destined as shown below, which said company (the word company being understood throughout this contract as meaning any person or corporation in possession of the property under the contract) agrees to carry to its usual place of delivery at said destination, if on its own railroad, water line, highway route or routes, or within the territory of its highway operations, otherwise to deliver to another carrier on the route to said destination. It is mutually agreed, as to each carrier of all or any of said property over all or any portion of said route to destination, and as to each party at any time interested in all or any of said property, that every service to be performed hereunder shall be subject to all the conditions not prohibited by law, whether printed or written, herein contained, including the conditions on back hereof, which are hereby agreed to by the shipper and accepted for himself and his assigns.

Consigned to ....

Destination.. Street, ... City,

.... County, ... State

Routing ....

Delivering Carrier .... Vehicle or Car Initial .... No. ....

Collect On Delivery $.. and remit to:

.... Street, ... City, ... State

C. O. D. charge | Shipper ☐
to be paid by | Consignee ☐

No. Pack-ages	Kind of Package, Description of Articles, Special Marks, and Exceptions	*Weight (Subject to Correction)	Class or Rate	Check Column	
					Subject to Section 7 of conditions, if this shipment is to be delivered to the consignee without recourse on the consignor, the consignor shall sign the following statement:
					The carrier shall not make delivery of this shipment without payment of freight and all other lawful charges.
					(Signature of consignor)
					If charges are to be prepaid write or stamp here "To be Prepaid."
					Received $.................... to apply in prepayment of the charges on the property described hereon.
					Agent or Cashier
					Per .... (The signature here acknowledges only the amount prepaid)

*If the shipment moves between two ports by a carrier by water, the law requires that the bill of lading shall state whether it is "carrier's or shipper's weight."

Note—Where the rate is dependent on value, shippers are required to state specifically in writing the agreed or declared value of the property.

The agreed or declared value of the property is hereby specifically stated by the shipper to be not exceeding

.... per ....

Charges advanced:

$ ....

Shipper .... Agent.

Per .... Per ....

Permanent address of Shipper: .... Street, ... City, ... State

**Recommended C. O. D. Section be Printed in Red.

Source: National Motor Freight Classification A-10, Washington, D.C.

consignee's bank, and after payment of the sight draft the consignee receives the original copy. The funds are then transferred to the consignor. After presentation of the original copy to the carrier, the consignee receives the goods.

If the original consignee cannot pay the sight draft, the consignor retains title to the goods and can seek out a new buyer. If the consignee sold the goods to another party, the carrier could not legally make delivery to the original consignee. In both situations, the party possessing the properly endorsed original copy would have title to the goods and the carrier would make delivery to this new owner.

Bill of Lading
Contract Terms

The terms of the contract for movement between the carrier and the shipper are specified on the bill of lading. One of the primary terms of the bill of lading contract is the specification of the carrier's liability, which was discussed in Chapter 7. The complete contract of carriage is found on the bill of lading, as well as the carrier's tariffs and ICC rules and regulations. A copy of the bill of lading contract is shown in Exhibit 9-2.

The major terms of the carrier's contract of carriage as found on the bill of lading are as follows.

1. *Carrier liability*: the carrier is held liable for all loss damage or delay to the goods except for the following: *Act of God* — loss resulting from any unavoidable catastrophe of nature. If the carrier had sufficient opportunity to avoid the catastrophe, the carrier is liable and cannot use this exception. *Act of Public Enemy* — loss resulting from armed aggression against our country. *Act of Shipper* — loss resulting from shipper's improper loading, packaging or concealment of goods being shipped. *Act of Public Authority* — loss resulting from public agencies taking or destroying goods by due process of law. *Inherent Nature of the Goods* — the normal or expected loss of the products, e.g., evaporation.

2. *Reasonable dispatch*: the carrier is held liable for the actual loss or damage as a result of unreasonable delay in transit. No specific rule has been established for determining reasonable time. The specifics of the shipment are examined to see if the delay was unreasonable given the circumstances.

3. *No recourse*: the carrier has no legal recourse back to the shipper for additional charges after delivery has been made. If the shipper signs the no recourse clause and the shipment is delivered, the carrier has recourse only to the consignee for additional freight charges for the shipment.

4. *Articles of extraordinary value*: the carrier is not obligated to carry documents or articles of extraordinary value unless such items are specifically rated in the classification or tariff. This is one area where a common carrier can refuse to provide service.

This brief discussion of the bill of lading contract terms describes the essence of the contract of carriage. The various rules and regulations found

EXHIBIT 9-2   Bill of lading contract.

NATIONAL MOTOR FREIGHT CLASSIFICATION A-10

CONTRACT TERMS AND CONDITIONS

Sec. 1. (a) The carrier or party in possession of any of the property herein described shall be liable as at common law for any loss thereof or damage thereto, except as hereinafter provided.

(b) No carrier or party in possession of all or any of the property herein described shall be liable for any loss thereof or damage thereto or delay caused by the Act of God, the public enemy, the authority of law, or the act or default of the shipper or owner, or for natural shrinkage. The carrier's liability shall be that of warehouseman, only, for loss, damage, or delay caused by fire occurring after the expiration of the free time (if any) allowed by tariffs lawfully on file (such free time to be computed as therein provided) after notice of the arrival of the property at destination or at the port of export (if intended for export) has been duly sent or given, and after placement of the property for delivery at destination, or tender of delivery of the property to the party entitled to receive it, has been made. Except in case of negligence of the carrier or party in possession (and the burden to prove freedom from such negligence shall be on the carrier or party in possession), the carrier or party in possession shall not be liable for loss, damage, or delay occurring while the property is stopped and held in transit upon the request of the shipper, owner, or party entitled to make such request, or resulting from a defect or vice in the property, or for country damage to cotton, or from riots or strikes. Except in case of carrier's negligence, no carrier or party in possession of all or any of the property herein described shall be liable for delay caused by highway obstruction, faulty or impassable highway, or lack of capacity of any highway, bridge or ferry, and the burden to prove freedom from such negligence shall be on the carrier or party in possession.

(c) In case of quarantine the property may be discharged at risk and expense of owners into quarantine depot or elsewhere, as required by quarantine regulations or authorities, or for the carrier's dispatch at nearest available point in carrier's judgment, and in any such case carrier's responsibility shall cease when property is so discharged, or property may be returned by carrier at owner's expense to shipping point, earning freight both ways. Quarantine expenses of whatever nature or kind upon or in respect to property shall be borne by the owners of the property or be a lien thereon. The carrier shall not be liable for loss or damage occasioned by fumigation or disinfection or other acts required or done by quarantine regulations or authorities even though the same may have been done by carrier's officers, agents, or employees, nor for detention, loss, or damage of any kind occasioned by quarantine or the enforcement thereof. No carrier shall be liable, except in the case of negligence, for any mistake or inaccuracy in any information furnished by the carrier, its agents, or officers, as to quarantine laws or regulations. The shipper shall hold the carriers harmless from any expense they may incur, or damages they may be required to pay, by reason of the introduction of the property covered by this contract into any place against the quarantine laws or regulations in effect at such place.

Sec. 2. (a) No carrier is bound to transport said property by any particular schedule, train, vehicle or vessel, or in time for any particular market or otherwise than with reasonable dispatch. Every carrier shall have the right in case of physical necessity to forward said property by any carrier or route between the point of shipment and the point of destination. In all cases not prohibited by law, where a lower value than actual value has been represented in writing by the shipper or has been agreed upon in writing as the released value of the property as determined by the classification or tariffs upon which the rate is based, such lower value plus freight charges if paid shall be the maximum amount to be recovered, whether or not such loss or damage occurs from negligence.

(b) As a condition precedent to recovery, claims must be filed in writing with the receiving or delivering carrier, or carrier issuing this bill of lading, or carrier on whose line the loss, damage, injury or delay occurred, or carrier in possession of the property when the loss, damage, injury or delay occured, within nine months after delivery of the property (or, in the case of export traffic, within nine months after delivery at port of export) or, in case of failure to make delivery, then within nine months after a reasonable time for delivery has elapsed; and suits shall be instituted against any carrier only within two years and one day from the day when notice in writing is given by the carrier to the claimant that the carrier has disallowed the claim or any part or parts thereof specified in the notice. Where claims are not filed or suits are not instituted thereon in accordance with the foregoing provisions, no carrier hereunder shall be liable, and such claims will not be paid.

(c) Any carrier or party liable on account of loss of or damage to any of said property shall have the full benefit of any insurance that may have been effected, upon or on account of said property, so far as this shall not avoid the policies or contracts of insurance: **PROVIDED,** That the carrier reimburse the claimant for the premium paid thereon.

Sec. 3. Except where such service is required as the result of carrier's negligence, all property shall be subject to necessary cooperage and baling at owner's cost. Each carrier over whose route cotton or cotton linters is to be transported hereunder shall have the privilege, at its own cost and risk, of compressing the same for greater convenience in handling or forwarding, and shall not be held responsible for deviation or unavoidable delays in procuring such compression. Grain in bulk consigned to a point where there is a railroad, public or licensed elevator, may (unless otherwise expressly noted herein, and then if it is not promptly unloaded) be there delivered, and placed with other grain of the same kind and grade without respect to ownership (and prompt notice thereof shall be given to the consignor), and if so delivered shall be subject to a lien for elevator charges in addition to all other charges hereunder.

Sec. 4. (a) Property not removed by the party entitled to receive it within the free time (if any) allowed by tariffs, lawfully on file (such free time to be computed as therein provided), after notice of the arrival of the property at destination or at the port of export (if intended for export) has been duly sent or given, and after placement of the property for delivery at destination has been made, or property not received, at time tender of delivery of the property to the party entitled to receive it has been made, may be kept in vessel, vehicle, car, depot, warehouse or place of business of the carrier, subject to the tariff charge for storage and to carrier's responsibility as warehouseman, only, or at the option of the carrier, may be removed to and stored in a public or licensed warehouse at the point of delivery or other available point, or if no such warehouse is availabe at point of delivery or at other available point, then in other available storage facility, at the cost of the owner and there held without liability on the part of the carrier, and subject to a lien for all freight and other lawful charges, including a reasonable charge for storage. In the event consignee cannot be found at address given for delivery, then in that event, notice of the placing of such goods in warehouse shall be mailed to the address given for delivery and mailed to any other address given on the bill of lading for notification, showing the warehouse in which such property has been placed, subject to the provisions of this paragraph.

(b) Where nonperishable property which has been transported to destination hereunder is refused by consignee or the party entitled to receive it upon tender of delivery, or said consignee or party entitled to receive it fails to receive or claim it within 15 days after notice of arrival shall have been duly sent or given, the carrier may sell the same at public auction to the highest bidder, at such place as may be designated by the carrier:

PROVIDED, That the carrier shall have first mailed, sent, or given to the consignor notice that the property has been refused or remains unclaimed, as the case may be, and that it will be subject to sale under the terms of the bill of lading if disposition be not arranged for, and shall have published notice containing a description of the property, the name of the party to whom consigned, or, if shipped order notify, the name of the party to be notified, and the time and place of sale, once a week for two successive weeks, in a newspaper of general circulation at the place of sale or nearest place where such newspaper is published. **PROVIDED,** That 30 days shall have elapsed before publication of notice of sale after said notice that the property was refused or remains unclaimed was mailed, sent or given.

(c) Where perishable property which has been transported hereunder to destination is refused by consignee or party entitled to receive it, or said consignee or party entitled to receive it shall fail to receive it promptly, the carrier may, in its discretion, to prevent deterioration or further deteriorations, sell the same to the best advantage at private or public sale: **PROVIDED,** That if time serves for notification to the consignor or owner of the refusal of the property or the failure to receive it and request for disposition of the property, such notification shall be given, in such manner as the exercise of due diligence requires, before the property is sold.

(d) Where the procedure provided for in the two paragraphs last preceding is not possible, it is agreed that nothing contained in said paragraphs shall be construed to abridge the right of the carrier at its option to sell the property under such circumstances and in such manner as may be authorized by law.

(e) The proceeds of any sale made under this section shall be applied by the carrier to the payment of freight, demurrage, storage, and any other lawful charges and the expense of notice, advertisement, sale, and other necessary expense and of caring for and maintaining the property, if proper care of same requires special expense, and should there be a balance it shall be paid to the owner of the property sold hereunder.

(f) Property destined to or taken from a station, wharf, landing or other place at which there is no regularly appointed freight agent, shall be entirely at risk of owner after unloaded from cars, vehicles or vessels or until loaded into cars, vehicles or vessels, and, except in case of carrier's negligence, when received from or delivered to such stations, wharf, landings, or other places, shall be at owner's risk until the cars are attached to and after they are detached from locomotive or train or until loaded into and after unloaded from vessels, or if property is transported in motor vehicle trailers or semi-trailers, until such trailers or semi-trailers are attached to and after they are detached from power units. Where a carrier is directed to unload or deliver property transported by motor vehicle at a particular location where consignee or consignee's agent is not regularly located, the risk after unloading, or delivery, shall be that of the owner.

Sec. 5. No carrier hereunder will carry or be liable in any way for any documents, specie, or for any articles of extraordinary value not specifically rated in the published classification or tariffs unless a special agreement to do so and a stipulated value of the articles are endorsed hereon.

Sec. 6. Every party, whether principal or agent, shipping explosives or dangerous goods, without previous full written disclosure to the carrier of their nature, shall be liable for and indemnify the carrier against all loss or damage caused by such goods, and such goods may be warehoused at owner's risk and expense or destroyed without compensation.

(Uniform Straight)

Source: National Motor Freight Classification A-10, Washington, D.C.

EXHIBIT 9-2 Continued.

NATIONAL MOTOR FREIGHT CLASSIFICATION A-10

Sec. 7. The owner or consignee shall pay the freight and average, if any, and all other lawful charges accruing on said property; but, except in those instances where it may lawfully be authorized to do so, no carrier shall deliver or relinquish possession at destination of the property covered by this bill of lading until all tariff rates and charges thereon have been paid. The consignor shall be liable for the freight and all other lawful charges, except that if the consignor stipulates, by signature, in the space provided for that purpose on the face of this bill of lading that the carrier shall not make delivery without requiring payment of such charges and the carrier, contrary to such stipulation shall make delivery without requiring such payment, the consignor (except as hereinafter provided) shall not be liable for such charges. **PROVIDED,** That, where the carrier has been instructed by the shipper or consignor to deliver said property to a consignee other than the shipper or consignor, such consignee shall not be legally liable for transportation charges in respect of the transportation of said property (beyond those billed against him at the time of delivery for which he is otherwise liable) which may be found to be due after the property has been delivered to him, if the consignee (a) is an agent only and has no beneficial title in said property, and (b) prior to delivery of said property has notified the delivering carrier in writing of the fact of such agency and absence of beneficial title, and, in the case of a shipment reconsigned or diverted to a point other than that specified in the original bill of lading, has also notified the delivering carrier in writing of the name and address of the beneficial owner of said property; and in such cases the shipper or consignor, or, in the case of a shipment so reconsigned or diverted, the beneficial owner shall be liable for such additional charges. If the consignee has given to the carrier erroneous information as to who the beneficial owner is, such consignee shall himself be liable for such additional charges. Nothing herein shall limit the right of the carrier to require at time of shipment the prepayment or guarantee of the charges. If upon inspection it is ascertained that the articles shipped are not those described in this bill of lading, the freight charges must be paid upon the articles actually shipped.

Sec. 8. If this bill of lading is issued on the order of the shipper, or his agent, in exchange or in substitution for another bill of lading, the shipper's signature to the prior bill of lading as to the statement of value or otherwise, or election of common law or bill of lading liability, in or in connection with such prior bill of lading, shall be considered a part of this bill of lading as fully as if the same were written or made in or in connection with this bill of lading.

Sec. 9. (a) If all or any part of said property is carried by water over any part of said route, such water carriage shall be performed subject to all the terms and provisions of, and all the exemptions from liability contained in, the Act of the Congress of the United States, approved on February 13, 1893, and entitled "An act relating to the navigation of vessels, etc.," and of other statutes of the United States according carriers by water the protection of limited liability, and to the conditions contained in this bill of lading not inconsistent therewith or with this section.

(b) No such carrier by water shall be liable for any loss or damage resulting from any fire happening to or on board the vessel, or from explosion, bursting of boilers or breakage of shafts, unless caused by the design or neglect of such carrier.

(c) If the owner shall have exercised due diligence in making the vessel in all respects seaworthy and properly manned, equipped and supplied, no such carrier shall be liable for any loss or damage resulting from the perils of the lakes, seas, or other waters, or from latent defects in hull, machinery, or appurtenances whether existing prior to, at the time of, or after sailing, or from collision, stranding, or other accidents of navigation, or from prolongation of the voyage. And, when for any reason it is necessary, any vessel carrying any or all of the property herein described shall be at liberty to call at any port or ports, in or out of the customary route, to tow and be towed, to transfer, trans-ship, or lighter, to load and discharge goods at any time, to assist vessels in distress, to deviate for the purpose of saving life or property, and for docking and repairs. Except in case of negligence such carrier shall not be responsible for any loss or damage to property if it be necessary or is usual to carry the same upon deck.

(d) General Average shall be payable according to the York-Antwerp Rules of 1924, Sections 1 to 15, inclusive, and Sections 17 to 22, inclusive, and as to matters not covered thereby according to the laws and usages of the Port of New York. If the owners shall have exercised due diligence to make the vessel in all respects seaworthy and properly manned, equipped and supplied, it is hereby agreed that in case of danger, damage or disaster resulting from faults or errors in navigation, or in the management of the vessel, or from any latent or other defects in the vessel, her machinery or appurtenances, or from unseaworthiness, whether existing at the time of shipment or at the beginning of the voyage (provided the latent or other defects or the unseaworthiness was not discoverable by the exercise of due diligence), the shippers, consignees and or owners of the cargo shall nevertheless pay salvage and any special charges incurred in respect of the cargo, and shall contribute with the shipowner in general average to the payment of any sacrifices, losses or expenses of a general average nature that may be made or incurred for the common benefit or to relieve the adventure from any common peril.

(e) If the property is being carried under a tariff which provides that any carrier or carriers party thereto shall be liable for loss from perils of the sea, then as to such carrier or carriers the provisions of this section shall be modified in accordance with the tariff provisions, which shall be regarded as incorporated into the conditions of this bill of lading.

(f) The term "water carriage" in this section shall not be construed as including lighterage in or across rivers, harbors, or lakes, when performed by or on behalf of carriers other than water.

Sec. 10. Any alteration, addition, or erasure in this bill of lading which shall be made without the special notation hereon of the agent of the carrier issuing this bill of lading, shall be without effect, and this bill of lading shall be enforceable according to its original tenor.

(Uniform Straight)

in the carrier's tariffs and those issued by the ICC provide the finer detail in the contract. These contract terms are subject to regulatory scrutiny for compliance to common carrier duties and other transportation regulations.

THE FREIGHT BILL

Definition

The freight bill is the carrier's invoice for the charges incurred in the movement of a given shipment. ICC regulations stipulate the credit terms the carriers are permitted to offer the shipper or consignee. The reason for regulation of credit terms is the preclusion of discrimination; i.e., it prevents the carrier from discriminating against a particular shipper by extending short credit times and granting others longer times. The shipper is required to comply with the credit payment periods. No discount is permitted for transportation charges.

Credit Terms

Railroads are permitted to extend a maximum of five days' credit, i.e., the freight charges must be paid within five days of presentation of the freight bill. For motor carrier shipments, the freight bill must be paid within seven days of presentation. The carriers can require prepayment of charges if, in the opinion of the carrier, the value of the commodity being shipped is less than the transportation charges.

Freight bills may be either prepaid or collect. The prepaid or collect basis determines when the freight bill will be presented and not necessarily whether the charges are paid in advance or after completion of the movement. On a prepaid shipment, the freight bill is presented on the effective day of shipment. On a collect shipment, the freight bill is presented on the effective day of delivery. In both cases, the bills must be paid within maximum days of credit from presentation, but with the collect basis, the due date for payment is extended by the length of the transit time.

In order to meet the prescribed credit period, companies will perform only a cursory preaudit of the freight bill (check for correct math). A more thorough audit (determination of correctness of rate given routing, weight, carrier, etc.) is made at a later date but within three years of the shipment date. Claims for overcharges may be filed with the carrier within three years of delivery of the shipment.

Freight bill auditing may be performed internally by the traffic personnel. Internal auditing requires personnel with an extensive expertise in the area of carrier tariffs and rates. For companies that do not have the inhouse expertise, external auditors are available. External auditors usually receive a percentage of the overcharge claims paid.

CLAIMS

Definition

The freight claim is the document (no prescribed format) filed with the carrier to recoup monetary losses incurred as a result of loss, damage, or delay to the shipment or to recover overcharge payments. As noted above, the common carrier is liable for all loss, damage, or delay, with limited exception (Act of God, Act of Public Enemy, Act of Shipper, Act of Public Authority, and Inherent Nature of the Goods).

Nature of Claims

Freight claims must be filed in writing with the carrier (originating, delivering, or on whose line damage occurred) within nine months of delivery, or, in the case of loss, within nine months of reasonable delivery. The carrier is required to acknowledge in writing the receipt of the claim within 30 days. The carrier must inform the claimant within 120 days after receipt if the claim will be paid or refused. If the claim is not disposed of within 120 days, the carrier must notify the claimant of the reasons for failure to settle the claim at the end of each 60 succeeding days. If the carrier disallows the claim, the filing party has two years from the time of disallowance to bring legal action through the courts against the carrier.

Damage Claims

Damage may be either visible or concealed. Visible damage is that detected prior to opening the package and is usually discovered at delivery. Concealed damage is that which is not detected until the package is opened. A problem arises with the latter in determining whether the concealed damage occurred while the goods were in the carriers' possession or the consignee's possession. Many carrier's have adopted the policy that concealed damage claims must be filed within 15 days of delivery. However, this does not overrule the nine-month limitation, but the carrier will look more favorably upon the claim if it is filed within the stated policy period.

To support the claim, the claimant is required to submit the original bill of lading, the original paid freight bill, and some indication of the commodity's value (invoice, price catalog, etc.). If the consignee notes on the bill of lading that the goods were damaged when tendered for delivery and there is no such indication of damage when the carrier picked up the shipment, the claimant has a *prima facie* case against the carrier. The original paid freight bill is used to determine the amount the carrier will reimburse the claimant, since the courts have concluded that the carrier is held liable for the market value of the commodity at destination less any unpaid freight charges.

The value of the damage claim is derived from the following principle: The claimant shall be put in as good condition as he would have been had the goods been delivered safely. To determine this value, the claimant will utilize the original invoice, price catalog, etc., to show what the market value of the commodity would be at destination. For commodities that do not have a ready market value, e.g., one-of-a-kind items, the claimant may use cost accounting records to determine the value.

The logistics manager must recognize that there is a cost involved in the filing of a claim. This cost includes labor, communication and overhead. This cost of filing a claim establishes the minimum damage value required before a claim is filed. For example, if the cost to file a claim is $40, only claims for more than $40 would be filed with the carrier.

Damage to goods results in considerable "hidden" costs. In addition to the direct cost of filing a claim, the intended user experiences a loss associated with the inability to use the product. Stockout costs (lost profit or lost productivity) may be incurred, as well as ill will between the buyer and seller. To prevent the cost and disruption associated with damage in transit, the logistics manager may improve upon the protective packaging or utilize a different carrier. A total cost analysis comparing the saving in reduced damage to the added cost of packaging or transportation cost would be utilized.

F.O.B. TERMS OF SALE

The F.O.B. terms of sale determine the logistics responsibility that the buyer and seller will incur. Originally, *F.O.B.* referred to the seller's making the product free of transportation charges to the ship, or "free on board." More specifically, the F.O.B. terms of sale delineate (1) who is to incur transportation charges, (2) who is to control movement of the shipment, and (3) where the title passes to the buyer.

The F.O.B. term has associated with it a named point which specifies the point to which the seller incurs transportation charges and responsibility and relinquishes title to the buyer. For example, "F.O.B., delivered" indicates that the seller incurs all transportation charges and responsibility to the destination of the buyer and title passes to the buyer at delivery. "F.O.B., plant" is the exact opposite; the buyer incurs all transportation charges and responsibility and title passes to the buyer at the origin of the shipment.

The terms of sale utilized by the firm for sale of its products or purchase of its raw material have a direct bearing upon the magnitude of the transportation function. A firm that purchases raw materials F.O.B., origin and sells its finished product F.O.B., delivered would require a rather extensive transportation management department. In such a situation the firm is controlling carrier selection and warehousing, and is also incurring transportation charges for all commodity movements. This responsibility can be passed on to the buyer or supplier by altering the terms of sale and thereby lessening the importance of transportation management for the firm.

The F.O.B. term also defines the party who has the responsibility for filing a damage claim. The party that possesses title to the goods must file the claim. If damage occurs after the shipment reached the named point, the buyer would be responsible for filing the claim. Conversely, if damage occurred prior to the shipment reaching the named point, the seller would file the claim.

PRIVATE CARRIAGE

In almost every company, private carriage has either been given serious consideration or been implemented as an alternative to common carrier (for-hire) transportation. The desire for better service or lower cost is the motivating force behind the use of private carriage. Since private carriage is a link alternative, the logistics manager is directly involved in the evaluation of the potential for private carriage and, if private carriage is undertaken, in its operation.

Types

Companies have utilized private carriage in rail (private rail cars), water, air, and truck transportation, but private trucking is by far the most widely used form of private carriage. Private rail carriage consists of shipper owned or leased rail cars moved by the railroad, which provides a car allowance to the shipper. Shipper owned (leased) rail cars are frequently found in companies utilizing unit train moves, e.g., coal and grain shipments.

Rather extensive use of private water transportation is made by shippers of grain, coal, oil, and other bulk commodities. In private water transportation, the shipper not only owns (leases) the equipment, but also operates the private fleet.

Private air transportation is primarily utilized to transport company personnel. Very few private air carriage operations are designed to transport freight; an occasional emergency shipment will be moved by a private aircraft.

As noted above, private trucking is the most widely used form of private carriage. Private trucking is easy to start — all that is needed is a truck and a driver. It has been estimated that in 1975 there were approximately 103,000 private trucking operations.[1] The actual number of private carriers is difficult to determine since the private carrier is not required to report to a government agency.

Since private trucking is the most frequently used and most pervasive form of private carriage, this section will emphasize the management decision areas concerned with private truck operations. Attention will be directed to the reasons companies use private trucking, the legal requirements for bona fide private trucking, the feasibility (reevaluation) study and the private truck operations.

Rationale for Private Trucking

Private trucking is primarily used to improve service or to lower costs. Private trucking permits a shipper to provide better service to customers and thereby increase the marketability of its product. Better service (than provided by common carrier) results from the firm's ability to exercise greater control over the provision of the link service.

By having a direct control over the dispatching, routing, etc., of the private fleet, a company can provide lower transit times and more convenient delivery schedules to customers and can reduce damage (the driver is an employee of the shipper). These service improvements can result in reduced inventories for the buyer. Improved customer service resulting from the use of private trucking permits the seller (shipper) to differentiate the product, thereby gaining a competitive edge in the marketplace.

Within the improved service reasons, one finds companies being "forced" into private trucking because for-hire carriers either cannot or will not provide the desired service. The two most frequent service areas are the movement of freight requiring special equipment (e.g., high cube capacity trailers) and driver-salesman operations (e.g., bread or milk deliveries). In the latter case, the company does not have to rely upon the for-hire carrier to act as its sales agent, while, in the first case, the carrier may deem the purchase of special equipment to be uneconomical.

The other common reason for using private carriage is to reduce costs. If a private fleet is operated as efficiently as a common carrier, the cost of private transportation should be lower than common carriage, since the common carrier profit is eliminated. Products that have high density and high value and move in large volumes (truckload quantities) are logical shipments for realization of lower costs via private truck.

It must be pointed out that achieving both lower costs and improved service may not be possible for a private fleet. For example, to achieve lower costs, a firm may consolidate shipments to achieve a full truckload before dispatching a vehicle to a market area. This consolidation may require delays in dispatching shipments, which may result in longer transit times. Most companies will attempt to lower costs given some acceptable level of service.

Companies that emphasize the lower cost goal should establish the private truck operation as a profit center. The private truck division will assess an internal charge to the division, department, plant, etc., that uses the fleet. This "paper" fee usually is based upon a rate schedule that is a percentage (90%-95%) of the common carrier rate or that is based upon the actual cost of operation.

The profit center concept must permit the user (division, plant, etc.) to choose between the private fleet and a common carrier. This "competitive" use provides some inherent control over the conflicts that may result from the philosophy that because the private fleet is in place it must be used regardless of the for-hire charges. Accurate accountability of the total cost of private trucking is very critical to the viability of the profit center approach; if costs are overstated, a beneficial private trucking operation may be discarded since the center may not be able to "charge" a competitive fee (competitive with for-hire carriers) that is high enough to cover its costs and, thus, not make a profit (and vice versa for costs that are understated).

The Feasibility (Reevaluation) Study

Analyze Changes in Current Approach

Before the decision is made to implement private trucking, the existing for-hire system must be examined for potential cost reductions. Rate negotiations with common carriers must be explored for possible rate decreases. Increasing the weight per shipment, using more protective packaging, increasing the density, providing the carrier with a balanced load pattern (finished goods out and raw materials in), and reducing the handling required (palletization) are logistics area changes that offer potential for rate reductions. In addition, for-hire carrier services such as stopping in transit offer possibilities for lower transportation charges.

Investigate Other Alternatives

Consideration should be given to the use of contract carriers (see Chapter 7). The contract carrier can provide essentially the same service as private trucking. Special equipment, unique pick-up and delivery times and lower transit times are all possible with the use of a contract carrier. The contract carrier will, however, include a profit in the rates charged, which may result in higher costs than from private trucking.

The feasibility (reevaluation) study of private trucking compares the cost and service of private trucking to that of for-hire carriage. The study should consider private trucking for only a portion of the company, not for all transportation requirements. Furthermore, the study should be restricted to the movement of high-value, high-density commodities, and to links that offer regular, high-volume, two-way load patterns (no empty backhaul).

Uneconomical private trucking usually emanates from underutilization of the equipment. This underutilization stems from low, irregular volume of freight to be moved and from empty backhauls. To guard against this, a company will select a link that will generate truckload moves in both directions. If this is not possible, efforts should be made to keep the number of empty miles as low as possible.

For example, a large corporation that manufactures industrial products found that with more than 36 percent empty miles private trucking was more expensive than for-hire carriage. This discovery was made at the study stage and was extremely useful in delineating the operating scope of the fleet after implementation.

Starting Point

The point of departure in the study is the amount of freight to be shipped and the origin/destination of the moves. This information will define the amount of equipment needed and the number of miles the equipment will be operated. By knowing how much equipment is required and the mileage it will be driven, the evaluator can determine the fixed and operating costs (total costs) of the proposed private fleet.

For example, if over a given link 80,000 pounds a day is moved in one direction, the minimum number of tractor/trailer combinations required is two. Current state maximum weight limits permit a maximum net weight per vehicle of about 40,000 to 45,000 pounds. Thus, two trucks, each carrying 40,000 pounds, are necessary to transport the 80,000 pounds generated over the link.*

Cost Analysis

Once the number of trucks to be used is known, the next step is to calculate the total cost of the proposed private trucking operation. Exhibit

---

* Product density (weight/cubic foot) has a direct bearing upon the maximum payload a vehicle may carry and, thus, the number of vehicles required. Assuming that the 80,000 pounds of commodity to be transported has a density of 10 lbs./ft.^{3} and that a trailer being used has 2,600 ft.^{3} (40' long × 8' high × 8' wide), then a minimum of three units would be required. This is determined as follows: Each unit can transport 26,000 lbs. (10 lbs./ft.^{3} × 2,600 ft.^{3}/trailer = 26,000 lbs./trailer). Then, 80,000 lbs. divided by 26,000 lbs./trailer equals 3+ trailers.

EXHIBIT 9-3   Private trucking costs.

1. Fixed costs
   a. depreciation
      1. straight trucks
      2. tractors
      3. trailers
      4. garage and shop equipment
   b. interest on investment
      1. straight trucks
      2. tractors
      3. trailers
      4. garage and shop equipment
   c. management costs
      1. salaries of management and garage supervisors
      2. office and garage salaries
      3. workman's compensation, taxes
      4. FICA
      5. fringes: insurance—life and health, vacation and holiday pay, bonuses
      6. entertainment and travel
      7. education/professional development
      8. dues and subscriptions
   d. office costs
      1. utilities—heat, electricity, water/sewage
      2. telephone, teletype
      3. office space—rent or allocated cost, property taxes
      4. equipment, supplies and repairs
      5. postage
   e. garage costs
      1. utilities
      2. rent or property cost
      3. supplies (uniforms, soap, cleaning fluid)
      4. special equipment (racks, storage bins)
      5. insurance (fire, theft)
   f. other:
      1. tarps
      2. chains
2. Operating costs
   a. drivers and helpers
      1. wages
      2. meal, lodging allowances for layovers
      3. workman's compensation
      4. FICA
      5. fringes: life and health insurance, vacation, holiday and sick pay
   b. vehicle operating costs
      1. fuel, oil, grease, filers
      2. tires and tubes, repairs
      3. repairs and parts (in house)
      4. outside repairs (parts and labor)
      5. road service
      6. tolls
      7. washing
      8. painting
      9. protective services
      10. antifreeze
   c. insurance
      1. comprehensive on vehicles
      2. collision
      3. public liability and property damage
      4. cargo
   d. licenses and registration fees
   e. highway use taxes: fuel, ton-miles

9-3 contains a list of the costs that must be considered. Cost estimates may be obtained from suppliers, other private fleet operators, and internal records and trade associations (e.g., Private Carrier Conference of the American Trucking Associations, Inc.).

The costs are categorized into fixed and operating. The fixed costs include depreciation of the trucks, trailers, and maintenance facility; interest; management; office; garage; and special equipment. The one area where fixed costs are usually understated is management cost. The time management spends controlling, directing, etc., the fleet must be allocated to the private fleet rather than to general administration, overhead, etc. Many companies have found that management spends more time managing the fleet than originally anticipated since the private fleet operation is new and is different than the company's primary business.

The operating cost area includes driver and helper costs, vehicle operating costs, insurance, registration fees, and highway use taxes. In each of these major cost areas, there are many specific costs that must be considered so as to get an accurate measure of the total operating costs. Since operating costs (variable) are approximately 90 percent of the total cost of a trucking operation, an accurate assessment of total operating costs is very critical.

After the total cost of private trucking is estimated, a comparison is made to the cost of shipping the same volume of freight by for-hire carriage (common or contract). If private trucking costs are lower, the logistics manager should use this savings to compute a return-on-investment (R.O.I. equals savings per year divided by the investment). This R.O.I. is then compared to the return the company normally realizes and if the private truck R.O.I. is equal to or greater than the normal return, the private truck operation is acceptable.

However, as indicated earlier, cost saving is not the only reason for utilizing private trucking. The improved service must also be weighed in making the final decision. If private trucking costs are higher than for-hire transportation, the decision rests upon whether the private truck service is worth the added cost.

Own vs. Lease Decision.   An integral part of the private truck feasibility study or operation is the question of equipment leasing. Equipment leasing is found in many private trucking operations and this section will consider the factors that are to be considered in the analysis of truck leasing.

Types of Leases   Basically, there are two types of lease arrangements available: finance lease and full service lease. Under the finance lease, the lessee pays a monthly fee that covers the equipment purchase price plus a lessor's finance charge. The lessor provides no other services. The finance lease is quite popular for trailer leasing.

The full service lease, as the name implies, includes the provision of a variety of support services. Such services as licensing, maintenance, insurance, towing, and washing, and providing fuel, substitute vehicles, road services, and highway use tax reports are all available. The leasing charge is dependent upon the amount of services requested. The full service lease is a common form of truck leasing.

Leasing offers the advantage of reducing the demands upon company funds. As capital becomes increasingly more costly and scarce, the leasing option becomes more advantageous. Existing capital is not drained away from use in the primary business of the company.

If full service leasing is used, a company can eliminate much of the private trucking risk. The fixed and operating costs (fuel, maintenance, etc.)

are known throughout the term of the lease. The full service lease is ideal for a firm starting a private fleet and lacking operating knowledge.

Leasing does have some disadvantages. Leasing may cost more than owning.* If the company has excess capital, investment in a private fleet may be a desirable use of the funds. The company may possess operating experience and would gain little benefit from full service leasing.

Private Fleet Operation

The purpose of this section is to draw attention to the major operating areas of private carriage. Emphasis is placed upon regulatory controls and intra-organizational conflicts.

As noted in Chapter 7, private trucking is exempt from Federal economic regulations, but it is subject to Federal safety regulations. To be exempt from economic regulations, the private carrier must show that trucking is not the company's primary business. To comply with the primary business test, the firm must be able to prove that it takes the normal risks associated with a nontrucking business, e.g., it manufactures a product, maintains a sales force, holds inventory, etc.

The economic exemption simply requires that the private fleet be used in the furtherance of the firm's primary business. However, as firms have merged and conglomerates have been formed, a question has been raised as to the legality of using the private fleet of one subsidiary to transport the freight of another subsidiary. The ICC has held that intercorporate hauling via a private fleet is legal as long as *no* fee is charged, e.g., the service is free. When a fee is charged, the ICC has ruled that this is for-hire service and an operating authority as a common carrier is required.

Backhaul Problem   As noted earlier, the empty backhaul is one of the major problems to economical private trucking. Many private carriers attempt to secure revenue generating loads on the return haul. In order to comply with economic regulations, the private carrier is permitted to transport only certain types of commodities, namely agricultural, fish, and horticultural products. In addition, the private carrier is permitted to transport within 35 miles of an airport freight that will be or has been moved by air transportation. Such for-hire transportation, while generating revenue to offset the backhaul costs, distracts from the primary use of the private fleet. Equipment availability, flexibility of operation, and customer service may be adversely affected and one of the major goals of the private fleet— improved service—may not be achieved.

Safety Regulations   The primary Federal regulatory constraints imposed upon private carriers operating in interstate commerce are the safety regulations. Federal safety regulations impose rules in the following areas:

---

* For a presentation on the use of present value to the cost analysis, see: Kenneth A. Miller, "Lease vs. Buy?" *Distribution Worldwide*, March 1977, pp. 77-78.

1. Qualifications of drivers.
2. Driving of motor vehicles.
3. Parts and accessories necessary for safe operation.
4. Notification, reporting, and recording of accidents.
5. Hours of service of drivers.
6. Inspection and maintenance.
7. Transportation of hazardous materials.

The hours of service of drivers (driving time) regulation directly affects the utilization of drivers. The regulation states that a driver is permitted to drive a maximum of 10 hours. After 10 hours, the driver must accumulate 8 consecutive hours off-duty before driving again. In addition, a driver is permitted a maximum of 60 hours on-duty (driving, loading and unloading) in 7 consecutive days or 70 hours in 8 days.

These driving time regulations affect the level of service the private fleet can offer. For example, if a destination is 12 hours driving time from origin, the delivery will require at least 20 hours (10 hours driving plus 8 hours off-duty plus 2 hours driving) with one driver. For long-distance runs, driver teams are utilized so that one driver is driving while the other one is sleeping (off-duty) in the sleeper berth of the vehicle.

Another major operating area that requires managerial attention is intra-organizational conflict. More specifically, intra-organizational conflict refers to the departmental or divisional demands that do not agree with the goals of the private fleet operation.

The most common form of conflict is best described as the "free" transportation concept. The department assumes that the cost of using the private fleet is zero since the fleet is already in existence. Many shipments suddenly take on an emergency nature (the plant will close, the customer will be lost) and, therefore, the private truck must be used to give the special service needed.

To combat the idea of private trucking being free transportation, many companies will assess internal charges (paper costs) to the user department. These internal fees are included in the costs incurred by the division just as though the department has utilized a for-hire carrier. The user does not have free use of the private trucks.

The internal fee approach becomes the basis for organizing the private fleet as a profit center. The manager of the private fleet is evaluated on the basis of the "profit" (paper profit) generated by the fleet. The profit center approach is an ideal structure when the objective of the private fleet is lower costs.

If the profit center approach is used, the users should not be forced to use the private fleet at any cost so as to assure the private fleet operates profitably. The user should have the option to utilize for-hire carriers when the private trucking charges are higher than common carrrier rates.

The conflict between cost minimization and service maximization is constantly present in private trucking. An acceptable (desirable) level of service must be established and then costs can be minimized for this level of service. Without establishing desired service levels, it is very difficult to control private fleet costs.

Summary

In this section attention has been directed toward the use of private trucking, the most frequently used form of private carriage. The major reasons for using private trucking are to improve service and to reduce costs. The feasibility study must start with an examination of cost reductions and service improvements in the present system and then proceed to an examination of total private trucking costs, including operating cost. Finally, attention was given to the operating areas of regulatory compliance and intra-organizational conflicts.

In the next section, international traffic management is discussed.

INTERNATIONAL LOGISTICS

During the past decade, many companies have come to the realization that the world, not just the United States, is the marketplace. Foreign markets offer opportunities to sell additional units and thereby increase profits. Likewise, the United States has turned to foreign countries for raw materials, component parts, and finished products. As international trade grows for a company, international logistics becomes more important. The increased shipping distances and the multiplicity of regulations and foreign transportation systems associated with international business have contributed to the uniqueness and complexity of international logistics.

In this section, attention is directed toward international business functions that affect the logistics area.* The discussion will concentrate upon documentation, packaging, transportation alternatives, and carrier liability.

Documentation

Documentation for exportation is far more complicated than that required for domestic shipments. Since different nations are involved, the political as well as the economic consideration of the transaction affect the documentation required. The specific documentation requirements vary widely from country to country, but it is necessary to complete each document accurately, for a mistake may mean that the delivery of the shipment will be delayed.

For discussion purposes, the various documents will be grouped into two categories: sales and transportation. Much of the information required by the documents is similar, but each document serves a different purpose.

* For an overall treatment of international business, see: John D. Daniels, Ernest W. Ogram, Jr., and Lee H. Radebaugh, *International Business: Environments and Operations* (Reading, Mass.: Addison-Wesley, 1976).

Sales Documents   The initial document in any international business transaction is the sales contract. There is little uniformity in export sales contracts but, to reduce time and cost, the export sales contract should be complete so that all parties can understand the nature and specifics of the agreement.

The export sales contract should contain the following information:

1. Description of the commodities.
2. Price of the commodities.
3. Method and terms of payment.
4. Quality and quantity of the commodities.
5. Who bears the risk in transit.
6. Where title to the goods passes.
7. Insurance requirements and responsibilities.
8. Packaging, marking, and labeling requirements.
9. Port of exit.
10. Steamship line or air carrier.
11. Importer's permit number.
12. Any other special requirements of the buyer, carrier, or destination country.[2]

Once the sales contract has been negotiated, the method of payment must be determined. The letter of credit is the most common method of payment (cash, consignment, and open account are other forms used) and provides a high degree of protection. The letter of credit is an assurance by a bank that payment will be made as long as the sales terms (export sales contract terms) agreed to by the buyer and seller are met. When the seller complies with the sales conditions as stated in the letter of credit and presents a draft drawn in compliance with the letter of credit, payment is made to the exporter.

After agreement is reached as to sales and credit terms, the exporter prepares an export declaration. The export declaration (see Exhibit 9-4) provides the Department of Commerce with information as to the nature, value, etc., of export activity. The export declaration is filed with the Collector of Customs at the exit port or border point.

The commercial invoice is basically the seller's invoice for the commodities sold. However, the commercial invoice is used to determine the value of the commodity less freight and other charges and is often required by the letter of credit and by companies or agencies to determine the correct value for insurance purposes, assessing import duties, etc. Some countries have special requirements (language, information requested, etc.) for the commercial invoice, while some countries require a special form called the consular invoice to be used. (The consular invoice permits collection of import statistics.)

A certificate of origin is often required by a destination country when a treaty agreement has been made to give favorable import duty treatment to certain U.S. goods. The certificate of origin certifies that the origin of the goods is the United States so as to prevent application of the favorable import duty to goods that were merely reshipped from the United States after originating in another country.

The purpose of the above discussion of export sales documentation was to draw attention to the various documents needed in international transaction. Assistance with the documents required and their preparation is

EXHIBIT 9-4   Shipper's export declaration.

available from local financial institutions, area Chambers of Commerce, and local offices of the U.S. Department of Commerce.

The initiating document for any international shipment is the bill of lading. One bill of lading, the export bill of lading, could be issued to govern the domestic portion of the move (from plant to port of exit), the intercountry portion (ocean), and the foreign portion (from port of entry to final destination in foreign country). In practice, the majority of shipments move under a combination of bills of lading, domestic and ocean.

The ocean bill of lading is similar to the domestic bill of lading discussed earlier in this chapter. The ocean bill of lading serves as the contract of carriage, a receipt and, if applicable, a certificate of title. Little uniformity has been achieved in the ocean bill of lading and the carrier is able to add conditions to the bill of lading contract as long as the additions are not contrary to law.

The primary bill of lading contract term is concerned with the ocean carrier's liability. The Carriage of Goods by Sea Act of 1936 states that the ocean carrier is responsible to use due diligence to make its vessel seaworthy and is held liable for losses resulting from negligence. The shipper is liable for losses resulting from perils of the sea, acts of God, acts of the public enemy, inherent defects of the cargo, or shipper negligence. Thus, the liability of the ocean carrier is less than that imposed upon a domestic carrier.*

After the goods have been delivered at the dock, a dock receipt is issued by a steamship agent. The dock receipt merely indicates that the shipment has been delivered to the steamship company by the domestic carrier. The dock receipt can be used to show compliance with the letter of credit requirements for payment and to support damage claims.

Packaging

Export shipments moving via ocean transportation require more stringent packaging than normally used for domestic shipments. An export shipment is handled more: loaded at origin, unloaded at the dock, loaded onto ship, unloaded from ship at port, loaded onto delivery vehicle, unloaded at destination. This handling is usually made under unfavorable conditions—inclement weather, antiquated handling equipment, etc.

In addition, the shipper will find it very difficult to settle liability claims for damage. There are usually a multiplicity of firms involved in the freight handling and these firms are located in different countries. Claim prevention through more stringent packaging is the key to reduced liability claims for export shipments.

More protective packaging (increased packaging costs) for export shipments is justifiable when consideration is given to the stockout costs.

---

* Marine insurance is an integral part of ocean shipping since the ocean carrier's liability is rather limited. For a discussion of marine insurance, see: Kenneth U. Flood, *Traffic Management*, 3rd ed. (Dubuque, Iowa: Wm. C. Brown Company, 1975), pp. 384-388.

The distance involved is often so great that the length of time (two to four months) required to receive a reordered shipment may result in extremely high stockout costs to the buyer and seller. The buyer may resort to an alternate supply source and the original seller may lose the business.

The package size—weight, length, width, height—must conform to the customer's instructions. Packaging dimensions usually reflect the transportation physical constraints existing in the buyer's country. For example, the 40' × 8' × 8' container that is common in the United States may be nontransportable in a foreign country. The container may not fit the existing transportation equipment, height, and lateral constraints of the highways, bridges, overpasses, etc., of that country. If the package cannot be transported, the shipment will be repackaged and this additional handling adds costs, delay, and increased risk of loss or damage to the shipment.

As noted in Chapter 7, containers are used quite frequently for international shipping. The frequency of handling the actual commodity is greatly reduced by containerization, and with reduced commodity handling comes reduced risk of loss and damage as well as greater time efficiency in the transfer among modes. The decision to use containers must reflect the savings noted above as well as the added cost of the container, return freight costs on the container, and any additional costs of handling and storing the container.

Lastly, the package marking requirements for international shipments differ from domestic requirements. On domestic shipments, package markings provide much detail concerning the shipment content, consignee, etc. On export shipments, little information about the shipment is provided on the package. Large geometric symbols, numbers, letters, and various codes are used. The symbols (⬆, "This End Up," for example) provide handling instruction to foreign material handlers who normally cannot read English or any other language. The use of codes conceals the identity of the shipper, the consignee, and the goods so as to reduce the possibility of pilferage.

Transportation Alternatives

Two basic modes of transportation are available for the movement of international shipments from or to the United States: ocean and air transportation. The movement into and out of the port or airport will not be discussed in this section. Rather, the specifics of ocean and air transportation as they relate to international shipping will be emphasized.

Ocean Transportation.   Ocean transportation has a distinct advantage over air transportation in the area of rates. Ocean rates are lower than air rates. The lower transportation rate is the primary reason that the majority of international transportation is performed by ocean carriers.

Service Characteristics   Ocean transportation is slow. Long delays may occur at the ports of exit and entry. In addition, the frequency of service may be quite low or too erratic to certain countries, which increases the delay at the port and the total transit time.

The use of ocean transportation requires the selection of a departure port and a destination port. The relative proximity of the shipper and buyer to a port may be a major port selection determinant. However, consideration must be given to inland rates (to and from ports), carrier availability, (e.g., frequency, direct service between ports), and special port facilities (e.g., lift cranes, storage facilities).

Types of Carriers
There are two basic types of ocean carriers available: tramp and conference carriers. The tramp carrier does not follow a regular trade route. Rather, the tramp carrier goes from port to port following the trade, and this nomadic service poses problems as to carrier availability. Tramp carrier rates are not published and the specific rate charged is determined by the marketplace (demand of and supply for service).

The conference carriers are individual steamship companies who form a conference for the purpose of providing regular service over given shipping lanes at a published rate. Most conferences utilize a dual-rate system whereby a shipper who agrees to exclusively use conference carriers will receive a discount from the published noncontract rate. If the shipper does enter into a contract with the conference, a reduction of 8 to 15 percent is given to the exclusive-patronage shipper.

Rates
Ocean freight rates are assessed upon either weight or measurement of the shipment and the carrier will utilize the basis that results in the greatest charge. For the weight basis, the rate is assessed on the number of long tons (2,240 lbs.). On the measurement basis, the rate is assessed on the number of measurement tons which is defined as 40 ft.^{3}, i.e., a 4,000 ft.^{3} shipment equals 100 measurement tons.

Service
Air Carriers. The primary advantage of air transportation is low transit time. The tremendous speed of the airplane plus frequently scheduled flights permits servicing most foreign destinations in the matter of a few days, if not a few hours. The speed of air transportation has opened new foreign markets that previously were too far away in terms of ocean transit time. This has been especially true for companies exporting perishable products.

In addition to low transit time, air transportation offers an advantage in packaging. Less stringent packaging is required since the shipment will not be exposed to rough handling at the port, a rough ride on the oceans, and the climatic exposure of ocean transportation. It is possible to use the same packaging for international shipping as for domestic shipping when air transportation is used.

The primary disadvantage of air carriage is high freight rates. This high freight rate has prohibited many international shipments from being moved by air. Generally, commodities that are high in value, highly perishable and/or urgently needed are moved by air freight.

Foreign Freight Forwarders. For a company that has little expertise with international shipping, the foreign freight forwarder is the answer. The

Functions

foreign freight forwarder employs individuals that are knowledgeable in all aspects of international shipping, and most small international shippers find it uneconomical to employ such individuals in their traffic departments.

The primary function of the foreign freight forwarder is to make certain that the client's shipment is delivered to the foreign buyer. Most forwarders are capable of performing the following functions:

- Quoting steamship or other foreign carrier rates.
- Chartering vessels or obtaining necessary space.
- Obtaining export licenses.
- Obtaining port warehouse space.
- Tracing shipments in transit and expediting them through port of exit facilities.
- Paying freight charges.
- Obtaining dock receipts.
- Issuing export declarations for the shipper.
- Obtaining and preparing consular invoices.
- Preparing commercial invoices.
- Compiling ocean bills of lading and checking them against packing lists, weights and measures, etc.
- Preparing certificates of origin.
- Obtaining insurance.
- Presenting documents to the bank or forwarding them to other destinations.
- Collecting and submitting money for shipments.[3]

Since no two international sales transactions are exactly alike and shippers have varying capabilities for international traffic, the forwarder usually performs the portion of the export work that cannot be handled by the shipper. The logistics manager must weigh the forwarder's cost against the cost of hiring personnel to perform the same tasks.

Summary

As new and better inventions and ideas increase the scope of the business world, more and more companies are reaching out to foreign markets as a way of meeting the challenge of competitors. The coming years should see a quickening of this trend as more and more companies realize the potential markets open to them in other countries or find it necessary to turn to foreign nations for raw materials, components, or even finished products. And as international markets become more common, international logistics will grow increasingly more important.

Study Questions

1. What is the purpose of a bill of lading?
2. Distinguish between a straight bill of lading and an order bill of lading.
3. Discuss the nature of the contract of carriage as defined on the bill of lading.
4. Why are freight bill credit periods regulated? Discuss the credit terms and their impact upon the shipper.
5. Outline the procedure, documentation, and carrier responsibility in settling claims for damage.
6. Determine the logistics responsibilities described by the following F.O.B. terms: (a) F.O.B. port of entry; (b) F.O.B. origin, freight prepaid; (c) F.O.B. Toledo.
7. Why do firms operate private truck fleets?
8. Outline the major steps in a private truck feasibility study.
9. What are the advantages and disadvantages of leasing?
10. Discuss the economic and safety regulations imposed upon private trucking.
11. Comment upon the major private trucking operation problems and the solutions to these problems.
12. Discuss the purpose of the various documents required in international distribution.
13. Compare the liability of a railroad with the liability of an ocean carrier.
14. Discuss the packaging requirements of international shipments.

Notes

1. Charles A. Taff, *Commercial Motor Transportation*, 5th ed., (Cambridge, Md.: Cornell Maritime Press, 1975), p. 471

2. Durward L. Brooks, "Exporting Without Tears," *Transportation and Distribution Management*, June 1972, p. 44.

3. Durward L. Brooks, "Exporting Without Tears," *Transportation and Distribution Management*, December 1972, p.38.

Case 9-1
Make-It-While-You-Can Company

The Make-It-While-You-Can Company (Can Co.), located in St. Clair, Pennsylvania, is a leading manufacturer of tin cans for use in the commercial canning industry. Can Company sold over 5 million cans last year, for a total sales revenue of slightly over $2 million. Currently, Can Company receives the sheet tin from suppliers by rail and delivers the finished tin cans by common motor carrier. Tom Lynagh, the manager of Can Company, has instructed his staff to undertake a feasibility study of the possible advantages and disadvantages of the Can Company purchasing its own tractor-trailer units to make the finished goods delivery. He stated: "Because we deliver such a large quantity of tin cans, it may be wise for our company to look into the concept of private carriage. Buying our own trucks and making our own deliveries may be much cheaper and more efficient than hiring common motor carriers to do the job. I expect the final report from my staff in one week because I see no difficulties in fully evaluating this prospect." At the end of one week, Mr. Lynagh was dismayed to learn that the report was far from finished. The staff encountered problems in determining the appropriate number of tractors and trailers, in efficiently allocating costs and implementing pricing schedules, and deciding how to acquire drivers, among other operating dilemmas. A functional problem also arose as to where the transportation/logistics function should be located in the department hierarchy. Locating it in the marketing department was a possibility, but the sales effort might oversell production capacity to satisfy the company's motor carrier capacity. Locating the transportation/logistics function in other departments was also discussed, with no final recommendation formulated.

If you were on Mr. Lynagh's staff, what problems do you think you would encounter when studying the feasibility of your company going into private carriage? How could you attempt to solve these problems? Where in the company could this transportation/logistics function be located? Where would you locate it for maximum efficiency and overall coordination? Explain your reasoning.

SELECTED BIBLIOGRAPHY FOR PART III

BALLOU, RONALD H., and DANNIEL W. DeHAYES, Jr., "Transport Selection by Interfirm Analysis," *Transportation and Distribution Management*, Volume 7, Number 6, June 1967, pp. 33-37.

BARDI, EDWARD J., "Carrier Selection From One Mode," *Transportation Journal*, Volume 13, Number 1, Fall 1973, pp. 23-29.

COYLE, JOHN J., "The Compatibility of the Rule of Ratemaking and the National Transportation Policy," *ICC Practitioners' Journal*, March-April 1971, pp. 340-53.

DeHAYES, DANNIEL W., Jr., "Industrial Transportation Planning: Estimating Transit Time For Rail Carload Shipments." *Transportation Research Forum Papers*, 1969.

FAIR, MARVIN L., and ERNEST W. WILLIAMS, Jr., *Economics of Transportation and Logistics*, Dallas, Texas: Business Publications, Inc., 1975.

FAIR, MARVIN L., and JOHN GUANDOLO, *Transportation Regulation*, 8th Edition, Dubuque, Iowa: Wm. C. Brown Company, 1979.

FARRIS, MARTIN T., and PAUL T. McELHINEY, ed., *Modern Transportation Selected Reading*, 2nd ed., Boston: Houghton Mifflin Company, 1973.

FLOOD, KENNETH U., *Traffic Management*, 3rd ed., Dubuque, Iowa: Wm. C. Brown Company, 1975.

HARPER, DONALD V., *Transportation in America*, Englewood Cliffs, N.J.: Prentice-Hall, Inc., 1978.

HILLE, STANLEY J., and RICHARD F. POIST, Jr., eds., *Transportation: Principles and Perspectives*, Danville, Illinois: The Interstate Printers and Publishers, Inc., 1974.

LIEB, ROBERT C., *Transportation: The Domestic System*, Reston, Va.: Reston Publishing Co., Inc., 1978.

LOCKLIN, D. PHILIP, *Economics of Transportation*, 7th ed., Homewood, Illinois: Richard D. Irwin, Inc., 1972.

MILNE, A. M., and J. C. LAIGHT, *The Economics of Inland Transportation*, 2nd ed., London: Sir Isaac Pittman and Sons, 1963.

PEGRUM, DUDLEY F., *Transportation Economics and Public Policy*; 3rd ed., Homewood, Illinois: Richard D. Irwin, Inc., 1973.

SAMPSON, ROY J., and MARTIN T. FARRIS, *Domestic Transportation: Practice Theory, and Policy, 4th ed., Boston: Houghton Mifflin Company, 1979.*

SIGMON, RICHARD R., *Miller's Law of Freight Loss and Damage*, 4th ed., Dubuque, Iowa: Wm. C. Brown Company, 1974.

STEPHENSON, P. RONALD, and RONALD P. WILLET, "Selling with Physical Distribution Services," *Business Horizons*, Volume XI, Number 6, December 1968, pp. 75-85.

TAFF, CHARLES A., *Commercial Motor Transportation*, 5th ed., Cambridge, Md.: Cornell Maritime Press, Inc. 1975.

TAFF, CHARLES A., *Management of Physical Distribution and Transportation*, 6th ed., Homewood, Illinois: Richard D. Irwin, Inc., 1978.

WILLIAMS, ERNEST W., Jr., ed., *The Future of American Transportation*, Englewood Cliffs, New Jersey: Prentice-Hall, Inc., 1971.

WILSON, GEORGE W., *Essays on Some Unsettled Questions in the Economics of Transportation*, Bloomington, Indiana: Indiana University Business Report, Number 42, 1962.

Part IV

The previous sections have acquainted the reader with the specifics of the major functional areas of logistics and with the application of the particulars to the immediate short-run decision making in these areas. In this section our attention is focused upon the broader (long-run, less frequent) decision-making areas dealing with the overall management and control of nodal linking and nodal location decisions, organizational structuring, customer service levels and the design of logistics systems.

In the nodal location chapter a discussion of the logistics variables impacting the nodal location decision and an application of logistics oriented location techniques are presented. The relationship of logistics service levels upon the marketability of a firm's product and the procedures for establishing and controlling logistics service levels is considered in the customer service chapter. The final chapters consider organizational and control issues of the logistics system and a look at future issues.

Chapter 10

Nodal Location

After studying this chapter, you should be able to:

- Discuss the importance of location to logistics systems.

- Present an overview of the important factors affecting the location of fixed facilities such as plants and warehouses.

- Analyze certain quantitative techniques that can be used in making location decisions.

- Provide an understanding of some of the practical aspects of ratemaking practices of carriers that affect the location decision.

- Examine a procedure for linking the appropriate nodes in a logistics system.

The location of the various nodes in a firm's logistics system establishes constraints upon the efficiency of time and place utility creation. The geographic placement of a node directly affects the costs incurred in moving goods into and out of the node as well as the time required to do so and the resultant costs of inventory and logistics service. Once the nodal location decision has been made, the logistics manager can manipulate other logistics variables (link service, materials handling, order processing, etc.) to maximize time and place utility at minimum total cost. Our concern in this chapter is to examine the logistical variables pertinent to the nodal location decision.

The previous definition of a node, that is, a fixed point in the logistics system, suggests to the reader that the node is a logistics input variable that cannot be manipulated. This implication is both true and false. First, it is true that a node cannot be altered on a day-to-day basis; that is, a warehouse, for example, cannot be located in Detroit one day, Cleveland the next, and Toledo the third day. The physical and financial limitations required to move inventory would preclude such actions. The investment, lease contract, or public warehousing fees associated with the node would make such day-to-day changes uneconomical. Lastly, the availability of suitable warehouse space in the locations mentioned would be a pragmatic constraint. Thus, one is led to the conclusion that in the short run the location of a node is not manipulable.

Importance

But, in the long run, the location of a node is subject to managerial decision and is a variable input in the logistics system. The nodal location decision has a direct influence upon the costs of transporting and storing goods as well as upon the level and cost of service provided to the customers. The importance of the location decision is magnified by the inability, because of physical and financial considerations, to change a nodal location in the short run.* The nodal location decision made today has ramifications upon the logistics department, as well as marketing, production, and finance, for many years into the future.

The expansion into new market areas, shifts in population, development of new product lines, technological changes, competitive pressures, and other factors have caused many firms to analyze the location for a new node or change the location of existing nodes. The aforementioned factors may cause the firm to question the location of existing nodes to serve new market areas, for example, or the location of a new node to best serve this new market area. Production, marketing, or logistical factors can also be the motivating force for relocation of an existing facility; that is, the existing node may be inefficient based upon one or more of these factors. The nodal location is a major element in the success or degree of success a firm achieves in today's dynamic business environment.

---

*   If a firm is utilizing public warehousing, the short run may be something less than a year. But for privately owned or leased warehouses and for plants the short run is five, ten, or more years.

The criteria utilized to determine where a node is to be located are many and varied. Some criteria are quantifiable in terms of their impact upon costs and profits while others are nonquantifiable such as the cultural, educational, and recreational opportunities available to the firm's employees with a particular location. The location decision usually begins with an examination of the quantifiable determinants and then proceeds to the nonquantifiable factors.

The quantifiable determinants generally considered to answer the question of where a facility should be located are grouped as follows: market areas, raw material sources, land, labor, capital, and transportation/logistics. A potential nodal site is analyzed as to the cost to be occasioned with regard to the above determinants. The purpose of this chapter is to concentrate upon the latter determinant, transportation/logistics, as it affects the nodal location decision. Attention is given to an overview of all factors impacting the location decision and to a transportation cost minimization technique. Finally, the question of market territory for a node is analyzed. Appendices to this chapter discuss the classical location theories and the application of linear programming to the market territory question.

OVERVIEW OF NODAL LOCATION FACTORS

As noted earlier, there are many factors that must be considered in determining the location of a plant or warehouse (nonretail facility). Although this chapter will emphasize the logistical factors in the nodal location decision, the reader must remember that logistics is but one of many factors determining the location.

Major Location Determinants

Our discussion of the nodal location factors will center around the following three major determinants: (1) logistics; (2) operating costs; and (3) community factors. Exhibit 10-1 indicates the relative importance hierarchy of these location determinants in the decision process and the specific factors within the major determinants.

As is indicated in Exhibit 10-1, logistics determinants are usually considered first in a nonretail facility location. This factor usually eliminates areas from consideration and permits the decision maker to concentrate attention, i.e., gather very specific data about a community, upon a limited number of sites. The next sections treat the logistics determinant in greater detail.

The relative importance of these determinants will vary by type of facility being located and the importance of any one factor in the overall operation of the company. For example, a home office or data-processing facility location would not give logistics cost much attention. The cost of labor is very significant for a labor intensive production facility. Or, the availability of fuel, for example, may become the overriding determinant for a plant that requires heat in its production process.

EXHIBIT 10-1   Major determinants in the location decision process.

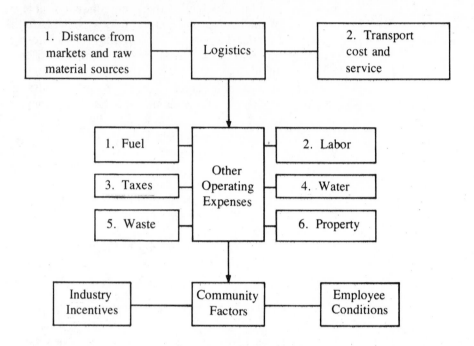

*Logistics
Determinants*

The reader will note that the logistics factor also considers markets and raw material sources. It is usually an implicit assumption that market and raw material source locations are known. It is true that existing markets and raw material sources would be known, but this is usually not the case when a plant or warehouse is being designed for a new territory. For a new territory, the marketing and production departments would analyze the area for potential buyers and suppliers.

*Operating Expense
Determinants*

The operating expense determinant of fuel includes both the cost and availability of fuel. The cost and availability of fuel affects both the cost of operating and the ability to continue operation of a facility. During the natural gas shortage, many companies requiring natural gas were considering plant locations in Southern states that had abundant supplies of natural gas. In other situations, the availability and cost of electricity, coal, or oil would be more significant. However, if the desired fuel is not available, a plant location decision will be made in areas where such fuel is available so as to permit continued operation. The location of a facility in an area where a desired fuel is available will usually be at the expense of (trade off of) higher costs in other operating or logistics factors.

As with fuel, both the cost and the availability of labor are significant. The location of production facilities that are labor intensive tend to be pulled toward low labor cost areas, for example, the South. But the location facilities requiring labor that possesses technical expertise will emphasize the availability of such labor rather than the cost. In addition, the labor factor will include labor management harmony, or the number of man-days lost due to work stoppages, and some measure of labor's productivity, value added/production worker.

The area of taxes includes both business and personal taxes. The taxes upon business reflect the cost of operating in an area whereas the taxes upon the individual indirectly reflect the cost of living and the wages that must be paid. The taxes usually considered are: real property, inventory, machinery and equipment, intangibles, sales, income (both state and local) and unemployment compensation. Care must be exercised in evaluating taxes among alternative sites so as to give full attention to overall tax burden (all taxes) and assessment rates. This requires certain assumptions as to investment in plant, property, inventories, income, and labor costs.

The remaining operations factors of water, waste, and property are usually not that significant in comparison to the other operating factors. If water is a significant raw material in the production process, then the cost and availability of water at a potential location will be given more importance. Likewise, the cost and capacity of waste removal will be more important in the location of certain production facilities. The availability of suitable land determines whether a specific city will even be considered. Suitable land would include consideration of surrounding properties, zoning restrictions, land for future expansion, and cost.

Community Determinants

The final major determinant area, community factors, is normally the final stage of the location decision and will usually provide the fine distinction among a limited number of sites that have "passed" the above determinants. The two determinants considered here are employee conditions and industrial development incentives. Industrial development incentives will have a direct impact upon the cost of operating the facility at a given location, whereas the employee conditions of a community do not have a direct impact upon operating costs.

Industrial development incentives are those "carrots" offered by states and local communities to companies who locate in a particular area. Some examples of industrial development incentives are tax incentives (reduced rates on or exclusion from property, inventory, sales, etc.), financing arrangements (state loans), reduced water and sewage rates, and rent-free buildings that are built to the company's specifications. Most states have an industrial development commission that provides information about the inducements available in the state and local communties.

Employee conditions have a direct bearing upon the quality of life in a community. Some examples of the factors considered in this area are:

1. Population—size, density, age distribution, income.
2. Physical environment—climate, pollution.

3. Education—number of public and private schools, number of universities and trade schools, quality of education.
4. Recreational facilities—parks, boating, skiing, etc.
5. Culture—museums, a symphony, theaters.
6. Community services—police and fire protection, libraries, hospitals, etc.

Although the above is not a complete list of the employee condition factors, it does give some indication that the companies do consider the quality of life for employees in various locations.

The preceding discussion of the overall nodal location determinants and their relative importance must be considered in light of the specific needs of a company. Before undertaking any nodal location analysis, the decision maker must have some indication from top management as to the company policy regarding facility locations. These policies will alleviate much wasted time and effort by the analyst who does not concentrate upon a location determinant deemed very important by top management.

For example, a company may have a policy of locating all new facilities in the "sunbelt." Thus, all possible locations in the "coldbelt" should be excluded from consideration. Or, a company may have a policy of locating warehouses in areas where competitors have located warehouses. These policies may vary for different types of facilities (plant vs. warehouse vs. technical center). But, whatever the policy, the decision makers should be informed so as to establish the appropriate determinant hierarchy and thereby eliminate wasted time and cost.

NODAL LOCATION AND LOGISTICS

As noted, above, the location of a node has a direct impact upon the creation of time and place utility in goods by the logistics function. An improper nodal location can result in added costs and/or unacceptable levels of logistics service. For example, an improper nodal location may be characterized by (1) not having sufficient carriers available to provide link service; (2) being located outside the commercial zone of a city which means the rates quoted to the city will not apply for movements into or out of the node; (3) incurring higher costs of total transportation resulting from uneconomical moves for raw materials and/or finished goods; and (4) increasing transit times and thereby reducing service to customers and/or increasing inventory carrying costs.

Nodal location analysis is in essence a staff function for a logistics department. The logistics department must be involved in the location decision so that alternative sites for a node are evaluated as to their impact upon the cost and quality of logistics service to be incurred. This analysis must be accomplished in light of the firm's policy regarding service levels and of the operational constraints imposed upon the logistics system by production and marketing.

The material in succeeding sections will emphasize transportation costs as a locational determinant. Justification for this lies in the direct relationship between nodal location and the cost of producing place utility—the link service. The location decision most often begins with determining the least transportation cost area for the node. The analysis then proceeds to consider the other nonlogistic determinants such as availability and cost of land, power, labor, etc., as well as such nonquantifiable factors as cultural, recreational, and educational opportunities of a site. Thus, the logistics determinant provides a starting point for the nodal location decision.

The first screening by the logistics determinant will usually eliminate logistically uneconomical areas which, in essence, reduces the number of alternatives to consider. For example, consider the potential number of alternative sites available for locating a warehouse to serve the Northeast market area. Applying the logistics location determinant, the decision maker may find that the logistically optimum location is in eastern Pennsylvania. This definitely reduces the number of potential sites to consider and now enables the location analysis to continue, but to be directed toward a specific area rather than the horrendous number of alternative locations associated with the original problem.

The logistics determinant can be used also in the selection of specific site locations. Consideration is given to such factors as total logistics costs from the various sites proposed in the specific area, the accessibility of transport modes from and to the proposed sites, etc. Thus, the logistics determinant will usually be used at various stages in the location decision.

Before turning our attention to the transport cost determinant, it would be desirable to comment on the effects of service level policy statements upon nodal location, especially warehouse location. If corporate policy dictates that 95 percent of demand is to be serviced with two-day transit time, the warehouse location must be established such that 95 percent of demand is served with a two-day transit time. Any potential location that does not meet this requirement, given the mode of transport being utilized, is eliminated. However, the decision maker must be aware of the economies of operating various size warehouses and may be forced to expand the geographic area served by the warehouse to increase utilization of the facility and thereby reduce warehousing costs. But to achieve the desired service level, a more expedient mode (one providing lower transit time) may be required since the territory served by the node was increased to achieve increased utilization; that is, a trade-off exists between warehousing costs and link costs to achieve the desired level of service.

The location decision is another example of the required coordination of logistics and other functional departments of the firm. The nodal location has a direct impact upon logistics costs and the level of logistics service provided. These two logistics areas affect product price and competitiveness, cost of manufacturing, and firm financing. These factors must be considered in determining the optimum location for a node.

In the next section our attention is directed to logistics cost as a locational determinant.

TRANSPORTATION AND THE LOCATION DECISION

As indicated in Appendix 10-A, the classical theories of location considered transportation cost as the major locational determinant for a node. The location of a node with respect to markets and raw material sources impacted the total cost of transportation and, thereby, profitability. Emphasis was upon selecting that location that minimized total transportation costs and, by implicit assumption, maximized profits.

Most location analyses today emphasize transportation cost minimization. The location selected for a new industrial facility is that which minimizes the inbound transportation cost plus the outbound transportation costs. An average transportation cost per ton per mile is applied to the tonnage purchased at raw material sources and sold at markets and to the distance this tonnage is moved to and from a proposed site. The grid technique utilizes this concept.

GRID TECHNIQUE

Nature of Approach The grid technique helps determine a least-cost facility location for situations with multiple markets and raw material sources. Essentially the grid tecnhique is an approach that attempts to determine a fixed facility (plant, warehouse) location that is the least-cost center of moving both raw materials and finished goods in relation to a grid system. The technique determines the low cost "center of gravity" with respect to raw materials and finished goods movement.

Approach This technique assumes that the raw material sources and finished goods markets are fixed and the amounts of each type of product consumed or sold is known. A grid is then superimposed upon the geographic area where the raw material sources and finished good markets are located. The zero point on the grid, then, corresponds to an exact geographic location as do other points on the grid. Thus, each source and market can be identified in terms of its grid coordinates.

Figure 10-1 is an example of a firm's supply source and market environment in which the firm is attempting to locate a plant. The grid has been superimposed over the exact geographic locations of the sources and markets. The location of these points can be defined in terms of their grid coordinates. For example, the market, FG_1, located at the lower left of the grid, has a horizontal coordinate of 100 and a vertical coordinate of 100 or (100, 100). The raw material source, RM_1, at the upper left of the grid, has a coordinate location of (100, 900).

FIGURE 10-1   Grid locations of sources and markets.

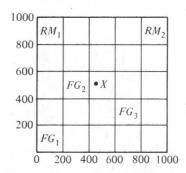

RM = raw material source locations
FG = finished good market location
X = least cost location

The concept underlying this technique is best visualized as a series of strings to which are attached weights corresponding to the weight of raw materials consumed at each source and of finished goods sold at each market. The strings are threaded through holes in a flat plain; the holes correspond to the location of the sources and markets. The other end of the strings are tied together and the weights are then permitted to exert their respective pulls on the knot. The knotted end of the strings will finally reach an equilibrium; this equilibrium will be the center of mass or the ton-mile center.

The above concept can be computed mathematically; the ton-mile or center of mass is given as follows:

$$M = \frac{\sum_{1}^{n} D_i FG_i + \sum_{1}^{m} d_i RM_i}{\sum_{1}^{n} FG_i + \sum_{1}^{m} RM_i}$$

where:

D_i = distance from 0 point on grid to the grid location of finished good (i)

d_i = distance from 0 point on grid to the grid location of raw material (i)

FG_i = weight (volume) of finished goods sold in market (i)

RM_i = weight of raw material purchased at source (i)

The above equation will generate the least cost location if transportation rates are the same for raw materials and finished goods. But as we have already seen, transportation rates vary among commodities and, therefore, the ton-mile center equation does not reflect differences in the cost of

TABLE 10-1

Example Data for Grid Technique Analysis

	Tons	Rate/Ton/Mile	Grid Location*
RM_1	100	$ .50	100,900
RM_2	100	$ .50	900,900
FG_1	50	$1.00	100,100
FG_2	50	$1.00	300,500
FG_3	50	$1.00	700,300

*From Figure 10-1

moving the commodities. The impact of the transportation rate is to pull the location toward the location of the commodity with the higher rate. That is, the higher rates for finished goods as opposed to raw materials will draw the least cost location toward the market and thereby reduce the distance the higher rated commodity (finished goods) is moved and increasing the distance the lower rated commodity (raw material) is transported.

Thus we must incorporate into our analysis the transportation rate of moving the different type of products. This modification is:

$$M = \frac{\sum_{1}^{n} R_i D_i FG_i + \sum_{1}^{m} r_i d_i RM_i}{\sum_{1}^{n} R_i FG_i + \sum_{1}^{m} r_i RM_i}$$

where:

R_i = finished good transportation rate/distance unit for finished good (i)

r_i = raw material rate/distance unit for raw material (i)

The R_i and r_i are the transportation rates per distance unit and are assumed to be linear with respect to distance. This assumption does not correspond to the tapering principle of rates, but it simplifies the analysis. The decision maker could relax this assumption by incorporating an equation that relates the actual relationship of the rate to distance. This is beyond the scope of our presentation and will not be considered here.

Example　　It is appropriate at this point to present an example. Table 10-1 presents the relevant data for the example. The grid coordinates of the raw material sources and markets correspond to the locations of same on the grid in Figure 10-1. For simplicity we have assumed that this firm utilizes only one type of raw material and produces only one type of finished good. The result of this assumption is that the rate for the raw materials is the same and likewise for the finished good.

To determine the least-cost center on the grid two grid coordinates must be computed, one for moving the commodities in the vertical direction and one for moving the commodities in the horizontal direction. The two coordinates are computed by using the above formula for each direction.

The computations for this example are as follows (the subscripts have been omitted):

$$M_H = \frac{(1)(100)(50) + (1)(300)(50) + (1)(700)(50) + (.5)(100)(100) + (.5)(900)(100)}{(1)(50) + (1)(50) + (1)(50) + (.5)(100) + (.5)(100)}$$

$$= \frac{10,500 \; \$ \cdot Ton \cdot Mile}{250 \; \$ \cdot Ton}$$

M_H = 420 miles in the horizontal direction.

And for the vertical direction:

$$M_V = \frac{(1)(100)(50) + (1)(500)(50) + (1)(300)(50) + (.5)(900)(100) + (.5)(900)(100)}{(1)(50) + (1)(50) + (1)(50) + (.5)(100) + (.5)(100)}$$

$$= \frac{135,000 \; \$ \cdot Ton \cdot Mile}{250 \; \$ \cdot Ton}$$

M_V = 540 miles in the vertical direction.

Thus the least-cost center for the plant location in this example is 420 miles in the horizontal direction and 540 miles in the vertical direction, both distances from the zero point on the grid and indicated as points X in Figure 10-1.

The strengths of the grid technique are in its simplicity and its ability to provide a starting point for the location analysis. The technique is relatively easy, computationally, to use. The data necessary can be generated from sales figures, purchase records, and transportation documents (either the bill of lading or freight bill). More exact coding of the market and source locations is possible as well as the previous modification mentioned regarding quantification or rate, distance relationship. Such refinements would easily be handled on a computer.

The grid technique also provides a starting point for the location decision. As suggested earlier transportation cost is not the only locational determinant. Use of the grid technique can eliminate certain areas from consideration and thereby permit the decision maker to focus attention to the particular area that is advantageous from the logistics viewpoint. For example, the solution from the grid technique to a problem of locating a plant to serve the Ohio, Michigan, Indiana, and Illinois market area may suggest Toledo, Ohio, as the least-cost location. This has eliminated consideration of Chicago, Indianapolis, etc., and permits the decision maker to concentrate the location analysis in northwestern Ohio and southeastern Michigan. This is a tremendous step forward in the location decision process.

There are limitations to the grid technique that the decision maker must recognize. First, it is a static approach and the solution is optimum for only one point in time. Changes in volumes purchased or sold, changes in transportation rates, or changes in raw material source or market locations will shift the least cost location. Second, linear transportation rates are assumed, while actual transportation rates increase with distance, but less than proportional. Third, the technique does not consider the topographic conditions existing at the optimum location, e.g., the optimum site may be in the middle of a lake. Fourth, it does not consider the proper direction of movement; most moves are made along a straight line between two points, not vertically and then horizontally.

Application to Warehouse Location in a City

The preceding discussion concentrated upon utilizing the grid technique to solve plant location decisions. The technique can be used to solve warehousing location problems as well. The same procedure would be followed with the exception that the raw material sources would be the firm's plants. The least-cost center of moving finished goods into the warehouse from the firm's plant and of moving the finished goods from the warehouse to the various markets will be generated by the grid technique.

The grid technique must be modified to eliminate the raw material movement which will not affect the location decision. The technique is then concerned with the least-cost center of moving finished goods from the warehouse to the customer locations.

The equation with this modification becomes:

$$M = \frac{R \sum_{1}^{n} D_i FG_i}{R \sum_{1}^{n} FG_i}$$

Since the R is the same, i.e., the cost of distributing the commodity throughout the city will be the same, it cancels out and the equation is reduced to:

$$M = \frac{\sum_{1}^{n} D_i FG_i}{\sum_{1}^{n} FG_i} \quad \text{or, a ton-mile center.}$$

As before, the grid technique will permit the decision maker to eliminate certain areas of the city and concentrate the analysis upon those sites in the general vicinity indicated by the grid technique. Consideration must be given to land availability and cost, access to highways, etc., to determine the exact site.

OTHER QUANTITATIVE TECHNIQUES

Thus far our discussion has centered upon the fundamental relationships existing between logistics variables and the location decision. The grid technique was suggested as a quantitative approach to determining a least transportation cost location for a node. Other quantitative techniques, linear programming, heuristic programming, and simulation, have been used in the location decision analysis. Our purpose here is to present a general discussion of the technique rather than an indepth application of same.

Linear Programming

Linear programming (LP)* is a technique that produces an optimum solution within the bounds imposed by constraints upon the decision. The LP technique is most useful for considering the distribution problem among nodes where supply and demand limitations at plants, warehouses, or market areas are constraints upon the system. Through a series of iterations, each iteration bringing the decision maker closer to an optimum solution, the LP technique defines the optimum distribution pattern among the nodes consistent with the demand-supply constraints of the problem. (The LP technique will be utilized in Appendix 10-B when considering the nodal linking decision.) The LP approach can then be used to evaluate the distribution patterns and resultant costs of alternative nodal locations in light of existing nodal locations (plants, warehouses, demand areas) and corresponding supply-demand constraints.

Heuristic Programming

Heuristic programming† is similar to the human thought process. The problem is reduced to manageable size by heuristic programming and it then searches automatically through possible alternatives in an attempt to find a better solution. Heuristic programming does not guarantee an optimum solution but it can provide a good approximation to the least-cost location in a complex location decision problem. Assumptions regarding the location characteristics the decision maker considers important for an optimum site are incorporated into the heuristic program to reduce the number of alternatives to be evaluated.

Simulation

Simulation‡ is a highly sophisticated tool with which the decision maker develops a mathematical model of the system under consideration.

* For an application of LP see R. M. Burstall, R. A. Leaver, and J. E. Sussans, "Evaluation of Transport Cost for Alternative Factory Sites—A Case Study" *Operations Research Quarterly* December 1962, pp. 345-54.

† For example, see Alfred A. Kuehn and Michael J. Hamburger, "A Heuristic Program for Locating Warehouses," *Management Science*, IX, No. 4 (1963), pp. 643-66.

‡ For a discussion of simulation see Martin L. Gerson and Richard B. Maffei, "Technical Characteristics of Distribution Simulators," *Management Science*, X, No. 1, (1963), pp. 62-69.

For location analysis, simulation affords the opportunity to test the effects upon costs and service levels of alternative nodal locations. The modeling requires extensive data collection and anlysis to determine the interaction of various system factors such as transportation, warehousing, inventory, materials handling, labor costs, etc. The alternative sites selected by the decision maker are evaluated by the simulation process to determine respective costs. However, simulation does not guarantee an optimum solution; rather, it can evaluate the alternatives fed into the process by the decision maker.

All of the above techniques are valuable aids to the decision maker, but each has certain limitations. LP use is limited by the capacity of the computer to handle large-size LP problems. Heuristics can handle any size problem but it does not guarantee an optimal location as does LP. Simulation requires considerable data and expertise to develop the mathematical model which can become quite prohibitive; it has no size limit but does not guarantee an optimum solution.

TRANSPORTATION PRAGMATICS*

The previous discussion has shown the importance of the transportation factor in the nodal location decision. Certain assumptions were made regarding the transportation rate—the linear relationship of rates to distance—to emphasize the locational pull of the transportation factor. In this section our attention is directed toward the effects of the actual transportation rate construction upon the nodal location decision. Consideration is given to the tapering nature of rates, blanket rates, commercial zones, and in-transit privileges.

Tapering Nature of Rates

As pointed out in Chapter 8, transportation rates increase with distance, but less than proportional to the distance increase. The reason for this is the carrier's ability to spread certain shipment fixed costs—loading, billing costs, etc.—over a greater number of distance units. As Hoover† noted the impact of this rate characteristic is to influence the nodal location at the supply source or market in the one source one market situations.

To illustrate this effect, Table 10-2 and Figure 10-2 are used. In Table 10-2, the rates are assumed to be the same for the raw material consumed at *A* and the finished product sold at *B*. The rates increase with distance but not in direct proportion. As shown in Figure 10-2, the location that produces the lowest total transportation cost per unit is at either *A* or *B*, but not in between. At *A* or *B* the total transportation cost is $.73 but at a point 30 miles from *A* (20 miles from *B*) the cost is $.86 per unit. Thus, the tapering nature of rates pulls the location toward the end points—the raw material source or market place.

* Adapted from Edward J. Taaffe and Howard L. Gauthier, Jr., *Geography of Transportation (Englewood Cliffs, N.J.: Prentice-Hall, Inc., 1973), pp. 41-43.*

† See Appendix 10-A.

TABLE 10-2

**Tapering Nature of Rates Locational Effects
With the Constant Rate Assumption**

Distance From A	Transport Cost From A	Distance From B	Transport Cost From B	Total Transport Cost
0	0	50	.73	.73
10	.20	40	.62	.82
20	.36	30	.50	.86
30	.50	20	.36	.86
40	.62	10	.20	.82
50	.73	0	0	.73

FIGURE 10-2   Locational effects of tapering rates with constant rate assumption.

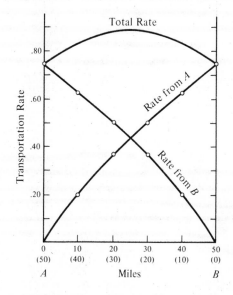

If we relax the assumption of constancy of rates between raw materials and finished goods we find the location is pulled toward the market point B. Table 10-3 contains the rates for various distances from A and B increased to reflect the higher cost associated with the movement of finished goods. As can be seen in Figure 10-3, the least transport cost location is at point B where a total transportation cost of $.73 per unit is incurred.

Blanket Rates   A noted exception to the above structure of rates is the blanket rate. The blanket rate does not increase with distance; that is, the rate is the same from one origin to all points in the blanket area. The carriers establish such prices to insure that the price for a product in a given area will be competitive with

TABLE 10-3

Tapering Nature of Rates Location Effects Without Constant Rate Assumption

Distance From A	Transport Cost From A	Distance From B	Transport Cost From B	Total Transport Cost
0	.0	50	.83	.83
10	.20	40	.72	.92
20	.36	30	.60	.96
30	.50	20	.46	.96
40	.62	10	.30	.92
50	.73	0	.0	.73

competing products and thereby resulting in the demand for a product and a demand for transportation of said product. An example of a blanket would be the same rate on wine from the West Coast to all points east of the Rocky Mountains to compete with imported wines entering the East Coast.

The blanket rate eliminates any transportation cost advantage or disadvantage associated with a given location. In the case of the wine blanket rates, the West Coast wine producers can effectively compete in the East Coast market area with East Coast and foreign producers. The blanket rate, then, is a mutation of the basic rate-distance relationship that eliminates the transportation rate factor as a locational determinant.

The blanket rate is not the normal type of transportation rate structure faced by a firm. The blanket rate must be approved by the transportation regulatory agencies which require demonstration of the detrimental effects of the tapering rate upon the demand for the product and the consequent demand for transportation of the product. Thus, the blanket rate is the exception rather than the rule in transportation rates.

Commercial Zones   A specific and quite common type of blanket area is the commercial zone. The commercial zone is the transportation definition of a particular city or town. It includes the municipality itself plus varying degrees of surrounding areas determined by a formula.* The relevant attribute of the commercial zone is that the rates quoted to a particular town or city also apply to points in the surrounding area delineated as being within the commercial zone.

The locational impact of the commercial zone is evidenced in the latter stages of the nodal location decision process, that is, at the decision stage where the specific site is being selected. If the specific site is beyond the commercial zone of a municipality, the various commodity rates applicable

---

* For a greater discussion of commercial zones see: Charles A. Taff, *Commercial Motor Transportation*, 5th ed., (Cambridge, Md: Cornell Press, Inc.), pp. 139-43.

FIGURE 10-3 Locational effects of tapering rates without constant rate assumption.

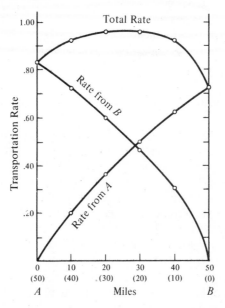

to the city will *not* be applicable to the site selected. Also, the availability of carriers is reduced if the site is not within the commercial zone, especially for motor carriers which have their operating scopes defined in terms of point to point operations.

Therefore, sites beyond the commercial zone will require use of local transportation (an extra cost) to get the commodities into the city where the carriers are authorized to serve, the incurrence of additional pick-up and/or delivery charges and possibly the incurrence of costs associated with assisting carriers in obtaining additional operating authority or negotiating with carriers to publish commodity rates to this site. Consideration of the commercial zone is definitely important in the specific site selection aspect of the nodal location decision.

Transit Privileges   The final pragmatic aspect of transportation to be considered is the transit privilege. Basically the transit privilege permits the shipper to stop the shipment in transit and to perform some function that physically changes the characteristic of the product. The lower through rate (the tapering rate principle) applies from origin to final desitnation rather than the higher combination of rates from origin to transit point and transit point to final destination.

The transit privilege essentially causes intermediate locations to be optimum as well as the end points—origins or destinations. The transit privilege eliminates any geographic disadvantage associated with a producer's location. That is, the intermediate point designated as a transit point enjoys the lower, long-distance, through rate that is applicable at either the origin or destination location.

Like the blanket rate, the transit privilege is not available at all locations nor for all commodities, only those sites and commodities specified by the carrier with regulatory sanction. If a commodity is benefited with the availability of a transit privilege, the limited points specified in the carrier tariffs will be prime alternatives for the location of the node.

NODAL LINKING DECISIONS

In previous sections the nodal location decision was discussed with the assumption that the nodal pairs to be linked had been determined. The purpose of this section is to provide an analytical framework that delineates the nodal pairs to be linked. Associated with the nodal linking decision is the question relating to the volume of goods to be transferred among the nodal pairs. Thus, the nodal linking decision requires recognition of two problem areas: (1) Which nodes are to be linked? and (2) What quantity is to be shipped between the nodal pair?

If a firm has a very simple logistics system, for example, one supply source, one plant and no warehouse, the nodal linking decision is equally simple. That is, the one raw material source is linked to the one plant and the one plant is linked to all customers. Unfortunately, the real-world situation is not as simple as described above. Most firms have multiple supply sources, plants and finished good warehouses. The logistics manager faces a multiplicity of alternative nodal pairs to consider in light of the system's objectives of minimization of total logistics costs.

All too often the geographic configuration of supply sources and plants and of the market (sales) territories has been utilized to arrive at the nodal linking decision. That is, the raw material supply sources near plant A are linked to plant A and those near plant B are linked to plant B. Likewise, a warehouse located within sales territory A serves customers in that territory, etc. Such a decision rule is pragmatically simple to implement, but it does not guarantee the lowest total costs. It may be economical to link certain customers in sales territory B with a warehouse situated in sales territory A. The configuration of a sales territory in most cases is not determined in light of logistics variables and therefore does not guarantee an economical delineation of nodal linking patterns.

The purpose of this section is to acquaint the reader with the methodology applicable to solving the nodal linking decision, both as to the nodes to be linked and the volume to be transferred between each nodal pair. Our attention is initially directed toward the early location theory concerned with market area determination—a plant (warehouse) to customer nodal linking decision. This provides the basis for a nonrigorous methodology applicable to other nodal linking decision areas. In Appendix 10-B the transportation method of linear programming is utilized to determine the nodes to be linked and the volume to be transported between each.

EXTENT OF THE MARKET AREA

The work of Frank Fetter, an American economist, and August Losch,* a German economist, has stressed the determination of the market area for a production facility. The extent of the market area for a facility is defined as the geographic point where the laid down costs are equal for a given product of two competing producers. Given the assumption of rational and informed buyers and sellers, and no product quality differences, the buyers will be indifferent at the point where the producers have equal laid down costs.

The laid down cost is defined as the delivered cost of a product to a particular geographic point. The delivered cost includes the cost of production (production, marketing and normal profit) plus the cost of transporting the product from origin to any given destination (buyer location). (Transportation costs are assumed to be linear with respect to distance, which we know from previous discussion is not the real-world situation.) The above relationship is quantified as follows:

$$LCD = P + T(X)$$

where

LDC = laid down or delivered costs/unit

P = production cost/unit

T = transportation rate/distance unit, and

X = distance from origin.

An implicit assumption in the analysis is that the buyers make a purchase decision upon the basis of price only. This further assumes that the competing products are identical, i.e., there is no product differentiation. Thus, the price (delivered cost) of the product is the only criterion the buyers utilize in evaluating alternative supplies.

The market area for a seller will be that area where the seller has a laid down cost advantage. At any given point the buyers will purchase from the seller that has the lowest laid down cost. The seller will not attempt to market his product in an area where his laid down cost is higher than the competitor's laid down cost since the buyer purchases the product with the lowest price. Thus, a seller's market area is defined as that region in which the seller has laid down cost advantage.

Let us now turn our attention to an application of the above framework to the situation described in Figure 10-4. Two producers, A and B, are located 100 miles apart and sell identical products. Each producer incurs a production cost of $50 per unit and a transportation cost of $.10 per unit per mile transported. This is an example where each seller has equal costs.

* For an additional discussion of Fetter and Losch see: Roy J. Sampson and Martin T. Farris, *Domestic Transportation*, 4th ed. (Boston: Houghton Mifflin Company, 1979, pp. 239-42.

FIGURE 10-4   Extent of market for sellers with equal costs.

100 miles

A 50 miles   50 miles B

$P_a = \$50/unit$ $P_B = \$50/unit$
$T_a = \$.10/unit/mile$ Y $T_B = \$.10/unit/mile$

To determine the extent of the market between these two sellers, we set the laid down costs of A equal to the laid down costs of B and solve for X, the distance factor, that equates the two costs, or:

$$LDC_A = LDC_B$$

$$P_A + T_A(X) = P_B + T_B(100 - X)$$

where: $(100 - X)$ is the distance from B's plant to the indifference point, i.e., the total distance between the two minus the distance from A to the indifference point. Substituting the appropriate costs and solving for X:

$$\$50 + .10(X) = \$50 + .10(100 - X)$$

$$X = 50 \text{ miles}$$

That is, the extent of the market area for this example is 50 miles from A and 50 miles from B, point Y in Figure 10-4. To the left of point Y, A has a price (laid down cost) advantage over B (the converse is true for B for the area to the right of point Y).* The areas to the left of A and to the right of B are natural market areas for A and B, respectively. The extent of the market areas to the left of A and to the right of B will be delineated by the elasticity of demand for the product. The extent of the market area between the two producers is a vertical line since the costs are equal for both producers.

The effects of a decrease (increase) in costs for one producer with the costs of the other held constant is an increase (decrease) in the extent of the market area for that producer. In Figure 10-5 the transportation cost for A has been reduced to $\$.08/unit/mile$. All other costs remain the same as in Figure 10-4. The impact of this reduced transportation rate is to increase the extent of the market area for A. This is given as follows:

$$LDC_A = LDC_B$$

$$\$50 + \$.08(X) = \$50 + \$.10(100 - X)$$

$$X = 55.5 \text{ miles}$$

* The reader can verify this by determining the LDC for A and B at any point to the left or right of Y.

FIGURE 10-5 Extent of market area for two sellers with unequal transportation costs.

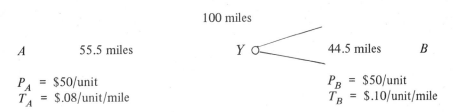

100 miles

A 55.5 miles Y 44.5 miles B

P_A = \$50/unit
T_A = \$.08/unit/mile

P_B = \$50/unit
T_B = \$.10/unit/mile

For the example given in Figure 10-5, the market area for A has been increased by 5.5 miles (55.5 miles as compared to 50 miles in Figure 10-4) as a result of a decrease in transportation costs. The market area is backward bending toward B since A has a rate advantage.

The implication to the logistics manager is that a reduction in the transportation costs or logistics costs will enable the firm to increase its market area. The reader is again confronted with the interdependence of logistics and marketing. Modifications of the logistics sytem will enable the firm to expand into new market areas that formerly were not economical to serve.

Establishment of a Distribution Center

To fortify the above conclusion let us consider the situation described in Figure 10-6. Here, seller A has established a distribution center (DC) at a distance of 40 miles from A's plant. The goods are shipped into the DC in bulk at lower volume rates and distributed from the DC at \$.10/unit/mile. The cost of operating the DC is \$2/unit, which includes inbound transportation cost.

The impact of the distribution center is to increase the extent of the market as follows:

$$LDC_A = LDC_B$$

$$P_A + W_A + T_A (X) = P_B + T_B (60 - X)$$

where: $(60 - X)$ is the market area between B and DC.
Substituting the appropriate costs and solving for X:

$$\$50 + \$2 + .10(X) = \$50 + .10(60 - X)$$

$X = 20$ miles from the DC or the extent of the market area for A is 60 miles (20 miles from DC) and is an increase over that found in Figure 10-4.

FIGURE 10-6 **Extent of market for two sellers with one seller establishing a distribution center.**

100 miles

A ———————————— DC 20 miles $\quad$ 40 miles $\qquad$ B

Y

$$P_A = \$50/\text{unit} \qquad W_A = \$2/\text{unit} \qquad P_B = \$50/\text{unit}$$
$$T_A = .10/\text{unit} \qquad T_{DC} = .10/\text{unit/mile} \qquad T_A = .10/\text{unit/mile}$$

The example in Figure 10-6 presents the essence of the internal nodal linking question, i.e., What is the extent of the market area to be served from the plant at A and from the DC respectively? The framework presented above, determining the point when the laid down costs are equal, is utilized to answer this question. The extent of the market between the two nodes of firm A is:

$$LDC_A = LDC_{DC}$$

$$\$50 + \$.10\,(X) = \$50 + \$2 + .10\,(40 - X)$$

$$X = 30 \text{ miles from } A$$

The above analysis tells us that customers 30 miles from A will be served by A and customers 10 miles from DC will be served by the DC. This analysis defines the economical service limits of the two nodes in A's logistics system.

Nodal Market Limits

The last example given above provides the basis for the decision process utilized in defining the market territories for various nodes in a firm's logistics system. Essentially, the extent of the service territory between nodes is the area where the laid down costs are equal from the different nodes. If we assume that the cost of the product is equal at all nodes in the system, the transportation cost factor can be used solely as the nodal market boundary determinant.

Consider the analysis suggested in Figure 10-7. In this situation the firm has three warehouses in the system, and it is assumed that the product cost at each node is equal and that the transportation rate per mile is the same for each. The limits of the market territories for each is delimited by those points where the transportation rates from two nodal points are equal (the points where the laid down costs are equal).

The circles radiating from each node are similar to the isodapanes set forth in the discussion of Weber's location theory. At any point on a given isodapane the transportation costs to ship from that node are the same.

FIGURE 10-7   Defining market territory for many nodes in the system.

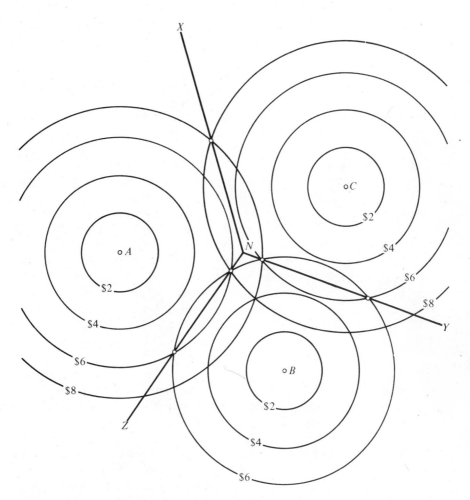

Where equal isodapanes from two nodes cross, the cost of serving this point is the same from each node. These equal transport cost points will define the territory for each node. Examination of Figure 10-7 reveals that the market area for node *A* is to the left of the lines *XNZ*; for node *B* it is the area below the lines *ZNY*; and for node *D* it is the area above the lines *XNY*.

The above analysis can be modified to consider differences in product costs at each node. For example, if the nodes in Figure 10-7 are plants, each plant will probably have a different product cost. Likewise for warehouses, the cost of landing the goods at and the cost of operating each warehouse are likely to be different. To take this into consideration, the circles radiating out from the nodes would be lines of equal laid down (landed) costs from each, i.e., each isodapane in Figure 10-7 would include the production costs plus transportation costs for each node.

In actual situations, the market areas for the nodes in Figure 10-7 will be irregular with notable indentations. This will be the result of specific volume (commodity) rates quoted between particular nodal pairs. The linearity of rates with distance assumption must be modified to give due regard for pragmatics of the rate structures faced by the firm.

The analytical framework presented thus far enables the logistics manager to define the geographic territory to be served by various nodes. The basis for this delineation is the point where the laid down costs from various nodes are equal or, more specifically, the shipments will be made between those nodal pairs where the cost of laying down the product is the lowest.

The analysis thus far has not explicitly considered what volume is to be transported between the linked nodal pair. It has been implicitly assumed that the supplying node can accommodate all the demand present in the nodal territory delineated. This usually is not the real world situation. Plant or warehouse supply capacity may not be sufficient to serve all nodal demand in the territory or, conversely, the supplying node may have greater capacity than the demand in the territory. Thus, the logistics manager must modify the territory to recognize the demand supply constraints imposed by the pragmatic requirements of the nodes.

The material in Appendix 10-B addresses the problem defined above. Specifically, attention is given to use of linear programming to solve the allocation of goods among the nodes.

SUMMARY

In this chapter attention has been directed toward the logistics variables affecting the location of a node. The logistics variables of transportation cost and service are important determinants in a nodal location decision. Emphasis was given to the determination of a nodal location based upon the logistics cost criterion. Such an analysis provides a starting point in the nodal location decision. Although logistics variables are not the only locational determinants, they do play a significant role in determining the efficiency of operating a logistics system associated with alternative nodal sites. In addition, attention was given to the nodal linking decision utilizing laid down costs as the linking determinant. The laid-down costs determine which plants will serve which warehouses or which warehouses will serve which customers.

Study Questions

1. To what extent does node location establish constraints upon efficiency of time and place utility creation?
2. List some factors which would cause firms to analyze nodal locations.
3. Discuss the qualifiable and nonqualifiable determinants considered in nodal locations.

4. Why is logistics considered in nodal location decisions?

5. What are the advantages and disadvantages of the grid technique?

6. Explain the effects of tapering rates and blanket rates upon nodal location.

7. What is the effect of transit privileges upon nodal location decisions?

8. What two problem areas can be recognized in nodal linking decisions?

9. Discuss laid down cost and identify the costs associated with it.

10. What effect does unequal transportation cost have on sellers in a market area?

11. Discuss the impact of customer service levels upon nodal linking decisions.

12. Determine the extent of the market area between two warehouses (A and B) that are 400 miles apart. Both warehouses incur a distribution cost of 10 cents per unit per mile but the cost of laying down the product at A is $40 per unit and at B it is $42 per unit.

13. Using the grid technique determine the least cost location for the problems given in Exhibits 10-2 and 10-3.

EXHIBIT 10-2   Example of plant location.

	Tons	Rates	Grid Coordinates
RM_1	200	.50	2, 14
RM_2	300	.60	6, 10
FG_1	100	1.00	2, 2
FG_2	100	2.00	10, 14
FG_3	100	1.00	14, 18
FG_4	100	2.00	14, 6
			(H) (V)

EXHIBIT 10-3   Example of warehouse location.

Customer	Tons	Grid location
A	100	1, 11
B	300	7, 11
C	200	5, 9
D	500	7, 7
E	1000	1, 1
		(H) (V)

Case 10-1
Maple Company

The Maple Company, a major producer of spiral-type college notebooks, has experienced a drop in profits in its eastern sales region. Maple competes with the Aries Notebook Company for the market area between their plants, i.e., the eastern region.

In a recent staff meeting, Andrew Key, the marketing director, made it quite clear that Maple should increase its marketing and thus bring sales in the eastern region back to the expected level. In contrast, the logistics manager, Jack Martin, argued that the primary step which Maple should implement is that of determining their exact market boundary, in relation to that of Aries. By determining the market boundaries, Maple will then be able to decide how extensive a marketing program to initiate. Additionally, this will prepare the logistics department for any potential increases in production and distribution.

Maple, being a cautious firm, has decided to follow Mr. Martin's advice and to specifically define the market boundaries.

Given the following information, determine the market boundary for both firms. The plants are located 800 miles apart.

	Yearly Production Cost	Yearly Demand	Transport Cost Per Mile
Maple	200,000	100,000	.20
Aries	300,000	200,000	.30

Maple's market boundary is _____ miles.
Aries' market boundary is _____ miles.

Questions for discussion:

1. Was the market boundary analysis a good idea?
2. Based on your calculations, what should Maple do?

Case 10-2
Choco Cupcake Company

The Choco Cupcake Company, a major producer of baked goods in New York City, has decided to expand its present operations and build a new plant in the "sunbelt" region of the United States.

Choco, having no logistics department, has contracted the Guiness Logistics Consulting Company to evaluate the situation and to recommend the new plant location.

In order for Guiness to make the optimal location decision for Choco, they must obtain information pertaining to product input, input weight, input source, and input contribution to the final product.

The information needed is presented below.

Input	*Input Wt.*	*Input Source*	*Input Contribution to Final Product*
Chocolate	1.0 oz.	Ft. Worth	1.0 oz.
Flour	3.5 oz.	Houston	3.0 oz.
Yeast	1.5 oz.	New Orleans	1.0 oz.
Water	2.0 oz.	Anywhere	1.0 oz.

With the information provided, determine the location of the new plant.

1. Compute the material index.
2. Compute the location weights for all relevant inputs.
3. Where would you recommend the plant be located? Show how you arrived at your decision.

Appendix 10-A:
Classical Theories of Location

The purpose of this section is to indicate the development of location theory and the importance of transportation factors in this theoretical development. The theories of Von Thunen, Weber, Hoover and Greenhut are discussed. This discussion provides the basis of the transportation location decision found in the chapter.

VON THUNEN[1]

One of the first writers to attempt to theorize the factors of production with respect to facility location was Johann Heinrich von Thunen. Von Thunen was a German agriculturist concerned with the location of agriculture production. His theory is predicated upon cost minimization (transportation cost) as the locational determinant.

The assumptions utilized by von Thunen reduced the complexity of the problem and enabled concentration upon the transportation variable. First, von Thunen assumed an isolated city state that was surrounded by a plain of equal fertility. The plain ended in wilderness and the city was the only market for the agriculture products. Production of any product could occur anywhere in the plain and at the same cost. Transportation was assumed to be equally accessible to all locations in the plain and, further, transportation costs were a function of weight and distance, i.e., transportation cost was a constant rate per ton-mile for all commodities.

The location of agriculture production would take place at the point where the farmer would maximize profits. Profits were determined as follows: profits equal market price minus production costs and transportation costs. With the market price and production costs the same for a given product at any production location, the transportation cost factor was the major locational determinant.

According to von Thunen, locations a greater distance from the city (market) would incur a greater transportation cost. Such locations would not be economically feasible for the production of products with a low value and high weight. For such products, the more distant locations from the city would result in very high transportation costs which they could not bear because of their low value to weight relationships. Thus, von Thunen concluded that products with low value to weight could not bear the burden of large transfer costs associated with long-distance moves (the higher weight and longer distance incurs higher transportation costs resulting in lower profits) and should be produced (located) near the city to minimize transport cost.

Another transport attribute recognized by von Thunen as a locational determinant was transit time. Perishable products, fresh vegetables, would be produced near the city; the influential determinant was not transportation cost, but the time required to move the goods to the markets.* Such products could not sustain long transit time and thus had to be produced near the city to ensure nonperishability on the good while in transit.

The analysis was continued for various types of agricultural products and culminated in the development of a series of concentric rings about the city. The rings, von Thunen's belts, delineated the products that should be produced at various distances from the city. Perishable products and products of low value to weight relations would be produced in the "belts" nearest the city. Products of high value to weight would be produced in the rings more distant from the city.

The simplifying assumptions and concentration upon agricultural production location makes von Thunen's theory seem unrealistic for the modern business firm. But his work remains as a major part of the foundation upon which our present location theory is predicated. It stands as a threshold to the delineation of the relationships between transportation costs and location theory. One also finds that the general conclusions are still valid today. For example, land close to urban areas is expensive and must be used intensively (warehouses would have to be multi-storied).

WEBER[2]

Alfred Weber, a German economist, developed a theory for the location of industrial production facilities. Unlike von Thunen, Weber started with a given industry and determined the best location for this industry. Weber assumed equally accessible transportation, constant transportation costs with respect to weight and distance. Raw material and consumption points are known and labor is geographically fixed and available at a given dollar amount.

Like von Thunen, Weber's analysis defines the optimum location as that point that is the least-cost location. More specifically, the least-cost site is the location that minimizes total transportation costs, the costs of transferring raw materials to the plant and finished goods to the market. Thus, total transportation cost is the criterion used to evaluate alternative plant locations.

Weber recognized that from a logistics standpoint raw materials were different. Raw materials possess two characteristics that have a direct relation to the total transportation costs incurred: geographic availability and weight lost in processing. With regard to geographic availability, a raw material is either ubiquitous or localized. A ubiquity is a raw material that is

---

* Mechanical refrigeration was non-existent at this time, so this was a practical solution to the problem. However, perishability is still a factor today in spite of our technology.

found everywhere (for example, water and air), and a localized material is one that is found only in certain locations (for example, coal and iron ore). In addition, a raw material has the quality of either being pure or weight-losing. A pure raw material does not lose weight in processing (the entire weight of a pure raw material is entered into the weight of the finished product) and a weight-losing raw material is one that does lose weight in the production process (only a portion of the weight of a weight-losing raw material is entered into the weight of the finished product). Therefore, a raw material may be: ubiquitous and pure, ubiquitous and weight-losing, localized and pure, or localized and weight-losing.

The ubiquitous or localized characteristic defines geographic fixity of raw materials and the need for transportation of same in relation to proposed plant locations. By definition, ubiquities are found everywhere and thus would not impose a need for transporting the ubiquitous material to the plant site. Regardless of the proposed plant location, the ubiquitous material is available at that location and no transportation cost is incurred for this input. Thus, ubiquities place no constraints upon the location of a production facility. However, ubiquities generally favor location in the market as we shall see in the analysis which follows.

A localized raw material is not found everywhere and therefore such a raw material necessitates transportation (and corresponding transportation costs) for any location other than at the supply source. The greater the distance the plant is located from the localized material source, the greater will usually be the transportation costs of moving the input to the plant since transport costs increase with distance. But one must be cognizant of the weight lost in processing since this raw material characteristic affects the total transportation cost for localized raw materials and finished goods.

The pure or weight-losing characteristics directly affect the total amount of weight to be transported and corresponding total transportation costs (for raw material and finished goods) at the various plant location sites. Since localized pure raw materials do not lose weight in processing, the entire weight of the input is entered into the weight of the finished product. Assuming only one input and one market, the total weight to be transported will be the same with a localized pure raw material. However, with a localized weight-losing material, a location at the supply source can minimize the weight to be transported and consequently the transportation costs. That is, the weight lost in processing is not transported when the location is at the weight-losing raw material supply source.

One Market, One Supply Source

At this juncture it is worthwhile to consider some examples of Weber's location theory. To accomplish this we will utilize the situation described in Figure 10A-1. We will determine the least cost location for a production facility in which raw materials of different characteristics are utilized in the

FIGURE 10A-1 One market, one raw material source.

RM = raw material source
M = market
X = midpoint between RM and M

production process. The transportation rate is $1.00 per ton-mile for both raw material and finished good movements.

First, if the one raw material used is ubiquitous, either pure or weight-losing, the least cost location is at M. At M, no cost of raw material or finished good movement is incurred. This location is possible since by definition the ubiquity is available at RM as well as M. A good example of such a situation is the soft drink industry. With water being the primary raw material and an ubiquity, the soft drink bottlers are located in the various local markets. With such a location, the bottler can eliminate the transportation of basically water from, for example, New York to the Toledo market area. Since water is available in Toledo as well as New York, a bottler can minimize total transportation costs by locating in Toledo and not incur transport costs for the movement of water.

Second, assume a pure localized raw material weighing one ton is used to produce one unit of finished good (FG) weighing one ton. To determine the least cost location, one must analyze the total transportation cost at various locations for the plant. If the plant is located at RM, the total transportation cost per unit is $100 ($RM$ = 1 ton, 0 miles or $0; FG = 1 ton, 100 miles or $100); the total transportation costs per unit is also $100 for a plant located at M (RM = 1 ton, 100 miles or $100; FG = 1 ton, 0 miles or $0). If the plant is located at point X in Figure 10A-1, the total transportation cost per unit is also $100 ($RM$ = 1 ton, 50 miles or $50; FG = 1 ton, 50 miles or $50). Thus, the least cost location using a pure, localized raw material is RM, M or anywhere in between on a straight line connecting the two. This led Weber to conclude that pure materials can not bind production to their deposits.

Third, assume a localized, weight-losing material weighing one ton is used to produce one unit of finished good weighing 1/2 ton. Again the alternative plant locations are analyzed as to the total transportation costs to be incurred. A location at RM will result in a total per unit transportation cost of $50 ($RM$ = 1 ton, 0 miles or $0 and FG = 1/2 ton, 100 miles or $50). The locations at X and M will result in total per unit transportation costs of $75 and $100, respectively. The least cost location for a localized, weight-losing raw material is the raw material source; at this location the weight lost in processing is not transported.

Consideration of the one raw material source, one market situation enables one to grasp the fundamental relationships between transportation costs and the location of a production facility under varying raw material situations. However, it is highly unlikely that an industrial firm operates in such a simplified situation. Weber expanded his analysis to consider two sources and one market. This is considered below.

Two Raw Material Sources and One Market

Weber approached this problem by considering the advantage of locating the production facility in relation to the three terminals of this situation (the market, and the two raw material sources). The effects of raw material characteristics upon transportation costs as discussed now becomes complicated by the two supply sources.

The location influence of the relative weights and results of transportation costs of the products at the various terminals was formalized by Weber into a material index. The material index is defined as the ratio of the sum of the localized raw material weights to the weight of the finished product. If greater than one, the least cost location is not the market but pulled toward the raw material sources.

To determine which raw material source is the least cost location when the material index is greater than one, Weber considered the relative pull exercised by the weight of the localized raw material. This is accomplished through the location weight index (LWI) which is defined as the ratio of weight of the material at a terminal to the weight of the finished product. Then, the least-cost location is that raw material source where the LWI is greater than the sum of the other LWI's. (The reader should envisage a flat board with the market and raw material sources located in a triangle. A hole is drilled at each terminal and a string passed through each. To one end of each string is attached a weight corresponding to the localized raw material and finished good weight at the terminal. The other ends of the string are tied together on top of the board. The weights are released and their respective locational pulls transferred to the knot. The final resting point of the knot is the optimum location.)

Consider the four situations with differing raw material and finished good weights shown in Figure 10A-2. We will attempt to determine the optimum plant location for each again with the assumption of a constant transportation rate per weight/distance.

Example A in Figure 10A-2 is a situation in which a ubiquitous raw material weighing 4 lbs. is combined with two localized materials weighing 4 lbs. and 2 lbs. The material index is 3/4 (4 + 2 ÷ 8) which is less than one and this tells us that the least-cost locaion is the market. The influence of the ubiquity pulling the location toward the market is evidence in this example

FIGURE 10A-2   Two raw material sources, one market.

Example A	Example B	Example C	Example D
(FG = 8 lb.)	(FG = 4 lb.)	(FG = 1/2 lb.)	(FG = 3 lb.)

(4 lb.) (2 lb.)   (2 lb.) (2 lb.)   (2 lb.) (3 lb.)   (4 lb.) (2 lb.)

(ubiquity = 4 lb.)

M = market
R = raw material source locations
FG = finished good
number in parentheses is the product weight

as in the previous one source, one market example. (The reader should justify the conclusion of this example as well as the ones that follow by assuming distances between each terminal pair and a transportation rate and then calculating total transportation costs for various alternative locations.)

A situation in which two pure raw materials are utilized in the production process is given by example B in Figure 10A-2. The material index is one (2 + 2 ÷ 4) and we conclude that the optimum location is the market. Any other location would increase the distance the commodities are transported and thereby would be a higher cost location.

In example C both raw materials are weight-losing. The material index is 10 (2 + 3 ÷ 1/2) and we conclude that the location should not be at the market but toward the source of deposits. To determine which deposit location, we make use of the location weight index. The LWI for R_1 = 4(2 ÷ 1/2), for R_2 = 6(3 ÷ 1/2), and for M = 1(1/2 ÷ 1/2). (The LWI for the market terminal is always one.) Next, we compare the LWI for one terminal to the sum of the others and find that the LWI for R_2 is greater than the sum of the others (6 > 4 + 1). Our conclusion is that the location will be pulled toward the R_2 location.

The last example, D, in Figure 10A-2 is another situation of two weight-losing raw materials, but the location decision is to not locate at any one of the three terminals. The material index of 2 (4 + 2 ÷ 3) tells us to not locate at the market. The LWI's are as follows: $R1$ = 4/3, $R2$ = 2/3, and M = 1. No LWI is greater than the sum of the others and the conclusion is to not locate at any one of the terminals. The optimum location will be somewhere inside the triangle.

The optimum location for the last example, D, can be determined by evaluating the total transportation costs incurred at the many alternative sites inside the triangle. However, this is a cumbersome mathematical process. Consideration of more than two sources is likewise cumbersome. There is an approach, grid technique, that is basically an expansion of the Weber approach that can facilitate many origins and many destinations in determining the least transportation cost location of a facility.

Labor and Agglomeration Factors

Thus far we have concentrated upon the effects of transportation in the location decision. Weber then considered the locational pull of labor by recognizing that labor costs vary at different locations. If labor can be purchased at a lower price in a location other than the least transportation cost site, the firm will locate at the lower labor cost point providing the labor savings offset the increased transportation costs. In essence, a cost trade-off is involved between labor and transportation costs.

The effect of the labor savings or other production cost savings can be shown by the use of isodapanes. Isodapanes are lines of equal though not minimal transportation costs about the least transportation cost site. Figure 10A-3 shows a series of isodapanes constructed for one market, two source situation. Point M (the market) is the least transportation cost ($10) location. Any location on the isodapane labeled $12 will incur $12 total transportation costs. If at point Y which is on the $14 isodapane (a transportation cost point $4 greater than the least transfer cost point) labor can be purchased at a savings of $4 or more over that at M, the decision to locate at Y rather than M would be economically sound. Other alternative sites would be analyzed in a similar manner, analyzing the trade-off between labor savings and the increased transportation costs. The use of isodapanes enables ready examination of these trade-offs.

In a similar cost trade-off analysis, Weber introduces another locational determinant that he calls agglomeration. Agglomeration is a net advantage gained by a common location with other firms. A common location precipitates benefits such as supply of skilled labor, better marketing outlets, proximity to auxiliary industries, etc. (A net disadvantage from common location is termed deglomeration.) Again utilizing Figure 10A-3, point Y will be a desirable location if the agglomeration benefits are $4 or more to offset the higher transfer costs at point Y than at M.

In summary, Weber's location analysis is a least-cost approach with emphasis upon transportation costs. The assumption regarding a constant, linear transportation rate is not realistic, but the constant assumption can be eliminated by applying the actual rate for different raw materials or finished goods. Although Weber's theory does not adequately handle the more complex location decisions, its benefit lies in its easy application, and it can provide the decision maker with a starting point in the location analysis. The alternatives to be considered can be reduced which brings the decision maker one step closer to determining the exact location. Weber's emphasis

FIGURE 10A-3 Example of isodapanes.

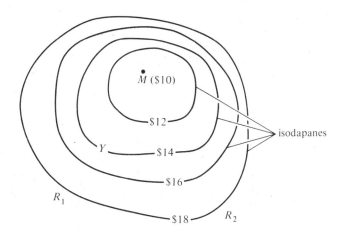

upon transportation costs as a locational determinant for industrial facilities is the basis of many other locational works.

HOOVER[3]

Edgar M. Hoover, an American theorist, considered the optimum location of industrial facilities based upon cost factors. He also considered demand factors which were not considered by von Thunen or Weber. His demand consideration relates to the definition of what the market area will be after the location has been determined. He recognizes the effect of distribution costs upon the price of the product and resultant demand.

In the area of cost factors, Hoover greatly expanded the analysis over that of previous authors. He considered transportation costs, agglomerative forces and industrial costs. In all three areas Hoover's treatment is more inclusive than Weber's.

With regard to transportation costs, Hoover pointed out that rates are not linear with respect to distance. The majority of rates follow the tapering principle—rates increase with distance but at a decreasing rate. This alters the conclusions reached by Weber for localized pure raw materials in the one market-one source situation. Instead of there being three location choices (the market, raw material source, or anywhere in between), the nonlinearity of rates makes the location at either the market or the raw material source cheaper than an in-between location. Location in between would result in the rates for the two separate movements being greater than the one rate from raw material source to market.

Availability of transportation companies (link suppliers) is not homogeneous throughout all areas which Hoover also noted. The areas that have high concentrations of carriers, therefore, are more desirable for location since they provide a greater supply of alternative vendors to meet the varied link requirements of a logistics system.

Hoover pointed out that the importance of transportation costs as a locational determinant varies for different firms. Transportation costs may be of lesser importance for firms capable of shipping in carload or truckload quantities compared to firms shipping in LCL or LTL quantities. Product characteristics have an impact upon the rates charged also and consequently influence importance of transportation costs as a locational determinant.

Hoover's main contribution to location theory was his more inclusive analysis of the cost factors affecting the location decision. Basically his approach is based upon cost minimization.

GREENHUT[4]

Melvin L. Greenhut, another American theorist, placed emphasis upon demand as a locational determinant. He pointed out that demand is a variable which enables different profits to be realized at different locations; thus, the location that maximizes profits is the optimum site which may not necessarily coincide with the least-cost definition.

The locational determinants deemed important by Greenhut are grouped into demand, cost, and purely personal factors. Demand and cost factors are influential in all site selections while personal considerations, which partially determine demand or production costs, should be included with demand or production costs determinants. Exhibit 10A-1 contains a list of Greenhut's locational determinants.

The reader may be concerned at this point with the difference in location between the cost minimization and profit maximization criteria. If one assumes constant demand, then the two criteria will result in the same location. Given differing elasticity of demand at different locations, a high-cost location may provide higher profits resulting from the ability to charge higher prices.

Notes

1. C.M. Warnenburg (trans.) and Peter Hall (ed.), *Von Thunen's Isolated State* (Oxford: Pergamon Press, 1966).

2. Carl J. Friedrich (trans.) *Alfred Weber's Theory of the Location of Industries* (Chicago: University of Chicago Press, 1929).

3. Edgar M. Hoover, *The Location of Economic Activity* (New York: McGraw-Hill Book Co., 1948).

4. Melvin L. Greenhut, *Plant Location in Theory and in Practice*, (Chapel Hill: The University of North Carolina Press, 1956).

EXHIBIT 10A-1   Greenhut's locational determinants.

Demand Factors
1. The shape of the demand curve for a given product.
2. The location of competitors, which in turn partially determines
   a. the magnitude of the demand, and
   b. the cross-elasticity of demand at different places.
3. The significance of proximity, type of service, and speed of service; prejudices of consumers.
4. The relationship between personal contacts and sales.
5. The extent of the market area, which itself is partially determined by cost factors and pricing policies.
6. The competitiveness of the industry in location and price; certainty and uncertainty.

Cost Factors
1. The cost of land, which includes
   a. the rent of land;
   b. the tax on land;
   c. the availability of capital, which partially depends upon
      1. the banking facilities and financial resources, and
      2. personal contacts;
   d. the availability of capital, which is also partially dependent upon
      1. the banking facilities and financial resources and
      2. the type of climate;
   e. the insurance rates at different sites, which in turn partially depend upon
      1. the banking facilities and financial resources,
      2. police and fire protection, and
      3. the type of climate;
   f. the cost of fuel and power, which is partially dependent upon
      1. natural resources,
      2. topography, and
      3. climate.
2. The cost of labor and management, which is influenced by
   a. The health of the community, the park and education facilities, housing facilities, wage differences, etc., and
   b. state laws
3. The cost of materials and equipment which is partially determined by
   a. the location of competitors (sellers and buyers),
   b. the price system in the supply area (f.o.b. mill, equalizing or other forms of discriminatory delivered prices),
   c. the extent of the supply area, which in turn is partially dependent upon

EXHIBIT 10A-1   Continued

          1. personal contacts and

          2. price policy

4. The cost of transportation, which is partially determined by

    a. the topography

    b. the transport facilities and

    c. the characteristics of the product.

Purely Personal Factors

1. The importance of psychic income (size of plant).

2. Environmental preferences.

3. The security motive.

Source: Melvin L. Greenhut, *Plant Location in Theory and in Practice* (Chapel Hill: The University of North Carolina Press, 1956) pp. 279–81.

Appendix 10-B:
Nodal Linking Using
Linear Programming

The nodal linking decision considered here is approached from the basis of the least-cost method of linking nodes given the constraints of supply and demand at each node and the cost of laying down the commodity at each demand node from the different supply nodes. This will be accomplished by using the transportation method of linear programming.

We will use as our explanatory vehicle the problem situation identified in Table 10B-1. In this example the firm has three plants (labeled 1, 2, and 3) and four warehouses (labeled *A*, *B*, *C*, and *D*). The cost matrix contains the transportation cost/unit from each plant to each warehouse. The unit cost of production at each plant is also given as well as the capacity of each plant and the demand at each warehouse.

The questions posed by this example are: Which plants are to be linked to which warehouses—the nodal linking decision—and What quantity is to be shipped between each—the allocation problem. The criterion utilized to answer these questions is the minimization of total laid down costs.

The quantitative technique used to solve this problem is the transportation method of linear programming. Before continuing with the example it is worthwhile to briefly identify the requirements associated with this technique.* First we assume that the costs are known and linear, i.e., it will cost $1.20/unit to ship one unit or 200 units from plant 1 to warehouse *A*. Second, the demand requirements must equal the supply requirements. If this does not exist for an actual problem, "dummy" warehouses or plants are introduced into the matrix. Any products produced at or shipped to a "dummy" will in reality not be produced or shipped. Finally, the transportation method requires complete divisibility of units, i.e., we can ship or produce a portion (fraction) of one unit.

Basically, the transportation method is a formalized search procedure by which the decision maker moves closer and closer to an optimum solution through a series of successive iterations. It has a tremendous advantage over the trial and error method. A minimum proficiency in mathematics is required and the technique is readily adaptable to computer application (most computer system packages contain transportation method programs).

To begin the application of the transportation method to the problem set forth in Table 10B-1, we must set up a laid down cost matrix, i.e., the

---

*   For an additional discussion of linear programming see: Frederick S. Hiller and Gerald J. Lieberman, *Introduction to Operations Research* (San Francisco: Holden-Day, Inc., 1967), chapters 5 and 6.

TABLE 10B-1

Example Problem for Linear Programming Application to Nodal Linking Decision

Warehouses	Plants			Warehouse Demand	Production Cost/Unit
	1	*2*	*3*		
A	1.20	1.30	1.10	1,000	1 = 4.00
B	.80	1.10	1.20	2,000	2 = 3.50
C	1.10	.80	.50	1,000	3 = 3.75
D	1.20	1.00	1.00	500	
Plant Capacity	1,500	1,000	2,000	4,500	

transportation cost between each node must be modified by the production costs incurred at the respective origin (plant) nodes. This laid down cost matrix is found in Figure 10B-1.

We will utilize the "northwest corner" rule to find an initial solution. That is, we will start with cell $A1$, allocate as much as possible to this cell, given the demand-capacity restraints; continue to cell $A2$, etc. This procedure is continued until all capacity is utilized and all warehouse demands are fulfilled. Figure 10B-2 contains the initial solution.

The allocation must equal the number of rows plus the number of columns − 1 (4 + 3 − 1 = 6 in our example) otherwise the problem will be degenerate and the analysis can not continue. Degeneracy is handled by allocating an infinitesimal (zero) amount to the number of cells required for a nondegenerate assignment.

Is the initial allocation the optimum nodal linking decision? To answer this, we will determine the opportunity costs of shipping one additional unit into the unused cells (those plant-warehouse nodal pairs to which commodities moves were not assigned). This is accomplished by use of row and column costs (U and V respectively) and then modifying the original cost matrix by these row and column costs to arrive at the opportunity cost matrix.

First, we arbitrarily assign a zero (0) value to any one row (U) or column (V) cost. In Figure 10B-3, U_A is set equal to zero. The remaining U and V values are determined such that the opportunity costs equals zero for those cells that have allocations, i.e., the opportunity cost for a given cell is computed by subtracting from the original laid down cost in the cell the sum of the $U + V$ costs for that cell or original cost $- U - V =$ opportunity cost.

For example, in Figure 10B-3, the row U_A is arbitrarily set equal to zero. The other U and V values are determined from those cells that have allocation. That is, the value for $V_1 = 5.20$ is computed by subtracting from the OR for cell $1A$ the sum of $U_A + V_1$ or $V_1 = OR - U_A$ ($V_1 = 5.20 - 0 = 5.20$). U_B is calculated by using the OR for $1B$ and V_1. This process,

FIGURE 10B-1   Laid down cost matrix.

Warehouses	Plants			Demand (units)
	1	2	3	
A	5.20	4.80	4.85	1,000
B	4.80	4.60	4.95	2,000
C	5.10	4.30	4.25	1,000
D	5.20	4.50	4.75	500
Capacity (units)	1,500	1,000	2,000	

FIGURE 10B-2   Initial allocation to problem.

Warehouses	Plants			Demand
	1	2	3	
A	1,000			1,000
B	500	1,000	500	2,000
C			1,000	1,000
D			500	500
Capacity	1,500	1,000	2,000	

utilizing the cells that have allocations, is continued until all U and V values are determined.

The opportunity costs for each cell (nodal pair) is determined as follows: $OP = OR - U - V$, the original cost for the cell minus the row and column values for that cell. Referring to Figure 10B-3, the opportunity cost for cell 1D is $5.20 - (-.60) - 5.20 = .60$. This procedure is followed for each cell. (*Note*: the opportunity costs is zero for the cells that have allocations.)

The opportunity cost matrix tells us the possibility for total cost reduction if we change the existing allocation. For cells that have positive opportunity cost, allocating one additional unit to that cell will increase the total costs over the initial allocation. For cells that have negative opportunity cost, allocating one unit to that cell will reduce total costs over the original allocation. As found in Figure 10B-3, cells 2A and 3A have negative costs

FIGURE 10B-3   Opportunity cost matrix for first allocation.

Plants

Warehouses	1		2		3		Row Costs
	OR	OP	OR	OP	OR	OP	
A	(5.20)	0	4.80	−20	4.85	−.50	$U_A = 0$
B	(4.80)	0	(4.60)	0	(4.95)	0	$U_B = -.40$
C	5.10	1.00	4.30	.40	(4.25)	0	$U_C = -1.10$
D	5.20	.60	4.50	.10	(4.75)	0	$U_D = -.60$
Column costs	$V_1 = 5.20$		$V_2 = 5.00$		$V_3 = 5.35$		

OR = Original cost   OP = Opportunity cost

Parentheses indicate cells with allocation.

FIGURE 10B-4   Second allocation.

Plants

Warehouse	1	2	3	Demand
A	500		500	1,000
B	1,000	1,000		2,000
C			1,000	1,000
D			500	500
Capacity	1,500	1,000	2,000	

indicating that our initial solution is not optimum, i.e., by reallocating units to anyone of these cells a lower total laid down costs will be realized.

The formalized search nature of the transportation method requires reallocation to only one cell with a negative opportunity cost. (If reallocation is made to all negative cost cells we would in essence have another initial solution, not a systematic approach.) Cell 3*A* is selected since this cell offers the greatest cost saving per unit ($.50).

The reallocation procedure requires the transfer of units from allocated cells to the empty cell making certain the reallocation complies with the demand-supply constraints. To shift units into cell 3*A* we move in a clockwise direction taking 500 units from cell 1*A* adding 500 units to cell 3*A*, subtracting 500 units from cell 3*B* and adding 500 units to cell 1*B*. Our shifting occurs at right angles and the maximum amount shifted is governed

FIGURE 10B-5   Opportunity cost matrix for second allocation.

Plants

Warehouses	1		2		3		Row Cost
	OR	OP	OR	OP	OR	OP	
A	(5.20)	0	4.80	−.20	(4.85)	0	U_A = .40
B	(4.80)	0	(4.60)	0	4.95	.50	U_B = 0
C	5.10	.50	4.30	.10	(4.25)	0	U_C = −.20
D	5.20	.10	4.50	−.40	(4.75)	0	U_D = .30
Column Costs	V_1 = 4.80		V_2 = 4.60		V_3 = 4.45		

OR = Original cost   OP = Opportunity cost

Parentheses indicate cells with allocation.

FIGURE 10B-6   Third allocation.

Plants

Warehouse	1	2	3	Demand
A	.		1,000	1,000
B	1,500	500		2,000
C			1,000	1,000
D		500	λ	500
Capacity	1,500	1,000	2,000	

λ = infinitesimal amount (zero units)

by the demand-supply constraints. The second allocation is given in Figure 10B-4. (*Note*: The allocations to cells 2*B*, 3*C*, and 3*D* are not changed.)

Again we must determine if the second allocation in Figure 10B-4 is the optimum. The same procedure as outlined above is utilized to develop the opportunity cost matrix. Figure 10B-5 contains the opportunity cost matrix for the second allocation. Cell 2*D* offers the greatest opportunity to reduce total laid down costs, thus, we allocate as many units as possible to this cell. Cells 3*D*, 2*B*, 1*B*, 1*A*, and 3*A* are involved in the shift and a maximum of 500 units are shifted. The new (third) allocation is given in Figure 10B-6.

The third allocation is evaluated following the procedure above. A unique problem is encountered with this allocation. That is, the number of

FIGURE 10B-7   Opportunity cost matrix for third allocation.

	Plants						
Warehouses	1		2		3		
	OR	OP	OR	OP	OR	OP	Row Costs
A	5.20	.40	4.80	.20	(4.85)	0	U_A = 0
B	(4.80)	0	(4.60)	0	4.95	.10	U_B = 0
C	5.10	.90	4.30	.30	(4.25)	0	U_C = −.60
D	5.20	.50	(4.50)	0	(4.75)	0	U_D = −.10
Column Costs	V_1 = 4.80		V_2 = 4.60		V_3 = 4.85		

OR = Original cost   OP = Opportunity cost

Parentheses indicate cells with allocation.

allocations is less than six, the number required for a nondegenerate solution. The quantity λ, zero, is allocated to cell 3D (the lowest cost cell of the empty cells (1A and 3D) created by shifting) to get the required number of allocations so as to enable the determination of the U and V values and resultant opportunity costs. The opportunity cost matrix for this allocation is given in Figure 10B-7.

The opportunity cost matrix in Figure 10B-7 indicates that we have an optimum solution to our nodal linking problem. Since all opportunity costs are zero or positive, any reallocation will result in increased total costs. The optimum nodal linking pattern, volumes to be shipped between each pair and the total distribution costs are:

1 to B	1,500 units @ 4.80	$ 7,200
2 to B	500 units @ 4.60	2,300
2 to D	500 units @ 4.50	2,250
3 to A	1,000 units @ 4.85	4,850
3 to C	1,000 units @ 4.25	4,250
	Total cost:	$20,850

To fortify the idea that the *TM* is a systematic search procedure that brings the decision maker closer to an optimum solution through a series of iterations, the total costs for each allocation is presented below. As can be seen, each successive iteration resulted in a lower total cost. Any allocation other than the third (optimum) will result in higher total laid down costs.

Allocation	Total Costs
Initial	$21,300
Second	$21,050
Third	$20,850

In summary, the transportation method of linear programming enables the logistics manager to determine the least-cost nodal linking pattern and to delineate the volume to be shipped over each link. This is a substantial improvement over the decision framework suggested at the outset of this chapter, that is, determining only the market area, nodal pairs to be linked, and assuming that all demand nodes in that market area will be served by that supply node.

SENSITIVITY ANALYSIS

The optimum nodal linking and allocation decision delineated by the transportation method is subject to change over time. This change stems from fluctuations in the costs of laying down the goods over a given link or from variations in the demand or supply constraints. The logistics manager must be cognizant of the changes and recognize that the changes will alter the optimum nodal linking decision.

The most common cost variable to change is the transportation rate. The logistics manager is constantly involved in rate negotiations with carriers and it is desirable to determine what is the minimum rate reduction that is necessary before the original optimum allocation would be revised, i.e., what rate reduction would result in lower total laid down costs. For cells (nodal pairs) where allocations are presently made, any rate reduction would produce a lower total laid down cost.

For reallocated cells (nodal pairs) the opportunity cost matrix for the optimum allocation provides the logistics manager with the minimum rate reduction necessary. For example, let us assume that the logistics manager is involved in a rate negotiation with a carrier serving the Plant 2 to warehouse A nodal pair. In Figure 10B-7, the opportunity cost for this cell is $.20. Remembering the iteration procedure, a new assignment is made only when the opportunity cost is negative. To make the opportunity cost negative for cell $2B$, the transportation rate must be reduced by at least $.21 per unit. Therefore, the minimum rate reduction necessary is $.21 per unit.

A similar examination of the opportunity cost matrix indicates to the logistics manager the effects of cost increases upon the nodal linking decision. Cost increases for unallocated cells have no impact upon the optimum nodal linking decision. Cost increases in allocated cells may cause a reallocation.

To determine if a reallocation is required let us consider a rate increase of $.20 per unit occurring for cell $1B$. The effects of this increase is found by considering the cells that would be affected in a reallocation—cells $1B$, $1D$, $2D$, and $2B$. The absolute (original) costs are used to determine the total cost effect of shifting one unit out of cell $1B$ into cell $1D$, and one unit from $2D$, and one unit from $2D$ into $2B$. If the sum of the positive costs is less than the sum of the negative costs then an iteration can be performed with lower total laid down costs. For example:

Since the sum of the negative signs is less than the positive, a reallocation would entail a higher total costs. Thus, the cost increase of $.20 per unit for cell $1B$ would not change the optimum nodal linking allocation. Total costs, however, would increase.

Examination of the opportunity cost matrix for the optimum allocation provides the logistics manager with readily accessible information for determining the effect of cost changes upon the nodal linking patterns.

OTHER APPLICATIONS OF THE TECHNIQUE

Linking Customers to Supply Nodes

The application of the transportation method to the above problem concerned linking plants to warehouses and allocating volumes among same. The technique can be applied to the delineation of market areas for warehouses or plants, i.e., to determine which customers will be served from the various supply nodes, and to the delineation of supply sources to be linked to plants.

Application of the transportation method to the linking of customers to supply nodes presents somewhat of a problem in terms of the multiplicity of customers locations, demand centers, and the resultant mechanical perplexity (especially if manually manipulated) associated with large-size matrices. Computer applications of the transportation method enables fairly large-size problems to be solved quickly, but most computers have limits as to the number of origins and destinations that can be facilitated.

Thus, the decision maker must aggregate customers into a limited number of demand centers to apply this technique to the market area nodal linking decision. Certain customers are naturals for this combination; customers located in the same city will incur the same transportation costs and, therefore, all customers in one city can be considered as one demand unit. In other situations the decision maker must consolidate customers in larger areas with consequent adjustments as to the average laid down costs in this market area.

Nodal Location Analysis

As alluded to in the nodal location chapter, the transportation method can be utilized to analyze alternative location sites for a node. It is used to evaluate alternative nodal sites that have previously been elected as potential locations. (The reader will recognize that some decision-making process is required to define which potential sites are to be evaluated by the transportation method. The material presented in the nodal location chapter is used to minimize the number of alternative sites to be considered.)

Specifically, the transportation method can be used in two ways to analyze potential locations. First, each alternative can be separately analyzed with existing nodes to determine the nodal linking pattern, and resultant total laid down costs for each. A comparison of the total costs for each potential node is made and the one that results in the lowest total cost is selected.

The second approach is to simultaneously consider all potential supply (plant) sites at one time. The existing demand nodes are utilized with their corresponding capacity and demand constraints. The laid down costs from the proposed plant sites as well as existing plants are developed for each nodal pair. Since the *TM* technique requires demand to equal supply, a "dummy" warehouse is added with a cost of zero from any supply source. Thus, potential nodal sites shipping to the dummy warehouse should not produce any output and, therefore, are not optimum locations.

Certain problems may arise in the second approach, such as all potential plants linked to some actual demand nodes or some existing plants linked to dummy. The decision maker is forced to consider the magnitude of the allocation of each plant. That is, if the allocation results in one potential plant having 95 percent of its output linked to actual demand nodes, this plant in all likelihood is the site to select.

Transshipment Problem

Another application of the transportation method is the analysis of consolidating shipments from one source to one destination and then reshipping from the destination to other destinations. This is known as the transshipment problem. The original matrix is augmented so that each source becomes a destination and each destination a source. (The iterative procedure described above is applied to solve the augmented matrix.) It is then possible to consider the total costs of nodal linking patterns in which goods are shipped from one plant to another plant and then reshipped to a warehouse or customer.

SUMMARY

In this section the transportation method of linear programming was applied to the nodal linking decision. The advantage of *TM* is its ability to determine the optimum (least cost) nodal linking patterns and the volume to be shipped over each link. Application of *TM* to other decision areas was also discussed.

A word of caution is required here. First, the use of *TM* requires knowledge of the technique's assumptions, i.e., the real-world problem may not meet the requirements of the technique so the decision maker must "force" the problem to fit the technique and then give consideration to the problem pragmatics. Second, the dynamics of the real world can result in changes for the *TM* determined nodal linking decision. Such factors as demand changes transportation and production costs increases will alter the original optimum decision. Thus, the decision maker is faced with a necessity to reevaluate the nodal linking decision over time.

Study Problems

1. Determine the least cost nodal linking pattern for the following problems. The cell costs are laid down costs.

Warehouse

A.	Plant	A	B	C	Capacity
	P_1	$12	$10	$9	30
	P_2	$8	$12	$6	12
	Demand	15	18	12	

Note: Dummy warehouse needed.

B.

	Market			
Warehouse	1	2	3	Capacity
W_A	$15	$7	$3	10
W_B	$10	$20	$9	20
W_C	$8	$5	$25	30
Demand	10	20	30	

Chapter 11	Customer Service

After studying this chapter, you should be able to:

- Provide an overview of customer service and its relationship to logistics.
- Analyze the elements of customer service.
- Discuss the cost of levels of customer service.
- Discuss how customer service standards are established.

Early View of
Customer Service

As pointed out in Chapter 1, the objective of business logistics is the minimization of total cost with the maximization of time and place utility in goods. Much of the early work in the field was concerned with the realization of cost savings. But this cost saving concern was by no means unconstrained. Customer service levels provided an inherent constraint upon the logistics system. Logistics costs, i.e., transportation, warehousing, inventory, order processing, etc., are directly related to the level of service provided. No rational cost reduction decision can be implemented without consideration being given to the level of customer service necessary for a firm to retain its competitive position in the market place.

Recent View

As the logistics concept matures, the customer service level is being viewed as a variable that can differentiate the product in the market place and thereby improve upon the product's competitiveness. The logistics department is being called upon to develop customer service levels in light of its (customer service level) sales effect and corresponding cost. Thus, the logistics manager must build into the objective function both the cost of providing various customer service levels and the related benefits (sales or profits) to the firm as a whole.

Customer service may take several forms depending on the needs or wants of the buyer and the ability and willingness of the seller to provide them. It should be pointed out here that these desires on the part of the buyer do not, in and of themselves, impose constraints upon the seller's system; rather, the establishment of customer service standards creates the logistics system constraints. For example, a customer's desire for one-day delivery time does not become a constraint until the seller establishes a one-day delivery service level policy.

Problem of
Definition

Anyone who has ever struggled to define customer service will soon realize the difficulty of such an endeavor, for the term "customer service" is quite nebulous. Customer service functions, which impact every area of the firm, attempt to ensure customer satisfaction by the provision of aid or assistance to that customer. Examples of the various forms that customer service may take care of are as follows:

- The revamping of a billing procedure to accommodate a customer's request.
- Guaranteed delivery within specified time periods.
- Provision of prompt and congenial sales representatives.
- Extending the option to sell on consignment.
- Providing material to aid in the customer's sales presentation.
- Product installation.
- Maintenance of satisfactory repair parts, inventories, etc.

Definition and
Philosophies

For our purposes at this point, we can use the following definition of customer service: "Those activities that occur at the interface between the customer and the corporation which enhance or facilitate the sale and use of the corporation's products or services.''[1] Another source has suggested that the following statements typify some corporate philosophies about customer service:

> Customer service is providing the right products in the right quantities at the right place at the right time.
>
> Customer service is meeting the expectations of customers at a reasonable cost.
>
> Customer service is a plan of action for accomplishing product delivery within established standards of quality, quantity, form, and time.[2]

The first and third philosophies are very close to descriptions that we used for business logistics. Therefore, one can see very easily why customer service has to be given special consideration in our discussion managing the business logistics system.

CUSTOMER SERVICE AND LOGISTICS

It may be well to pause at this moment and reflect some more upon the logistician's concern with customer service. In much the same way as customers respond to price reduction, they are sensitive to changes in customer service. (This usually is brought about by incurring additional customer service expenditures.) A general rule is that the higher the level of service provided, the greater will be the revenue received relative to the competition, other factors being held constant.

Explanation of Importance

The customer is concerned with the total product being purchased, not merely the physical characteristics of the goods. The level of logistics (customer) service provided is a basic product quality, similar to price and other physical characteristics. The logistics function is the final phase of the buyer-seller transaction. The final phase is in essence, the physical transfer of goods. Some level of customer service, good or bad, is automatically produced when this transfer function occurs. "Good" logistics service, enhances a firm's product while "poor" service detracts from it.

Customer service is an important basis for incurring logistics costs. Economic advantages generally accrue to the customer by virtue of better supplier service. As an example, customer inventories can be lowered by utilizing air as opposed to rail transportation. Lower inventory costs result from the lower transit time of air but the link costs by air will be higher than via rail transportation. The logistics manager must balance the desire of the customer for high service and the resultant benefit from possible increased sales revenues against the cost of providing that service. The logistician cannot provide extremely high customer service and incur tremendous costs without offsetting or greater profits (sales). By the same token, service must not be sacrificed in order to obtain low costs. A balance must be struck between customer service levels, total logistics costs and total benefits to the firm.

As can easily be seen, customer service is a complex collection of demand-related factors under the control of the firm but whose importance in determining supplier patronage is ultimately evaluated by the customer receiving the service.[3] The sellers should receive some information on the service revenue functions if they wish to evaluate the customer service levels necessary for their products. All too often this information stems from customer complaints which lead to the logistics manager frantically "fighting fires" started by poor service to customers. Or, if all is going well, the logistics manager may fall victim to the feeling that the customer service level is satisfactory since no customer is complaining; but customer silence may conceal the customer's plans to switch to the competition. The buyer-seller communication is essential to fully understanding the revenue generating attributes of customer service.

Customer Service Factors Related to Logistics

As has been previously mentioned, customer service may affect all areas within a firm. However, we are primarily concerned with customer logistics service, or those aspects of customer service under the control of the firm's logistics function. A study by Hutchinson and Stolle identified seven such factors of interest to the logistics manager:

1. *Order processing time*: elapsed time from receipt of the customer's order until it is ready for assembly.
2. *Order assembly time*: time required to prepare the order for shipment.
3. *Delivery time*: time in transit to the customer.
4. *Inventory reliability*: stockouts, back orders, percentage of demand filled, omission rate, percentage of orders complete, and so on.
5. *Order size constraint*: minimum order size and allowable order frequency.
6. *Consolidation allowed*: ability to consolidate items from several locations into a single shipment.
7. *Consistency*: range of variation occuring in each of the previous elements.[4]

It is apparent from the above that logistics may not have direct control over all elements of customer service. However, by granting logistics the customer service elements relevant to the creation of time and place utility in goods, the manager is able to have direct control over the customer's service variables for which logistics is held responsible. Thus, logistics does not become subservient to marketing or finance in the performance and establishment of customer service levels. At the same time, logistics must work closely with other departments in the establishment of customer service levels so that the firm as a whole is benefited, not just logistics.

CONCEPTUAL EVALUATION OF CUSTOMER SERVICE IN LOGISTICS SYSTEMS

As has been indicated in numerous instances in this text, customer service plays a very relevant role in the design and operation of logistics systems.

**FIGURE 11-1   General relationship between required inventory and cus-
tomer service.**

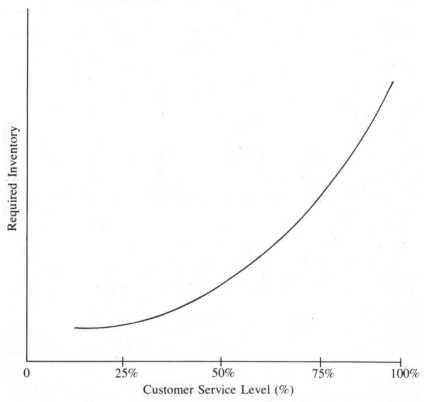

Before turning to some of practical or descriptive dimensions of customer
service, it would be useful to discuss the basic principles of logistics as they
relate specifically to customer service.[5]

*Customer Service
and Inventory*

In Chapter 2, it was stated that the cost of lost sales could be decreased
by increasing inventory levels. Essentially what was being stated was that
customer service levels have a direct effect upon inventory. In other words,
high customer service levels require high levels of inventory.[6] The relationships which has been depicted previously is shown in Figure 11-1.

The change in the required inventory is obvious from Figure 11-1, and
we can see that as customer service levels approaches 75% the required
inventory increases at an increasing rate. The obvious question is whether it
is worth the additional cost. The significant implication of this rhetorical
question is that it points up the most important interface between logistics
and marketing. The decision about customer service levels then has to be
analyzed in the familiar framework of the relevant trade-offs, i.e., the
increased sales associated with the improved customer service against the
increased costs associated with logistics and other relevant areas.

*Order Cycle and
Customer Service*

It was also noted previously that customer service is a convenient
means of competition in the marketplace that frequently supplants price

FIGURE 11-2   **Relationship between order cycle length and required inventory levels from the perspective of the buyer.**

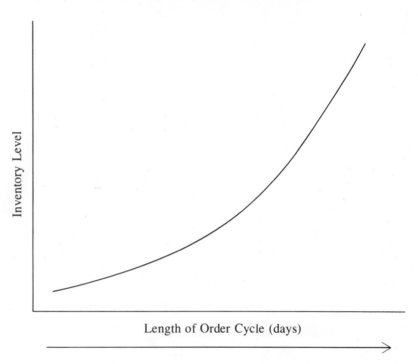

Length of Order Cycle (days)

competition, particularly in oligopolistic markets. As will be discussed in some detail in the next section, the length of the order cycle as measured in convenient time units is an important measure of customer service level. A shorter order cycle will usually result in lower inventory costs to customers.[7]

The order cycle has a particularly direct impact upon safety stock and process inventory.[8] The underlying logic is based upon customers being able to respond more quickly to rapid increases in their demand without carrying excess safety stock to protect against stockouts. As consumers in our households, we see the extreme of this principle in our consumption (use) of water and electricity. The suppliers (electric companies and water companies) provide instant response to customers who want to use their products. So we turn the spigot and out comes water, or we flip the switch to receive the electricity for the light bulb.

Most companies cannot provide like water and electric companies what is essentially a zero order cycle time to their customers. However, they may use market warehouses located strategically to the market, faster modes of transportation to respond more quickly to customers, and/or faster communication to transmit the order.

It should be clear by this point in the text that order cycle time can also be viewed as lead time or replenishment time. Also, it should be noted that

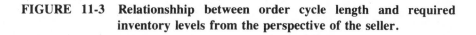

FIGURE 11-3 **Relationshhip between order cycle length and required inventory levels from the perspective of the seller.**

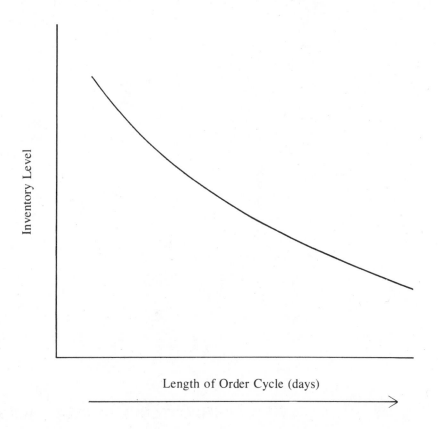

Length of Order Cycle (days)

order cycle time or lead time has the opposite impact on inventory requirements to that viewed in Figure 11-2 if viewed from the side of the seller. Figure 11-3 shows the impact on inventory from the perspective of the seller.

The logic of Figure 11-3 can be explained by the fact that the seller would not have to keep as much safety stock or process inventory on hand to meet its customers' requirements, i.e., it could, perhaps, produce after receiving orders or maintain a level of production and inventory that accepted a certain number of stockouts.

Once again we have a trade-off perspective. The cost of the shorter cycle time has to be viewed against the extra cost of inventory. There could also be other logistics costs affected, such as transportation.

At this point, you should have a good overview of customer service and its relationship to logistics. It would be useful, therefore, to now examine the importance of customer service in a more analytical manner in the context of the total company.

TABLE 11-1

Importance of Variables Affecting Sales

Category	Product	Price	Customer Service	Sales Effort	Total
ALL RESPONDENTS	36	23	23	18	100
ALL MANUFACTURING	38	24	20	18	100
Chemicals and Plastics	38	26	18	18	100
Food	36	27	15	22	100
Pharmaceuticals	47	20	12	21	100
Electrical	48	14	22	16	100
Paper	29	26	24	21	100
Machine Tools	43	30	20	7	100
All Other	38	25	22	15	100
ALL MERCHANDISING	30	22	27	21	100
Consumer	31	23	23	23	100
Industrial	28	17	39	16	100

Source: B. J. LaLonde and P. H. Zinszer, *Customer Service: Meaning and Measurement,* National Council of Physical Distribution Management, 1976.

OVERVIEW OF IMPORTANCE OF CUSTOMER SERVICE

Before delving into some of the more detailed aspects of customer service, consideration should be given to how important customer service is in relation to other variables affecting sales for various industry groups. Also, some attention should be given to the importance of various components of customer service as viewed by users and suppliers.

Table 11-1 shows the results of the most comprehensive study undertaken to develop empirical evidence about the importance of customer service. The information shows that overall customer service was tied for second in importance. It is interesting to note that it ranked ahead of sales effort in most instances, and in one instance, it ranked ahead of the appropriate product.

Logistics and Product Design

The importance of the product, as a variable as indicated in Table 11-1, is worth discussing. You can see that this variable ranks first in all but one instance. It is safe to say that historically either manufacturing or marketing has had the primary responsibility for product design. In industrial product companies, it has tended to be the manufacturing segment of the organization, whereas with consumer nondurables, it has been the marketing group in the organization with primary input. In consumer durables, there is

TABLE 11-2

Importance of Major Customer Service Variables by Industry

Respondent	Product Availability	Order Cycle	Service Flexibility	Service Information	Service Malfunction	Post Sale Product Support
ALL RESPONDENTS	42.4	20.7	11.5	12.6	7.7	4.5
ALL MANUFACTURERS	42.7	19.4	11.6	12.4	8.0	5.1
Chemicals and Plastics	44.5	17.4	10.6	11.7	9.1	6.2
Food	37.1	21.4	12.9	14.8	10.3	2.3
Pharmaceuticals	39.7	28.0	10.6	9.0	7.8	2.9
Electrical	32.7	17.4	12.9	16.7	7.9	11.7
Paper	41.3	12.3	18.5	20.1	4.5	1.8
Machine Tools	56.3	10.7	17.3	1.0	4.0	10.0
All Other	50.5	18.0	12.4	9.5	5.4	4.1
ALL MERCHANDISING	43.1	25.5	10.1	11.8	7.2	2.3
Consumer	40.5	26.2	9.0	14.0	8.2	2.0
Industrial	43.9	20.2	12.9	8.0	10.0	5.0

Source: B. J. LaLonde and P. H. Zinszer, *Customer Service: Meaning and Measurement,* National Council of Physical Distribution Management, 1976.

frequently a strong input in the product area from both marketing and manufacturing.

There is mounting evidence of the need for more logistics input in the product design area in all products, but most importantly for industrial products and consumer durables. The cost of logistics, as it relates to product design, is much too important not to consider.

The same study also provides some detailed information about the importance of the various components of customer service. The study classifies the elements of customer service somewhat differently than it has been described in the previous section. Product availability is included in our concept of dependability. In addition, system malfunction would be included in dependability, since the authors define it to include damage, incorrect orders, delayed shipment, etc.[9] System flexibility refers to the ability of the logistics system to respond to stockouts and problems, e.g., able to expedite orders, back order, substitute items, etc. This latter category would be covered by our concepts of time and dependability.

Importance of Dependability   The most interesting aspect of the findings shown in Table 11-2 is that they substantiate all the other studies; i.e., dependability, as we have defined it, is the most important variable. In the summary for all respondents, note that the sum of product availability, flexibility, and malfunction adds up to over 60 points of a total of 100. Even if we only included product availability and service malfunction, these two categories would account for over 50 points of the total of 100 in almost every instance. Adding in some part of the service flexibility would easily push dependability over 50 points in all instances, clearly indicating its importance for all respondents.

Another variable in Table 11-2 that should be noted is the past product support. For industrial products and consumer durables, this is an important variable which does not show up as well as it perhaps should in this study. You should note that for the electrical group and machine tool group the product support variable is quite important. Not enough attention is devoted to this area in most instances.

CUSTOMER SERVICE ELEMENTS

From the above discussion it is apparent that customer service has four main dimensions: time, dependability, communication, and convenience. The cost centers, for both the buyer and the seller, are affected by these elements. The cost effects are considered as we examine each of these areas below.

Time

As suggested previously, the time factor is usually viewed as order cycle time, particularly as the seller looks at customer service. On the other hand, the buyer usually regards the time dimension as lead time or replenishment time, whatever the perspective or term utilized, there are several basic components or variables that affect the time factor.

The seller does have control over lead time. Manipulation of the basic elements of lead time—order transmittal, order processing, order preparation, and order shipment—permits the seller to change lead time offered to buyers. Direct control is possible in order transmittal and order processing stages with possibly limited control over order shipment (especially if common carriage is utilized).

Order Transmittal

Order transmittal is associated with the time that elapses from the time the customer develops the order until the order is received by the seller. Order transmittal time can vary from a few minutes by telephone to a number of days by mail. As the seller moves from slow to fast order transmittal, lead time is reduced, but the cost of order transmittal is increased.

Order Processing

Order processing is that time required to process the customer's order and make it ready for shipment. This function usually involves customer credit check, transferral of information to sales records, order transference to inventory area, and preparation of shipping documents. Many of these functions can occur simultaneously. The use of electronic data-processing equipment can significantly reduce the information time for transferral functions, while automated materials handling systems can reduce the time for the physical phase of order processing. Such changes have associated increases in cost, the fixed costs of a more capital intensive order processing system.

Order Preparation

Order preparation time involves the "picking" of the order, as previously described in Chapter 5, and packaging the item for shipment along with all the appropriate checks. In Chapters 5 and 6, the impact of various types of materials handling systems on order filling and preparation was discussed. These systems can vary from a simple manual system to a very highly automated system. Consequently, the time can vary considerably. The costs and benefits of the alternatives have to be considered.

Order Shipment

Order shipment time extends from the moment the order is placed upon the vehicle for movement until it is received and unloaded at the buyer's destination. It is usually difficult to measure and control order shipment time when for-hire carriage is used. Information from the carrier may be unreliable. The use of response cards to be completed by the buyer permits the seller to measure transit time of for-hire carriage. If the for-hire carriage transit time is to be reduced, the seller must use a faster (lower transit time) carrier within the mode presently used or utilize a faster mode of transport with a corresponding increase in transportation cost. Direct control of transit time is possible with a private fleet.

Modifications on all four areas may be too costly. It is possible, therefore, to make cost modifications in one area and permit the others to operate at the existing level. For example, it may be financially unwise for the firm to invest in automated materials handling equipment. To take account of this higher manual order processing time, the firm could switch from mail to telephone order transmittal and the use of motor transportation instead of rail. This would permit a reduction in lead time without an increase in capital investment for automated materials handling equipment.

The guarantee of a given level of lead time is one of the more important advancements in logistics management. Its impact may be seen both in the efficiencies that accrue to the customer (inventory costs) and to the seller's logistics system and market position. But, the concept of time, by itself, is rather meaningless without a consideration of dependability.

Dependability

Most often dependability is more important than lead time to a customer. The customer can adjust his inventory to a minimum level if lead time is fixed. That is, if lead time is known with 100 percent assurance to be ten days, customers can adjust inventory level to correspond to the average demand (usage) during the ten days. There would be no need for safety stock to guard against stockouts resulting from fluctuating lead times.

Lead Time

Dependability of lead time, then, has a direct impact upon the customer's inventory level and stockout costs. The provision of dependable lead time reduces some of the uncertainty faced by a customer. If the customer can be assured of a given level of lead time, plus some small tolerance, the seller has established a distinct differentiation for its product over that of its competitor. The seller that provides dependable lead time permits the buyer to minimize the total cost of holding inventory, stockouts, order processing, and production scheduling.

The concept of dependability encompasses more than just the variability of lead time. More generally, dependability refers to the delivery of a customer's order with regular, consistent lead time, in safe condition and in harmony with the type and quality of items ordered.

Safe Delivery

Safe delivery of an order is the ultimate goal of any logistics system. As noted earlier, the logistics function is the culmination of the selling function, and if the goods arrive in a damaged condition (or are lost) the customer can not make use of the goods as intended. The arrival of a shipment containing damaged goods aggravates a number of customer cost centers—inventory, production, and/or marketing.

The receipt of a damaged shipment means the customer may not use the damaged items for sale or production. This sets up the possibility for stockout costs (foregone profits or production) to be increased. The hedge against these costs is an increase in the level of inventory held. Thus, unsafe delivery causes the buyer to incur higher inventory carrying costs or foregone profits or production.

In addition to the above costs, an unsafe delivery may cause the customer to incur the cost of filing a claim with the carrier and/or returning the damaged item to the seller for repair or credit. (Depending upon the F.O.B. terms of sale and other stipulations of the sales agreement, the seller, not the buyer, may be responsible for these costs.) The seller will probably be aware of these two cost areas since it will be more or less directly involved in corrective actions.

Correct Orders

Finally, dependability embraces the correct filling of orders. It is not uncommon for a customer who is anxiously awaiting the arrival of an urgently needed shipment to discover upon receipt of the shipment that the seller made an error in filling the order. The customer has not received what was requested and may face potential lost sales or production. An improperly filled order necessitates a reorder by the customer, if the customer is not angered to the point of buying from another supplier. Also, if a stockout is experienced by a customer who is an intermediary in the marketing channel, the cost of the stockout (lost sales) directly impacts the seller.

The two vital logistics areas in the order filling function are the communication of customer order information to the order filling area and the actual process of picking out of inventory the items ordered. In the order information stage, the use of EDP can reduce the possibility of error in transferring order information from the order to the warehouse receipt. Product identification (codes, etc.) must be simplified so that the chances for an order picker to make an error are reduced.

The logistics manager must continually monitor the dependability of transit time, safety, and order filling. In most instances this monitoring function involves feedback, either through a formalized information gathering procedure or an informal, word-of-mouth process from customer as to the quality of logistics dependability. The informal feedback will indicate blatant errors or problems, such as, four shipments were three days late, etc., but this procedure does not guarantee access to the complete information required. The informal monitoring does not give the accuracy and completeness necessary to effectively make decisions regarding dependability. The formal feedback method usually involves some mechanism, possibly a short questionnaire or a response card that elicits the desired information regarding time, safety, and order filling dependability.

Communication

As noted above, communication with the customers is a vital link in monitoring the customer service levels relating to dependability. Customer communication is essential to the design of logistics service levels. The communication channel must be constantly open and readily accessible to all customers, for this is the source to the major external constraints imposed upon logistics. Without customer contact, the logistics manager is unable to provide the most efficient and economical service; i.e., the logistics manager would be playing the ball game without full knowledge of the game rules.

However, the communication must be a two-way street. The seller must be capable of transmitting vital logistics service information to the customer. For example, the supplier would be well advised to inform the buyer of potential reductions in the level of service provided so as to permit the buyer to make the necessary operational adjustments.

In addition, many customers request information on the logistics status of shipment. Questions concerning shipment date, carrier, route, etc., are not uncommon. The logistics manager is expected (by the customer) to provide the answers, for the answers are needed by the customer to plan operations.

Convenience

Convenience is another way of stating that the logistics service level must be flexible. From the standpoint of logistics operation it would be ideal to have one or a few standard service levels that applied to all customers. But this assumes that all customers are homogeneous as to their logistics requirements. This, by all means, is not the situation in reality. For example, one customer may require all shipments to be palletized and shipped via rail; another may require truck delivery only, with no palletization; or, special delivery times may be requested. Basically the logistics requirements differ with regard to packaging, mode and carrier required, routing, and delivery times.

Essentially, the convenience factor recognizes the different requirements of customers. It is usually possible to group customer requirements by
customer size, market area, product line purchased, etc. This grouping
(market segmentation) enables the logistics manager to recognize the
customer service requirements and attempt to fulfill these demands in the
most economical manner.

The need for convenience in logistics service levels is attributable to the
differing consequences the service levels have on the many customers. More
specifically, the cost of lost sales will differ among the customer groups. For
example, the lost sales resulting from a customer that purchases 30 percent
of a firm's output is much greater than the lost sales cost resulting from a
firm buying less than .01 percent of the output. Also, the degree of
competitiveness in market areas will differ; those market areas that are
highly competitive will require a higher level of service and vice versa for
lesser competitive areas. The level of profitability with regard to different
product lines in a firm's marketbasket will limit the level of service that can
be offered; i.e., low-profit product lines may have a lower service level
provided than for a high-profit product line.

However, the logistics manager must place the convenience factor in
proper operational perspective. Customer service level convenience can be
carried to the extreme situation characterized by a specific service level
policy for each customer. Such a situation sets the stage for operational
chaos; the logistics function can not be optimized because of the plethora of
service level policies. The need for flexibility in service level policies is
warranted, but it should be restricted to easily identifiable customer groups.
The trade-off between the benefits (improved sales and profits or elimination
of lost profits) and the costs associated with unique service levels must be
examined in the specific situation.

THE COST OF LOGISTICS SERVICE LEVELS: A CONCEPTUAL OVERVIEW

Thus far in our discussion attention has been directed toward the examination of customer service levels and their benefits to the firm (supplier). It is
not intended in the above discussion to imply that increases in customer
service levels are costless. The costs to be incurred to establish and operate a
given customer service level must be examined and weighed against the
benefits to be realized from such levels of service. If the benefits (improved
sales and profits or elimination of lost profits) are greater than the total costs
of a proposed service level the firm as a whole will be benefited, and the
logistics manager should make the necessary logistics changes to implement
this level of service.

Example

To realize changes in the level of service provided, the logistics
functional areas of transportation, warehousing, inventory, materials handling, and/or order processing must be manipulated with a corresponding

increase in the cost of the functional areas altered. For example, if a supplier is providing a service level in which 85 percent of customer orders are processed and shipped two days after receipt, a $100,000 investment in inventory may be required. To increase this to 90 percent of customer orders processed in five days, the supplier may be required to invest an additional $150,000 in inventory. In addition, this new service level may require additional investment in automated materials handling and order selection equipment as well as expenditures for automated order processing equipment.

Distribution Centers and Customer Service

A recent trend in the area of customer service is use of the distribution center concept in the logistics system. The distribution center permits the supplier to ship bulk loads (CL or TL) of his many products into the market area distribution center from various plants to realize savings in transportation cost. The customer orders are processed and shipped from the distribution center at higher LTL or LCL rates but a shorter distance, thus realizing lower total transportation costs. The lead time element is reduced, thereby improving customer services.

The above example is utilized to indicate the cost trade-offs within the logistics areas. As the number of warehouses increases, the supplier realizes a reduction in the transport cost from the factory to the customer. This is attributable to the shipment of larger quantities (CL or TL) at lower rates to the warehouse rather than smaller quantities at higher LCL or LTL rates from the factory to the consumer. However, at some time, too many warehouses may exist in the system, causing an increase in the transportation cost from the factory to the warehouse. As the number of warehouses increases, the total business at each is reduced, which may result in the shipping of less-than-volume loads at higher transportation rates between the factories and warehouses.

The outbound transportation cost from the warehouse to the customer decreases as the number of warehouses increases. The greater the number of warehouses, the closer inventory will be to the customer; this reduces the distances from warehouses to customers and lowers the cost of transportation. Theoretically, this warehouse-to-customer transport is minimized when each customer has a warehouse.

The notion of having a warehouse at each customer's location has associated with it very high service levels. The customer would have almost immediate access to inventory, thus very low lead times. However, the cost of such a system would be prohibitive. The cost of holding the inventory at each location and of operating the tremendous number of warehouses would make such a system very uneconomical.

Warehousing costs are directly related to the size of a warehouse and the amount of use made of the facility. Usually larger warehouses offer economies of a scale associated with the large investment for automated materials handling equipment necessary to achieve acceptable order processing times. In addition, there are cost economies in the construction and operation of larger size warehouses.

FIGURE 11-4   The relationship of logistics inputs trade-offs to the level of customer service derived.

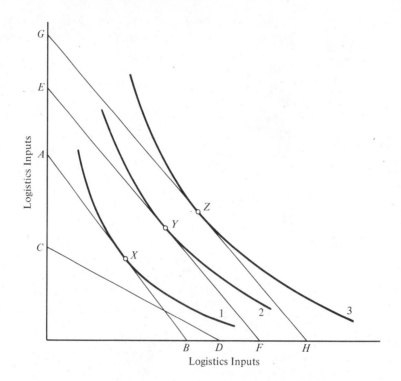

The investment associated with holding inventory at each customer's location would be tremendous. Take, for example, a supplier with 2,000 or more customers. The investment in inventory for 2,000 warehouses would be much greater than that required for 15 or 20 warehouses to serve these customers.

The foregoing discussion of logistics costs should give the reader some feel for the importance of customer service and its effect on the logistics system. It must be remembered that there is a great deal of interplay among costs. For example, a given level of customer service may be obtained through the use of premium transportation and low warehouse inventories. The same level of service may be provided by high warehouse stockage and a lower quality mode of transportation. There are system trade-offs possible which are used to give a minimum total cost for a given service level. One might view these trade-offs in terms of isocosts and isoquants.

Isocosts

Isocosts, in this instance, will be used to denote the combination of logistics inputs that can be purchased with given input costs and fixed amount of money. Isoquants will refer to equal levels of customer service.

Isoquants

FIGURE 11-5   Relationship between logistics costs and service levels.

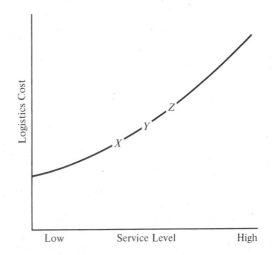

Isoquants are convex to the origin and may never intersect one another, for, if they did, it would be the equivalent of being able to produce two given levels of customer service with the same combination of logistics inputs. In Figure 11-4, lines 1, 2, and 3 are isoquants representing higher levels of customer service for a given time period. The axes represent inputs to the logistics system. These inputs may be transportation, warehousing, inventories, handling and processing, etc. The isocost lines (*A-B, C-D, E-F,* and *G-H*) show the cost for a given combination of inputs into the logistics system.

Let us first look at isocost *A-B*. We see that it intersects isoquant 1 at point *X*; this is the minimum cost of obtaining customer service level 1. The combination of inputs expressed by line *E-F* will also produce customer service level 1, but at a higher than optimal cost. The logistics manager must make trade-offs within his system so as to produce the given level of results at the least possible cost. Continuing, the reader will note that *E-F* and *G-H* are tangent to isoquants 2 and 3, respectively, meaning that these combinations of inputs will result in achievement of these service levels at the lowest total cost. (*Note*: isocost *C-D* does not permit the attainment of the service levels being considered.) If we now draw a line through the low cost points (*X, Y,* and *Z*) we would obtain the curve given in Figure 11-5.

In general, the costs of providing higher levels of service increase at an increasing rate. For example, one firm has found that to increase on-time delivery from 95 percent to 100 percent the per unit cost index increased from about 30 to 100, or approximately a threefold increase.[10] In another situation, the cost of switching from an 85 percent customer service level—mail order transmittal, water transportation, and low inventories—to a 96 percent level—telephone order transmittal, truck transport, and high inventories—increased 320 percent.[11]

The decision to alter customer service levels has far reaching and interrelated logistics cost effects. Such a decision can not be made without careful analysis of the logistics cost impacts. Any customer service level decision requires a prudent blending of the various logistics functions to produce the least-cost system that will enable realizations of the given service level benefits.

THE COST OF CUSTOMER SERVICE: A PRAGMATIC APPROACH

The previous section looked at customer service costs using a theoretical approach, which necessitates gathering a significant amount of data. In some instances, such a detailed approach would not be possible and the logistics manager would need a simpler and faster way to reasonably approximate the costs involved.

A suggested approach is based on a procedure consisting of three steps:[12]

1. Determine a reasonable cost for stockouts.
2. Establish realistic probabilities for losses.
3. Develop the best service policy.

As pointed out in Chapter 3, stockout costs can be viewed as consisting of a short-run and/or long-run component. In the short run at the retail level, a stockout may mean that the customer will substitute another similar product. Consequently, the stockout will cost us the profit on each item times the number of units that were not sold. It should be noted that there is some brand loyalty at the retail level which has been estimated at the level of 50 percent; i.e., about 50 percent of U.S. consumers cannot be sold a substitute product.[13]

As has been indicated previously, it is usually too costly, particularly for consumer products, to have a 100 percent customer service level, i.e., no stockouts. Therefore, as suggested above, some level of stockouts must be accepted; we may aim for 95 percent service level, for example.

Role of Expediting   Related to the above idea of a certain level of stockouts, the logistics manager should view the level of customer service within a framework that includes the possibility of trading off against the cost of expediting shipments. In other words, the manager should use expediting as an alternative to a stockout situation.[14] Stated as simply as possible, if the cost of a stockout is greater than the cost of expediting, then an order should be expedited.

Probabilities   The second step, as indicated, implies establishing reasonable and realistic probabilities of losses associated with a stockout. These probabilities are dependent upon the stocking policies of the company's customers. The identification of such policies will lead to establishment of the appropriate probabilities or odds.[15]

Service Policy

The final step is the development of a best service policy. The evaluation involves the assessment of two costs. The first is a determination of the cost of carrying an additional unit of inventory to render better service. The second is the cost of the profit which is foregone because of the stockout.[16] The inventory required to render varying levels of service will differ. This difference increases at an accelerating rate as the desired service level is increased. For example, if a company raises its service level to 96 percent from 95 percent, they will require 6 percent more safety stock. If the service level is raised 1 percent from 98 percent to 99 percent, the new service level requires 14 percent more safety stock.[17]

PHYSICAL SUPPLY SERVICE LEVELS

Up to this point we have been considering customer service levels from the physical distribution side of logistics. A brief digression into customer service levels for physical supply will show a great deal of similarity to that for physical distribution.

The requirement for 100 percent customer service is almost a necessity on the physical supply side. As previously noted, disruptions, i.e., incorrect orders, undependable lead times, etc., in the flow of goods to the consumer aggravate the consumer's costs. However, in many situations the consumer (user) has the ability to substitute products, or, if substitutes are not available, the cost of the foregone sales and profits during the stockout is quite small in comparison to the stockout cost on the physical supply side.

The possibility for substituting raw materials usually does not exist with short lead times. First, the existence of raw material suppliers is not as plentiful and widely available as suppliers of finished goods. Second, there may be technical standards of a particular raw material that preclude the substitution of a like material with different standards. In short the lack of sufficient geographically accessible alternative raw material suppliers coupled with the possible technical incompatibility of raw materials from different suppliers greatly restrains the firm's ability to substitute raw materials during a stockout.

Cost of Physical Supply Stockout

Without this substitution possibility, the disruption in the physical supply service may create a potential plant closing, temporary layoffs, and high start-up costs when the raw material finally arrives. Temporary closing of a plant may mean paying labor for a partial day's wage (depending upon union contract terms) even though no production occurs during this time. If the temporary stockout is prolonged, labor will be furloughed, causing future unemployment compensation rates to increase. In addition, once the stockout is alleviated, overtime production might be necessary to replace reduced finished goods inventory or to fill back orders of the finished goods. If finished goods inventory is depleted, foregone profits will be incurred as well. Lastly, the overhead costs of the plant are incurred throughout the period of nonproductivity.

In short, the cost of a physical supply stockout is very great. This extremely high cost greatly increases the "value" of a raw material facing stockout; i.e., the item takes on an emergency value which is much higher than the price of the item. The emergency value of raw material requires and enables the logistics manager to utilize movement and storage functions that would not be a normal operating procedure.

For example, consider a possible stockout of a door handle at a plant manufacturing auto bodies. The stockout of this handle would cause the stopping of the auto body assembly line with the corresponding cost of labor, lost productivity, and overhead. In addition other assembly lines will be affected if the work stoppage at the body plant is prolonged; the auto assembly plants dependent upon the stopped body plant will face closing as well. In this situation, the stockout of a raw material at one plant has an impact upon the operations of other manufacturing plants in the firm's system. To offset the stockout of the door handle, one would find the firm utilizing air freight, at very high transportation rates.

For bulk raw materials (coal, iron ore, sand, etc.) the provision of uninterrupted supply service normally utilizes high inventory levels rather than premium transportation. The physical characteristics of bulk commodities permit the use of inexpensive warehousing facilities—an open air (on the ground) type of facility is usually adequate—and preclude the use of air freight. In addition, the value of the bulk material is relatively low, thereby not requiring inordinately high capital investment.

If one considers an electric utility company utilizing coal one will find anywhere from 60-120 day supply of coal stockpiled. In this example the potential costs of stockouts (the social and economic costs to all users of electricity) are astronomical. Also, the volume of coal used in one day would make the use of premium transportation (air or even truck) a physical impossibility; the vehicle carrying capacity of these modes would require a large number of vehicles. Therefore, the capital investment associated with a 90-day inventory of coal is quite justifiable in light of the potentially devastating cost of an electric supply stoppage.

In summary, the cost of inadequate physical supply service is so excessive that firms assure a 100 percent service level either by use of premium transportation or increased inventory levels.

CUSTOMER SERVICE STANDARDS

The development of customer service standards requires the firm to determine the types of customer service desired by its customers, the cost of providing alternative services, and the measures to be used in evaluating service performance. Inherent to this development is a market analysis of customers by market area, customer size, and product or product lines. Such information is the basis for the analysis of required customer service levels, costs and standards for measurement.

Establishing Standards

Analysis of Demand   The establishment of a customer service policy must start with an analysis of customer demand. The degree of product substitutability and number of competitors determine the amount of units of lost sales and the resultant cost of these lost sales units that can be expected during a stockout. For those products that have a high degree of substitutability the need for high inventory levels or use of premium transportation is greater than for products with lesser substitutability. More specifically, the firm must determine for each product or product line if its customers will wait until stocked out items are replenished or if during the stockout the customers will purchase from competitors. The analysis must be performed for various market territories, for the number of competitors, customer brand loyalty, etc., will differ among territories thereby requiring specific service levels for specific territories.

Costs are Different   It should also be noted that the stockout cost is not homogeneous for all customers. Customer size (volume of purchases) determines the potential long-run cost of a stockout. For example, the long-run lost profit associated with a customer who shifts to a competitor's product during a stockout and does not return afterwards is much greater for a customer who purchases 25 percent of a firm's output than for a buyer who purchases less than one-tenth of one percent. Thus, the size of the customer may warrant different service policies.

Operational Needs   Consideration must also be given to the customer's operational needs. That is, the customer may have definite requirements for delivery dates so as to enable the customer to effect efficiencies in production processes, marketing campaigns, etc. Such requirements must be known so that the seller may tailor (differentiate) product offering and thereby increase or at least maintain sales and profits.

Competitor's Service   Finally, the market analysis must concern itself with an examination of current competitor service levels. At the minimum, a firm must establish a service level policy that equals that of its competitors. Any service levels less than that provided by competitors means that the firm is placing itself in a competitively disadvantageous position. The real concern is whether the firm can provide better service than competitors at a cost that does not place the firm at a price disadvantage.

This market analysis must not be a "one shot" function performed for the customer service level development. It must be an ongoing process to monitor changes in customer demands and competition performance. The continued customer service analysis provides the necessary feedback to evaluate and effect changes in the established policy. The marketing department can be of tremendous assistance in both the initial and post analysis of customer service needs and competitor service levels.

Framework of Analysis   One must not get the impression that service levels are established only to reduce stockout costs or to emulate competitor offerings. The establishment of service level policies must be looked upon as a tool or device that can differentiate the firm's product and consequently increase sales. The provision of lower lead times, less product damage, and fewer stockout situations than that of competitors is a definite marketing edge for the firm to emphasize in its marketing tactics. However, the advantages, increased sales and profits, must be weighed against the costs associated with the increased service; i.e., the total trade-off to the firm must be analyzed. If the marginal benefits are less than the marginal costs of the increased service, then the firm will be in a better position without the increased service and vice versa.

The establishment of customer service standards has associated with it the question of who should develop the policies. It is imperative that the department responsible for the implementation of customer service standards also have some authority in the establishment of the policies. That is, the department held accountable for the realization of the established service levels is logistics and it should be involved in the policy-making decision.

The initiative for determining the required level of customer service should rest with the logistics department. This does not mean that logistics is to be the sole contributor in the standard development. To the contrary, logistics must seek and utilize customer service information from marketing, finance and production; the input from these departments is essential to the development of a customer service policy that is beneficial to the firm as a whole, not one individual department or function.

Objectivity in evaluating customer service level needs, benefits, and costs is paramount. The customer service policy decision must not be overshadowed by marketing's objective of increased sales or finance's concern for reduced costs. The logistics department provides the necessary objectivity (neutrality) to recognize the marketing benefits and the financial constraints and thereby establish a customer service level policy, which logistics will be responsible for implementing and controlling, that is beneficial to the firm as a whole.

Service Level Standards

Useful customer service levels must be defined in a manner that permits quantifiable measurement. Such policy statements as "90 percent customer satisfaction" are not readily measurable and therefore difficult to achieve and control. An ambiguous, nonquantifiable policy does not establish the necessary standard to evaluate the system's performance and to control customer service costs.

The logistics functional areas involving time, inventory, and product safety are essentially the service standards that permit quantification. The time element refers to the level and consistency of lead time, inventory involves measurement of the seller's ability to fill customer orders, and product safety concerns the frequency and magnitude of damage.

Importance of Time   Time is the main service element concern of the customer. Basically, a purchaser is interested in knowing "how long it will take the seller to get the order to me." This question can be translated into a measurement of lead time and the establishment of lead time standards for serving customers. The time dimension can be utilized to encompass both inventory availability and product damage standards since the latter two measures directly impact the length of time required to complete the customer order transaction.

For practical applications, the time element is usually measured from receipt of customer order to ultimate delivery of order. That is, the customer service time standard may not include the order transmittal phase of lead time. The pragmatics associated with measurement of order transmittal time (checking postmark dates, for example) are cumbersome, costly, and time-consuming, but this does not imply that the logistics manager should overlook control and analysis of order transmittal procedures.

One often finds the customer service time element policy stated as a given percentage of deliveries completed within a given number of days after order receipt, e.g., 90 percent of deliveries made within three days after order receipts. The example policy means that the seller expects 90 percent of the orders to be in the hands of customers within three days of receipt of the order. Some customers will receive orders in less than three days, but only 10 percent of the orders will be delivered after three days of receipt of order.

The given percentage of orders and the time element of the policy standard is determined from the customer analysis and the analysis of costs. The greater the percentage of customers served in shorter time period, the greater the logistics costs. For example, if a firm wishes to increase the service levels from "80 percent deliveries within five days" to "90 percent deliveries within two days," the firm may be required to modify its logistics system by such measures as increasing the number of warehouses, increasing inventory levels, utilizing automated materials handling equipment, and/or purchasing premium, low-transit-time transportation service. The logistics manager is confronted with a trade-off consideration between the benefits of improved customer service standards and the costs of this improvement.

Control of Time   To determine if the logistics function is meeting the desired customer
Policy   service time policy, the logistics manager merely develops a cumulative frequency distribution of the actual delivery times and compares this to the stated policy. For example, if the stated policy is "90 percent deliveries within three days of order receipt" the logistics manager would analyze the order delivery times to determine the number of orders delivered within three days and the number beyond three days. A random sample of orders or a comprehensive analysis (if computerized operation) of orders for all or particular markets could be used in the development of the actual service time performance to determine time compliance with stated policy.

Correct Order   The second logistics service standard of the seller's ability to fill
Policy   customer orders is concerned with order filling reliability. One measure of

order filling reliability considers stockouts. In particular, Magee[18] suggests the use of the fraction of order cycles with no stockouts and expected stockouts per time period as standards for order filling reliability. If one establishes a policy of 95 percent of order cycles (stock replenishments) with no stockout, actual performance should occasion only five stockouts in 100 order cycles for a particular product or, if the 95 percent reliability is applied to a group of 100 products, only five items should be stocked out per order cycle. The expected stockout per time unit measures the number of stockouts for a given item in a given time period and is desirable when the firm desires the same stockout frequency for all items.

The correct filling of orders is also a measure of a seller's ability to fill orders on time. An incorrectly filled order is essentially equal to nonreceipt of an order. For example, a purchaser who orders 20 gallons of red paint but receives 20 gallons of green paint is in the same position as not receiving the order at all. In addition, the seller may be required to incur the cost of returning the incorrect order or the customer incurs the inventory costs of the unwanted items as well as being dissatisfied with the seller's service.

The firm must develop standards relating to the number or percentage of correctly filled orders per time period. Deviations from this established policy indicate an analysis of the order filling function. In many cases, human error is involved in transferring order information and in picking the ordered items from inventory; use of electronic data processing can minimize the former and simplified product identification schemes the latter.

Safety

The final logistics service area of product safety can be viewed as an incomplete order or as an increased level of lead time. An order that is received in a damaged condition means the customer cannot use the damaged item, or, essentially, the nonreceipt of an order. Additional time is required as well as added seller expense to supply the customer with a usable item. Thus, the delivery of damaged products reduces a firm's customer service level and increases logistics costs.

The establishment of an "acceptable" dollar amount of product damage per time period per logistics functional unit as well as an "acceptable" frequency of damage per time per logistics functional unit is a prerequisite to effective control of product damages. The frequency as well as dollar amount of damage must be stated, for there are many purchasers who have an established policy that damages of less than $45 to $50 will not be filed since the cost of filing the claim is greater than the recoverable damage value. Thus, the frequent occurrence of smaller dollar damages could pose a serious problem in the aggregate to a customer and the supplier.

Ascertainment of the reported damages presents no real problem to the supplier; the firm will have an in-house record of the customer's damage claims. But the unreported claims require initiative on the seller's part to secure this information from the customer. Use of questionnaires or salesmen's contracts provides a ready solution to ascertaining this "silent" threat to a firm's customer service.

FIGURE 11-6 **Examples of customer service elements.**

Service Element	Service Standard
Time	95% of orders delivered in two days
	90% of orders processed in one day
	90% of orders processed and delivered in five days
Order Filling	98% of orders accurately filled
	95% of order cycles with no stockouts
Safety	5% of shipments damaged
	$100,000 in damage claims per year
	$5,000 in damage claims per carrier, warehouse, etc.

As indicated above, the product damage policy must be stated by logistics functional unit. By doing so, the logistics manager has the necessary criteria to analyze and to take corrective actions regarding specific product handling facets (warehouses, carriers, etc.) of the logistics systems. For example, aggregate dollar amount and frequency damage data do not permit corrective actions; the source of the damage must be known as well.

For the customer service elements of time, order filling, and safety, examples of customer service standards are given in Figure 11-6. It should be noted that the use of the specific limits of the examples given varies widely in practice. The exact service level policy utilized is dependent upon the specific characteristics of the firm's environment—products, competition, and demand—and the resultant cost and benefits of different service levels.

The standards developed for time and order filling elements are minimums. That is, the firm desires at least 95 percent of demand to be delivered in two days. Any level less than 95 percent will not be acceptable. Conversely, the levels established for the safety element are maximums. That is, the firm will tolerate only 5 percent of shipment being damaged. If actual performance levels are above those established for time and order filling or below those for safety, the logistics manager, on the surface, may seem to be doing an excellent job, but this better-than-normal or expected performance must be analyzed as to the actual costs being incurred. The provision of a 96 percent service level rather than the 95 percent standard established is beneficial as long as the additional costs do not offset the additional benefits.

In conclusion, the customer service standards developed for a firm must be quantifiable so as to be functional. The logistics areas of time, inventory and product damage provide useful areas for customer service policy standards.

SUMMARY

In this chapter attention was given to the establishment of customer service levels and the operation of the logistics system. The level of customer service provided has a direct impact upon the cost and operation of the logistics function. The establishment and control of customer service policies is the responsbility of logistics, but input from marketing, finance, and production is essential for provision of customer service levels that are beneficial to the firm as a whole.

Study Questions

1. Discuss the role logistics plays in the development and implementation of customer service level policies.
2. Discuss the impact of customer service levels upon marketing and finance.
3. Identify the main customer service elements and indicate the important characteristics of each.
4. Explain the nature of the cost trade-offs inherent in the establishment of customer service levels.
5. Compare the differences (similarities) between the customer service levels for physical supply vs. physical distribution.
6. Describe the procedure that would be used to establish a customer service level policy.
7. Discuss the criteria and the rationale for such criteria for measuring the performance of a company's customer service level.

Notes

1. B. J. LaLonde and P. H. Zinszer, *Customer Service: Meaning and Measurement* (National Council of Physical Distribution, 1976), p. 2.
2. Warren Rose, *Logistics Management* (Dubuque, Iowa: William C. Brown Company, 11979), pp. 280-281.
3. R. H. Ballou, *Business Logistics Management* (Englewood Cliffs, N.J.: Prentice-Hall, Inc., 1973), p. 96.
4. William Hutchinson and J. F. Stolle, "How to Manage Customer Service," *Harvard Business Review,* November-December 1968, p. 88.
5. Roy Dale Voorhees and Merrill Kim Sharp, "The Principles of Logistics Revisited," *Transportation Journal,* Fall 1978, pp. 71-73.
6. *Ibid.*
7. Warren Rose, *Logistics Management* (Dubuque, Iowa: William C. Brown Company, 1979), pp. 284-86.
8. Voorhees, op. cit., pp. 80-81.

9. *Ibid.*, pp. 118-19.

10. "The Basic Problem: Skyrocketing Costs," *Purchasing Week,* October 25 1971, p. 18.

11. R. H. Ballou, *op. cit.,* p 106.

12. This approach is based on: H. N. Shycon and C. R. Sprague, "Put A Price Tag On Your Customer Service Levels," *Harvard Business Review,* July-August 1975, pp. 73-78; and Appendix 4-B of this text.

13. *Ibid.*

14. David P. Herron, "Managing Physical Distribution for Profit," *Harvard Business Review*, May-June 1979, pp. 126-127.

15. H. N. Shycon and C. R. Sprague, *op cit.*, pp. 74-75.

16. *Ibid.*

17. *Ibid.*, p. 76.

18. John F. Magee, *Industrial Logistics* (New York: McGraw-Hill, 1968, pp. 91-92.

Case 11-1
Petro-Chem, Inc.

Petro-Chem, Inc., is a large manufacturer of motor coolants and petroleum products. The firm is two years old, and all physical distribution activities have taken place through a large petroleum products distributor in Los Angeles.

Since Petro-Chem feels that it has established itself in the petroleum products market, a logistics department has been formed in order to establish a physical distribution system for the firm. Within this system, a private motor carrier fleet will be implemented.

In addition to the transportation responsibilities, the logistics department has been ordered to establish a customer service section within the department. The customer service personnel will be charged with the responsibilities of establishment of customer service policies and the estimated level of this service. Petro-Chem has started the construction of a large distribution center warehouse beside its manufacturing location.

As the newly appointed director of the customer service department:

1. Describe and list the important elements which must be considered in the establishment of a customer service department.
2. Discuss the procedures used in establishing the "level" of customer service.
3. Make any additional recommendations with respect to the customer service aspects of a logistics department.
4. Do you think it was a wise decision for Petro-Chem to establish its own distribution and customer service departments? (Discuss).

| **Chapter 12** | Management of Logistics: Information Systems and Cost Control |

After studying this chapter, you should be able to:

- Explain the role and importance of information systems in the logistics area.
- Discuss the types of information required for effective logistics systems.
- Illustrate the use of information systems in logistics.
- Discuss the need for good cost control in logistics.
- Explain the problems of developing cost data and standards in logistics.

The preceding chapters have pointed out the need for effective information systems for control of logistics systems. For example, the volume of data necessary for inventory control, as discussed in Chapters 3 and 4, indicates the need for good information systems. In fact, it could be argued that every chapter has mentioned or implied the importance of good information systems in logistics. The topic of information systems deserves more attention than we can devote to it in an introductory text, but in this chapter we give some attention to the basic concepts of information systems and the types of information needed by the logistics manager.

In addition to a good information base, the logistics manager requires good cost data in order to administer the logistics system. We have noted the need for cost data in our discussions of the various trade-offs in logistics systems. In fact, we need more than just historical data to measure trade-offs. We also require estimates of cost under alternate approaches. Therefore, we need to discuss some of the basic issues involved in cost control and such coverage will be provided in this chapter. We will turn our attention initially to a discussion of information systems.

INFORMATION SYSTEMS: AID TO LOGISTICS MANAGEMENT

Decision making is a process by which input is received, weighed against stored factors and other input, and a decision is made (output) which may or may not initiate action. The main ingredient in the decision-making process is information.

Information is a patterned relationship between events. It is what is transmitted in the communication process. Communication systems act as vehicles through which the key management functions can be integrated and administered. Information is in the form of data, objectives, strategies, alternatives, probabilities, and consequences.

The overall organization and management framework facilitates the flow of information and makes appropriate decisions. In this vein, the communication system appears paramount with the organizational structure around it as a framework. The term information-decision system highlights the point that the information developed should be formulated in light of the decisions to be made. Thus, it should be designed with the end use of both input and output elements of decision making.

This theory can be applied to the practical side when it is used in conjunction with the decision points necessary in the firm. These points range from the bottom (operational decisions) to the top (policy decisions). Each point is analyzed in terms of what system function it performs and what decisions it makes. This establishes the informational needs of each decision point.

It should be noted that transmitted information is of two types. The first is "real time" in nature. It is active and used in day-to-day control mechanisms; this information facilitates flow and control. Information of this type includes order documents, picking instructions, inventory levels, etc. The second type of information is of the ''summary'' type, which is used for planning and organizing because it contains long-term trend and performance data.

Example

As an example of a real-time information system, consider the following freight bill pre-audit system. A large consumer goods manufacturer discovered that post-audits (after payment) of freight bills resulted in $150,000 annual overcharge claims filed against carriers and that the company was two years behind in auditing freight bills (a shipper has three years to file for overcharge claims). In addition, the majority of the overcharges resulted from errors—math, weights, and rates. A pre-audit before payment would permit the company to utilize this $150,000 per year and realize an investment income ($15,000 at 10%, for example) rather than giving this money to the carrier for two years without realizing any interest when returned (overcharge claim paid).

To permit pre-auditing of carrier freight bills, a real time information system, as indicated in Figure 12-1, was developed. The carrier's freight bill was matched against the bill of lading to assure the assessed charges were for the goods shipped and to prevent duplicate payments. If the freight bill and bill of lading matched, the system checked for correct weights, rates, and math. Errors were corrected and the corrected amount paid to the carrier.

A freight bill file was then created. This file provided the basis for developing summary information on carrier utilization, shipping patterns, customer purchases, etc. With the summary freight bill information, the company was able to analyze shipping patterns so as to permit greater efficiency in the scheduling of carrier equipment, warehouse utilization, and shipment consolidation. A report indicating the amount of business given to various carriers was helpful to effective rate negotiations, claim settlements, etc., with the carriers. Since the company in this example had over 2,000 major origin-destination pairs and used hundreds of carriers, the summary freight bill information was very critical to planning.

As a guideline to information needs, each manager should have the information required to measure performance and should receive it soon enough to make any changes necessary.[1]

All too often the only information available to a manager in a specific area is that which was developed and used by another corporate function (accounting, production, or marketing systems).[2] This deficiency leads to having to make assumptions about and adjustments to the available data, a process which many times leads to uncertainty and loss of confidence in the decision-making process. Another problem is that system performance measurement is difficult in most firms because managers were trained, organized, and evaluated on the basis of traditional management functions.

Finally, managements tend to perform only half a job in reorganization. They often lose sight of simple relationships between an organization-management structure and information needs. Many times they fail to follow

FIGURE 12-1   Real time and summary information system.

```
┌──────────────────┐                            ┌──────────────────┐
│  BILL OF LADING   │                            │     CARRIER      │
│                   │                            │     FREIGHT      │
└──────────────────┘                            └──────────────────┘
          │                                               │
          │         ┌──────────────────────┐              │
          └────────▶│      MATCHING:        │◀─────────────┘
                    │   Shipment Date.      │
                    │  Commodity. Weight.   │
                    │  Rate. Prior Payment  │
                    └──────────────────────┘
                               │
                               ▼
                    ┌──────────────────────┐
                    │   CORRECT ERRORS      │
                    └──────────────────────┘
                               │
                               ▼
                    ┌──────────────────────┐
                    │    CHECK MATH         │
                    └──────────────────────┘
                               │
                               ▼
                    ┌──────────────────────┐        ┌──────────────────┐
                    │    CORRECTED          │───────▶│  FREIGHT BILL    │
                    │   FREIGHT BILL        │        │     FILE         │
                    └──────────────────────┘        └──────────────────┘
                               │                              │
                               ▼                              ▼
                    ┌──────────────────────┐        ┌──────────────────────┐
                    │   ISSUE PAYMENT       │        │   SUMMARY REPORTS:    │
                    └──────────────────────┘        │   Carriers Used - $   │
                                                    │   Shipping Patterns   │
                                                    │  Customer's Order Size│
                                                    │        Etc.           │
                                                    └──────────────────────┘
```

up a reorganization with a reappraisal of the information system; thus managers are given new responsibilities and decision-making authorities, but do not receive all the information components required for effective performance.[3]

Three Types of Data

Information is the operation, control, and planning medium in logistics. Distribution departments need and use cost and service information as *communication links* between dispersed system components, as *detection devices* that report areas where critical performance items are out of line, and as *planning tools* that are inputs to periodic performance evaluations, policy reviews and revisions, and overall system adjustments.[4]

Communication

Communication links and detection devices are found on the day-to-day operating level. This flow consists of "direction type" information which facilitates the actual product flow from factory to consumers. In this category fall production orders, warehouse inventory status data, bills of lading, waybill copies, customer order forms, loss and damage claims, order picking instructions, and service level data. Selectivity of information at this level is limited to periodic reviews only. Detection device information consists of variations in any one of the above sub-sub-system performance beyond a certain predetermined standard (e.g., a weekly order to customer *A* takes 7 days instead of the usual 3 days, or carrier *X* has damaged two shipments in one month when its L&D record is historically lower). This is decision information in that it signals a need for corrective action by the responsible sub-system manager who will determine a solution within his scope of authority. These two types of data are accumulated into a data bank of system product flows, along with associated cost and service performance.[5]

On the planning and organizing level, summarized product flow information is required for use in system element performance reviews, trade-off analysis, policy revisions, and system adjustment planning.[6]

Trade-off analysis, as will be recalled, occurs when the inputs of one sub-system are analyzed in conjunction with the inputs of another, the end result directed toward increased effectiveness or lower total cost to the system. Overall system costs and service information is analyzed here to answer such questions as: Since our 90 percent service time system cost $500,000 last year, should we go to $750,000 to meet our competitor's 98 percent two-day service? Environmental factors are combined with marketing, production, financial, and logistical considerations. Logistics management might review the cost record of a certain warehouse against the trend of business generated there to determine if it should be modernized or abandoned. On a more detailed level, the high variation record of a certain sub-sub-system might warrant investigation to determine if an unplanned factor is present, if a new flow trend is taking place, or if the manager's performance is deficient.[7]

Due to the long-run nature of the decisions that are made and the fact that some variables are slow changing, the trade-off analysis and policy revision process usually take place annually. For example, the question of determining a minimum economic customer order quantity need not be determined weekly; a monthly or annual review is all that may be necessary. Much of the trade-off analysis might not be performed by use of automated reports, but rather by a one-time engineering study of, say, materials handling time and costs.[8]

Before establishing standard costs and measurement devices, input from the managers must be considered. All too often, the omission of this input leads to failure or ineffectiveness. Such input helps shape the system with minor elements often overlooked by top management and it brings forth problems before they are discovered expensively. Managers should participate in the goal-setting and measurement process because they are the ones who must live with them. Further, the system should not be used for appraisal until all the measurement system bugs are ironed out.[9]

Another important item often overlooked by management is the creation of a logistics controller function. This staff can provide valuable financial analysis to logistics activities and acquisition plans. It serves as a link to the corporate controller's office and further acts as a powerful interface component in logistics-marketing and logistics-production areas. This controller should report directly to the top distribution executive.[10]

A primary information problem in logistics is the quantification of service. This problem is two-fold in nature. First, there are difficulties inherent in the determination of service standards (truthfulness of the customer, plausibility of the company salesman, etc.). Second, the energy and cost required for measuring actual service are high. The firm must often rely on external systems such as trucking firms and customers, and must have clerical force or some automated component matching up his feedback to each particular bill of lading. Many firms conduct this activity on a rotating or spot basis.

One reason for the slow development of reliable and timely cost information in logistics is because these costs do not exist in present accounting systems. These traditional systems do not enter costs into the accounting data bank in the form of fixed and variable elements to specific warehouses and products.[11] The next section considers this problem in more detail.

COST CONTROL IN LOGISTICS

Nature of Problem As mentioned above, the important aspect of accounting in business logistics is the provision of information. The basic inputs for many of the sophisticated decision techniques used is the cost that has been or is to be incurred in the situation under consideration. The purpose of accounting is to make available the information, delineated by the logistics manager, that is necessary for the analysis.

The above statement is not to imply that the accounting department is to provide voluminous data at mere request. The implication is that the logistics manager must stipulate explicitly the nature of the information that is needed for control and analysis functions performed in the department. As will be pointed out below, this lack of explicitly defining the information needed from the accounting department has been a contributing factor to the present accounting problem in this area.

Role of Accounting The information flow network necessary for control purposes has an important geographical constraint that can be overcome by accounting. The various functions controlled by logistics (warehousing, transportation, etc.) are performed at many different locations other than the firm's plant location. The accounting system can overcome this spatial barrier to information by collecting the information pertinent to the cost centers at the various locations. Thus, accounting provides the necessary link for effective analysis, control, and planning of the spatially separated logistics functions.

In the past, accountants have concentrated their efforts upon production costs. This concentration has provided a detailed cost-accounting system that specifically (or almost) meets the needs of the production department. But, this is not the situation in logistics. Despite a growing management emphasis on business logistics, these subjects (control, analysis, and planning) have been neglected by accountants, both in theory and in practice.[12]

The entire blame cannot be foisted upon the accountant, for in the past management has emphasized the production and the accounting for same. But as more attention is given to logistics by top management, more emphasis will be placed upon accounting for logistics costs.

The logisticians, as well, must accept some of the responsibility for this problem. There are cases in which the logistics manager knows that the present accounting information is not adequate, but does not know exactly what additional information is required. More specifically, the logistics manager has failed in many situations to provide the accounting department with specific requests as to the nature of the information desired.

Specific Problem

The goal of logistics cost analysis is to establish a base for cost management and control through an improved understanding of cost patterns and behavior.[13] The problems encountered in reaching this objective are as follows: (1) separating and identifying logistics costs, (2) establishing accounting cost centers which are capable of providing the type of information necessary for continuing logistics cost analyses, and (3) analyzing the results of changes in the performance of a system after new concepts have been implemented.[14]

Present accounting procedures are designed to meet the needs of financial officers, inventory valuation, the S.E.C., and tax officials, often without regard for the needs of internal control functions.[15] The generally accepted accounting practice of classifying expenses on a natural basis (based on what the expenditure buys, auto expense, wages, etc.) and then assigning them to functions is not adequate for effective control and logistics cost analysis.[16]

Source of Problem　　The breakdown of natural accounts into functional accounts and the assignment by standard costs to customers, products, locations, etc., is made *after* the accumulation of the data. This is the exact opposite of the procedure used in production cost accounting in which the analysis starts at the source of the cost, the various cost centers, and proceeds to aggregate costs. This allocation of aggregate logistics costs in the opposite manner prevents accurate detection of the variations in logistics costs at their source.[17]

Averages and natural accounts also preclude the logistics manager from performing analyses upon customers, territories, products, and order sizes. It is necessary for the logistics manager to know more than just the average cost of such functions as transportation, materials handling, etc. He must be aware of the costs incurred for different customers, territories, etc., so that any inefficiencies can be detected and corrected.

The allocation of aggregate warehousing costs to all products (average warehousing cost per unit produced) does not give the logistics manager any indication of which products incurred more or less than this allocated (average) cost. That is, some shipments move directly from the plant to the customer, whereas others require extensive warehousing. Thus, the logistics manager cannot detect the excessive warehousing costs that may be incurred by a particular product line in a particular marketing area.

However, the analysis of customers, products, territories, and order sizes cannot be made independently. These four segments are interrelated. To say that serving customer Y is unprofitable (based upon the allocation of total logistics costs to all customers) does not take into consideration that Y may purchase large quantities at one time, buy the most profitable product produced, and is located in a low-cost (transportation and warehousing) territory. These factors could not be determined if each segment is considered independently.

It is desirable to dwell somewhat on the territory segment to emphasize its relevance to logistics. There is a tendency to overlook geographic cost variations and to concentrate on customers, products and order sizes. The very nature of logistics implies a spatial variation to costs. The complexity of the current rate structures prohibits an overall average logistics cost from having any meaning. For a logistics manager to effectively analyze and control costs, the geographic cost variations must be recognized and known.

Example

For example, a firm may be using an average logistics cost of $1.00/sales unit in the market area depicted in Figure 12-2. The use of an average logistics cost implies that transportation, warehousing, and materials handling costs are homogeneous, when, in fact, they are definitely heterogeneous and vary with distance and order size.

Further analysis in our example may show that the cost of serving customer A is $1.25/sales unit and $.95/sales unit for customer B. Assuming A and B purchase the same quantity, this cost difference is attributable to the increased transportation costs associated with serving A, which is a greater distance from the warehouse, W. In effect, the firm must utilize a weighted average of transportation costs so that the customer located nearer the warehouse provides sufficient subsidy to offset the increased transportation costs (actual-average) of servicing the more distant customers. The weighted average transportation cost is subject to variations resulting from shifts in the volumes moved to each customer and must be constantly monitored to insure that sufficient logistics costs are included in the selling price.

Finally, Figure 12-2 suggests that customer C, who purchases in large quantities, is served directly from the plant, bypassing the market warehouse. The effects of this distribution pattern is the elimination of the warehousing and materials handling costs associated with serving customers from the warehouse. Thus, the logistics costs for customer C will be less

FIGURE 12-2   Simple logistics channel.

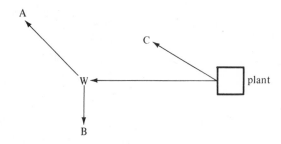

than the $1.00/sales unit average used in pricing the product in this market area and the savings can be used to subsidize the greater than average logistics cost customers or to justify offering quantity discounts.

Related Problem   Another problem common to many firms is the charging of obvious logistics costs to departments other than logistics. The physical supply costs of freight warehousing and materials handling may be charged to the production department or to overhead, whereas these are definitely logistics costs. If portions of logistics costs are made the responsibility of other departments, it is very difficult for the logistics department to control these costs and to efficiently and economically provide service for the firm.

The above discussion has attempted to analyze the problems that exist in the application of current accounting practices to logistics. The following section tries to present some possible solutions to these problems.

The problems discussed above are the ones that can be overcome by a joint effort of logistics and accounting. The logistics people can set up the objectives they desire in accounting information. With these criteria, accounting can then proceed in developing an accounting system that is simple and operable while providing the information desired.

An accounting system for logistics would be based upon the present system with the following areas of modification: classification of accounts and basis for allocation of costs.

The accounts must be reclassified so as to eliminate the practice of charging logistics costs to other departments. This will permit the logistics manager to grasp the entire logistics function, not just a portion of these functions. The following is a list of accounts that should be transferred from production to logistics: packaging labor and material costs; materials handling, labor, equipment, and maintenance costs; warehousing costs; taxes and insurance on inventories; and order handling costs. On the physical distribution side, such costs as warehousing, order processing, and packaging charged to marketing or sales would be assigned to logistics.

The allocation problem can be somewhat solved by switching from aggregate natural accounts to the use of explicitly identified cost centers — customers, products, order sizes, and territories. With this identification of cost centers, it is then possible to record the various functional costs incurred for each. In this manner, an analysis of transportation, for example, is possible for each cost center. It is now possible to develop standard costs that have as a basis the costs incurred in the various cost centers, rather than upon the basis of some allocation process.

A solution to the geographic variability of logistics costs has been put forth by Richard J. Lewis.[18] Using 1° latitude and longitude quadrilaterals he develops a spherical grid system covering the entire country. (This could be restricted to the particular operational area of the firm.) Each customer and raw material source can be identified by its location coordinates. By adding additional digits to the locational coordinates, a customer (supplier) identification code is developed.

The identification code permits specific costs to be assigned to an individual customer in a particular area. From such internal documents as the sales order and freight bill, the specific costs can be found. This system will provide specific cost information, by customers and marketing zones, that might otherwise be concealed by averages. The specific costs that will be excluded will be warehousing and inventory costs. But this system permits the four cost centers to be isolated: the customer is known, the product (from sales order) is shown, and the territory is likewise known. The transportation cost associated with each cost center is taken from the freight bill, which eliminates the necessity of allocation at a later date.

The above system would give the logistics manager valuable information as to the specific and direct logistics cost incurred to serve an area and customer. But this may not be the system that should be used by all firms. The economics of instituting and operating such a system may be prohibitive for some firms. For this reason and others, no one accounting system can be established for all firms. The above system may be desirable as a "model" or basis upon which a particular accounting system that meets the requirements of an individual firm can be developed.

The suggestions presented here for possible solutions to the existing problem of accounting in logistics are directed toward improving the information logistics receives, so as to permit better analysis, control, and planning of the logistics function. Without these and other modifications in the present accounting system, the logistics department will not be able to effectively and efficiently provide service to the firm as well as to customers.

SUMMARY

The focus in this chapter has been upon aids to the logistics manager. Initially, a discussion was presented of information systems and the importance to logistics management and decision making. Emphasis was placed upon the different types of information. Also, Appendix 12-A presents a good illustration of an information system along with some guidelines.

Study Questions

1. Discuss the three basic types of cost and service information needed by a logistics department.
2. Why is it important to have good cost information for effective planning and control of logistics activities?
3. Distinguish between real time vs. summary information. Give logistics examples of each.
4. You have been asked to develop a logistics cost accounting system. What costs would you include in the system and why?
5. Discuss the interrelationships that exist among logistics organizational structure, cost control, and the information system.

Notes

1. Heskett, R. Ivie, and N. Glasowsky, *Business Logistics* (New York: Ronald Press, 1964), p. 563.
2. J. Bowersox, et al., *Physical Distribution Management* (New York: Macmillan Company, 1968), p.8.
3. *Ibid.*, p. 36.
4. *Ibid.*,
5. *Ibid.*,
6. James Arbury and others, *A New Approach to Physical Distribution* (New York: American Management Association, 1968), pp. 50-54.
7. *Ibid.*
8. *Ibid.*
9. Michael Schiff, *Accounting and Control in Physical Distribution Management* (Chicago: NCPDM, 1972), pp. 53-72.
10. *Ibid.*
11. Raymond Lakashman and John Stolle, "The Total Cost Approach to Distribution," *Business Horizons,* (Winter 1965), p. 33.
12. Ronald J. Lewis, "Strengthening Control of Physical Distribution Costs," *Management Services,* 5 (Jan-Feb., 1968), p. 37.
13. James A. Constatin, *Principles of Logistics Management* (New York: Appleton-Century-Crofts, 1966)' p. 184.
14. Heskett et al., *op. cit.,* p. 455.
15. Ronald J. Lewis, *op. cit.,* p. 41.
16. Richard J. Lewis, "A Business Logistics Information and Accounting System for Marketing Analysis," reprinted in *Readings in Business Logistics* by David McConaughy (ed.). (Homewood: Richard D. Irwin, Inc., 1969), p. 154.
17. *Ibid.*
18. *Ibid.*, pp. 154-57.

Case 12-1
P. S. Company

The P. S. Company, a large manufacturer of smoke detectors and fire alarms, has recently experienced its largest single increase in sales volume in years. Bob Rossi, marketing vice president, has expressed his satisfaction for the efforts of his sales force: "This has been our best year ever. My sales personnel are working night and day to consummate sales in order to make our firm the industry leader." A few days after Mr. Rossi made this statement, he was flooded with calls from his salesmen asking why they have not been receiving their merchandise. Their calls have repeatedly mentioned customers' threats of cancelling their orders because of failure to deliver. Mr. Rossi became furious at hearing this and immediately requested a meeting with both the vice-president of logistics and the vice-president of production, assuming that failures in these departments have led to his dilemma.

At the meeting, Mr. Rossi presented his case by stating that his department is maximizing its resources by creating sales but concurrently realizing lost customers. Pointing the finger of blame at the vice-presidents of production and logistics, Mr. Rossi vehemently suggested that these two departments review their operations and make the necessary adjustments to remedy the situation.

When Mr. Rossi had finished his argument the other two vice-presidents made their presentation. Both accused Mr. Rossi's department of failing to accurately predict sales and of not notifying their respective departments of his big sales push. The vice-president of logistics stated that his department is currently set up to handle normal demand and that currently he is experiencing a high level of stockout costs which is hurting the company as a whole. The vice-president of production also claimed that the current sales push is causing him extensive overtime and set-up costs since his production process is designed to accommodate normal demand.

As president of this company, you are sitting in on this meeting because you were not aware of any problems but can now see how the present situation will affect the company's operations. As president, what do you see as the immediate problems? What would be their eventual consequences? How would you suggest remedying these problems?

Appendix 12-A
Guidelines to Consider in a
Management Information
System Study*

Standardization of Data

This entails the definition of terms to be used on a consistent basis throughout the entire system. For example, a firm may refer to a notification to the warehouse to ship as a movement directive, material release order, or a shipping order. All three terms are synonymous but one must be selected and used consistently. Also, product lines must be catalogued on a standard numerical and descriptive basis. For example,

Cot, steel folding 1242 561 2407 1 ea

identifies a steel cot in standard terms of nomenclature, stock number, and unit of issue.

Automation of Source Data

Whenever feasible, data should be captured at the source of the information. The best time for source data automation is when a transaction takes place. This allows the data to be captured in a machine readable format which permits entry into a data processing system without further manual transcription or conversion. For example, salesmen can be equipped with pre-scored Hollerith cards which list products and quantities to be ordered. By using a porta punch device and by scoring cards with a stylus, a salesman can automate orders at the source. Other examples of SDA devices are cash register tapes used to tally sales by product line, charge-a-plates, and Magnetic Ink Character Representation (MICR). MICR offers the advantages of being both machine and human readable. All bank checking accounts use MICR on individual checks.

Maximum Use of Standard Formats

Sometimes referred to as integrated data processing, this guideline refers to the use of multipurpose forms and standard data descriptions. If possible,

---

*   The authors are indebted to Major Walter Bawell, U.S. Army, for his contributions to this section of the book.

one form should be used to accomplish more than one function. Ideally the same form could be used for a customer order, inventory posting, and release order.

Standard data formats used on punched cards or magnetic tape refers to the reservation of data fields for specific data. Using the steel cot example, consider a customer request for 10 cots when only 5 cots are on hand. The transaction calls for a material release order for the 5 on hand, a back order for five more, and special inventory since zero balance was reached. The 11 digit stock number on the customer order would be perpetuated from the order to reserve 11 digit fields for each of the documents created.

Management by Exception

This principle keeps the manager away from routine operations and allows him to manage the overall operation. His attention is needed only when consequential problems arise. Within the design of an information system the framework of management indicators or red warning lights must be identified and included in the system. Indicators should be able to be monitored quickly and they should allow enough time for remedial action. For example, the following are indicators which may be used for inventory control activity:

> Customer satisfaction falls below 90%.
> Zero balance lines above 10%.
> Warehouse denials above 2%.
> Order processing time is in excess of 3 days.
> Materials handling equipment deadline rate over 10%.

All exception reports and indicators must be enumerated from the start. These requirements are met when designing the output data for the new system.

Psychological Aspect

In any systems study and especially when considering the use of automatic data processing, employees may feel their jobs will be taken away. Staff briefings and orientations should serve the purpose of alleviating the fear of job security by informing all personnel exactly as to what will take place. This will help prevent rumors and provide better employee cooperation.

Time Scheduling

Once the goals have been set, a time schedule for completion of phases of the study should be set. A helpful technique for a project of this nature is the use of PERT (Program Evaluation Review Technique) which helps identify important events and critical paths through the system.

STUDY OF THE PRESENT SYSTEM

Initial Survey

In order to design a better system a thorough understanding of organizational charts, functions, policies, and operating procedures is necessary. Once these areas are thoroughly understood by the systems analyst the first step in the study of the present system is collection of documents and reports.

Collection of Documents and Reports

The purpose of this step is to gather all data in order to determine how it is processed. Management has the responsibility of defining the scope of the study in order to collect data from the departments that will be a part of the new system. The scope of a given study could entail a system design for a collection of retail activities, a network of servicing depots and retail outlets, or both.

All documents must be validated by the highest level of management associated with each report. The systems analyst conducts an interview of persons preparing and using the documents in order to determine validity.

Document Analysis

After validation, each document is classified as to one of four types:

Source Input.   This is the vehicle on which data first enters the processing system. Example—a customer order.

Basic Record.   A document or report used for day-to-day administration and operation. Example—a credit file.

Intermediate Record.   A record maintained as a means of deriving data for further processing. Example—an analysis of market sales.

Final Output Record.   The end product of data processing. Further information is never generated from this record. Example—a listing of sales by-product line for the first quarter of the fiscal year.

After classification, the following characteristics of each document are analyzed:

- Frequency of preparation
- Volume
- Number of copies received and forwarded
- Disposition
- Documents originating from and updated by this report
- Access requirements

Narrative Flow Charting

A narrative flow chart is a graphical representation with a narrative description of the logical processing of data. It insures the analyst understands the system and it enhances communication between operating personnel and management. A narrative flow chart can uncover duplication of effort by separate but related departments that otherwise would have gone undetected. It is used as a basic tool to aid in the integration of functional areas of the firm. Another tool used in the study of the present system is the use of decision tables that use "if then" logic. These tables eliminate excess verbiage contained in operating procedures and they show step by step system logic. The combination of narrative flow charting and decision tables portrays the present system as it exists in a precise, logical method.

Documentation and Data Analysis

The flow charting and analysis of individual documents are combined to study the overall system. All documents are collected and sorted as to service input, basic record, intermediate record, and final output. This information is usually placed on a large document analysis sheet which reflects all documents and data. This helps uncover documents that do not support output documents and documents that may have been collected outside the scope of study. A check is also made to see that all outputs are supported by input documents. All reports and documents discovered as not being essential to the system are eliminated. Within a large firm some reports that may have been required as a matter of previous policy no longer may be needed. This phase of systems design helps to identify this situation. The cost savings and possible decrease in data-processing time can have an effect on product price plus allow for a reduction in inventory levels. Note that cost reduction can be effected before the purchase of ADP equipment. Potential areas for file modification are identified and considered. Also, redundancy of input and output of information is examined for possible automation.

DESIGN OF THE NEW SYSTEM

Determine Output Requirements

The first consideration in the design of a new system is the output. Management establishes the needs of the system and determines the requirement for new output documents that were not possible under the old system. Exception reports (or systems redlights) are identified and included in order to provide for management on an exception basis. In determining information needs the systems analyst provides the technical assistance and expertise to the functional area specialists (managers).

Using the data analysis study, the systems analyst designs new documents and presents them to management for approval. In the design of documents the systems analyst classifies data as to:

> Variable elements
>> Reported—example: customer order
>> Generated—example: replenishment requisition
> Fixed elements
>> Identifying—example: nomenclature
>> Quantitative—example: unit price
>> Constant—example: date

This classification of data assists in document design and helps to determine the construction of the data base and master files. Usually, cost considerations are critical at this point since the amount of information required to be stored, accessed, and processed varies directly with cost. It is quite possible that output requirements may have to be modified in order to lower the costs of storage and retrieval devices.

Determine Input Requirements

Input is next determined on the basis as to information needed to update master files and to provide required output. Use of source data automation is weighed against speed and cost of implementation. Input form design considerations are ease of preparation, simplicity, and ability for clear interpretation by users.

Below is a list of considerations for input/output design:

1. Identifying elements of data should be at a minimum on input documents and at a maximum in the data banks. This helps increase the speed of form preparation and helps to cut down on clerical errors.
2. Constant elements of data should be included in the program or keyed from the console. Example: 25% carrying cost for inventory.
3. Generated elements of data should not be on input or output document format since they are determined by the program.
4. Quantitative elements of data should be in the master file. Example: current price for a given product line.
5. Reported elements of data should be on input documents format only.

Systems Charting

After determining output, input, records, and master files, the entire system is charted by the use of flow symbols. A narrative for the chart is written and both are used to write programs for the new system. All program logic is documented to show logical steps and each run. Documentation is essential especially during program "debugging" because it allows the systems analyst to retrace programming steps in order to correct program errors.

System Specifications and Costs

From the systems study, a clear, concise description of the proposed system is written. Vendors are usually invited to submit their equipment configurations that will best accommodate systems specifications. During this phase, consideration should be given to the purchase or lease of second-hand equipment. Since the physical life of a computer system outlasts the technological life there is an abundant supply of used systems that can be either leased or purchased at a substantial cost savings.

Because cost of sophisticated equipment may be prohibitive, a more economical approach is to time share. If a system is characterized by the use of one central processing unit used by many users such as that used by the airlines, time sharing is feasible. This allows for simultaneous use of a computer by independent users through a number of input/output stations linked with the central processor.

Advantages of time sharing are relatively low cost, flexibility of terminal locations, and service to user on a real-time basis. Disadvantages are system complexity, data base security, and possibility of a systems breakdown.

Interface Costs

In systems analysis jargon, interface is often referred to as the communication link necessary to hook up one computer system with another. Interface may be required when there are a large number of retail stock record keeping outlets that are serviced by an inventory control center that controls servicing depots. The state of the art for interface communications is not advanced as to provide a 100 percent link and at present, due to its high cost, implementation of 100 percent interface is prohibitive.

Nevertheless, data transmission requirements do exist for output media and they must be evaluated in the light of improved customer service and reduced transmission time versus cost trade-offs.

Trade-off Analysis

Using the objectives of our systems study; namely, to:

- Increase sales through better service;
- Reduce costs;

- Anticipate and respond rapidly to customer demand;
- Establish a reliable, timely information system as a competitive advantage;

a trade-off analysis of equipment costs versus degree of customer service level desired is necessary for each objective. During systems design, the objectives must be constantly referred to in order to conduct a trade-off that will produce the best equipment configuration in accordance with cost and service constraints.

Chapter 13	Management of Logistics: Organization

After studying this chapter, you should be able to:

- Examine the organizational problems resulting from the nontraditional horizontal authority relationships of logistics to other departments.

- Identify the advantages and disadvantages of organizing logistics on the basis of line vs. staff functions and on centralized vs. decentralized basis.

- Develop a systems approach to logistics organization.

- Examine the pragmatics of logistics reorganization.

Unlike production, marketing, or finance, which have a relatively long history and functions common to every manufacturing firm, business logistics, as has been indicated, is relatively new to the business scene. The evolution of logistics in individual firms has been neither easy nor uniform. The postwar business era, as noted, was marked with forces and conditions that heretofore had not existed. Firms now had to compete under new rules. New products were introduced which added to the firm's inventory and made stock control and production planning more difficult tasks.

The magnitude of the problems has been documented in many places. One study, for example, conducted to measure the effect of increased product line variation on inventory levels (holding all other factors equal) found that the addition of one product to an existing single product line increases total inventory needs by 60 percent. Thus, to maintain the same sales volume and customer service level as before, the addition of even one product line has no small effect.[1] Managements became aware of a whole host of increasing indirect costs which were hard to control under the previous methods of operation.

Consequently, companies began to investigate the possible adoption of a business logistics approach which provided opportunities for cost reduction through trade-offs, allowed some control of the rising "indirect" costs of marketing, and promised to help resolve some of the traditional conflicts that existed between production, marketing, and finance.[2]

While the logistics or physical distribution approach was being accepted in many industries, the application of logistics in each firm was often different. Each company had specific individual problem areas inherent to their products, distribution channels, competitive relations, formal organizational structure, and personalities of managers. Some firms initiated efforts toward the systems concept by modernizing their troubled inventory systems. Such actions, while solving one problem, tended to ignore connecting logistics components. Many of these firms found that the purchase of sophisticated computer hardware did not alone construct an efficient logistics system. Other managements collected previously separated areas from various functions, such as warehousing, transportation, order processing, etc., and created new physical distribution or logistics departments with the goal of reduced cost, maximized service or some related mission. But even in the latter cases, many of the new departments lacked specific authority to carry out their responsibilities, or were given goals that were difficult to attain.[3]

Use of computer hardware, top management recognition of the total system need, and even reorganization are no guarantee to productive logistical applications. For many firms, the evolutionary change to a logistics organization can be described as patchwork. For many others, however, the transition and current logistics operations are successful. The initial part of this chapter examines the organizational problem of the logistics area to provide insight into how a company can set up a logistics department or section.

ORGANIZATION FOR LOGISTICS

The adoption of a complete business logistics or physical distribution area tended to create some problems in the traditional organizational structure of the firm. Business logistics was not a customary function, such as production, marketing or finance, performed by firms. The functions incorporated within the logistics area were controlled in several departmental groups which created the need to coordinate and combine these functions into a logistics organizational unit to achieve cost reductions and service improvements that were not possible under the traditional production, marketing, and finance functional organizational structure.

Organizational Problems

Corporate management usually accepted the interdependence of the logistics areas and the need for organizational change, but the form the reorganization should take was a difficult question faced by many corporate executives. Some firms resolved the problem by adding to their corporate structure a vice-presidential position for logistics or physical distribution at the same level with the traditional vice-presidents of marketing, finance, or manufacturing. The restructuring of the organization was usually an attempt to solve the many logistical problems associated with growing product lines and diverse markets and to realize the inherent cost savings and service improvements proponents of the logistics system approach advocated. Often coupled with the new vice-presidential position was the addition of sophisticated hardware and the collection of organizationally scattered functions such as warehousing, transportation, packaging, etc. Such attempts were aimed at applying the logistics system concept to the real-world business environment.

The relatively fast implementation of the logistics function in the manner described above sometimes proved to be disadvantageous:

> The psychology was all wrong . . . the exponents of physical distribution promised the world but, in order to deliver, they needed the president to agree to appoint a vice-president-distribution, and to give the new crown prince segments of the marketing organization, segments of the manufacturing organization, and in some cases, segments of the finance organizations.

> The results of this approach, of course, were that you had in the executive suite a vice-president of distribution (who typically had been a traffic or warehousing manager) who had the vice-president-marketing, vice-president-manufacturing and the vice-president-finance . . . if not mad at him . . . at least displaying a lot of passive resistance to whatever he was going to do.

> This new vice-president was so anxious to make some of the cost saving promises come true (to make his mark on the corporate hierarchy) that he started questioning some of the requirements registered on his group by marketing and manufacturing groups respectively.[4]

The foregoing comments may lead the reader to conclude that the establishment of a separate logistics department is not necessary or beneficial. However, such manifestations of change are to be expected and in spite of the problems, valuable lessons were learned and many problems solved. Larger firms with a complex distribution pattern usually need a formal and established logistics department which provides the structure for the effective integration of diverse activities to achieve desired service at an acceptable cost level.

Organization for logistics is a prerequisite to effective application for the logistics concept. But as pointed out by Ballou,[5] the organization does not need to be a formal mechanism. Some firms operate the logistics function very well with informal relationships and understandings while other firms with apparently sound organizational structures on paper have found application of same somewhat less than desirable. The moral of the story is: There is no one best organizational structure which is appropriate for all firms. The objective of this section is to discuss the problem areas and examine the organizational alternatives.

Logistics and Traditional Managements

Traditional management techniques stress the organizational structure based upon vertical, hierarchical relationships, differentiation or specialization of tasks, and the coordination of the separated tasks so as to form a cohesive whole. Traditional techniques, therefore, suggest the segregation of work and activities so as to achieve technical and economic efficiency through specialization of labor with the corporate management coordinating the specialized efforts.

Horizontal Nature of Activities

These traditional techniques were satisfactory for manufacturing, marketing, and finance where well-defined activities and work units are amenable to specialization and hierarchical relationships. However, logistics activities are basically horizontal. The horizontal nature is evident in the structuring of the various logistics functional areas into any of the three primary functions, i.e., transportation has been included in marketing, production or both. Figure 13-1 reveals the fragmentation of logistics activities and related activities in traditional departments.

As many firms developed, the traditional departments adopted required facets of logistics to accomplish the departmental objectives and, as a consequence, the respective departments annexed the relevant logistics activities into an existing hierarchical structure. Such annexation usually resulted in an inability to realize corporate goals and led to duplication of efforts and uneconomic use of resources.[6]

A common symptom of the fragmentation of logistics activities is the "Not I, But He" syndrome. The various departments were foisting the blame for inefficient logistics actions upon some other department because there was no one individual or department responsible for all logistics activities.

Need for Systems Approach

Application of the logistics systems approach to achieve corporate goals is also beset with certain human problems. The traditional organiza-

FIGURE 13-1   Logistics activities in traditional functional areas.

Production	Marketing	Finance and Control
Plant warehousing	Distribution warehouse	Order processing
Plant inventory	location and operation	Computers
Physical supply	Finished goods inventory	Cost analysis
transportation	Customer service levels	Investment and
Packaging	Quantity discounts	acquisitions
Materials handling	Channels of distribution	Operations research
Plant location	Sales forecasting	
Physical distribution		
transportation		

Source: Adapted from Felix Wentworth, *Physical Distribution Management* (Boston: Cahners Books, 1970), ch. 2.

tional reward system uses as its criterion the efficiency with which a particular manager performs a specialized task. Such measures as the cost of performing the task are used to evaluate the manager's performance from one time period to the next. With the systems approach operating, the transportation manager, for example, may be asked to utilize a more expensive link service so that overall corporate costs (inventory, lost sales, etc.) will be reduced. But such a decision does not place a "feather" in the transportation manager's cap; the existing reward system views this department's operation negatively. Thus, there is no incentive for the manager to make decisions that are not favorable to the department directly.

Organizational Conflicts

Application of the systems approach to logistics requires cutting across the traditional organizational lines to group related logistics activities. At the same time this requires implementation of decisions that may not be in the best interests (benefit) of a particular department or segment of a department, but are nevertheless desirable for the firm as a whole. Such decisions can not be made under the shadow of the goals established by traditional organizational structuring. Conflicts arise as to the objectives to be attained with respect to various logistics functions. The result of the conflict is a nonconcerted effort toward the logistics function or, stated alternatively, an attempt by various organizational units to manipulate the logistics area to its own betterment without regard to the implication to the firm as a whole.

Typical Conflicts   An example of the traditional organizational conflict is given in Figure 13-2. The marketing department desires larger inventories, field warehousing, fast delivery and order processing, and frequent, short production runs to achieve "satisfactory" customer service levels and to increase demand.

FIGURE 13-2   Objective conflicts in typical manufacturing firm.

Marketing	*Finance and Accounting*	*Production*
Increase inventory	Reduce inventory	Increase inventory
More production runs	Low production cost	Long production runs
Rapid order processing	Cheap order processing	
Rapid delivery to customers		Low cost routing
Many Market warehouses	Less warehousing space	Plant warehousing

Source: Adapted from John F. Stolle, "How to Manage Physical Distribution," *Harvard Business Review* (July-August 1967), p. 95.

Finance and accounting attempt to reduce investments in inventory and warehouses while the production objective is long production runs (resulting in higher inventories), plant warehousing, and low-cost transportation (not necessarily fast transport service). Only the president, in this situation, has ultimate authority to resolve such conflicts.

Probably the most common problem encountered in organizing for logistics is that traditionally the logistics activities have been fragmented throughout the organization. The logical regrouping of logistics activities into a unified group is met with resistance associated with the giving up of responsibilities and authority to this new unit.[7]

Positioning Logistics

Early Proposals   The above discussion of the problems of organizing for logistics suggests an additional question as to where in the organization the logistics function should be placed. Early writers* suggested that for effective operation, the logistics function should be placed in a high position reporting directly to either the president or an executive vice-president. Such a positioning, it was suggested, would enable logistics to make more objective decisions that affect the traditional departments and would provide the authority to implement the decisions.

It was further suggested that to annex the logistics function (assuming all related logistics activities have been grouped) onto an existing department tends to place logistics in a subordinate position to the annexing department and its goals. In such a situation the logistics decisions often can not be made without bias toward the parent department. The company, therefore, should not relegate logistics to a secondary role and expect to realize service improvements and cost benefits. The conflicting objectives as noted in Figure 13-2, cast a shadow over the objectivity or neutrality of logistics decisions.[8]

---

*   See: Philip F. Cannon, "Organizing for Effective Physical Distribution Management," *AMA Report No. 40,* 1960.

Placing logistics under marketing, it was felt, would result in increased customer service, warehouses, and inventories and limited attention to production requirements. If located in the existing transportation department, emphasis would be placed upon rates, carrier negotiations, etc., which are important elements in logistics but not ends unto themselves. Likewise, if incorporated into production, difficulty could arise in administering to the needs of marketing, since primary attention is directed toward production with logistics serving as a supporting element to production.[9]

Alternate Strategies   However, a word of caution is warranted at this point. The need to establish a logistics department in a high position on a par with marketing and production may not be necessary or satisfactory for all firms. The particular characteristics of the firm may require the placing of logistics under marketing, production, or finance. The Schiff study revealed that a high level of logistics effectiveness has been achieved in some firms regardless of its positioning in the organization.[10]

The earlier writers suggested the establishment of an independent, high-ranking logistics department, whereas some current findings suggest that this is not always a necessity for effective logistics management.[11] The difference of opinion stems from the mechanism utilized in the implementation of the logistics concept. Two important points in this apparent conflict are the organization of the related logistics activities into one department and the recognition by corporate management of the importance of these activities. If both of the above are achieved, the positioning or level of logistics in the corporate structure may not be as critical; top corporate awareness of logistics importance will enable the logistics manager to accomplish the decision making in an objective manner and such decisions will be implemented with the authority vested in the corporate hierarchy. The subordination to marketing or production, however, will rarely allow the necessary objectivity to analyze alternate strategies and programs to achieve overall corporate objectives.

Recent Findings   A recent study of distribution executives revealed that fewer logistics managers are reporting to functional (production, marketing, etc.) vice-presidents.[12] As more companies recognize the need for logistics to be at the vice-presidential level, logistics is reporting to top management (president, group vice-president, etc.). Such positioning permits logistics to function with the objectivity necessary to accomplish system efficiency.

Logistics Department Organization

Two additional aspects of organization germane to our discussion are the questions of line vs. staff functions and centralized vs. decentralized authority. We consider the former initially and then turn our attention to the latter.

Definitions and Explanation   **Line vs. Staff.**   Traditional organization theory suggests the use of line and staff functions within the structure to achieve overall efficiency through specialization of labor in the hierarchical structuring. The line authority emphasizes superior-subordinate relationships and a delegation of responsibility over specific tasks; each line member, then, has complete authority over his particular area of the firm's operation. The line manager is responsible for making decisions that affect daily operations of the firm. Contrasted with this is the staff function, which literally means the provision of support or advice to the line authority in the daily management of the firm. Staff functions aid line managers through developing plans, designing new techniques, and collecting data that enable the line manager to achieve operational objectives. In essence, the staff function is a delegation of authority laterally, not the vertical or hierarchical relationship encompassed in the line authority.

Examples

For a logistics department, line activities would include such functions as transportation and traffic, inventory control, warehousing, order processing, and packaging. The staff activities could include warehouse location, system designing and planning, customer service strategies, inventory and cost analysis, analysis of private transportation alternatives, etc.

The establishment of a logistics department as solely line or staff has associated with it the problem of effectively controlling the other area. For example, if a logistics department is organized with line authority exclusively, authority for developing system designs and objectives is vested in other departments. Conversely, if logistics is organized as staff only, the implementation of system designs on a day-to-day basis rests with other departments.

Staff Organization.   The acceptance of the logistics concept by corporate management means the company is faced with the pragmatic problem of how this department is to be structured. The separation of logistics staff activities from traditional departments with the line activities remaining in former functional departments such as marketing and production is convenient to initiate.[13] An example of such an organization is given in Figure 13-3.

Problems

Such a structuring as illustrated in Figure 13-3 permits the new department to analyze and design a new logistics system and to provide the needed coordination among the remaining diversified grouping of logistics line activities. The problem with this structure rests with the authority the staff position has over the various logistics line activities. Under such a grouping, logistics line activities are not included in the logistics department and may remain subordinate to goals of the traditional departments. Thus, logistics organized in this manner lacks authority for implementation of staff decisions into daily operations.

However, the positioning of the logistics department in the organizational structure and/or the corporate attitude toward logistics can make this a desirable and effective structure for a logistics department. For example, if the firm is logistics oriented, corporate management has the authority to effect the necessary changes in line operations to implement the

FIGURE 13-3   Grouping of logistics staff activities.

```
                     ┌─────────────────────────┐
                     │    Logistics Manager    │
                     └─────────────────────────┘
                                  │
        ┌─────────────────┬───────┴───────┬─────────────────┐
   ┌─────────┐      ┌──────────┐    ┌─────────────┐    ┌─────────────┐
   │Planning │      │ Analysis │    │Coordination │    │ Engineering │
   └─────────┘      └──────────┘    └─────────────┘    └─────────────┘
```

Planning	Analysis	Coordination	Engineering
Spatial patterns	Operational cost	Sales	Materials handling
Warehouse locations	Customer service requirements	Production	Transportation equipment
Budgets	Inventory levels	Finance	Packaging
Product development	Transportation rates and service	Other	Systems and procedures

Source: Adapted from John F. Stolle, "How to Manage Physical Distribution Standards," *Harvard Business Review* (July-August 1967), p. 97.

decisions—system design, service levels, etc.—developed by the logistics department organized in staff role. In companies which are highly decentralized and have diverse operations, a staff approach with consulting sources is often desirable. However, in the typical company the strict staff approach leaves much to be desired.

Line Organization.   Since traditional organization concepts favor hierarchical relationships, many firms have organized the logistics department by grouping line activities. Such a structure has advantages but often does not permit economical grouping of analytical skills (staff functions) required for effective logistics planning, design, and analysis. Such staff functions then must be performed by a logistics manager who is capable of both administering day-to-day operations as well as analyzing, planning, and designing logistics activities. The other alternative is to have another area such as production, marketing, etc., perform the staff functions but this may result in some sub-optimal strategies. Figure 13-4 depicts a logistics department in which line activities are grouped.

Advantages   The organizational procedure exhibited in Figure 13-4 permits a unified approach to the day-to-day logistics activities by delegating responsibility for these activities to one individual. The logistics manager is now held accountable for total logistics cost and service levels. The "not I but " syndrome utilized to foist the blame upon some other department for excess costs or poor service is truncated with this structure. If logistics cost and/or service is not acceptable, the "not I, but " rationalization becomes "not I, but logistics." Thus, grouping line activities delegates *responsibility* to the

FIGURE 13-4   Grouping line activities.

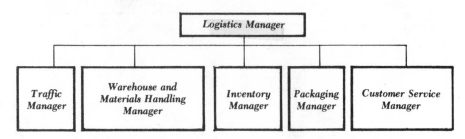

Source: Adapted from John F. Stolle, "How to Manage Physical Distribution," *Harvard Busi-ness Review* (July-August 1967), p. 96.

logistics manager for a unified approach to daily logistics activities and makes one individual accountable for logistics costs and service.

Line and Staff Organization.   As suggested above, the structuring of a logistics department on the basis of line or staff activities solely has certain pitfalls. The logical solution is to combine the line and staff activities into one department. An example of such a grouping is given in Figure 13-5.

Combination of line and staff functions provides the logistics depart-ment with the analytical skills to design, plan, and analyze existing and proposed logistics systems and with the authority to exercise control over the administration of these staff decisions to the day-to-day operations. Such an organizational structuring eliminates the subordinate role of logistics.

This does not mean that logistics will now operate in a vacuum, divorced from all other firm functions. The staff functions of planning, coordination, etc., must work closely with other departments to effect system changes that benefit the firm as a whole, not merely the logistics department. After the intrafirm relationships are examined and a system designed, the line functions of transportation, warehousing, etc., have the responsibility of implementing the system in accordance with the system objectives. With this line and staff organization, logistics is not operated as *subordinate* to the traditional department, but as *functionally dependent*.

Matrix Organization.   As alluded to in a preceding section, the horizontal flow of authority inherent to logistics created certain problems in organizing logistics in the traditional vertical or hierarchical structure. DeHayes and Taylor[14] have suggested the use of the matrix organization for logistics (see Figure 13-6) as a solution to the horizontal flow of authority and the cutting across traditional departmental lines inherent in the logistics concept.

The matrix structure would have logistics as a program with the logistics manager responsible for total logistics costs and services. Logistics would have a horizontal emphasis with the line organization (vertical flow) in a supporting role.

FIGURE 13-5   Grouping line and staff activites.

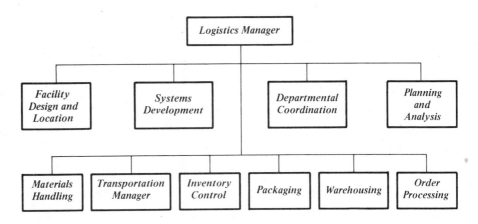

Source: Adapted from John F. Stolle, "How to Manage Physical Distribution," *Harvard Business Review* (July-August 1967), p. 98.

Advantages   DeHayes and Taylor cite three advantages of the matrix organization in logistics: (1) it establishes logistics as a responsibility center, permitting management by objective; (2) its application is flexible to meet the specific needs of any firm; and (3) it permits the logistics manager to integrate plans and designs rather than responding to problems only.[15] However, there are disadvantages associated with the matrix organization. For example, because of the two-way flow of control the responsibility and authority relations are at times unclear and lead to conflict or uncoordinated effort.

While no organizational approach is perfect, the line and staff grouping has been the most successful. In some cases, in decentralized operations the line responsibilities can be carried out at the plant or operational level while the headquarters group provides staff and consulting services.

Centralization vs. Decentralization

The question of centralized vs. decentralized organization is a question that is directed toward the degree of operating authority delegated. It is not a question of spatial location.[16] If one views centralization vs. decentralization from the spatial criteria, logistics would tend to be decentralized since logistics operations and decisions often occur at diverse locations. Decisions regarding warehousing, transportation, etc., are frequently required at the spatially separated market areas, plants, and warehouses in the firm's system.* Thus, one might expect decentralization to prevail for logistics.

* See: John F. Magee, *Industrial Logistics* (New York: McGraw-Hill, 1968), pp. 335-42.

FIGURE 13-6   Logistics in a matrix organization.

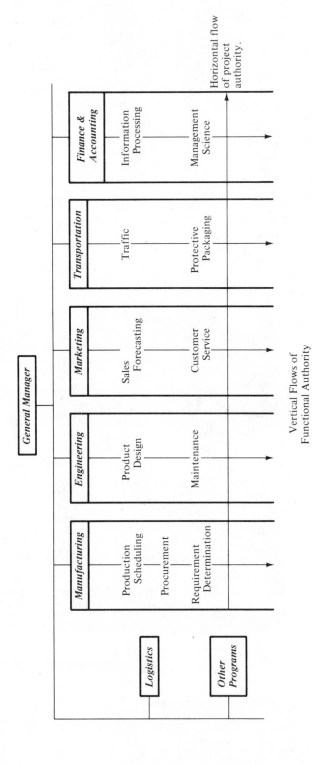

Source: Daniel W. DeHayes. Jr., and Robert L. Taylor. "Making Logistics Work in a Firm," *Business Horizons* (June 1972), p. 44.

The answer to the centralization-decentralization question may appear to rest with certain operational characteristics of the firm; such as size and homogeneity of markets. Schiff[17] claims that the centralization vs. decentralization question is not a function of size, nor of the markets served. However, in regard to the latter, there is some consistency with regard to type of industry. In the consumer products group where firms have homogeneous markets, centralization of logistics authority exists. Firms producing industrial consumable products, where diverse markets exist, utilized decentralization. But, industrial equipment manufacturers have often established centralized control even though they have diverse markets.

What is suggested is that neither approach is ideal for all companies and careful study is necessary in selecting the right approach. One solution is to follow the patterns established for control over other areas of the firm. For example, if a company is decentralized upon a product line division, it would follow that logistics should be decentralized upon the same basis. This, in fact, often does occur and is a logical arrangement, especially if the product divisions have widely diverse market areas. In such a situation, the logistics division organization is concerned with the movement and storage functions of that particular division.

Problems of Decentralization

However, decentralization may not permit the degree of coordination necessary to achieve economies of logistics operation. More specifically, many logistics costs are directly related to the volume of product flow. Transportation, warehousing, information processing, etc., for example, are logistics areas where grouping of activities permits realization of economies of scale. Underutilized warehouse facilities may be eliminated by establishment of a single warehouse system facilitating the many product lines, thereby increasing warehouse utilization and reducing per unit cost. Service may also be improved.

Problems of Centralization

Centralization of logistics in a firm that is organized on a decentralized basis, for example by product division, possesses certain problems. The product divisions may not be logistically compatible. The products produced may have completely different link and node requirements such as liquid chemicals and frozen foods. The transport and warehouse requirements for chemicals are physically noncompatible with that of the frozen food division. One may also find that the market areas are spatially diverse, i.e., the frozen foods market is in the southeast whereas the chemical market is in the Northeast. Such noncompatibility of logistics requirements among divisions somewhat eliminates the advantages associated with centralization.

A possible solution to the centralization of logistics (to achieve the inherent economies) in a decentralized firm is one of compromise through coordination at the staff level. At the staff level, the logistics system is designed to take into consideration the nature of the product flow for various divisions. It may be advantageous to group, or centralize, the logistics staff functions of the several divisions to help achieve sufficient volume for realization of logistics economies (cost reductions and/or service improvements) within the constraints imposed by requirements of the various divisions.

While we have discussed the major aspects of organization including line vs. staff and centralized vs. decentralized approaches as well as positioning, there is still a need to investigate how one would design and implement a logistics organization. In the next section a systems approach to serve as a guide is developed.

A Systems Approach to Logistics Organization

There are no clear-cut rules or guidelines to help one design and implement a logistics department using the systems approach. The process of developing the organization will often go hand-in-hand with designing the distribution system hardware (the warehouses, computers, trucks, order processing systems, etc.). But one can not simply add people to the "hardware" and begin operations. Though the system's physical components have been designed and can be treated as a "given" structure, an organization must be built around the hardware.

First Step

Systems design begins with top management's stated goal, translated into a set of logistics objectives for the logistics system in the form of delivery times, inventory levels, or logistics cost.

Second Step

The second step in the design stage is to relate the given resources and hardware to the environment. Environmental factors consist of such items as Bowersox's eight external system factors, which are:

1. Trade channel alliances
2. Economic conditions
3. Exchange channel alliances
4. Competitive tactics
5. Network of service industries
6. Government and legal regulation
7. Geomarket differentials
8. Industry structure[18]

The logistics design can start with the original mission and subtract or add the relevant external factors to arrive at "net" service or cost performance missions for the internal logistics organization.

An example of this analysis includes the quantification of competitive delivery times and subtracting from that amount the speed at which available transportation firms deliver; this determined net time figure is the margin within which the firm's logistical system must operate.

Third Step

The third step converts the key factors determined in step two into activity requirements. This means developing a clear-cut list of activities to be performed by the system. An example: all units of Product *A* sold in the Southeast will be (1) produced in the Memphis plant and (2) shipped in

FIGURE 13-7   A basic element applied to a traffic office.

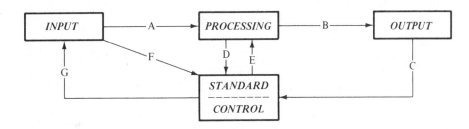

INPUT: Machinery to select carrier
to move a particular shipment
(routing guide, phone, order call).

PROCESSING: Carrier picks up shipment
and carries to destination.

OUTPUT: Delivery by carrier.

Link A: time from call to actual pick up

Link B: time and rate for shipment

Link C: cost and service measured against
a standard for each movement

Link D: trigger mechanism pinpointing too
long a delivery time

Link E: tracing activity

Link G: select or reject carrier for
future movements

Link F: determine if shipment is too small
or has some other extraordinary
characteristic apart from normal
procedure.

carload lots to (3) the Atlanta distribution center. The goods will then be (4) shipped to customers in LTL lots by trucking firms whose service permits at least 48-hour delivery. Activities then include: warehousing, order processing, unit loading, shipping, etc.

Fourth Step   The fourth step breaks the specific tasks that support the activity requirements into sub-sub-systems. Using the step three example, this would mean that the Atlanta distribution center would be sub-system to the firm that would have supporting sub-sub-systems consisting of one warehouse system, a shipping system, an order processing system, etc. This is the most elementary system level. Figure 13-7 illustrates how the sub-sub-shipping system would apply in this case. Interfacing with this shipping system would be the order processing, storage and materials handling, and sales service sub-sub-systems.

It will be noted that the logistics system should be a closed one so that its output can be continually measured and its subsequent input modified to correct deviations. Bowersox states that feedback and control in logistics should be one of management by exception, and that management review be limited to deviations from anticipated results.[19] Significant exceptions that are creating a trend, though, indicate the need for system evaluation and possible change.

FIGURE 13-8 **The three layer organization structure applied to logistics.**

Rank   *Activity*

VP Logistics — MASTER PLANNING

Overall system audit and change plans
  when needed.
Refine system design
Appraise system and sub-system performances
Coordinate policies and actions with
  other functions in the firm
Translate environmental forces into
  logistics policies and actions
Administer change in the system
Establish specific cost and service
  standards for the system.

Manager — Distribution Center A — PROGRAMMED MANAGEMENT

Administer warehouse, order processing,
  materials handling and shipping
  functions in Center A
Translate top management policies into
  specific guidelines for each
  sub-sub-system within Center A
  command
Coordinate all sub-sub-systems to
  produce desired goals and missions
Act on variances in each of the
  responsible sub-sub-system
  components
Summarize and report performance and
  exceptions to top management

Traffic Manager — Center A — OPERATIONS MANAGEMENT

Supervise the traffic function: order
  shipments, trace, expedite, handle
  claims and billing, etc.
Act on shipments whose performance is
  out of line (too late, etc.)
Report trends of exceptions to programmed
  level
Operate system within constraints in time
  and costs as established by
  programmed management
Report listing of complete time and cost
  performance to programmed level

Fifth Step

The fifth step places these system elements into the three-layer management organization scheme consisting of the physical operating level, programmed management, and the master planning level. Figure 13-8 shows how these layers relate to one another.

In concluding the logistics system development section, it should be remembered that because of competitive, productive, and product peculiarities of each firm, and different personalities involved, no two firms (even using the systems concept) will develop similar "optimum" logistics organizations.

Further, by its nature as a closed system, the logistics activity must always be on the lookout for and ready to accommodate change. Dynamic factors such as changing market forces and demands, altered production technology, differing information handling techniques, new carrier awareness for shipper-carrier cost-sharing opportunities, changes in product lines, shifting markets, fluid changes in financial considerations, etc., constantly play on logistics. So the system cannot be built once; it has to be built to accept change both passively and actively.

The job of managing the logistics activity is not definable in a concise and clear-cut manner. Where production management is basically defined as that task of adminstering productive resources in a most efficient manner and under established guidelines, logistics must do much more than administer its own system. Logistics department management must concern itself with such diverse functions as system design and development, physical distribution policy formulation, system administration, coordination with related functions, and public relations and representation factors.[20]

First Tier

The three-layer framework provides the basic structure and operational activity of the entire organization (See Figure 13-8). Starting at the bottom of the organization is the operational (or physical) systems components. These are the most elementary system activities and every one of these tasks (a sub-sub-system) is viewed as having one or more very limited goals. The shipping department for one plant may, for example, have four employees. Its input are the personnel and facilities used, orders to be shipped, labeling, and shipment documentation activities. The processing is the actual shipment, expediting, tracing, miscellaneous carrier contact work, and loss and damage work. The output is measured in terms of tons, shipments or the number of each product units shipped, their total shipment costs plus losses and damages and a realistic allocation of overhead costs attributable to the shipping department (e.g., supervisor's salary, direct phone expenses, floor space costs, supplies, and tariff book costs). The output is measured by feedback reports to the supervisor, who is considered the control mechanism. The supervisor initiates action on shipments that exceed normal delivery times (tracing and follow up), compares actual shipment preparation time and costs (wrapping and overall shipping dock throughput time) against a norm or desired standard (e.g., all shipments take no more than 15 man-minutes to prepare and must clear the dock within the same day). The actual management activity here is very routine in that it is limited to specific control and administrative activities. Very little managerial discretion is required because for each problem there is a very defined method of approach or solution. The manager's performance is very easy to measure since the job goals are specifically defined.

Second Tier

The second tier of management encompasses that person or group of persons who control and administer two or more of the individual sub-sub-systems. This level would include the manager of an entire distribution

warehouse or director of a whole product line. This is the programmed level
of management; that is, the control activities are concerned with making
programmed decisions on exceptions—problems of the sub-sub-systems.
The decisions on this level are also limited in that there is not a wide latitude
of discretionary powers resting here. This manager's responsibility is to
manage his or her sector of the firm (several sub-sub-systems) under a stated
cost, profit or service constraint. Upon facing a problem of one or more
sub-sub-systems (shipping, warehousing, etc.), this manager must take
corrective action and/or initiate investigation to determine the reasons for
problem reoccurrence. His or her administrative aspects are those of
implementing changes in the systems under jurisdiction, coordinating
related functions within and interfacing the overall sub-system, and he or
she might maintain a small support staff whose role it is to audit the
sub-system, conduct continual research to refine and adopt the sub-system to
change, and to represent the sub-system in dealings with external functions
(rate negotiations, etc.).

Third Tier

The top management tier is the master planning level. This is the
nonprogrammed level where very little routine work is done. Input is the
performance and exceptions problems of the sub-systems, and factors
external to the entire system (competitive forces and other changed
environmental considerations). Processing is mostly analytical work (research and engineering studies). Output is the decisions and orders concerning corrective sub-system actions, or new policies and overall system
guidelines, and actions on large distribution system capital acquisition
programs. This level typically consists of a top logistics office (with a
supporting staff of controllers, engineers, and analysts who continually
audit, consider, and plan changes in the system) and members of top
management who are concerned with policy matters of the entire firm
(overall roles, service, ROI, and corporate strategy).

The management of various activities under one executive (several
sub-sub-systems under one sub-system manager, etc.) is usually the most
effective way to manage logistics activities. When related activities are
grouped under one manager, decisions affecting two or more of these
activities are more likely to be made objectively, with a view toward
optimizing total effect on the firm rather than one activity.[21]

Logistics Reorganization

The most complex task facing top management interested in logistics is that
it must often form a department from already existing people, offices, and
hardware. It would be much simpler to draw up a plan forming a new
department, then hire the necessary people and buy the needed equipment.
What makes the implementation task difficult is the fact that the logistics
department must collect present activities and personnel that have been
operating in traditional departments in various phases of sophistication with
entrenched relationships and techniques.

A changeover plan should be developed to include first, the objective to be attained, and second, the techniques of the change itself. Since the phase-in of these many components might require as much as several years, intermediate performance goals should be established within the framework of the overall plan.

An initial and prerequisite step in any logistics reorganization process is the determination of the status of the logistics function in the company. Before any effective plans can be formulated regarding logistics reorganization, a company must have a benchmark (current status) from which the change will proceed. By knowing the *how much, where, what,* and *how* of the current logistics system, a company can then develop a logical plan to reorganize logistics so as to meet stated objectives.

The reorganization objectives usually follow from the logistics status study. The study will normally reveal ''surprising'' problem areas that need correcting. For example, a company completed the logistics status study and found excessive costs of transportation and long transit times, both for raw materials and finished products. An analysis indicated that coordination between traffic and purchasing and traffic and sales so as to permit shipment consolidation could reduce costs and improve service. This coordination objective resulted in a reorganization objective to establish a logistics department that contained traffic, order processing, and purchasing.

The above starting point suggests the need for logistics analysis, planning, and system design. More specifically, it suggests the initial logistics reorganization might take the form of a staff function. In fact, the staff organization for logistics is the easiest (least disruptive, least objectionable to existing personnel) first step in logistics reorganization and a plan that has been followed by many companies in the early 1970's.[22]

The final reorganized logistics will include both line and staff activities.[23] The actual line activities included will be determined by both internal and external factors (product demand, shipping characteristics, competitor's practices, etc.). In addition, one big factor in determining the exact organization form for logistics is people.

People will tend to resist such changes because they bring possible disruption in economic security, job status, established group relations, and superior-subordinate contact, can bring about uncertainty and increasing job complexity, and can meet resistance from union attitudes. These factors cannot be cast aside as unimportant. Managers should be as skillful not only at *what* needs to be changed, but also at *how* to change.

Resistance to the mission-oriented view is to be expected, because it goes against the grain of established traditional viewpoints. The person with the old department outlook no longer has that identity for now he or she is part of a ''system.'' Thus resistance appears in the form of both identity and political sources.[24]

The methods of ''people changing'' cover a wide range. Beginning with unilateral power, there is the decree approach (a one-way announcement), a replacement approach (people are replaced in key positions), or a structural approach (where changes in organizational structure are assumed to change relations and behavior accordingly). Moving further, there are the shared power approaches, where group discussions or group problem-solving approaches are used. Finally, at the other end of the spectrum are the delegated power approaches which incorporate many of the concepts used in sensitivity training.

No hard and fast rules exist for deciding which one of these methods is used or is best for logistical change, and literature in this area is scarce. One thing does stand out; firms are moving away from organization-change-by-rule-obeyance and closely structured behavior (traditional change) to an active participative approach by all involved.[25] Much of this "active participation" may be due to the recognition that logistics is treading on new waters and that coordination is only obtained through participation.

THE LOGISTICS ORGANIZATION: AN EXAMPLE

An attempt has been made to present the material about the logistics organization in a concise and straightforward manner using examples. However, the discussion would be enhanced by viewing an example which covers a description of the organization, the manager's responsibilities, and his or her role in the organization. While it is difficult to describe a typical situation, let us assume that we are dealing with a logistics area in a chemicals company where it is a recognized cost center.

The title of our top logistics executive is vice-president of logistics and he/she reports to a senior executive vice-president in the organization. The job description for our vice-president of logistics indicates that the individual is responsible for the management of logistical distribution, including inventory; materials control, including support systems; and customer service.
Figure 13-9 shows in more detail what the three major areas indicated above include and also provides insight into the staff coordinating activities.

The vice-president of logistics has two very important interfaces, as was explained in Chapter 2—intrafirm, functional relationships and customers. In terms of the first interface, the vice-president of logistics acts as a coordinator among the functional areas of marketing, production, and finance. This means mediating conflicting needs and interests in close cooperation with the appropriate managers. However, the outcome has to meet established performance standards that have been set as a result of the compromises.

As far as the customer interface is concerned, the logistics function is required to provide a reliable and responsive distribution system allowing the company to have a strong competitive position in the marketplace. The distribution system should be viewed as being complementary to the marketing strategy in pricing, promotion, sales, and product quality.

The information provided about the logistics organization (Figure 13-9) in terms of its activities and responsibilities should be relatively easy to

FIGURE 13-9   Key logistical functions and activities.

Logistical Coordination

Integration of Various Activities
Coordination of Sales Budgets
Coordination of Supply Budgets
Strategic Planning
Operations Planning
Evaluation of Performance Standards
Review of Information Systems

Physical Distribution	*Materials Control*	*Customer Service*
Storage	Forecasting	Order Processing
Transportation	Procurement	Records Management
Packaging	Inventory Control	Customer Inquiries
Warehouse Requirements		

understand at this point in the text. Also, Figure 13-9 lends additional insight to the discussion above about the customer and intrafirm interfaces. Our insight into a typical organization would be aided by two additional types of information, *viz.*, specific responsibilities and performance standards. This information for our hypothetical company is contained in Figures 13-10 and 13-11 respectively.

Figure 13-10 sets out a set of responsibilities for the vice-president of logistics to illustrate what can be done. Figure 13-11 relates to Figure 13-10 by setting specific standards against which performance can be evaluated. Finally, Figure 13-12 places in an organizational setting the activity and responsibilities laid out in Figure 13-9.

The reader should have a good overview of the organizational problems and approaches in logistics at this point. Our attention is next turned to the management of business logistics in the future.

SUMMARY

One of the most critical areas of concern is the development of the appropriate organization structure for the logistics function. There are a number of important decisions to be made, including which activities to include in the logistics area, whether to include line and staff responsibilities and authority, and whether to take a decentralized or centralized approach to authority and responsibility. All of these issues have been treated in this chapter, along with some additional items of importance in organization.

FIGURE 13-10   Responsibilities of vice-president of logistics.

FIGURE 13-11   Performance standards, vice-president of logistics.

1. Maintain inventory at four-month level during current year. Reduce to three-month level over the course of the next two years.
2. Establish and maintain a customer service level of 92 percent product availablity of all regular line items being ready for shipment within five days of receipt of order.
3. Develop procedures to maintain operating expenses of logistics at 3.5 percent of sales during current year.
4. Reduce transportation expenses including private fleet, to 2.5 percent of sales during current year and reduce to 2.4 percent next year.
5. Reduce damage rate for freight shipments to 1 percent of total sales.
6. Maintain 98 percent accuracy level in order filling.
7. Maintain employee turnover rate at 12 percent per year.

FIGURE 13-12

Study Questions

1. Discuss the organizational conflicts likely to arise when a new logistics department in a company is being established.
2. Where should logistics be positioned in the organizational hierarchy of a firm?
3. Discuss the advantages and disadvantages of a line vs. staff organizational structure for a logistics department.
4. Should a logistics department be organized on a centralized or decentralized basis? Discuss.
5. Develop a plan to establish a logistics department in a company that has been organized on the basis of traditional functional areas (production, sales, traffic, purchasing, etc.). What problem areas do you foresee in the reorganization and how would you alleviate these problems?

Notes

1. John F. Magee, "The Logistics of Distribution," *Harvard Business Review*, July-August 1960, p. 90.
2. Felix Wentworth, *Physical Distribution Management* (Boston, Massachusetts: Cahners Books, 1970), pp. 43-57.
3. *Ibid.*
4. Presentation by Ward F. Fredricks at St. Anselom's 16th Annual PDM Seminar, as reported in *Handling and Shipping*, Vol. 14, No. 7 (July 1973), p.55.
5. Ronald H. Ballou, *Business Logistics Management* (Englewood Cliffs, N.J.: Prentice-Hall, Inc., 1973), p. 424.
6. D.J.Bowersox, et al., *Physical Distribution Management* (New York: Macmillan Company, 1968), p. 102.
7. Michael Schiff, *Accounting and Control in Physical Distribution Management* (Chicago: NCPDM, 1972). p. 21.
8. Schiff, *op cit.,* pp. 2-11.
9. *Ibid.*
10. *Ibid.*
11. *Ibid.*
12. Bernard J. LaLonde and Jerome J. Cronin, "Distribution Career Patterns," *Distribution Worldwide,* March 1979, p. 68.
13. Donald J. Bowersox, "Emerging Patterns of Physical Distribution Organization," reprinted in Bowersox, et al., eds., *Readings in Physical Distribution Management* (New York: Macmillan, 1969), p. 279.
14. Donald W. DeHayes, Jr., and Robert L. Taylor, "Making Logistics Work in a Firm," *Business Horizons* (June 1972), pp. 37-46.

15. *Ibid.*

16. Bowersox, "Emerging Patterns of Physical Distribution Organization," p. 280.

17. Schiff, *op. cit.,* pp. 1-4.

18. D. Bowersox, B. LaLonde, and E. Smykay, *Physical Distribution Management* (New York: Macmillan, 1970), p.102.

19. *Ibid.*

20. J. Heskett, R. Ivie, N. Glaskowsky, *Business Logistics* (New York: Ronald Press, 1964), p. 448.

21. *Ibid.*

22. LaLonde and Cronin, *op cit.,* p. 70.

23. *Ibid.*

24. L. E. Graines, "Patterns of Organizational Change," *Harvard Business Review,* (May-June 1967), pp. 73-79.

25. Bowersox, *op cit.,* p. 376.

Case 13-1
Apollo Manufacturing, Inc.

Apollo Manufacturing, Inc., has made the decision to implement a logistics department into its organizational structure. Apollo has operated for the past three years without the services of a logistics department, with a large nationwide distributor initiating the needed physical distribution activities.

After an in-depth cost study and review of various trade-off elements by a local consulting firm, Apollo has decided that a logistics department would add to the overall effectiveness and efficiency of the firm by being able to exert more control over the flow of its commodities to the consignee.

Questions

1. Discuss any organizational problems which may occur due to the implementation of the logistics department into the firm.

2. Discuss how you would develop and design the new department so as it would blend into the present organization. (Be specific.)

3. Discuss information systems and how they might add to the efficiency of the logistics department.

Chapter 14	# Management of Logistics: A Look to the Future

After studying this chapter, you should be able to:

- Discuss some of the major developments in logistics.
- Discuss the current needs in logistics management.
- Analyze factors affecting logistics in the future.
- Discuss the changes and developments in logistics that are likely to occur in the future.

In his famous article written in 1962 for *Fortune*, Peter Drucker addressed the logistics-distribution area under the title of the "Economy's Dark Continent" and referred to it as a last frontier for significant cost reduction potential. In describing the situation at that time, Drucker made the following general observations:

> . . . distribution is one of the most sadly neglected but most promising areas of American Business. . . . We know little more about distribution today than Napoleon's contemporaries knew about the interior of Africa. We know it's there, and we know it's big; and that's about all. . . . Most of our present concepts focus on production or on the stream of money and credit, rather than on the flow of physical goods and its economic characteristics. . . . To get control of distribution, therefore, requires seeing—and managing—it as a distinct dimension of business and as a property of product and process rather than as a collection of technical jobs.[1]

Evidence of Developments

Reflecting back over the material covered in the previous chapters of this text, one is tempted to use the line of a popular comment—"We've come a long way, baby." Logistics has indeed come a long way, and there are many signs of successful achievement. For example, if you pick up the membership list of the National Council of Physical Distribution Management and review the list of major companies represented by individuals with titles of vice-president, director, etc., you cannot help but be impressed.

The annual program of the NCPDM and other logistics-related professional organizations such as the Society of Logistics Engineers, the American Society of Traffic and Transportation, Delta Nu Alpha, and the Transportation Research Forum contain impressive arrays of speaker topics, from the pragmatic to the theoretical. The quantity and quality of the presentations are evidence of the present level of attainment and sophistication. Another sign of the interest and improvement is the number of articles concerning various facets of logistics that have appeared in business journals such as *Harvard Business Review*, *Business Horizons*, etc., and the growing number of journals devoted exclusively to logistics-related articles. A further sign of interest and development is the growing number of academic institutions offering programs and/or courses in logistics.

More Growth and Development to Come

In spite of the developments that have occurred since World War II, we are really in the stage of rapid growth, as depicted in Figure 14-1. Even today at least 25 percent of the cost of almost everything manufactured goes to cover the expenses incured before an item gets to or after it leaves the production line, i.e., transportation, inventory, warehousing, packaging, and materials handling. As we have discussed, items that are difficult to transfer and handle, such as paper towels or lamps, frequently cost even more. One of our largest U.S. automobile producers spent close to $2 billion on transportation alone in one year.

The magnitude of the cost expenditure is further evidence of the need for effective management and control of the logistics system in the future.

FIGURE 14-1   Developments in logistics.

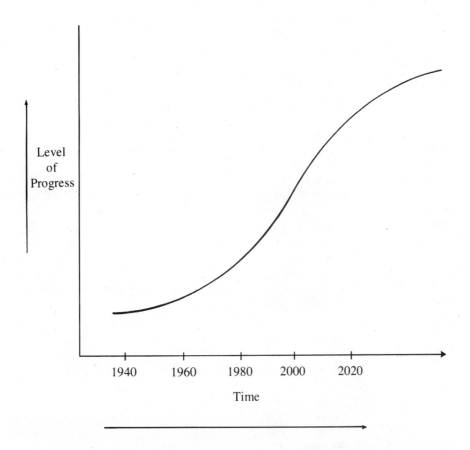

But, as we have noted, there are many reasons why the influence of logistics can continue to grow rapidly in business strategy in the future. For example, there are an increasing number of alternatives for meeting cost and service standards, coping with energy costs and shortages, controlling product lines and related inventory costs, obtaining less expensive, more flexible computer hardware and software, and coping with changing government regulations and controls.[2]

The logistics managers of today and tommorrow cannot stand complacent and count upon the above-cited factors to benefit their position in their organizations and industries. The managers of the future will have to keep abreast of the impact that these forces will have up on their organizations. They will have to adapt to these and other developments.

The above comments points out the importance of logistics and the need to develop more effective techniques, equipment and management strategies. Before looking at what will be coming in the future, it would seem appropriate to assess the current "state of the art" in logistics. The review will be a succinct and simplified version of what we have discussed in detail in previous chapters.

ASSESSMENT OF PRESENT STATUS

Three Areas of Review

In evaluating the present situation in logistics it would probably be useful to view it in three areas, *viz.*, hardware, software, and management. Looking first at the hardware area, one cannot help but think of computers. The rapid developments here are almost mind boggling and they are still coming. The age of the mini-computer is here and improving rapidly. However, the use of the computer has not kept up with the hardware development. There is much room for improvement. Many companies still use computers for record keeping and not for analysis. The potential here for logistics is great.

Hardware: Computers

Hardware: Transportation Equipment

Another dimension of hardware is transportation equipment. Once again, the technological change has been tremendous in all modes and also on an intermodal basis. While we have utilized the new equipment in transportation more effectively than we have used the computer, there is still much room for improvement by both carriers and shippers. The combination of computer utilization with equipment management has almost unlimited potential for improvement in the future.

The materials handling area is another facet of hardware. Once again, we have witnessed phenomenal developments in technology, and more change is to come. However, here again we can question whether we have really utilized the available equipment as effectively as possible.

Software: Inventory

The second area is software. Much attention has been devoted to improving the techniques for inventory control and forecasting. Textbooks and journals are full of applications and development of new techniques, but there is frequently a real gap between theory and practice. There is much potential for improvement in this area.

Software: Accounting and Control

Another aspect in the software area is accounting and control systems. We need to improve our measurement of inventory carrying cost and to develop better measures of stockout costs and back order costs. We also need to better measure the real cost of various customer service levels.

Software: System Design

Another dimension of software is system design. We have made important strides in the development of simulation models and mathematical programming models. However, there are many improvements possible. The present models are frequently expensive and difficult to implement.

Management

The final general area is management. We are still somewhat parochial and have communication problems with other functional areas. For example, at a recent conference on logistics topics, one panelist said that "those of us in the distribution field know our problems are caused by the people in marketing." I am sure that some marketing people say the same thing about logistics. We need a more integrative, cooperative perspective as logistics nanagers.

This brief overview of the present situation in logistics with a particular emphasis upon needs was obviously a somewhat abbreviated statement. It was primarily intended as a challenge and to provide some insights into what we can expect in the future. The next section treats the future aspect in more detail.

A LOOK TO THE FUTURE

Need for Change

As indicated above, in order for any system (including logistics systems) to survive and grow, it must possess the inherent flexibility to adapt to changes in technology, living standards, and the economy. This is of particular significance to business logistics systems, since the state-of-the-art of technology and business decision-making tools are continually changing. Logistics managers must not only stay abreast of new developments in industry and ways of meeting challenges and solving problems, but they must be able to integrate these changes into the daily business operation.

Framework of Discussion

With this thought in mind, we will address some of the changes, opportunities, and challenges that appear likely to occur in the years ahead, and we will discuss some of the ways and means that logistics will be able to profit from these changes. We will also look at the different logistical components to analyze the impact of the changes that are developing new and promise to play an even larger role in the future.

Transportation

We will first examine the transportation sector of the logistics system, since transportation has frequently been referred to as the most important economic activity in the business logistics mix. Often, transportation consumes two-thirds of a firm's dollars spent on all logistics activities. Two particular developments—energy and deregulation—appear to have the greatest potential consequence upon the transportation industry and, hence, the logistics system.

Dependence on Foreign Oil

The United States currently imports about 50 percent of its petroleum from foreign countries. Instability of foreign governments, collective price fixing via cartels, and arbitrary quotas, surcharges, etc., could have a severe impact on the financial health and service capabilities of the transportation industry, since it is very dependent on petroleum and its derivatives to meet their energy requirements. For example, oil accounts for 94 percent of truck energy.

These shortages and escalated price levels are going to be a fact of life, and therefore, they have to be dealt with. What are some of the options that are open to logistics managers so that they may confront the problem head-on?

All modes of transportation will have to make sure that their operations are conducted so that they get as much productivity as possible out of each drop of oil that is consumed. Vehicles will have to carry as much capacity (weight and/or physical bulk) as they possibly can; empty or "deadhead" mileage will have to be minimized; and certain governmental regulations which contribute to the inefficient utilization of fuel will have to be revised or eliminated to take into account actual operating conditions.

More efficient vehicles and components will have to be introduced. For example, in the years since the 1973 oil embargo, the trucking industry has come up with several new components that help the trucks get the maximum mileage out of each gallon of fuel consumed. For example, "fuel-squeezer" diesel engines have been introduced that minimize diesel waste, and wind deflectors are being installed on the roofs of truck-tractors and the "nose" of trailers so as to minimize the fuel consumption that occurs as a result of wind resistance. Radial tires are being used to increase fuel efficiency by producing less resistance to the pavement, etc. The development of improved technology to meet the energy challenges successfully will be an integral part of transportation research in the years ahead.

In an effort to reduce reliance on oil, other forms of energy will have to be investigated and developed to determine if they possess any potential applicability to the transportation/logistics field. Solar energy, our most abundant energy source, remains virtually untapped, as does the use of coal, synthetic fuels, etc. Massive sums of money will have to be allocated for the R&D efforts and production of these energy sources. While it is too early to predict with any degree of accuracy or reliability what the role of these alternate energy sources will be in transportation/logistics in the future, it is safe to say that they will receive some attention as we endeavor to shift our almost complete energy dependence on oil.

In addition to the actual availability of transportation services, the energy situation will result in a reallocation of our priorities among modes. Modes will have to be chosen, in part, for their effective use of energy over distance. We will probably see trucks used for hauls of 500 miles or less, while the railroads will probably recapture the bulk of the long-haul traffic. Some long-haul traffic will continue to move by truck, such as personal household goods and highly perishable fruits such as strawberries, since the rails do not have the equipment or the service capability to provide fast or damage-free service to these commodities. Rail service should improve because of investment in better roadbeds and rolling stock. We may see the initiation of truck-trailers that are equipped with the necessary mechanical features to be pulled by a train.

Related to the above constraints of the motor carrier will be a reduction in private trucking. As indicated in Chapter 9, there are instances when primary emphasis in evaluating the private trucking alternative is placed upon the service advantages, with limited attention to cost. The cost of fuel will necessitate a close scrutiny of the overall costs of private fleets. Obviously, situations which were on the borderline will probably not be economical with the rapid fuel cost increases. The threat of limited supplies of fuels will lead some companies to use for-hire transportation.

There could be a partial counterbalancing effect to the energy constraints if the trucking industry is deregulated or reregulated to the extent that private carriers are allowed to move into the for-hire sector. In this way, private trucking operations could solicit freight for empty backhauls which would make some such fleets economical in spite of increased fuel costs.

Need for Government Involvement

The energy problem will also call for increased government involvement, primarily on two fronts: policy making and planning, and economic regulation. On the policy making and planning front, the government will have to expand and improve its role. It will have to spend more effort in planning for changes, legislation, etc., that will encourage and promote a healthy and stable transportation system. The government will have to undertake policies to standardize some state regulations, such as truck size and weight limitations, which are wasteful of energy and add to the inflationary pressures felt by the economy. Since the Federal government funds such a large proportion of transportation projects for all modes, it is in a strong position to insist that certain standardization of regulations (such as vehicle size and weight and interstate licensing agreements) become effective as a prerequisite to receiving federal funding.

Need for Government Funding

In addition to planning and policy making, the government will have to continue to operate those sectors of transport activity that are too large or costly for the private sector to economically run, i.e., Amtrak, ConRail, the airports, etc. The government role in providing the crucial funding and operation of these activities will continue in the years ahead on a larger scale than now.

Need for Regulatory Change

The second major area of government involvement in the transportation sector is in the role of economic and safety regulation. The government, as we have seen, regulates transportation via the ICC, DOT, FMC, CAB, FAA, etc. The role of regulation will be radically changed in the coming years, so as to recognize the prevailing conditions and economic climate. Some regulation will be eliminated altogether if it has outgrown and/or outlived its usefulness. Regulation will emphasize competition more than it does now, particularly in the areas of entry and abandonment of routes and areas of operation, mergers, and ratemaking, to name just three. Some of the activities that are viewed as being anticompetitive in nature (e.g., collective ratemaking) will be, in all likelihood, dramatically changed or restructured.

Government regulation will most likely change to a system that fosters greater competitiveness with fewer restrictions. For example, regulations governing entry, exit, rail abandonment operating authority, and commodity exemptions will probably be eased or eliminated. Total deregulation of certain commodity carriers, etc., will probably be forthcoming, particularly if the current impetus and drive exhibited by the ICC is sustained.

Perhaps the most important aspect of regulation that needs to be discussed is: Are the costs (economic, social) of regulation less than the benefits that accrue because of regulation? The present regulatory system is not perfect; however, total deregulation has not proved to be idyllic, as experience in exempt-commodity agricultural trucking has shown. What will come about will be a regulatory renaissance, i.e., reregulation. Much of this effort is currently in the planning stage, yet it is practically certain that substantial regulatory changes applicable to all modes will be forthcoming.

In addition to regulatory and fuel-related changes in the transportation system, we will see further changes in the activities of the carriers themselves. As more uncertainty evolves in the common motor carrier segment (possible rate bureau abolishment, higher Teamster wage scales, limits on diesel fuel supply, etc.), more shippers will turn to alternate forms of carriage to fulfill their needs. These forms of carriage, e.g., private/leased rail-car fleets, contract barge service, etc., will play an increasingly greater role in intercity movements of freight. The big advantage of contract carriage is that it permits the firm to secure more cost and service control over the transportation function.

Growth of Cooperative Transport Arrangements

Inter- and intra-modal cooperation will also experience more growth, since energy, cost of service, and quality of service constraints will demand it. For example, shipments of highly delicate pieces of machinery that are time-sensitive will probably utilize truck for local pick-up and delivery and air freight for expedient linehaul. Piggyback, containerized, and freight forwarder services should all experience remarkable growth during the years ahead since they will meet the requirements for energy-efficient transportation and combine the cost and service advantages of the particular modes utilized for maximum benefit. Along these lines, we will most likely experience more inter- and intra-modal mergers. These mergers will reduce the total number of available carriers, yet offer the potential of better service due to single line coverage, more comprehensive authority, and greater diversity of services.

Customer Service

Customer service, as has been pointed out, can be an important variable in influencing a company's sales. Customer service is an intangible that can play a large role in determining whether a customer will place its order with one particular firm or one of its competitors. The customer service function should be "finely tuned" so as to keep the customer's operation running smoothly with a minimum of delay or interruption caused by the supplier.

Examples

In the future, order cycle and transportation consistency will probably become even more important, since customers will demand dependable estimates of performance. As an adjunct to the customer service function, we will see increasing standardization of many functions that contribute to the customer service concept. Commodity descriptions, carrier "Alpha codes," and point locations will be standardized in order to save time and trouble, and to make the transacting of business easier. Computers will handle increasingly more of the paperwork preparation activity, e.g., bill-of-lading preparation, freight rate calculations and freight bill preparation, order processing, inventory purchase and control, etc. The whole customer service area will be affected by the improvements and changes discussed in the next several sections.

Warehousing

The warehousing function, as we have seen, plays an important interfacing role between customer service and production on the physical distribution side of a company, and between vendors/suppliers and production on the physical supply side. The rising price of labor and the need for productivity improvements will keep the pressure on the organization to introduce more automation.

As was pointed out in Chapter 5, there was a significant increase in automation of warehouses during the 1960s, but there has been an even greater increase during the 1970s. We have noted the elaborate conveyor and crane systems based on computer programs that randomly assign and place stock in position in a warehouse on an automated basis and take the items out again when needed.

Automation
The one area in the warehouse which has not had the same degree of development of automation is the order picking area of physical distribution warehouses. The need for picking parts of full cartons has stymied attempts to introduce complete automation. So we still have much hand picking, and individuals push or pull some type of wheeled vehicle or cart through the order selection/picking area. During the 1980s we will see the development of more sophisticated materials handling equipment and packaging techniques which will gradually overcome the problems associated with automated order picking and preparation areas.

Paperwork
An almost obvious improvement which has already been covered to some extent in the customer service area is in the paperwork area of the warehouse. The computer has given rise to phenomenal developments in this area, but the availability of low-cost, compact computers, for example, that can be carried by sales persons and accessed by telephone, will expedite paperwork and processing even more.

Mini-computers
The hand calculator will be replaced to a large extent by the mini-computer. The small, inexpensive computer, along with more easily understood computer language and software packages will have a tremendous impact upon the efficiency of the overall logistics system, in particular, the warehousing functions.

Models
The control and management of warehouse inventories will be impacted by a number of the factors and variables discussed thus far. The continuing interest in inventory models and techniques will lead to more sophisticated decision making in terms of forecasting and economic order quantities. The availability of small, low-priced computers and software packages will also help the management and control of inventories. Our

overall efficiency in the inventory control area with its many facets will improve.

The energy situation previously described for transportation will obviously impact upon warehousing. The internal operations of the warehouse will have to be managed in an energy efficient manner. Various types of equipment, for example, forklift trucks, will be affected by the cost and shortage of gasoline. Alternate fuel sources, e.g., battery powered vehicles, will be more widely used.

Energy Constraints

As indicated previously, the energy shortage and higher energy costs will have an impact upon transportation services. In particular, they may constrain the alternatives in that motor carriers will likely be limited to distances of 500 miles or less. The fast, reliable service of motor carriers has enabled many companies to serve a wide geographic area from a limited number of strategically located warehouses. Some of these operations are based upon private truck fleets, which, as has been indicated, will probably be reduced or eliminated because of limited, high-cost fuel. The net result will be a reduced geographic area that can be served effectively on a cost and service basis for a warehouse.

The reduction in service area of warehouses should have a number of impacts. An obvious result will be more market warehouses with an increased need for good inbound rail service. The more limited markets areas to be served from these warehouses will mean more public warehousing. It is quite likely that we will see more public warehouses shipping consolidated loads of different companies to a retailer or wholesaler, which became quite common in the food industry during the later 1970s.

Overall, there will be a number of important changes in the warehousing segment of logistics systems. The changes will lead to improved warehousing and to better logistics systems. As was indicated, improvements in information systems will play a key role in some of the warehousing developments. A more detailed look at the information system area seems appropriate at this point.

Management Information Systems

Our prior discussion has pointed out a number of applications of computer-based information systems. In this section we will summarize these changes in terms of carriers and manufacturers.

· Equipment

For carriers, the improvements in information systems will lead to better utilization of equipment. Assignment of equipment to various terminals is presently being done by some carriers using computers. This will be expanded in the future. More importantly, we will probably see more short-run equipment decisions being made by the computer, e.g., in the daily dispatching area for motor carriers. While it may be hard to believe that the daily hectic pace of terminal area dispatching can be done by

Rating and Billing

computer, it is quite likely that we will see heuristic programs developed to assist in the dispatching area.

The rating and billing area will be another section where improvements will take place. We have already seen important changes in the billing area in terms of record keeping. More needs to be done in terms of analyzing the information provided by the bills, however. The big area for change will probably be in rating. We will see simpler tariffs which will lead to more computerization of tariffs. Such a development will have an important impact upon productivity and cost.

Maintenance

Maintenance of equipment has already benefitted from improved information systems. Once again, however, there will be continued improvements as we become more skilled with our systems.

Like maintenance, tracing and expediting of shipments has benefitted already from computer-based information systems. The improvements will continue here also. Overall, carrier service and performance should continue to improve in the 1980s because of the better information systems.

The logistics manager will also witness improvements related to better information systems as we progress through the 1980s. We have previously noted the important changes in inventory control. Also, mention has been made of the continuing improvements in order processing.

Planning Models

The most important change for the industrial user or shipper will be in planning. We are becoming increasingly sophisticated in developing simulation models for planning. The efforts in the past have been hampered by lack of data, limited modeling expertise, etc. This situation is rapidly changing, and the 1980s will show increasingly effective distribution planning efforts.

MANAGEMENT STRATEGY

In light of the various factors discussed above it appears quite likely that logistics will be systematically included in corporate strategy. As has been suggested elsewhere, there are compelling reasons why logistics will play a more important role in corporate strategy in the future including a decline in the growth rate of domestic markets, large incremental costs of energy, and an increasing emphasis on multinational markets.[3]

The situation was succinctly stated as follows:

> Attention to logistics can support expanded product lines in good times or provide a basis for gaining a competitive profit edge during periods of slow growth. Whether the goal is increased market shares or increased profits from existing or smaller market shares, logistics considerations can be basic to these accomplishments. If, as many have predicted, general management inevitably will have to spend an increasing proportion of its time dealing with low or no growth situations, it is not too early to put in place a process to ensure that logistical considerations will not be overlooked in formulating strategy.[4]

INTERFIRM RELATIONS

One of the major areas of development in the future will likely be interfirm relations. The development could come in the form of horizontal coordination, i.e., consolidation of inventories, shipments, and even facilities. While there are potential antitrust problems, there are some examples of success. In the food industry there are public warehouse companies that consolidate products of various manufacturers at strategic points and ship in "mixed" carload and truckload quantities direct from the warehouse to the wholesaler or retailer at considerable savings to all concerned.

Another possibility is vertical coordination between suppliers and customers, i.e., demand-supply coordination with more sophisticated materials requirements planning techniques. The result should be lower inventories and better facility utilization. The epitome of such coordination may be computer to computer communications.

NONPROFIT ORGANIZATIONS

As stated in Chapter 1, many of the early logistics developments after World War II can be traced to the military. In fact, the military has continued their strong interest in improving their logistical systems and management. There has frequently been close cooperation between the military and some manufacturing companies in exchanging information about logistically related developments in their respective situations to the mutual benefit of both. Frequently such exchanges have occurred through professional organizations such as the Society of Logistics Engineers (S.O.L.E.) and others previously mentioned.

While the military establishment has been the recognized leader in the nonprofit sector as far as logistics is concerned, there are many other government agencies and quasi-government agencies with a strong commitment and/or need for good logistical management. An obvious example would be the Post Office. While the Post Office could be viewed as a transportation company, it obviously offers services more comprehensive than the typical transport organization.

There are many other examples besides the Post Office and the military. The C.I.A. has an extensive and sophisticated logistics system. The Federal Reserve System has logistical needs with our money supply. We could go on and on. There is much need for effective logistical management in the nonprofit sector of our economy, and there are many areas where logistics has not received the attention that is necessary. This is true not only at the federal, state, and local levels of government, but also for other nonprofit organizations.

It would be most appropriate for us to end our discussion of future perspectives on logistics by focusing our attention on the education of tomorrow's logistics manager.

EDUCATION OF LOGISTICS PERSONNEL

It is safe to say that there will be an increasing emphasis upon management education in the future because of the sophistication that will be necessary to manage the changes in logistics that will be taking place. Colleges and universities will respond to this need by expanding their offerings in the logistics area. This will mean new programs at some schools and expanded programs at others. Such changes will take place at junior colleges and community colleges as well as at four-year colleges and universities.

The logistics manager will need to show competence in cost accounting, economics marketing, and production, as well as in other business areas. There will be a need for good communication skills and computer expertise. The need for a professional logistics manager is with us already, and this need will become more intensified. A manifestation of the need for the professional logistics manager will be more graduate degrees being earned.

Continuing education will also be an important aspect of these changes. The logistics manager will have to participate in special education opportunities in order to keep abreast of the rapid changes. The education will take place in a variety of ways, e.g., formal classes, professional meetings, executive development programs, and intensive self-study.

SUMMARY

Any discussion of the future, particularly with predictions, has to be approached with some reservation. It is difficult to assign probabilities to some of the predicted changes discussed in this chapter. Even if the predictions do not all come true, it is a meaningful exercise to try to analyze the impact of the variables likely to cause change. The analysis is helpful to the logistics manager to help him or her plan and not react. The most important point, however, is that the future for logistics managers looks bright in terms of their importance to their organizations and industries.

Study Questions

1. Discuss the major developments which have taken place in logistics in the post-World War II era.
2. Discuss the major factors that will affect logistics managers in the future.
3. Develop a rational statement for some government agency (use two specific examples) as to why it should put more emphasis on the management of its logistical activities.
4. Select some logistics activity, e.g., transportation, inventory, warehousing, etc., and do an in-depth analysis of future developments.

Notes

1. Peter F. Drucker, "The Economy's Dark Continent," *Fortune*, April 1962, pp. 103, 265-70.

2. James L. Heskett, "Logistics—Essential to Strategy," *Harvard Business Review*, November-December 1977, p. 86.

3. Heskett, *op cit.*, p. 95.

4. *Ibid.*

SELECTED BIBLIOGRAPHY FOR PART IV

BALLOU, RONALD H., *Business Logistics Management*. Englewood Cliffs, New Jersey: Prentice-Hall, Inc., 1973, Chapters 3, 8, 10, and 12.

BOWERSOX, DONALD J., *Logistical Management*, 2nd Edition. New York: Macmillan Publishing Company, Inc., 1978, Parts 3 and 4.

BURSTALL, R. M., R. A. LEAVER, and J. E. SUSSANS, "Evaluation of Transport Cost for Alternative Factory Sites—A Case Study," *Operations Research Quarterly* December 1962, pp. 345-54.

DeHAYES, DONALD W., and ROBERT L. TAYLOR, "Making Logistics Work in a Firm," *Business Horizons*, June 1972, pp. 37-46.

FRIEDRICH, CARL J., *Alfred Weber's Theory of the Locational Industries*. Chicago: University of Chicago Press, 1929.

GREENHUT, MELVIN L., *Plant Location in Theory and Practice*. Chapel Hill, North Carolina: University of North Carolina Press, 1956.

HESKETT, JAMES L., et al., *Business Logistics*, 2nd Edition. New York: The Ronald Press Company, 1973, Chapters 8, 12, 15, 20, and 21.

HILLER, FREDERICK S., and GERALD J. LIEBERMAN, *Introduction to Operations Research*. San Francisco: Holden-Day, Inc., 1967.

HOOVER, EDGAR M., *The Location of Economic Activity*. New York: McGraw-Hill Book Company, 1948.

HUTCHINSON, WILLIAM, and J. F. STOLLE, "How to Manage Customer Service," *Harvard Business Review*, November-December 1968.

KUEHN, ALFRED A., and MICHAEL J. HAMBURGER, "A Heuristic Program for Locating Warehouses," *Management Science*, IX, Number 4, 1963.

LEWIS, RICHARD J., "A Business Logistics Information and Accounting System for Marketing Analysis," Reprinted in: McConaughy, David, Editor, *Readings in Business Logistics*. Homewood, Illinois: Richard D. Irwin, Inc., 1969, pp. 153-57.

LEWIS, RONALD J., "Strengthening Control of Physical Distribution Costs," *Management Services*, Volume 5, January-February, 1968.

MAGEE, JOHN F., *Industrial Logistics*. New York: McGraw-Hill Book Company, 1968, Chapters 5, 7, 9, 10, and 14.

MAGEE, JOHN F., "The Logistics of Distribution," *Harvard Business Review*, July-August 1960.

REED, RUDDELL, Jr., *Plant Location, Layout, and Maintenance*. Homewood, Illinois: Richard D. Irwin, Inc., 1967.

RICHARDS, MAX D., and PAUL S. GREENLAW, *Management Decisions and Behavior*, Revised Edition. Homewood, Illinois: Richard D. Irwin, Inc., 1972.

SCHIFF, MICHAEL, *Accounting and Control in Physical Distribution Management*. Chicago: National Council of Physical Distribution Management, 1972.

STOLLE, JOHN F., "How to Manage Physical Distribution," *Harvard Business Review*, July-August 1967, pp. 93-100.

WARNERBURG, C. M., and PETER HALL, *Von Thunen's Isolated State*. Oxford: Pergamon Press, 1966.

WENTWORTH, FELIX, *Physical Distribution Management*, Boston, Massachusetts: Cahners Books, 1970.

Author Index

Subject Index

†